TOWARD A FIELD THEORY OF BEHAVIOR:

PERSONALITY AND SOCIAL STRUCTURE

Toward a Field Theory of Behavior

PERSONALITY AND SOCIAL STRUCTURE

J. MILTON YINGER

Professor of Sociology and Anthropology
Oberlin College

McGRAW-HILL BOOK COMPANY

New York · St. Louis · San Francisco

Toronto · London · Sydney

TOWARD A FIELD THEORY OF BEHAVIOR:
Personality and Social Structure

FOR WINNIE

Preface

This book is written in the conviction that the sciences of human behavior will be strengthened by explicit attention to their common theoretical base. For several years I have felt the need for a relatively brief systematic statement concerning the interdependence of the specialized disciplines—a statement that goes beyond pious affirmations of shared interests to an exploration of the research and theoretical implications of interdependence. There is now an extensive, and to me exciting, body of literature that cannot easily be placed in any one or two of the established special fields of knowledge. This literature is oriented toward a problem more than toward a discipline, toward an explanation of behavior more than toward the isolation of one factor in behavior causation.

If one asks today, "What are the sources of talent? What is involved in the process of aging? What causes discrimination against the members of a minority group? Why do people support the political movements they do? What is the origin of mental illness?" or any number of other questions, he will find answers—often tentative and incomplete, but based on thoughtful investigation—coming from many directions. Scientific advance is often most rapid at the point of contact of two or more disciplines. But what we are witnessing in behavioral science goes beyond this usual form of "hybrid vigor." A new frame of reference is being formed; a more complicated but also more powerful way of asking questions is developing. The tentative collaboration of anthropologist with psychologist, of psychiatrist with sociologist, of the student of economics or government with the student of personality or society, is growing into more persistent efforts to develop a shared perspective.

This development among the behavioral sciences seems similar to the process of learning a foreign language: for many scholars, not so long ago, the work of other disciplines was gibberish—a nonlanguage. Other scholars recognized the existence of related disciplines even if they did not understand them or find them particularly interesting— they were "Greek," but they were a language. More recently the number has increased who can read and speak one or more foreign tongues, even though with a noticeable accent and with a tendency to translate back into their native language for comprehension. We are only beginning to get, I believe, a number of persons who can *think* in interdisciplinary terms, who do not need to translate, who have mastered the more complex structure of questions essential to behavioral science.

Perhaps this book can be thought of as an effort to eliminate "foreign accents" from behavioral science—primarily from my own usages, but I hope from others' as well. It is not an attempt to synthesize existing knowledge in particular areas, although I shall comment upon a great deal of research. It is an effort to develop a perspective from which one can study the research in areas of his own interest more creatively and undertake his own research more effectively. My hope is to broaden the range of conversation among specialists and to persuade those who are entering careers in behavioral science to conceive of it from the first as multidisciplinary, even though their own work and interest may be highly specialized. This is no attempt to criticize the trend toward specialization or to imply that each of us must attempt to master the full range of the sciences of human behavior. It is, rather, a restatement of the context within which specialization must proceed.

For many persons, the established disciplinary approaches continue, quite appropriately, to be most attractive. For such persons, the need is for a greater awareness of the total empirical base from which they are abstracting. The psychologist who moves out of the university laboratory to a village in another society is quickly made aware that many variables which were "controlled" for him, so long as his attention was on a limited range of time and space, become critical for his research in a different setting. The anthropologist who develops a theory of behavior in a small society, homogeneous in race and religion, with relatively enduring patterns of socialization, is compelled to add new dimensions when he directs his attention to heterogeneous societies.

For some persons, specialization has taken a different form. They are interested in perception or drug addiction, in the origins of an "achievement motive" or delinquent behavior. Such scholars require not simply a recognition of the empirical world from which they abstract; they need to take account of the many sources of behavior, in gene and character, in group and norm, as they pursue their *specialized* interest in one segment of behavior.

In examining the issues raised by the development of behavioral science, I have commented on a wide range of subjects. Specialists will undoubtedly discover that when I have examined an area in which I have no particular subject matter competence, I have made errors of judgment. This I shall regret. I shall be even more regretful, however, if I have not effectively posed the questions related to the development of a behavioral science. In this day of specialization, the risk of knowing nothing about everything is generally regarded as considerably greater than the risk of knowing everything about nothing. I can only hope that this is a false dichotomy, that somewhere in the "excluded middle" there is room to plant one's feet.

These essays represent for me a third stage in what has been a long-standing interest in problems of a general theory of human behavior. During the first two stages, my interest was focused on two substantive areas: religious institutions and behavior, and the phenomena of prejudice and discrimination. The limitations imposed on specifically anthropological, psychological, or sociological approaches to these subjects have seemed more and more severe; and in other works I have made some hesitant moves toward drawing these approaches into one system. This volume is an attempt to examine that system in more general terms, drawing subject matter from a large number of research areas.

One piles up more debts than he can ever repay during the preparation of a book. My wife and family continue to treat me as if I had done nothing wrong. One repays such loyalty as best he can. Oberlin College has freed me of all teaching duties for a year and a half out of the last three years—a schedule that has permitted me to undertake the wide-ranging study demanded by the topic of this volume. Many persons have responded to letters of inquiry and to requests for a critical examination of parts of the manuscript. I want particularly to thank Drs. Kiyoshi Ikeda, Richard R. Myers, George E. Simpson, Ralph H. Turner, and Donald Warwick for their valuable comments. Miss June Wright has become so skilled at preparing good copy from my almost illegible first draft that I believe the next time she should prepare the first draft herself—why bother with a middleman? Thanks are also extended to the American Sociological Association, The University of Chicago Press, and The Society for the Scientific Study of Religion for permission to use portions of papers which I published originally in their journals: "Contraculture and Subculture," *American Sociological Review,* October, 1960; "Research Implications of a Field View of Personality," *American Journal of Sociology,* March, 1963; and "On Anomie," *Journal for the Scientific Study of Religion,* Spring, 1964.

J. Milton Yinger

Contents

Contents

Part ONE

THE DEVELOPMENT
OF A BEHAVIORAL SCIENCE

CHAPTER 1

Behavioral Science and Analytic Science

The historian of science may someday note that in the mid-twentieth century, the lines of distinction that had marked out separate sciences of human behavior became less clear. Research directed toward the full explanation of some human action produced disciplines that cut across several of the established subjects. Scientists came to see that even such an apparently individual fact as illness is a group fact as well. To comprehend it fully requires the study not only of the invasion of certain cells by virus, microbe, or poison, but also of the whole individual with his anxieties and desires (psychosomatic processes), the networks of interaction with which he is connected (his family and the hospital as a social structure, for example), and the cultural definitions of illness to which he has been trained (the sick role).

The perspective out of which such disciplines grew did not suddenly appear. It is implicit in the scientific tradition, along with other perspectives, and is strongly represented in twentieth-century philosophy and the humanities. It has always had some place among students of human behavior, so that most social scientists have been shaped in part by such observations as these:

In defending a social theory of mind we are defending a functional, as opposed to any form of substantive or entitive, view as to its course. And in particular, we are opposing all intracranial or intra-epidermal views as to its character and locus. ... If mind is socially constituted, then the field or locus of any given individual mind must extend as far as the social activity or apparatus of social relations which constitutes it extends; and hence that field cannot be bounded by the skin of the individual organism to which it belongs.

George Herbert Mead in *Mind, Self and Society*

But before I treat a patient like yourself
I need to know a great deal more about him,

Than the patient can always tell me.
Indeed, it is often the case that my patients
Are only pieces of a total situation
Which I have to explore. The single patient
Who is ill by himself is rather the exception.

T. S. Eliot in *The Cocktail Party*

Self and Society are twin-born, we know one as immediately as we know the other, and the notion of a separate and independent ego is an illusion.

Charles Horton Cooley in *Social Organization*

The idea of the self and the self-regarding sentiment are essentially social products;...their development is affected by constant interplay between personalities, between the self and society....

William McDougall in *Social Psychology*

You cannot think without abstractions; accordingly, it is of the greatest importance to be vigilant in critically revising your *modes* of abstraction.... A civilisation which cannot burst through its current abstractions is doomed to sterility after a very limited period of progress.

Alfred North Whitehead in *Science and the Modern World*

Something there is that doesn't love a wall....
Before I built a wall I'd ask to know
What I was walling in or walling out....

Robert Frost in "Mending Wall"

The theory of action is a conceptual scheme for the analysis of the behavior of living organisms. It conceives of this behavior as oriented to the attainment of ends in situations, by means of the normatively regulated expenditure of energy. There are four points to be noted in this conceptualization of behavior: (1) Behavior is oriented to the attainment of ends or goals or other anticipated states of affairs. (2) It takes place in situations. (3) It is normatively regulated. (4) It involves expenditure of energy or effort or "motivation" (which may be more or less organized independently of its involvement in action).

Talcott Parsons and Edward Shils in *Toward a General Theory of Action*

Chacun prend à l'adversaire, qu'il le veuille ou non. [One takes on the face of his opponent whether he wishes to or not.]

French proverb

One can't get very far in studying organisms without studying their environment—and vice versa. For the organism and the environment constitute a bi-polar field. The individual can be explained only in terms of his relatedness to others in his group. Patterns of interpersonal relations are influenced by the physical and biological environment of the group, by the number of persons in the group and the age and sex distribution of these, and by culture.

Clyde Kluckhohn and Henry A. Murray in *Personality in Nature, Society and Culture*

$B = f(P,E)$.... In this formula for behavior, the state of the person (P) and that of his environment (E) are not independent of each other. How a child sees a given physical setting (for instance, whether the frozen pond looks dangerous to him or not) depends upon the developmental state and the character of that child and upon his ideology.... The reverse is also true: The state of the person depends upon his environment.... The state of the person after encouragement is different from that after discouragement, that in an area of sympathy or security from that in an area of tension, that in a democratic group atmosphere from that in an autocratic atmosphere.

Kurt Lewin in *Field Theory in Social Science*

Such a miscellany as these quotations represent can perhaps suggest the outlines of the problem with which this book is concerned. They are not without contradictions, of course; and they only hint at the task involved in a research program that would transform a point of view into a theory.

I hope to show, however, that contemporary research on widely varying topics has taken the significant first steps in building a behavioral science. Just beneath the surface, if not yet fully in the clear, an important realignment is taking place among the sciences of human behavior. Direct examination of this process of realignment in several different substantive areas, and without regard for disciplinary starting points, may clarify its goals and alert us to its difficulties. Perhaps by viewing the highly diverse studies of society, culture, and personality within a common frame of reference, we can move toward a coherent system capable of explaining the observed facts and reducing the contradictions.

This book is essentially an essay in theory building and in the strategy of research. It is an attempt to ask the right questions for a contemporary science of human behavior. With the right questions asked, the tactics of specific research can be designed not only to test particular hypotheses but to contribute to the cumulative body of theory.

Developments in behavioral science are partly based on the advances achieved in specialized disciplines. Most interdisciplinary work today, in fact, represents the adding together of separate points of view rather than the synthesizing of a new and more complex unity. This can be illustrated by imagining what might be the summary statements of a group of specialists working together toward a shared perspective. If each were limited to one sentence, they all might agree on the first half of the statement given below and then add their own qualifier:

"It is true that behavior is the outcome of interaction among several influences, but let us not forget that...

First biologist: "man is an animal with certain inherited requirements, tendencies, and limits."

Second biologist: "—and those limits vary among individuals, as well as among species, and are affected by environment."

Geographer: "the physical environment also sets problems and limits which affect behavior in many ways."

Experimental psychologist: "man is a learning animal, capable of complex development as he responds to the stimuli which reach him through his senses."

Ego psychologist: "man is reflexive; he remembers the past and imposes some order on the inputs and outputs; there is a self, and a search for identity."

Psychoanalyst: "learned and inherited motives are often blocked, and much of behavior is a response to the blockage."

Social interactionist: "behavior is emergent in specific interactional settings, involving the cues and responses of significant others."

Sociologist: "man lives in groups that structure most interactions and define the alternatives for action; most satisfactions depend on others, and man is therefore motivated to view the world as others do, the better to deal with them."

Anthropologist: "most groups have designs for living, values and procedures which they prize and which they train their members to prize."

The ambivalence in these sentences may suggest that in their efforts to understand the world of nature, scientists have looked in two directions. First, they have sought to isolate laws of relationship that prevail under certain stated conditions, often of their own making: X will be followed by Y, all other things being equal; a sharp reduction in blood sugar will seriously disrupt brain function; on earth in a vacuum at sea level, an unsupported object will fall 16 feet the first second and 32 feet the second second, and it will accelerate at the rate of 32 feet per second per second; perception of the presumed movement of a spot of light in a darkened room will be influenced by the declared judgments of coperceivers. These statements are not, of course, equally abstract; that is, they do not equally exclude the effects of unmeasured variables; thus some are more "probabilistic" than others. They all illustrate, however, the desire to isolate from the complex empirical world some law of relationship. These laws are obscured in the normal course of affairs, because different relationships operating simultaneously in the same setting offset, reinforce, or deflect one another, thus requiring the analytic procedures of research for their discovery.

From a second perspective, scientific observers look at some segment of the world as it exists and ask "What various processes are operative there and what is the consequence of their *interaction?*" I shall call this perspective the *field perspective.* It is based on the more highly analytic procedures for determination of the important variables and the techniques for their measurement. This does not mean, however, that field research is useless until analytic research has been carried to a high level of accomplishment; nor does it mean that the field perspective is a simple addition of two or more specialized approaches. *The field is a new unit.* The point is not simply that one sees better with two eyes used simultaneously than with one—indeed, one may not see much better—but he sees differently; a new dimension is added. In mathematical terms, the combined results of two or more influences are a product, not a sum, of their interaction. (This is not to deny that various statistical procedures may be designed to get additive results.)

Among the sciences of human behavior, arguments for field-oriented research are particularly strong for two reasons. First, analytic research that requires manipulation of human subjects is severely limited. We do not set out to measure the effects of love deprivation or inconstancy among infants—its relationship to later schizophrenia, for example—by selecting an experimental group and a control group and systematically depriving the former of loving care. We observe behavior with the full range of forces at work, seeking by mathematical, statistical, or other symbolic processes, or by comparative study, to isolate the major forces. I do not mean to suggest that it is either impossible or scientifically undesirable to seek to isolate the influence of one variable in naturalistic, as opposed to laboratory, settings. I mean only that when human behavior in a natural situation is under analysis, studies concerned with the interplay of several variables are particularly valuable as complements to more abstract research procedures.

A second argument for field-oriented research among the sciences of human behavior is the fact that the final concern of most of us is not with the isolation of independent relationships but with the understanding and predicting of behavior. Not many are content with the type of proposition that states: This is the relationship of intelligence to delinquency, the influence of all other variables having been controlled. We want rather to be able to say: A given proportion of the youth under study became delinquent because of the *interaction* of these several variables. Even researchers who seek to isolate the influence of one variable seldom escape the temptation to try to explain behavior thereby. Analytic procedures may remove the influence of other forces from a relationship under observation, but these forces are not removed from nature.

There are situations, of course, when measurement of the influence of one factor alone may be necessary or wise. The researcher can disregard those forces that are constant and still achieve accurate prediction. But he must not mistake constancy for absence. He can avoid this error by noting the results when they are not constant. Social-psychological study of interpersonal relations, for example, can often disregard the normal physiological homeostatic processes in brain function. When these processes are disturbed by extreme hunger, fatigue, or illness, however, the researcher easily recognizes that they had been one of the forces affecting interpersonal relations all along. When the constant becomes a variable, it must be taken into account.

Closely related to the situation in which all forces but one can be disregarded as constant are the circumstances in which one factor is of such major importance that it dominates the outcome. At a given level of knowledge, major constitutional inadequacy of the brain, for example, may be accounted for by reference to biological and chemical influences, almost regardless of interpersonal experience and culture. (The reference is to constitutional inadequacy, not inadequacy produced or increased by illness, isolation, psychosis, or other causes.) But chemical and biological knowledge may grow to the point where we can prevent or cure "constitutional" or "inherited" deficiency. If inadequacy still exists, what then is the cause? Explanation in the new situation will have to take account not only of biochemical facts, but also of the presence or absence of certain cultural techniques. A constant has become a variable. It then becomes apparent that when we said, "The inadequacy was inherited," we were using a linguistic shortcut for the idea that certain biochemical processes interacting with a given environment (which for the particular situation had no "range"—it was the same for everyone) resulted in mental inadequacy. The same biochemical processes interacting with a different environment produce different results, a fact which indicates that our original "causal" explanation was insufficient. Environmental forces had always been involved. To say that one force dominates, in the sense that its variation explains the range of outcomes (and is the only one, therefore, that needs measurement to achieve prediction), is not to say that it determines the outcome.

Under other conditions, focusing attention on one or another of a series of variables may be the wisest course, from the point of view of the optimal use of available resources. Professional commitments, of course, are likely to affect the decision; independent criteria for determining the allocation of resources are lacking. The danger is, therefore, that limited perspectives, not wise strategy, will control the decision.

These points qualify the emphasis given in this book to the need for the simultaneous study of variables at different levels. But they do not, I believe, refute the argument that such a need exists in the examination of most of the issues of central concern to the social sciences. The test of this proposition, of course, is prediction.

Even a casual glance at human behavior under various conditions reveals an assortment of questions that no one discipline can handle. During and after the Korean War, for example, many Americans were shocked at the reported number of United States prisoners of war who were "unduly cooperative" with Chinese captors. Although only twenty-one persons remained under Communist rule, perhaps 15 per cent of all captives gave information, signed confessions, or otherwise cooperated with the Chinese. How does one explain such a phenomenon? Does it prove the power of certain drugs and thus require the interpretations of biochemistry? Does it indicate something about the "character structure" of the individuals (perhaps their softness) and thus require the interpretations of psychology? Does it demonstrate the influence of starvation, lack of sleep, and ill health on the functioning of the ego and thus likewise require psychology? Does it indicate the ways in which cultural values —or lack thereof—control human behavior, and therefore call for anthropology? Or does it show that the destruction of accustomed groups drastically changes the conditions within which human behavior occurs, thus suggesting the need for a sociological explanation?

I shall examine this particular question in a later chapter, but I wish to note here the several possible levels of interpretation and to suggest the inadequacy of each one by itself. Many laments appear in the literature concerning the isolation of disciplines, the one-factor determinisms, and the broader perspectives heeded in principle but not in research.[1] These expressions of unhappiness are, I believe, largely justified—largely, but not fully. It is the thesis of this book that important changes are occurring in research on interdisciplinary questions, changes which promise an integrated science of great strength. What I shall call field-oriented research is now appearing with increasing frequency, and the findings of much of the more specialized research can, because of their open-ended quality, be brought within the framework of larger theoretical systems.

Since the end of World War II to take an arbitrary date, studies of human behavior have begun to move from analytic separation to eclecticism to integration. There are a number of reasons for this development. Methodological work, particularly multivariate analysis and factor analysis, has helped us to organize large numbers of variables more meaningfully. Research centers with increased financial support have been able to get a larger supply of data. Computers have made it possible to use those data.[2] None of these factors, however, was sufficient or perhaps even strictly necessary to bring about the changes which have occurred in research orientation. At the least there had to be a readiness to use the new resources, and this readiness was evoked by a growing realization that many of the specialized disciplines by which we have sought to explain behavior are often inadequate to account for the complexities of the facts before us. Compile a list of the major areas of research in human behavior today, and almost every one will represent a field in which study is actively being carried on in two or more disciplines. Achievement motivation, the sources of talent, child rearing, prejudice, delinquency, social stratification, political behavior, abnormality, perception, gerontology, social change and economic development, anomie, alienation, identity—the list could be extended almost indefinitely—are commanding serious attention from psychologists and sociologists, from anthropologists and psychiatrists, not to mention able, if less frequent, participation by political scientists, economists, historians, biologists, mathematicians, and philosophers.

Perhaps we are beginning now to reap some of the benefits of the interdisciplinary departments and research centers which have developed in the last two decades. We are beginning to get over the sense of strangeness and "unnecessary complexity" in the work of those who have suggested new multilevel ways of asking the basic questions. Perhaps most important, the analytic disciplines are now sufficiently well developed that there is something to integrate.

The statement above that behavioral science is moving from analytic separation to eclecticism to integration requires some comment. Eclecticism is something of a swearword among theoretically sophisticated persons. There are good reasons for this: A statement that is "merely eclectic" may contain unresolved contradictions; it may contain propositions on different levels of generality without relating them; it may fail to expose gaps in the system of explanation; it may be inadequately parsimonious in the propositions used. Yet some protests against eclecticism mean simply that the critic's special explanatory principal is not given enough attention.

An eclectic adding together of separate explanations may help to reveal the insufficiencies of highly analytic models of explanation and lead the way to a general theory that is more systematic. On balance, an eclectic theory is a halfway station that serves best when it is most rapidly left behind. In explaining behavior, the researcher does better to add the influence of two factors than to leave one out; yet the final aim must be, not to add influences from two systems, but to bring them into one logically coherent system in order to measure their mutual influence.

AIMS OF THIS STUDY

If it is true that important steps have been taken toward a behavioral science, what is required to consolidate the gains and speed the process? That is the question posed in this study. I shall attempt to answer it in several ways.

First and most important, I am seeking to develop a theoretical point of view that is consistently interdisciplinary. The term "theory" has a strange double meaning in current usage.[3] In its sternest sense it means *demonstrated* relationships among a set of variables—or more fully, a series of propositions, tested by research, that indicate how a set of variables are related to each other under various conditions. When defined in this way, theory is both the capstone of research and the starting point for further research.

Theory is often used in another sense, however, to refer to a preparatory structure of presumed relationships that precedes and guides research. In this meaning, a theory specifies the variables that are thought to be of critical importance and the probable relationships among them. (If one opposes it, this is *mere theory*.) For referring to such a preparatory structure, *anticipatory theory* might be the best term.

We should not be misled by the several meanings of theory so that we misunderstand its place in science. Theory is continually interactive with research. Theory-nontheory is not a dichotomy; we do not go along without a theory for a long period and then break into the open with one. A wiser approach may be to speak of systematic statements of the relationships among a group of variables that have greater or lesser empirical grounding, that is, to speak of relatively untested, partially tested, and more fully tested theories. If the term used in this way lacks the connotations of thorough empirical demonstrations and internal consistency often associated with the word "theory," it nevertheless implies *some* empirical support and consistency. It is a step taken toward a firmer formulation.

A second goal may seem contradictory to, but is actually a corollary of, the first. I shall explore the widespread tendency to confuse social facts and individual facts. An adequate interdisciplinary theory will make clear *analytic* distinctions among different levels of variables. It will not produce "integration" by blurring those distinctions, by hidden or open reductionism, but will actually clarify the distinctions. It will seek then to tie the smaller systems of variables together into a larger system.[4]

Third, I shall attempt to develop a vocabulary of basic terms appropriate to the theory and sensitive to the dangers of reductionism. If the referent of a word is interlevel—simultaneously psychological and sociological, for example—this should be made explicit. Interlevel terms often both reflect and lead to confusion. In the literature today, such terms as "anomie" and "role" are used—almost indiscriminately, one is tempted to say—to refer to individual facts, cultural facts, social facts, or all at once. Doubtless there are many reasons for this, but in my judgment the primary one is the tendency most of us have to think in terms of one level of analysis only—to believe that level to be adequate to explain the full range of behavior. Our words, then, have to spread out to cover the neglected levels without our realizing it.

The cure for this creeping confusion is painful. We have to "impoverish" our words by peeling away connotations and double meanings. Since some words have a nice ring to them or have become the hallmarks of an educated mind, there is often competition over which meaning will prevail. And since many researchers have little time to read—especially across disciplinary lines—different and even contrary uses of words can continue for a long time, permitting a large literature to develop that requires translation if and when a precise terminology is adopted. A lexicon is needed; but since it is lacking, each researcher must make his own effort at clarification, bearing as he does so the responsibility for basing his work on careful study of the range of a word's uses. Simply adding another usage is of no value.

My fourth goal will be to survey some of the empirical work relevant to the study of personality, culture, and social structure. The research will be examined with one primary aim: to measure its contribution to an integrated theory of behavior. The task basically is to learn to ask a new and perhaps more complicated series of questions by examining various ways in which the problems have been studied.

THE RELATIONSHIP OF BEHAVIORAL SCIENCE TO ANALYTIC SCIENCE

When systematic efforts to apply science to human behavior began, the first task was to isolate and explore the different levels of analytic variables involved in behavior. Psychology and sociology, as abstract disciplines, emerged from these efforts, along with the branch of biology concerned with human processes. Anthropology did not develop so clearly as an abstract science of culture, but culture was a dominant theme in much of the work.

Economics and political science became differentiated, not because they worked at distinctive levels of analysis, but because their subject matters were of great importance. Adequate theory in both required a multidisciplinary approach, but this was avoided—in political science to a large degree by remaining nontheoretical (in the scientific sense) and in economics by developing its theory primarily in the context of industrial Western societies (thus controlling, at least roughly, many social, cultural, and psychological variables that become critical for an economic theory which is extended in space and time).

The development of separate analytic disciplines, however, was always accompanied, if not with full awareness of the implication, by a concern for particular issues or problems. Few scientists maintained an unwavering interest in the search for the system properties of the abstraction we call society or the abstraction we call the individual. Most wanted also to understand perception, or prejudice, or the range of cognitive responses to the world; they sought to interpret religious behavior, or delinquency, or mental illness; alcoholism or achievement motivation; political behavior or crowds.

These problem-oriented concerns required a different way of asking the questions. They required explorations on several levels—and not only additively, but interactively. In the context of strong disciplinary training, however, and at a time when understanding of the system properties at one level was still far from clear, the tendency was to use the modes of explanation that seemed valuable in analytic propositions to interpret behavior.

In the work of lesser scientists, limiting theoretical frames of reference coerced observations; their work thus did not profit from the self-correcting pressures that derive from stubborn facts. In the work of the

greater scientists—Boas, Durkheim, Freud, Lewin, McDougall, Weber—
their dedication to a limited theoretical perspective was not necessarily
less, but their keen powers of observation kept facts coming in that
demanded attention. Latent theories (insufficiently formulated but hinted
at) developed beneath and tangled with their manifest specialties. These
were critical starting points for more complex theories that could be
developed when manifest and latent propositions were brought into explicit
confrontation.

We are still far, of course, from adequate understanding of the properties of the abstract systems of the special sciences—of the processes and
potentialities of the biological individual, the psychological self, the society, and the cultural framework. For the foreseeable future, dedicated
specialists who are able and willing to work at the task of isolating and
measuring the analytic properties on one level alone are strongly needed.
Speaking as a sociologist, I would rank high the pleasure and excitement
of bringing into view, for myself or another, that invisible thing called
"society."

As we pursue such specialized tasks, however, we must be thoroughly
aware of other specialized disciplines in order to define boundaries of
competence and to escape the temptation of trying to explain the empirical world by our analytic scheme. The classic pattern of the experiment
(whether of a projected or a survey design) must be extended. To hold A,
B, and C constant so that the independent effects of D on E can be
measured is often insufficient.[5] The influence of D on E may depend
upon the extent to which A, B, or C is present. To measure the possible
effect of a "trait" on the probability of illegal behavior by studying only
persons from lower-class backgrounds (thus "controlling" for class) may
well obscure the possibility that the influence of the "trait," let us say of
aggression, may be a function of class: its importance for law violation
can be measured only by simultaneous attention to the *range* of class
backgrounds.

These statements suggest the need for interdisciplinary perspectives
even among specialists. A more decisive need for such perspectives, however, is the starting point of this book: Interest in behavior in its full
"natural" forms has become steadily stronger. In the last ten or fifteen
years, "problem-oriented" research has commanded the attention of a
large porportion of social scientists. Sometimes it appears, in fact, that
very few psychologists, anthropologists, or sociologists are left. Most of us
are stepping, noticed or unnoticed, across disciplinary lines. This shift to
behavioral questions doubtless reflects in part the growing sophistication
of the analytic disciplines and the growing number of requests from the
public—not to say from government bureaus with money to spend—for
practical guides to action. But most particularly, I believe, it demonstrates
the persisting interest that the social scientist has always had in understanding, not only the if-then world of his abstractions, but also the real
world around him.

This pressure toward a behavioral science may have developed too rapidly for optimum achievement of results, although I do not believe so. There is a great deal to be said for the claim—in some cases almost the lament—that "pure" psychology and "pure" sociology are being corrupted, the clarity of their concepts reduced, and the validity of research diminished by "premature" interest in behavior.[6] It is undoubtedly essential that many persons continue to claim this (and I continue to in part), provided that the claim is accompanied by pursuit of knowledge of system properties and relationships with full awareness of the abstractions involved.

It seems inevitable, nevertheless, that social science will become more "behavioral." If this is true, it is essential to realize what we are doing and what steps are necessary to improve our research and increase our understanding.

There is no sharp line of demarcation between analytic and behavioral science. Every science is analytic in the sense that it seeks to discover invariant relationships under stated conditions; and in some senses, every science is also behavioral. There is, however, an important difference in emphasis. By analysis one seeks to isolate a relationship in whatever constellation of other relationships it may be found. Behavioral science is directly concerned with these other relationships and with the consequences of their interaction. In an analytic approach a sociologist might ask, for example, whether an individual is more likely "to discriminate against minorities if he lives in a community where authoritarian values prevail than if he lives in one where they do not," *regardless of his personal tendencies*.[7] An affirmative answer indicates a structural effect that cannot be accounted for by the individual's own tendencies, which may work in the opposite direction. This is an important line of investigation. A behavioral science approach to the same problem begins with a different question: How do the external constraints and values of different structures, interacting with individuals with various tendencies toward discrimination, affect behavior? (See Chapter 11.)

If the trend toward problem-oriented research, as contrasted with what we might call system-oriented research, continues, there is a growing need for a redefinition of patterns of training—a need already recognized, of course, in several graduate and a few undergraduate programs. Specialized training in "government" does not prepare one to pursue questions concerning political behavior. Research in the latter requires the perspectives of cultural anthropology, sociology, and psychology. Some persons have shown, to be sure, that these perspectives can be acquired after specialized training; others have demonstrated the difficulty of doing this. Either they never learn to ask the full range of relevant questions, or they speak the language of behavioral research with a heavy accent—it is a foreign tongue to them, never entirely mastered. Specialized training in psychology does not prepare one adequately to study abnormal behavior, or perception, or motivation. Many students of psychology who have pridefully kept their contact with sociology and anthropology to a minimum have devoted or will devote a lifetime of research to topics for which knowledge of society and culture is mandatory as a complement to psychological knowledge.

I am not suggesting, of course, that every research problem requires observation on several levels. Those who can hold themselves to study of system properties and processes at one level—which I shall call *horizontal research*—need only to be aware of the boundaries of the system and the abstract quality of the propositions achieved. Even some problem-oriented study—which I shall call *vertical research*—can be pursued effectively from a specialized theoretical base, provided one is content with propositions fairly limited in space and time.

In a technical economic paper, Kenneth Strand and Thomas Dernburg have recently shown, for example, that official unemployment figures in the United States probably seriously underestimate the proportion of the potential labor force that is out of work. By a complicated statistical analysis they show that when unemployment grows, let us say, from a base rate of 4 per cent to 5 per cent, there is an additional loss of jobs (beyond the 1 per cent) of approximately ½ of 1 per cent. This results from the fact that many persons drop out of the labor force when unemployment rises—a reflection of the difficulty of finding jobs. Since "unemployed" means "out of work and actively seeking a job," they are not technically unemployed.[8] This finding, if substantiated, is important. Though it dealt with human behavior, the research used mainly the tools of mathematical economics. It yielded valuable knowledge about the economy of the United States in the mid-twentieth century.

Let us suppose, however, that the search had been for a stable economic law or laws, expressed as parsimoniously as possible. One would then need to isolate the conditions under which the discouragement factor operates. Knowledge of family structure ("Among what groups is there a high ratio of working wives?"), race relations ("Does the discouragement factor operate equally throughout society?"), demography of the labor force, consumer habits ("What are the pressures from an accustomed standard of living?"), social security measures ("What are the influences of different types of unemployment programs and retirement provisions?"), educational opportunities and attitudes, and doubtless other psychological and sociological factors would be essential. The fact that economics is a "vertical" or behavioral science has been obscured, partly by the fact that some of the variables with which it deals are quite stable, and partly by the lack of interest, until recently, in extending its propositions widely in time and space.

Because of their histories as disciplines and of "accidents" in the division of labor, and also no doubt, because their analytic perspectives alerted them to variables that were especially important (although never wholly determinative), the various special social sciences have assumed priority in the study of particular research areas, even of the problem-

oriented vertical type. Gradually, however, we are discovering the limitations on our ability to ask enough of the right questions. We turn to our
colleagues for short courses in question asking; we sit with them in
conferences; we publish books which at least put the various points of
view side by side in chapters where the Dewey decimal system cannot tear
them apart.

Now we need a generation of researchers for whom these efforts are
unnecessary, persons trained to ask the full range of questions focused
upon particular aspects of human behavior. The requirement for effective
pursuit of many of the research topics already prominent is basic training
in the analytic perspectives of anthropology, psychology, sociology, and
some aspects of biology—training well supported by a basic knowledge of
mathematics. A narrow major in any one of these is a hazard for future
work in the topics with which I shall be concerned in this book and for
many other topics. All this makes our lives more complicated than they
already are. But anything less sets severe limits on our ability to comprehend that complicated part of nature which the sciences of human behavior are trying to understand.

FOOTNOTES

*Note: The bracketed number following an author's name refers to the
footnote in which the source is cited in full.*

1. See Alex Inkeles, "Personality and Social Structure," in Robert
Merton, Leonard Broom, and Leonard S. Cottrell, Jr. (eds.), *Sociology
Today,* Basic Books, Inc., Publishers, 1959, chap. 11.

2. Although methodological questions will be raised at a number of
points, they would lead me too far from my major purpose to explore
them fully. For discussions relevant to my approach, see Paul F. Lazarsfeld, "Latent Structure Analysis," in Sigmund Koch (ed.), *Psychology:
A Study of a Science,* McGraw-Hill Book Company, 1959, vol. 3;
Paul F. Lazarsfeld, "Problems in Methodology," in Merton, Broom,
and Cottrell [1], chap. 2; Donald T. Campbell, "Factors Relevant to the
Validity of Experiments in Social Settings," *Psychological Bulletin,*
vol. 54, 1957, pp. 297–312; Robert McGinnis, "Randomization and Inference in Sociological Research," *American Sociological Review,* August,
1958, pp. 408–414; and Herbert Hyman, *Survey Design and Analysis,*
The Free Press of Glencoe, 1955. The periodical *Behavioral Science* is
a valuable source of methodological questions in general and of the use
of computers in behavioral research in particular.

3. See Robert K. Merton, "The Bearing of Sociological Theory on
Empirical Research," *Social Theory and Social Structure,* rev. ed., The
Free Press of Glencoe, 1957, for a discussion of several uses of the term
"theory." For a theoretical statement, see James G. Miller, "Toward a
General Theory for the Behavioral Sciences," *American Psychologist,*
September, 1955, pp. 513–531.

4. This is a major emphasis in many of the works cited throughout
this book, but see especially Talcott Parsons and Edward A. Shils

(eds.), *Toward a General Theory of Action,* Harvard University Press, 1951 (reprinted as a Harper Torchbook, 1962); John Gillin (ed.), *For a Science of Social Man,* The Macmillan Company, 1954; Henry A. Murray and Clyde Kluckhohn with David Schneider, *Personality in Nature, Society and Culture,* 2d ed., Alfred A. Knopf, Inc., 1953, pp. 3–67; Alex Inkeles and Daniel J. Levinson, "The Personal System and the Sociocultural System in Large-scale Organizations," *Sociometry,* June, 1963, pp. 217–229; Talcott Parsons, "An Approach to Psychological Theory in Terms of the Theory of Action," in Koch, [2], pp. 612–711. A number of Parsons' relevant papers have been drawn together in *Social Structure and Personality,* The Free Press of Glencoe, 1964. For a valuable compendium of knowledge, without regard to disciplinary lines, see Bernard Berelson and Gary A. Steiner, *Human Behavior: An Inventory of Scientific Findings,* Harcourt, Brace & World, Inc., 1964.

5. See Robin M. Williams, Jr., "Continuity and Change in Sociological Study," *American Sociological Review,* December, 1958, pp. 619–633.

6. Bolton has expresed concern lest the interest in behavior become a fad that obscures sociology's task and invites reductionism. See Charles D. Bolton, "Is Sociology a Behavioral Science?" *Pacific Sociological Review,* Spring, 1963, pp. 3–9. My answer to that question will be developed in the next chapter. Here I shall simply say that sociology is not a behavioral science as I am using that term; nor, for that matter, is psychology. Bolton points to possible dangers if they are allowed to become so without explicit attention to the transition. On this question, see Franz Adler's rejoinder in *Pacific Sociological Review,* Fall, 1963, pp. 80–81, and his paper "A Unit Concept for Sociology," *American Journal of Sociology,* January, 1960, pp. 356–364.

7. Peter Blau, "Structural Effects," *American Sociological Review,* April, 1960, p. 180.

8. Strictly speaking, the extent of withdrawal from the labor force is a net figure. Some persons are drawn into the labor force by "hard times"—the compulsion factor; others withdraw—the discouragement factor. The latter, as a national rate, is by far the larger. In November, 1962, the Bureau of Labor Statistics reported that 4,060,000 persons (5.62 per cent of the labor force) were unemployed. But if one adds those persons to the labor force who would have been in it if the unemployment rate were 4 per cent, the number rises to 7,110,000 (9.45 per cent). If 3 per cent is used as the base, the combined total of the unemployed by official definition and those out of work because of the discouragement factor is 7,825,000 (10.30 per cent). (From Kenneth Strand and Thomas Dernburg, "Cyclical Variation in Civilian Labor Force Participation," unpublished manuscript, July, 1963.)

Levels of Analysis

In formal statements there is general agreement that the science of human behavior must be carried forward on four levels—biological, individual, cultural, and social. These can be identified, roughly, with the four sciences of biology, psychology, anthropology, and sociology. This identity is rough, of course, because the sciences did not develop as neat subdivisions of a predesigned plan, but as products of the historical evolution of science, affected by the available knowledge at a given time, by academic structure, and by existing biases and intellectual styles which inclined thinkers toward the study of particular levels of influence. Above all, clear distinctions among these levels did not and have not developed because the lines of distinction are not in the behavior, which is the source of data for all the sciences, but rather in the analytic systems through which behavior is observed.[1]

It is exceedingly difficult to hold consistently to an abstract view of the world, particularly when one's ultimate interest tends to be in behavior. Under the circumstances, the specialized scientist is confronted with difficult choices: he must try to master the other behavioral sciences; or he must be ready to accept his own propositions as "if and when" statements that apply only to the analytic world of his own making; or he must subtly redefine his own field until it covers all the levels of analysis.

Although each of these processes is at work in the thinking of most of us, the last may be most prevalent. It is also the least satisfactory, because the effort to make one of the sciences a total science of behavior is more often carried out by reducing all the levels of influence to the one presumed basic level than by extending the reach of one's own theoretical scheme to include the other systems of variables. In a political figure of speech, one might say that we are more likely to have genocide than imperialism. Now imperialism is bad enough. When sociologists overrun psychology, or vice versa, they usually do a poor job of governing the new territory. Self-government is better; political scientists are generally agreed that no one can protect an individual's or a group's interests as well as the individual or group in question. What biologist or psychologist is content with one chapter on "human nature" in a sociology textbook; or what anthropologist is happy with one chapter on "culture" in a social psychology textbook written by a psychologist who knows that social psychology is simply one of psychology's specialties?

But if imperialism is bad, genocide is worse. It is one thing for a psychologist, for example, to pay some slight deference to the concepts of culture or role and to try to incorporate them into his system. It is another thing for him to say that only an individual can "behave" and that therefore the science of behavior is essentially the science of the individual—or will be as soon as we learn how to translate social facts into individual facts. Such a statement disregards the influence of the organization of parts into new wholes and the effects of *inter*action, which by definition cannot reside in individuals viewed separately.

Although they may be overlooked by the ambitious specialist at work, the weaknesses of reductionism (attempting to explain behavior by reference to one level of variables only) are well known. A random collection of motor parts is not a motor. The fact of "being a motor" resides in their *relationship,* their mutual involvement, the system of which they are a part. Yet each of the parts is also a system. A carburetor cannot be reduced to the bolts and springs and plates that make it up, because their organization is crucial. As every boy who ever took one apart knows, often to his dismay, the way in which the parts of a carburetor are interconnected is important. And further, each part is another system, a system of molecules of metal patterned in a certain way. The "behavior" of a bolt would be difficult to explain by the properties of the steel alloy of which it is made.

There is nothing sacrosanct about the four levels of analysis listed above.[2] As sciences emerge, new levels are isolated that prove to have sufficient systematic qualities that their separate examination as closed systems becomes worthwhile. Subsocieties, with their own partial systems of norms and interaction patterns, exist within a total society. They impose restraints on both the larger system of which they are a part and the smaller systems (groups and individuals) of which they are made. They are also constrained by these systems.[3] In recent years, physics has added to the familiar three states of matter—solid, liquid, and gas—a fourth, plasma. The behavior of matter in this fourth state cannot be explained by principles derived from analysis of the other states.

This book stems in part from a long-time and growing dissatisfaction with the tendency, not simply to disregard other levels of analysis in specialized research (to disregard them is not the same as to control them—to rule them out experimentally), but to subsume them in a limited model. At first, let me admit, my dissatisfaction was primarily with psychologists who denied the influence of social structural forces on behavior and with biologists who eliminated psychology. The heavy reliance of some anthropologists on culture as the basic factor in behavior also has reductionist aspects. But the eclectic views of most anthropologists, their strong interest in full description rather than in theoretical systems, perhaps their desire to live up to the very meaning of anthropology, "the science of man," have made them less reductionist than many other scientists and to some degree more open to a synthesizing view of human behavior. Only later did I begin to see the beam in my own eye and in the eyes of some of my fellow sociologists. Attempts to explain behavior by reference to the societal level or the sociocultural levels alone is[7] no more satisfactory than psychological or biological reductionism.

Paradoxically, there has often been a tendency among sociologists toward psychological and biological reductionism. The use of instincts, needs, and wishes as basic explanatory concepts was common in early sociological writing; and today a social structural or cultural fact is sometimes converted into an individual personality fact by introducing the concept of perception. Thus Gross, Mason, and McEachern define role conflict as "any situation in which the incumbent of a focal position perceives that he is confronted with incompatible expectations."[4] Incompatible expectations can exist independently of a person's perception of them and, as I shall discuss in Chapter 6, can affect his behavior whether or not they are perceived.

Perception does not determine the structure within which interactions occur or the available satisfactions in the environment and their "costs." Murray and others have distinguished between an *alpha* and a *beta* "press." The former are those elements in the objective environment, as seen or inferred by the trained observer, that can affect behavior. They need not necessarily be easily observed; in fact, perceived factors are often rationalizations. The beta press is made up of the forces acting upon an individual or group as perceived by them.[5] This is an essential distinction. With reference to the role illustration, both the social structural fact of role conflict and the psychological fact of its perception require attention.

Although a tendency toward biopsychological reductionism is not uncommon in sociology, sociocultural reductionism is doubtless more likely to occur. Individual variables are seldom disregarded entirely; they are treated as complicating variables that somewhat obscure and disturb a sound sociological interpretation. Dennis Wrong points out that there is a strong tendency in sociology virtually to eliminate the need for a personality theory by accepting a conception of human nature and socialization "that is tailor-made for special sociological problems. . . . The two-fold answer of contemporary theory is that man 'internalizes' social norms and seeks a favorable self-image by conforming to the 'expectations' of others."[6] In other terms, Wrong believes that modern sociology makes use of a "superego" concept but has separated it from any equivalent of id. "I think we must start with the recognition that *in the beginning there is the body.*"[7] Unfortunately, this last statement, in a useful effort to correct an "oversocialized conception of man," swings the pendulum too far. However one may want to describe primordial beginnings, for the infant, body and social experience arrive together. Sociologists cannot overcome reductionism by taking a stance equivalent to early Freud.

Tendencies toward reductionism are no less common among psychologists. Sometimes a rather full examination of the several levels of causation is carried out, but is labeled simply "psychology." But more often interindividual factors are disregarded. The group is readily seen, by a dedicated psychologist, as an epiphenomenon with no life of its own. In fact, some psychologists are oriented "down" to biology and chemistry, so that any emergent, systematic qualities of the individual are also treated as epiphenomena. Forces that support these tendencies are the greater prestige of the older sciences, the possibilities for more elegant research designs in the animal laboratory, the desire to support a "tough-minded" approach to the field (reflected in the fact that clinical and social psychology have only recently won status), and the almost complete lack of training in sociology and anthropology on the part of many psychologists.

Whatever the causes, psychological reductionism is no more satisfactory than sociological reductionism. Since the individual carries many distinct, even contradictory, tendencies within him, only some of which are facilitated or possible in a given situation, his behavior cannot be explained by reference to his internal "properties" alone. A large number of studies, many of which will be reported in the chapters that follow, have documented the ways in which the structural context affects behavior. The extent to which an individual will discriminate against minority-group members, support democratic policies in his union, serve as a leader of his group, or strive for academic values in his high school is not to be accounted for solely by his inner "traits." Shift the context and behavior often changes, because the new situation draws out other tendencies in him.

Put in different terms, what is abundantly clear is the tendency, in much specialized research, to commit the "fallacy of misplaced concreteness." By this telling phrase, Whitehead pointed up the danger that one may mistake analytic statements relevant to one level (A is related to B in such and such a way, all other things being equal) for descriptions of the empirical world, where forces other than A and B operate and are anything but equal.

INDIVIDUAL FACTS AND GROUP FACTS

One aspect of the tendency to blur levels of analysis is the fact that an important term may be used to refer to different systems of variables. Careful attention to context may permit one to make necessary translations; but often this is not possible or is not done. Since this problem will be dealt with at several points in the chapters that follow, I shall only illustrate it here by reference to a term to be explored carefully later.

Anomie, in Durkheim's formulation of the term,[8] was applied to a social situation in which there was low normative agreement *among* individuals. It cannot be measured or even conceptualized, as he defined it, except with reference to a group. To speak of an anomic individual would be meaningless. Strictly speaking, the term refers to the lack of cultural integration, the lack of consensus on norms. Anomie does not imply some particular individual tendency (an equivalent normative confusion within the person, for example); a wide range of different individual patterns can be found among the members of a group that is anomic. Nor does the term imply some particular pattern of social relationships.

Anomie is a cultural, a normative term. The patterns of human inter-relations that may occur within a group which is anomic are numerous; they are not implicit in the fact of anomie. There may be conflict, or movements toward cultural reintegration, or the imposition of norms by those who are powerful. To use the same term, as is sometimes done, to refer to a state of social structure, of culture, and of individuals is to imply a one-to-one relationship among the social, cultural, and person-ality facts. Such usage obscures the basic research questions: What *are* the patterns of social relationships that develop under conditions of low cultural consensus (anomie)? What *are* the various individual responses (which in turn become causes) to anomie?

This is not to imply that a cultural situation is a poor clue to probable individual and social structural facts. To know that individuals are living in an environment that is anomic is to have valuable information about their possible personality development and behavior, as Durkheim showed in his study of suicide. But Durkheim did not confuse the fact of an anomic cultural situation with individual facts. Only a tiny fraction of those living in highly anomic situations commit suicide. Others respond in different ways, perhaps destructive of individual and group values or perhaps creative.

Why do many terms refer to both individual and group levels without adequate discrimination between them? The confusion arises in part be-cause certain group and individual facts are found together empirically so often that one term seems to cover the complex of events in which they are embedded. An individual's perceived obligations often do have a close association with the culturally defined role. Anomie and individual normative confusion occur frequently together. Even when we are con-cerned with purely psychological or sociological questions, we must study behavior, from which alone we can *infer* the inner structure of the person or the patterns of the sociocultural system. It is scarcely surprising that we should sometimes confuse our inferences with the behavior from which they were derived.

The lack of precision in the vocabulary of studies of human behavior is related also to the pattern of academic training. Most students of human behavior have been trained in only one of the disciplines concerned with the topic. Few are willing to depart far from home territory—from the colleague group, the sources of prestige or promotion, the main reference group. In our home territory we find the continuing work being guided by the same models we have learned to use. Under such conditions, we are proud of and are rewarded in proportion to the "purity" of our research model. Yet insofar as we are interested in behavior, we are tempted to extend the reach of that model to cover all levels of influence. Our terms often reflect this tendency to explain the total range of facts by a partial theory.

The confusion of social and individual facts also rests partly on the measuring process. Group facts are often averages or ranges that derive from summation or aggregation of individual measures. To say that the average height of a group of men is 5 feet 10 inches tells nothing about any one individual, yet the group fact has been derived from a series of individual measures. To discover that schizophrenics come in larger proportion from highly mobile urban areas, measured in averages, is not to say that the specific individuals who become schizophrenic experience high mobility. It is now generally recognized as an "ecological error" to assume that the average measure of a heterogeneous area can be used to explain individual experiences therein. Not all persons in an area of high delinquency become delinquent; not all persons in an area of high anomie experience normlessness. Our vocabularies should be subtle enough to reflect the differences in levels of analysis to which we are referring at a particular time.[9]

Psychologically oriented persons sometimes assert that an aggregated fact has no importance in its own right, since it is derived from a series of individual facts. A moment's reflection will reveal, I believe, the error in this point of view. We readily speak of a "peasant society" or a "middle-class society" to refer to situations where large majorities can be identified as peasants or middle class. That is, the group designation is based on aggregated individual facts; but it is not confused with them. To be a peasant in a society where 80 per cent of one's fellows share the same status is one thing; to be a peasant in a middle-class society is something else. The proportion, which is a group fact, is of great importance in determining the meaing of the various individual facts, as can be recognized by comparing the implications of middle-class status in an "underdeveloped" country with its implications in a highly industrialized country.

Lazarsfeld and Menzel have distinguished between the kind of aggregative group property illustrated above, which they term analytical, and another group dimension derived from individual measures which is more readily recognized as a group characteristic. The appearance of "stars" in sociometric choices, for example, is based not only on individual selections but also on their patterning. Lazarsfeld and Menzel call this a structural property of groups. It is based on a relationship among the individual facts and thus cannot reside in them separately.[10]

There are in addition, of course, "integral" or "global" group properties that are not derived from facts about individuals. The use of money as a medium of exchange and the presence of written rules are examples.[11]

The characteristics of individuals can also be classified in various ways.

Cattell and Eysenck have sought to isolate "traits" by extensive factor analysis, a procedure that runs the risk of drawing an excessively sharp line between the individual and his situation, but is not inherently reductionist. Lazarsfeld and Menzel have noted that some individual characteristics imply relationships with others. They distinguish absolute properties, which can be obtained without further knowledge of relationships to others (income, age), relational properties (one's sociometric score), comparative properties (sibling order), and contextual properties (residence in a racially mixed neighborhood).[12]

The distinction between individual and group properties is sometimes overlooked because of an assumed parallel relationship between them. Social class status, for example, may be referred to as a "sociological variable." But as a measure of an individual's comparative level of income, education, and prestige, it is in fact an individual property. The average status level of his neighborhood is a group property. And the two measures may differ widely. Lack of parallelism is clearly illustrated by a hung jury—a group made indecisive by the very fact that its individual members are decisive and unwilling to yield their positions.[13]

In his examination of the mathematical study of small groups, Coleman has noted that many such studies are in fact concerned with individual behavior. "These experiments develop generalizations about the behavior of an individual under certain social conditions, leaving unexamined the behavior of the social system which constitutes these conditions." [14] Neither the analytic sciences of the individual and the group nor a behavioral science that studies their relationships can develop until their separate properties are clearly specified.

Some of those most inclined to interdisciplinary work are liable to the temptation to develop an interlevel terminology that blurs rather than integrates. In an excellent chapter on roles, for example, Sargent writes:

One reason sociologists have failed to agree upon a concept of role is that some have approached role as an objectively defined aspect of the culture pattern which can be considered apart from the persons who actually enact or play the roles. Other sociologists include personal variables in their concept. The social psychologist, always concerned with individuals, naturally leans toward the latter type of conceptualization. His problem is to frame a concept of role which is broad enough to cover such cases as those just mentioned, yet specific enough to have meaning. Can we then define role so as to embrace cultural patterning and personal modifications, including that elusive but very important individual perceptual factor?

With these considerations in mind, I venture the following definition: *A person's role is a pattern or type of social behavior which seems situationally appropriate to him in terms of the demands and expectations of those in his group.*[15]

Although by this definition Sargent seeks "to embrace cultural patterning and personal modifications," the cultural element in the definition is lost. What an individual sees as "situationally appropriate to him" may or may not correspond to a role viewed as "an objectively defined aspect of the culture pattern." One cannot use the same term to cover these two different facts without promoting a tendency to confuse one for the other. (In Chapter 6 I shall suggest a terminology to refer to the various levels involved in the concept of role.)

Sometimes individual facts can be used as an *index* of social facts if the operations involved are carefully specified. Selvin, for example, having no direct measure of the actual behavior of the officers in a military unit that might have been summed and averaged to arrive at a social measure of "leadership style," used the perceptions of the privates concerning their leaders' behavior.[16] Selvin was well aware that the perceptions of the privates were not the same thing as the leadership being measured; they simply comprised an index to that leadership. The only question in such usage would be "Is it a good index? Does it accurately measure what it is supposed to measure?" Although I have doubts about the value of this particular index (a problem I shall not explore here), the procedure is legitimate and often necessary. Properly used, the indexing process need not confuse different types of events. No one mistakes the rising and falling of mercury in a glass tube for the temperature changes which such variation records.

The confusion of social and individual facts rests, finally, on the kinds of units we have become accustomed to regard as "real." The boundaries of an individual can be comprehended by our senses; his reality seems self-evident. If a biochemist suggests that an individual is "nothing but" a series of interconnected cells, it is simple to emphasize that interconnectedness and to note that much which is important emerges only out of the pattern of their relationships. And, of course, the same applies to groups. Their reality lies in the relationships among individuals and cannot, therefore, rest with the individuals taken separately.[17]

Language patterns are the carriers, and in part the causes, of some of our difficulties in maintaining clarity in our view of analytic separation on one hand and empirical interaction on the other. I shall not explore here the thesis developed by Whitehead, Wittgenstein, Korzybski, and others that a philosophical picture of the world, broadly associated with Aristotle and reflected in the very structure of most European languages, distorts our perception and disrupts our logic.[18] It is now widely recognized that to say, e.g., "the rose is red" is to adopt a linguistic form that does violence to the process of observation and to nature. Less poetically but more accurately, we must note that redness is the result of the interaction of certain wave lengths and certain receptors in a particular situation: redness is field-determined. Thus we can reunite, in harmony with the natural world, what our linguistic habits have separated, which in this example is the perceiver and the perceived.

There is an opposite language problem, however, which also blocks understanding. Some terms are used as analytic constructs designed precisely to isolate some part of the empirical world, in order to study better the various combinations in which it may be found. If there is such a thing as substantial agreement among the members of a group regarding the proper ways for one of their members to behave when he occupies a given position, we need a name for that agreement. I shall call it a role. Now this is not behavior; nor is it the way the individual believes he should behave (although he may agree); it is an abstraction inferred from the words and actions of group members. It is a name for a consistent orientation to action shared by most group members. We need to conceptualize it independently in order to be able to inquire what happens when, for example, group agreement begins to fall off, or an individual who does not share the norms is confronted with expectations regarding them from others. What this means is that effective integration of a field or interlevel system requires, somewhat paradoxically, great clarity in the definition of single-level terms. I suppose saying this is to express some sympathy for the farmer in Robert Frost's poem who keeps insisting that "good fences make good neighbors." A wall, no; but a low fence, perhaps.

WHAT SHOULD A BEHAVIORAL SCIENCE BE CALLED?

One interesting, if relatively unimportant, aspect of the development of multidisciplinary work is the confusion that stems from lack of an agreed-upon name. "Social science" is inadequate and in some person's minds conjures up images of eleventh-grade civics. "Behavioral science," which I have been using in part, has connotations that are misleading, for it generally excludes experimental psychology and biology.

Social psychology has developed as the discipline most directly concerned with behavior; but there are somewhat confusing tendencies within this field. Some social psychologists have thought of the discipline as one of the several specialties among the sciences of man, with its own distinct analytic level of study; others interpret the field as a multilevel discipline which is built on the more specialized sciences.[19] But equally common is the tendency to view social psychology as a part of one of the "parent" disciplines, thus denying it any separate life, whether as a single or a multilevel field. Krech and Crutchfield, for example, declare that "social psychology does not differ in any fundamental way from psychology in general." [20] And Strauss holds that "social psychology . . . should have much to offer its sister fields, but only insofar as its practitioners can self-consciously tie their work back to the organizational heart of sociology and anthropology." [21] This is close to the view expressed by Rose that symbolic interaction ties society and the individual together "in such a way that sociology cannot be divorced from social psychology." [22]

The view that there are two social psychologies—which I suspect is an understatement—reaches back at least to 1908, when the first two books titled *Social Psychology*, written by E. A. Ross and William McDougall, were published within a few weeks of each other. There were significant differences between them. In recent years with the development of "psychological anthropology" or "cultural psychology," a third social psychology—or a field overlapping the other two—has appeared.

A case can be made for calling the interlevel field "sociology," if one goes by some of the strongest research and theoretical traditions of that subject and not by the literal meaning of its name. Many of its major writers, from Comte and Spencer to Weber and even the staunchly "patriotic" Durkheim, reached well beyond a strictly structuralist view. In the United States, the influence of Cooley, Thomas, Park, Faris, Znaniecki, and others is shown in the powerful emphasis on interaction.[23] Most of the eminent contemporary sociologists of whatever school would be difficult to classify as specialized students of society, if "society" is used to imply an analytically distinct system. This is notably true of Parsons, who has been the leader in the development of a theory of "action," [24] and of Sorokin,[25] MacIver, and Becker. But it is scarcely less true of Merton, Lazarsfeld, Davis, Homans, Blumer, and many others. This is a diverse list on many grounds, which makes more impressive the tendency of sociologists to act as behavioral scientists.[26]

In psychology, the gestalt approach of Koffka, Köhler, Wertheimer, and others broadened the theoretical range. It was a major influence in the development of Lewin's field theory. Freud's theories, which at first glance seem narrowly focused on the individual, as well as later developments in psychoanalytic theory, have also played an important part in making the self-other relationship central. Lewin credited Freud with the abolition of boundaries between the normal and pathological, the ordinary and the unusual, thus "homogenizing" psychology.[27] But Freud's "homogenizing" influence is much wider than that. Bronfenbrenner, in an excellent comparative study, notes that underneath the "class-theoretical" thinking, the either-or categories, the focus on the past, and other tendencies so much in opposition to field theory, Freud has a "latent" theory that compels attention to self-other interactions.[28] In recent years a broad definition of psychology's task has become much more common. A major encyclopedic work, *Psychology: A Study of a Science,* goes a long way, in the six volumes so far published, toward defining psychology as a behavioral science.[29]

Perhaps "anthropology" is the most appropriate name for a general science of man, whether we base this judgment on the literal meaning of the word or on the actual interests of some of its most distinguished representatives, particularly those working in recent years. Sapir, Linton, Kluckhohn, Mead, and many others have contributed greatly to a science of "society, culture, and personality." [30]

It would be difficult to redefine our present terms for the various disciplines. But if we were to ask the proverbial man from Mars—who may not remain proverbial—to make order out of the current situation, he might suggest that in our present state of knowledge there appear to be four analytic levels, which can be named human biology, psychology, sociology, and culturology, all of which together constitute anthropology. This terminology is nearly unthinkable, of course. "Culturology" [31] jangles our nerves, as most neologisms do; (we are used to the other "paleologisms"). Granted the reality we tend to invest in our words, biologists, psychologists, and sociologists are not likely to accept designation of their fields as branches of anthropology; nor are contemporary anthropologists likely to give up the name of their specialty. Nevertheless, as a way of alerting ourselves to both the analytic distinctions and the necessary connections among the sciences of human behavior, such a terminology may have some merit. We can also relate the specialized "vertical" studies to the Martian's terminology in the following way:

ILLUSTRATIVE RESEARCH AREAS

"Anthropology"

		Perception	Illness	Suicide	Talent	Discrimination	Economic behavior	Political behavior	Religious behavior	Motivation	Socialization
Analytic disciplines	Biology										
	Psychology										
	Sociology										
	Culturology										

Some of the "vertical" subjects are much more highly developed than others, of course. To emphasize their structural similarities I have listed fairly unimportant research areas side by side with major disciplines. And clearly the relevance of all four levels is not equal for every problem. Biological factors, for example, can be regarded as constants for many questions of human behavior or for the more limited area of "social action"—behavior relevant to self-other interactions. (The economist seldom has to be concerned with interference with the brain's supply of sugar or other disturbances of the steady state of the organism, although it is technically true that economic behavior may be affected by such organic processes.)

Before I sound too much like Auguste Comte, however, let me come back to a more realistic description of the present situation and possible future development. Most of the contributions of biology to a behavioral science, excluding the work of biologists on the analytic level, have been developed by psychologists or by theoretically inclined psychiatrists or other medical men. What we have seen, therefore, is three disciplines, each fairly clearly differentiated from the others on analytic grounds, but each tending, in some aspects of its development, to incorporate the others.[32] Perhaps the situation can accurately be charted in this way:

RELATIONSHIPS AMONG THE BEHAVIORAL SCIENCES

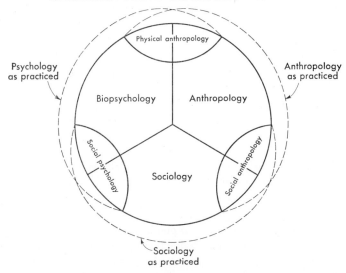

It is scarcely surprising that strong pressures for a multilevel science should emerge from each of the three disciplines, since they share the fundamental interest in understanding human behavior. The need for both analytic disciplines and a synthesizing discipline is clear. The tendency to develop a kind of halfway house between them, however, leads to serious problems. These are revealed most clearly when research on a particular question has been carried out primarily by persons who are trained to study one level of abstraction but who are interested in the study of behavior. Thus it has been over great obstacles that the study of mental illness has developed beyond first a biological and then a psychological orientation to include attention to the cultural and structural factors. Because sociologists became the first specialists in a theory of delinquency, it has been difficult to incorporate study of individual factors. Psychological interpretations of delinquency tend to be asserted as counterproposals rather than as parts of an interactive system. This situation is now changing in many substantive fields, as I shall show in later chapters; but skill in structuring problems so that they are appropriate to behavioral research, and skill in speaking a language designed to show the articulation of the several levels, are still in scarce supply.

No definitive name for these skills and the discipline within which they are employed emerges from this brief examination of the discipline's lines of development. I shall use the somewhat awkward phrase "behavioral science" most frequently, but on occasion I shall speak of social psychology or anthropology (my own preference) when I think the context will not lead to misunderstanding.

Two major disciplines, economics and political science, appear in the table given earlier which structures "anthropology." They are not listed as separate analytic levels, however, but as research areas. This is in no sense a judgment on their importance; it simply indicates that the behavior with which they are concerned is influenced by factors from several levels. I noted in Chapter 1 that the relationship of economics and political science to the other sciences of human behavior has been obscured because the two disciplines have focused on fairly stable and limited structures. That situation is now changing. Both fields are developing behavioral science branches of great promise. The vast increase in international contacts relevant to economic and political processes and the concomitant speed of change in prevailing structures have emphasized the need for attention to psychological and sociocultural variables. The research is being carried out both by economists and political scientists who have broadened the range of questions in which they are interested, and by anthropologists, psychologists, and sociologists who have applied their concepts to economic and governmental data.

The study of economic and political change in "underdeveloped" areas, for example, has demanded attention to psychological, cultural, and structural processes. As a newly discovered problem, it was not decisively claimed by any one of the disciplines; nor could a highly specialized approach do justice to the range of the facts. Factors that each of the five subjects had come to take for granted abruptly became variables which no one of the sciences alone was equipped to study. The result has been a somewhat disorganized and occasionally partisan, but basically exciting and fruitful, interdisciplinary effort.[33]

Economists found that their models of how a nation moves from a plateau of low productivity to self-sustaining economic growth fit only part of the facts. A geometric curve of technological development is inadequate, for there are plainly "take-off" points that seem to represent a discontinuity. Population and geographical factors are involved, but not decisively; for different rates of growth have been associated with similar demographic and environmental situations. Contact with more advanced societies explains little by itself, for the results may be as various as those in Jordan and Japan. More than half a century ago Weber argued persuasively that cultural values, particularly those embodied in religion, and their personality counterparts are crucial influences on the course of economic development, a point that is continually being documented by variation in rates of growth in the contemporary world. Yet cultural values are also dependent variables, deeply influenced by urbanization, culture contact, and technological change.

In my effort in this book to develop a systematic statement of behavioral science, I shall not undertake an interpretation or examination of "economic behavior" [34] or "political behavior." [35] I have chosen other research areas for my main illustrative cases. Nevertheless, a significant and growing proportion of the problems dealt with by economics and political science are behavioral science problems. They fall within the field as I am defining it, and the point of view developed here is relevant to their interpretation. It is my hope that a reader interested in economic or political behavior will discover that field theory structures his problems in a meaningful way.[36]

FOOTNOTES

Note: The bracketed number following an author's name refers to the footnote in which the source is cited in full.

1. Spiegel argues effectively for discarding the idea of levels, with its hierarchical implications, and using "foci" instead. He believes that the concept of focus better captures the idea of the different disciplines viewing the same phenomenon from different perspectives. See John Spiegel in Roy R. Grinker (ed.), *Toward a Unified Theory of Human Behavior,* Basic Books, Inc., Publishers, 1956, pp. 16–26. Such a view, however, may underplay the "system properties," the boundary-maintaining tendencies, and the emergence that a concept of levels permits. See also T. C. Schneirla, "The 'Levels' Concept in the Study of Social Organization in Animals," in John Rohrer and Muzafer Sherif (eds.), *Social Psychology at the Crossroads,* Harper & Row, Publishers, Incorporated, 1951, pp. 83–120; Abraham Edel, "The Concept of Levels in Social Theory," in Llewellyn Gross (ed.), *Symposium On Sociological Theory,* Harper & Row, Publishers, Incorporated, 1959, pp. 167–195; and Talcott Parsons, "An Approach to Psychological Theory in Terms of the Theory of Action," in Sigmund Koch (ed.), *Psychology: A Study of a Science,* McGraw-Hill Book Company, 1959, vol. 3, pp. 612–711.

If the concept of levels seems inevitably to imply a hierarchical structure of sciences or to increase the danger of reductionism, let us think of "foci," "modes," "levels," etc., as synonyms.

2. At many points in this essay I shall condense the four-level model into a two-level model for purposes of simplicity. But it is necessary to realize that reference simply to biopsychological and sociocultural influences involves some loss of information. There are system-maintenance processes on each level that may be obscured if they are not studied separately. This should not be taken as an inevitable fact, however. Discussions of "levels" and "reductionism" have too often been carried on in absolute terms, as if the issues were permanently resolvable on the basis of general principles. A wiser approach may be to argue the matter on the grounds that with *existing* theories and at *current* levels of knowledge, one level of organization can, or cannot, be subsumed under another level without loss of understanding. In behavioral science, arguments for the importance of "interaction," "emergence," and "organization" seem to me to be sound in the context of contemporary theories. I shall therefore take an "antireductionist" position. For an excellent discussion of this question, see Ernest Nagel, *The Structure of Science,* Harcourt, Brace & World, Inc., 1961, chap. 11.

3. Theodore Caplow, "The Criteria of Organizational Success," *Social Forces,* October, 1953, pp. 1–9, distinguishes four levels of association.

4. Neal Gross, Ward S. Mason, and A. W. McEachern, *Explorations in Role Analysis,* John Wiley & Sons, Inc., 1958, p. 248.

5. See George G. Stern, Morris Stein, and Benjamin Bloom, *Methods in Personality Assessment: Human Behavior in Complex Social Situations,* The Free Press of Glencoe, 1956, pp. 36–38.

6. Dennis H. Wrong, "The Oversocialized Conception of Man in Modern Sociology," *American Sociological Review,* April, 1961, p. 183.

7. *Ibid.,* p. 191.

8. See Émile Durkheim *Suicide,* The Free Press of Glencoe, 1951.

9. See W. S. Robinson, "Ecological Correlations and the Behavior of Individuals," *American Sociological Review,* June, 1950, pp. 351–357; Leo A. Goodman, "Ecological Regressions and Behavior of Individuals," *American Sociological Review,* December, 1953, pp. 663–664; Otis D. Duncan and Beverly Davis, "An Alternate to Ecological Correlation," *American Sociological Review,* December, 1953, pp. 665–666; John A. Clausen and Melvin Kohn, "The Ecological Approach in Social Psychiatry," *American Journal of Sociology,* September, 1954, pp. 140–151.

10. See Paul Lazarsfeld and Herbert Menzel, "On the Relation between Individual and Collective Properties," in Amatai Etzioni (ed.), *Complex Organizations,* Holt, Rinehart and Winston, Inc., 1961, pp. 422–440.

11. See *ibid.* and Hanan Selvin and Warren Hagstrom, "The Empirical Classification of Formal Groups," *American Sociological Review,* June, 1963, pp. 399–411. On the properties of groups see also Robert Merton, *Social Theory and Social Structure,* 2d ed., The Free Press of Glencoe, 1957, pp. 310–326; Raymond B. Cattell, "Types of Group Characteristics," in Harold Guetzkow (ed.), *Groups, Leadership, and Men,* Carnegie Press, 1951, pp. 16–52; Edgar F. Borgatta, Leonard Cottrell, Jr., and Henry J. Meyer, "On the Dimensions of Group Behavior," *Sociometry,* December, 1956, pp. 223–240; and John K. Hemphill and Charles M. Westie, "The Measurement of Group Dimensions," *Journal of Psychology,* April, 1950, pp. 325–341.

12. See R. B. Cattell, *Personality: A Systematic, Theoretical, and Factual Study,* McGraw-Hill Book Company, 1950; R. B. Cattell, *Personality and Motivation Structure and Measurement of Behavior,* World Book Company, 1957; H. J. Eysenck, *The Structure of Human Personality,* John Wiley & Sons, Inc., 1953; and Lazarsfeld and Menzel [10].

13. *Ibid.,* p. 430.

14. James S. Coleman in Herbert Solomon (ed.), *Mathematical Thinking in the Measurement of Behavior,* The Free Press of Glencoe, 1960, pp. 13–14. My preference would be to substitute the term "processes" for "behavior" in the phrase "behavior of the social system."

15. S. S. Sargent in Rohrer and Sherif, [1], pp. 359–360.

16. Hanan Selvin, *The Effects of Leadership,* The Free Press of Glencoe, 1960.

17. Émile Durkheim, *The Rules of Sociological Method,* The University of Chicago Press, 1938; C. K. Warriner, "Groups are Real: A

Reaffirmation," *American Sociological Review,* October, 1956, pp. 549–554.

18. See Alfred N. Whitehead, *Process and Reality,* The Macmillan Company, 1929; L. Wittgenstein, *Tractatus Logico-Philosophicus,* trans. D. F. Pears and B. F. McGuinness, Humanities Press, 1961; Alfred Korzybski, *Science and Sanity,* 2d ed., International Non-Aristotelian Library Publishing Company, 1941.

19. This group includes some of the most distinguished contributors to the theoretical perspective of this book. Without in any way implying that they agree with the propositions developed here, I would mention Urie Bronfenbrenner, Otto Klineberg, Theodore Newcomb, and Muzafer Sherif.

20. David Krech and Richard S. Crutchfield, *Theory and Problems of Social Psychology,* McGraw-Hill Book Company, 1948, p. 7. In the second edition (David Krech, Richard S. Crutchfield, and Egerton L. Ballachey, *Individual in Society,* McGraw-Hill Book Company, 1962), this position is considerably, but somehat ambiguously, modified. Social psychology is defined as "the science of interpersonal behavior events." It is different from "the social disciplines"—economics, political science, sociology, anthropology (pp. 3–4), but "builds on the findings of general psychology" modified to apply to social events (p. 9). Later, however, a synthesizing view of social psychology is given: "Our first objective in writing this book was to organize what man has learned about man—from general psychology, personality psychology, social psychology, anthropology, sociology—to make manifest the harmony which appeared to us to inhere in these accumulated facts, observations, and speculations. In other words, we have sought to present a science of social psychology as an organic whole—in so far as this is currently possible in this complex and fast-changing field without doing violence to the available facts. The critical reader will, we hope, find in these pages a synthesis of the behavioral sciences which will merit his attention" (p. 13).

It is no general criticism of their text, surely one of the best, to point out that social psychology in this statement is both one of the disciplines to be unified and the unifying discipline—a statement well designed to express a widespread ambiguity in the use of "social psychology."

21. Anselm Strauss, *Mirrors and Masks: The Search for Identity,* The Free Press of Glencoe, 1959, p. 11.

22. Arnold Rose (ed.), *Human Behavior and Social Processes,* Houghton Mifflin Company, 1962, p. 179.

23. See Roscoe Hinkle, "Antecedents of the Action Orientation in American Sociology before 1935," *American Sociological Review,* October, 1963, pp. 705–715.

24. See, for example, his *Structure of Social Action,* McGraw-Hill Book Company, 1937; *Toward a General Theory of Action* (edited with Edward A. Shils), Harper Torchbooks, Harper & Row, Publishers, Incorporated, 1962; and his essay in Koch [1].

25. Pitirim A. Sorokin, *Society, Culture, and Personality,* Harper & Row, Publishers, Incorporated, 1947. The subtitle is significant: "A System of General Sociology."

26. The interdisciplinary qualities of sociology are shown clearly in a recent major collection of historical and contemporary works

[Talcott Parsons, Edward Shils, Kaspar D. Naegele, and Jesse R. Pitts (eds.), *Theories of Society: The Foundations of Modern Sociological Theory*, 2 vols., The Free Press of Glencoe, 1961]. A substantial part of vol. 2 is given to interpretations of "Personality and the Social System." At least ten psychologists are represented, with Freud receiving major emphasis. More than a dozen anthropologists are included in the two volumes, as well as several economists, historians, and philosophers. To some degree, this "sociological" collection represents the "action theory" of Professor Parsons and his associates. Almost all the authors in another collection [Robert Merton, Leonard Broom, and Leonard Cottrell, Jr. (eds.), *Sociology Today*, Basic Books, Inc., Publishers, 1959] are sociologists. Yet many of the papers draw widely on psychology, psychiatry, and anthropology. There were also strong interdisciplinary qualities in an earlier collection: H. E. Barnes, Howard Becker, and Frances B. Becker (eds.), *Contemporary Social Theory*, D. Appleton–Century Company, Inc., 1940. In general, Blumer seems to me in error when he states that "sociological thought rarely recognizes or treats human societies as composed of individuals who have selves" (in Rose [22], pp. 184–185). Studies that isolate a purely structural influence are in fact less common than those in the symbolic interaction and social action traditions.

27. Kurt Lewin, *A Dynamic Theory of Personality*, McGraw-Hill Book Company, 1935, p. 22.

28. Urie Bronfenbrenner, "Toward an Integrated Theory of Personality," in Robert R. Blake and Glenn V. Ramsey (eds.), *Perception: An Approach to Personality*, The Ronald Press Company, 1951, pp. 206–257. In his comments on the convergences among Lewin, Freud, Rank, McDougall, Sullivan, and others, Bronfenbrenner, although he does not overlook their obvious dissimilarities, suggests a process among psychologists paralleling the description of convergence among the social scientists Weber, Durkheim, Pareto, and Marshall that Parsons develops in *The Structure of Social Action*. In Chapter 12 I shall explore some of the ways in which contemporary psychiatry has elaborated the aspects of Freud and others that are closest to a field view.

29. Sigmund Koch (ed.), McGraw-Hill Book Company, 1959–1963. This is not to suggest that the corpus of sociology and anthropology is included in the volumes. In fact, they lean much more heavily toward biology. But in vols. 3, 5, and 6, many of the problems dealt with by contemporary sociology and anthropology are explored. Several anthropologists and a few sociologists and economists are among the authors. *Psychology: A Study of a Science* is, in fact, scarcely less interdisciplinary than the *Handbook of Social Psychology* [Gardner Lindzey (ed.), 2 vols., Addison-Wesley Publishing Company, Inc., 1954], an indication, perhaps, of editorial judgment, but also I believe a sign of the strong tendencies toward an interdisciplinary perspective that are generating within psychology.

30. As in each of the other specialties, there is resistance to this trend in anthropology. Among the recent "inventories" I have cited, *Anthropology Today* [A. L. Kroeber (ed.), The University of Chicago Press, 1953] is the least broad. Several biologists and physicians are among the authors, but no psychologists or sociologists. And several of the chapters that deal with topics of shared concern draw almost entirely on anthropological sources (e.g., the chapters on projective tests, social structure, and ecology). Other interdisciplinary topics are based

on material drawn from a wider range of sources (e.g., Hallowell on "Culture, Personality, and Society," Mead on "National Character," and Caudill on "Applied Anthropology in Medicine").

31. See Leslie A. White, *The Science of Culture,* Fararr, Straus & Cudahy, Inc., 1949.

32. Much of the process in psychology and sociology has been carried out by persons who call themselves social psychologists, but most of whom, at least until recently, have also identified closely with one or the other of the "parent" disciplines. Strongly interdisciplinary branches or research emphases do exist, however. The study of small groups, interaction process, and group dynamics, for example, is largely field-oriented. "Group dynamics ... can be located within the social sciences. And yet it cannot be identified readily as a subpart of any of the traditional academic disciplines" [Dorwin Cartwright and Alvin Zander (eds.), *Group Dynamics,* 2d ed., Harper & Row, Publishers, Incorporated, 1960, p. 5]. "The study of small groups is thus a method for the study of social systems, of culture, and of personality—all three" (A. Paul Hare, Edgar F. Borgatta, and Robert F. Bales, *Small Groups,* Alfred A. Knopf, Inc., 1955, p. v.). And Bales, in his description of the method of "interaction process," refers to variation in personality, social organization, culture, and situation as important subjects of study. (*Interaction Process Analysis,* Addison-Wesley Publishing Company, Inc., 1950, p. 26.)

33. See Gabriel Almond and James S. Coleman (eds.), *The Politics of Developing Areas,* Princeton University Press, 1960; G. M. Foster, *Traditional Culture: And the Impact of Technological Change,* Harper & Row, Publishers, Incorporated, 1962; E. E. Hagen, *On the Theory of Social Change,* The Dorsey Press, 1962; Bert F. Hoselitz, *Sociological Aspects of Economic Growth,* The Free Press of Glencoe, 1960; Daniel Lerner, *The Passing of Traditional Society,* The Free Press of Glencoe, 1959; Daniel Lerner (guest ed.), "Attitude Research in Modernizing Areas," *Public Opinion Quarterly,* Fall, 1958, whole issue; Margaret Mead (ed.), *Cultural Patterns and Technical Change,* UNESCO (Mentor Books, New American Library of World Literature, Inc.), 1955; Gunnar Myrdal, *Rich Lands and Poor Lands,* Harper & Row, Publishers, Incorporated, 1957; Robert Redfield, *The Primitive World and Its Transformation,* Cornell University Press, 1953; W. Lyle Shannon (ed.), *Underdeveloped Areas: A Book of Readings and Research,* Harper & Row, Publishers, Incorporated, 1957; and the periodical *Economic Development and Cultural Change.*

34. Among the studies which I have found particularly valuable for an understanding of sociocultural and individual factors in economic behavior, in addition to those cited on the topic of economic development, are the following: M. J. Herskovits, *Economic Anthropology,* 2d ed., Alfred A. Knopf, Inc., 1952; C. A. Hickman and Manford H. Kuhn, *Individuals, Groups, and Economic Behavior,* Holt, Rinehart and Winston, Inc., 1956; Everett C. Hughes, *Men and Their Work,* The Free Press of Glencoe, 1958; Alex Inkeles, "Industrial Man: The Relation of Status to Experience, Perception, and Value," *American Journal of Sociology,* July, 1958, pp. 1–31; George Katona, *Psychological Analysis of Economic Behavior,* McGraw-Hill Book Company, 1951; Simon Kuznets (ed.), *Economic Growth: Brazil, India, Japan,* The Duke University Press, 1955; Albert Lauterbach, *Man, Motives, and Money: Psychological Frontiers of Economics,* Cornell University Press, 1954;

S. M. Lipset and Reinhard Bendix, *Social Mobility in Industrial Society*, University of California Press, 1959; David C. McClelland, *The Achieving Society*, D. Van Nostrand Company, Inc., 1961; Talcott Parsons and Neil Smelser, *Economy and Society*, The Free Press of Glencoe, 1956; Morris Rosenberg, *Occupations and Values*, The Free Press of Glencoe, 1957; W. W. Rostow, *The Process of Economic Growth*, W. W. Norton & Company, 1952; W. W. Rostow, "The Take-off into Self-sustained Growth," *Economic Journal*, March, 1956, pp. 25–48; J. J. Spengler, "Sociological Theory, Economic Analysis, and Economic Policy," *American Economic Review*, May, 1953, pp. 340–349; Max Weber, *The Protestant Ethic and the Spirit of Capitalism*, George Allen & Unwin Ltd., 1930; Max Weber, *The Theory of Social and Economic Organization*, Oxford University Press, 1947; Max Weber, *Sociology of Religion*, Beacon Press, 1963; Harold Wilensky, "Orderly Careers and Social Participation: The Impact of Work History on Social Integration in the Middle Mass," *American Sociological Review*, August, 1961, pp. 521–539. For a discussion of some of the vast literature that comments on Weber's work, see J. Milton Yinger, *Religion in the Struggle for Power*, The Duke University Press, 1946 (reprinted, Russell and Russell, 1961), chaps. 3 and 4.

35. An equally rich and to some degree overlapping literature is available on political behavior. See Gabriel Almond, *The Appeals of Communism*, Princeton University Press, 1954; E. C. Banfield, *Political Influence*, The Free Press of Glencoe, 1961; Daniel Bell, (ed.), *The Radical Right*, Doubleday & Company, Inc., 1963; Angus Campbell, P. E. Converse, W. E. Miller, and D. E. Stokes, *The American Voter*, John Wiley & Sons, Inc., 1960; Hadley Cantril, *The Politics of Despair*, Basic Books, Inc., Publishers, 1958; James C. Davies, *Human Nature in Politics*, John Wiley & Sons, Inc., 1963; Eric Fromm, *Escape from Freedom*, Holt, Rinehart and Winston, Inc., 1941; Stanley Hoffman, *Le Mouvement Poujade*, Libraire Armand Colin, 1956; Herbert Hyman, *Political Socialization: A Study in the Psychology of Political Behavior*, The Free Press of Glencoe, 1959; International Sociological Association, *The Nature of Conflict*, UNESCO, 1957; Morris Janowitz, *The Professional Soldier*, The Free Press of Glencoe, 1960; V. O. Key, Jr., *Public Opinion and American Democracy*, Alfred A. Knopf, Inc., 1961; William Kornhauser, *The Politics of Mass Society*, The Free Press of Glencoe, 1959; Robert Lane, *Political Life: Why People Get Involved in Politics*, The Free Press of Glencoe, 1959; Harold D. Lasswell, *Power and Personality*, W. W. Norton & Company, Inc., 1948; Gerhard Lenski, "Status Crystallization," *American Sociological Review*, August, 1954, pp. 405–413; Paul Lazarsfeld, Bernard Berelson, and William McPhee, *Voting*, The University of Chicago Press, 1954; Seymour M. Lipset, *Political Man*, Doubleday & Company, Inc., 1960; Lucy Mair, *New Nations*, The University of Chicago Press, 1963; C. Wright Mills, *The Power Elite*, Oxford University Press, 1956; Lucian Pye, *Guerilla Communism in Malaya: Its Social and Political Meaning*, Princeton University Press, 1956; J. David Singer, "The Relevance of the Behavioral Sciences to the Study of International Relations," *Behavioral Science*, October, 1961, pp. 324–335; Martin Trow, "Small Businessmen, Political Tolerance, and Support for McCarthy," *American Journal of Sociology*, November, 1958, pp. 270–281; Robert E. Ward, "Political Modernization and Political Culture in Japan," *World Politics*, July, 1963, pp. 569–596; Harold Wilensky and Hugh Edwards, "The Skidder: Ideological Adjustments of Downward Mobile Workers," *American*

Sociological Review, April, 1959, pp. 215–231. Valuable material on political behavior appears in almost every issue of *The Public Opinion Quarterly.*

36. The relationship of history to the development of behavioral science is complex. The German tradition which emphasizes the purely idiographic qualities of history stands strongly against any move toward a social and psychological approach. This tradition has powerful support among historians today. On the other hand, there have been many historians with strong social-scientific emphases, as the work of such men as Vernon Parrington, James H. Robinson, Charles H. Beard, Frederick J. Turner, Preserved Smith, R. H. Tawney, F. J. Teggart, Harry E. Barnes, and Arnold Toynbee will attest. Among contemporary historians, the interpretation of historical facts by locating them in their social and economic contexts, as in the work of Arthur Schlesinger, Jr., does not always entail an explicit awareness of one's social-scientific leanings. In recent years there has been some growth of a psychological perspective in history. See Stanley Elkins, *Slavery: A Problem in American Institutional and Intellectual Life,* The University of Chicago Press, 1959, and David Donald, *Charles Sumner and the Coming of the Civil War,* Alfred A. Knopf, Inc., 1960. Perhaps "hard times" promote some sociological leanings among historians, while 'good times" incline them more toward psychological interpretations.

CHAPTER 3

Field Theory
of Behavior

In the comments of the preceding chapter, there has been no intent, of course, to deny either the possibility or the value of analytic theories of behavior, so long as the nature of their abstractions is kept fully in mind. Continuing intensive research within the context of the more specialized disciplines is, in fact, essential to behavioral research. The isolation of the various sets of variables for precise measurement is a basic ingredient of interdisciplinary work. It is only necessary to realize that the victories of these sciences are in the abstract world of their own creation. In concentrating on one set of variables the researcher must control other variables, not simply disregard them.

For certain kinds of problems we can afford to accept the Newtonian view of the physical world. Modifications of our notions of time and space and changes in the mechanical conception of the stable structure of matter become necessary, however, when our curiosity leads us to explore outward to the reaches of the universe or inward to variations in processes inside the atom.

By analogy, a purely anthropological or sociological view of behavior, designed largely to study "social structure," "culture and personality," and "role," and a purely psychological view of personality, concerned primarily with the isolation and measurement of inner "traits" and their configuration, can contribute to the solution of some kinds of problems. Furthermore, under conditions in which sociocultural structure and individual experience are relatively stable and repetitive, *either* a purely sociological *or* a purely psychological approach to personality is effective, because the constructs of each are likely to be adequate *indexes* of the variables studied by the other. Thus under conditions of stability, definition of personality and prediction of behavior in terms of cultural norms and role requirements approximate the results obtained by analysis of the internal structure of the person. Likewise, under such conditions definition of personality and prediction of behavior in terms of inner traits and their configurations approximate the results obtained by a sociocultural approach to the same questions. Each discipline can partly afford to disregard the variables which are of interest to the other because of their relative stability. (One can afford to disregard the influence of altitude— or more generally, air pressure—on the boiling point of water if he seeks prediction at one altitude only.) The variables being neglected are no less operative because of their stability, but since their influence is constant it can be disregarded for purposes of prediction.

Under conditions of social change and mobility, however, the situation is quite different. If the psychologist seeks prediction simply by exploration of variation of inner "traits" (honesty, gregariousness, authoritarianism, aggressiveness, anxiety, persuasibility), he has to contend with the wide variation in situations within which these inner forces express themselves. And the sociologist or anthropologist who thinks of personality primarily in terms of cultural norms and roles is confronted, in changing societies, with wide variation in the extent and manner of their internalization. Under such conditions, a unit of analysis that is simultaneously psychological and sociological becomes essential.[1]

I shall use the term *field* in the sense employed by Lewin: "the totality of coexisting facts which are conceived of as mutually interdependent." [2] As a mode of analysis, field theory can be thought of analogically as an effort to overcome the perceptual problem in viewing reversible figures. In looking at "Rubin's goblet," for example, one sees either two faces or a goblet, but does not see both simultaneously or some "midway" figure. One is figure, the other is ground. In much the same way, in concentrating on the individual or on the situation, depending upon one's specialized interests, one loses the other in "ground." Field theory can be thought of as an attempt to surmount conceptual equivalents of the perceptual problem to make it possible to apprehend psychological and sociological facts simultaneously.[3] Awareness of the alternation can bring the previous perception into our judgments. And more important, what may be impossible perceptually is possible conceptually: in our mathematical and other statements, both kinds of observations can appear simultaneously.

Coutu has suggested that the constant reciprocity of inner and outer events can best be kept in view if we have words which express that relationship. He has designed the term "tinsit" (an abbreviation for tendency-in-situation). "If we know certain of John's tendencies-in-situation, we can say with some degree of assurance that John will tend to exhibit behavior B in situations of type X; but we cannot, merely by knowing John, say with any assurance that John will exhibit behavior B. That would be prophecy." [4] Such a term helpfully emphasizes interaction, but it is difficult to handle conceptually (Coutu departs from its field meaning when he speaks of John's tendencies-in-situation). Interlevel terms may also underplay the system qualities at each level. If in our interpretations of behavior we keep the full range of forces in mind, we can use—indeed, we need—terms that refer to each of the forces separately. We simply need to avoid using them as direct explanations of behavior. I shall use *tendency* to denote an inner disposition that is expressed only under certain conditions, thus implying the necessity for specification of conditions before its relevance for behavior is known.

Because "trait" usually carries the connotation of a fixed disposition, almost regardless of situation, I shall avoid the term. It could possibly be made a useful part of a field theoretical vocabulary by employing it somewhat after the manner of Gordon Allport. He defines a trait as "a generalized and focalized neuropsychic system (peculiar to the individual), with the capacity to render many stimuli functionally equivalent, and to initiate and guide consistent (equivalent) forms of adaptive and expressive behavior." [5] This he contrasts with "attitude" on various grounds, most helpfully, perhaps, in terms of its greater generality. An attitude is a predisposition focused on a specific object or class of objects; few stimuli are functionally equivalent. It may be close to some of his meaning to suggest a continuum of predispositions, ranging from the trait end (activated by many functionally equivalent stimuli) to the attitude end (activated by a specific stimulus). The words involved have such diverse meanings, however, that I prefer to think in terms of tendencies that have varying degrees of strength.

Strong ------------------------------------ Weak
(traits)　　　　　　　Tendencies　　　　　(attitudes)
(predispositions)

I know persons who like to play tennis if the weather is perfect, the opponents generous, the partners handsome, and the after-game refreshment plentiful. Others will sweep snow off the court, skip lunch, and play with anyone hardy enough to survive such enthusiasm. There is no doubt that the latter persons "render many stimuli functionally equivalent," to use Allport's phrase. An adequate vocabulary requires some way of stating the range in the strength of tendencies. Since it is a continuum, however, a wiser approach may be to avoid two or a few nouns and to describe the range in scale steps or mathematical terms. The concept of trait has an either-or quality that makes such formulations difficult.

If "trait" is inadequate as a concept and subject to misinterpretation as a term, our understanding is also limited if we are excessively situationist and overlook variations in individual tendency systems. When Lewin, Lippitt, and White, in their well-known studies of boys' clubs,[6] varied "group atmosphere" and process, they added significantly to our knowledge by isolating the influence of strictly social forces. They could predict certain *rates* of behavior without paying any attention to differences in individual propensity. But again, their success was partly a result of the fact that the tendencies of the boys involved varied over a narrow part of the imaginable range. Systematic variation in age, cultural and subcultural values, tendencies toward hostility, and the like, would be necessary for knowledge of how various people will respond to "democratic" and "autocratic" group situations. Do six-year-olds respond in the same way as sixteen-year-olds? Do insecure and self-confident boys react differently? Would results be the same in Japan, Russia, and the United States?

In a recent reexamination of their studies, White and Lippitt raise equivalent questions more fully than they did in the original work. Group atmosphere, it became clear, was not the only factor requiring measurement, for boys with different tendencies responded differently to the same atmosphere, even though the structure of the group also had important effects. "Conscientious individuals such as Eddie and Lyman are likely to contribute to the effective working of democracy, while self-assertive individuals such as Reilly and Fred are likely to have a disruptive influence. Unless constrained by autocratic controls, a group composed mainly of Reillys and Freds often becomes sheer anarchy." [7]

The need for simultaneous attention to the structure of the situation and the tendencies of the individuals is clearly stated by Murphy:

Gestalt will try to define organization within the organism first, and then look for organization in the situation, whereas in point of fact the organization *within* the organism depends partly on the organization of the situation. Similarly, situationism will try to define the organization of the situation first, before turning to the organism, forgetting that it is partly by virtue of the structure of the organism that the situation achieves structure. We cannot define the situation operationally except in reference to the specific organism which is involved; we cannot define the organism operationally, in such a way as to obtain predictive power for behavior, except in reference to the situation. Each serves to define the other; they are definable operationally while in the organism-situation field. [8]

DEVELOPMENT OF FIELD THEORY

After several centuries of development in physics, a field perspective has now perhaps become part of the world view of laymen. We require no serious effort of translation to realize that a lighter than air object rises, not simply because of its inner qualities, but because of the nature of its relationship to the environment. In a day of speculation about landing on the moon, even the more complex notion that the weight of an object itself is not intrinsic to it but is a function of the object in the environment may be part of common-sense thought. Quantum physics perceives or hypthesizes ever smaller particles, but their motion is always studied as part of a complex system of relationships.

Of greater potential significance for a science of human behavior is the development of a similar perspective in biology. The conception of the fixity of species was challenged in the nineteenth century and was decisively replaced by the theory of evolution. Thus a transaction between the organism and the environment was brought into the very process of inheritance.

Perhaps more important for our purposes, however, has been the extension of this point of view to cell differentiation and other organic processes. Even that most stable unit of heredity, the gene, is known to be affected by powerful external agents and perhaps even by normal contact with one of its alleles (partner genes).[9] Whether or not the environmental alteration of genes proves to be a normal process, cells are known to be field-determined. Their form and function are a result, not simply of inherited structure and capability, but of environmental influences as well. Their genetic endowment includes molecules that contain instructions for development of further cellular elements; but whether this development will in fact take place depends upon the environment. *"Euglena* is a protozoan-like organism that is capable of photosynthesis and contains about 10 chloroplasts per cell. When grown in the dark, where it generates energy not by photosynthesis but by oxidation of organic nutrients, the chloroplasts disappear. The instructions for making chloroplasts are still intact, but whether or not the cell does make them is decided by the light; when *Euglena* is once again exposed to light, chloroplasts are again formed." [10]

In view of such evidence, the conception of a fixed hereditary "program" built into cell and tissue inadequately explains the observed facts. Because of the stability of environment for most organisms, its influence is overlooked. Drastic changes of environment, however, reveal its importance. In his pioneering work on this question, Child noted that some organisms could be so significantly changed by outside influences that "we should never recognize them as belonging to the same species, or in the more extreme cases, to the same class, or perhaps even the same phylum" as organisms developing under the usual conditions.[11]

There are *multiple possibilities* in every cell and biological structure, particular ones of which are facilitated or drawn out by the environment. Transplant a cell in the early stages of its development (and in some instances at later stages) from one tissue environment to another, and it will show characteristics appropriate to its new location. Within limits, cells normally "destined" to produce certain structures can be removed from an embryo and yet a normal product will result; other cells take over the necessary development.[12] In the words of Jennings: "What any particular cell of the individual produces is largely determined by the surroundings of that cell—by the cells in contact with it, and by the hormones that bathe it; in short, by the 'internal environment'—so that the same set of genes produces different results in different cases." [13] One can add, of course, that the same environment produces different results when it influences cells with different capabilities.

Cellular flexibility is essential to the development and maintenance of the total organism as a system; if each cell were fixed and autonomous, there could be no adjustment to changes in the environment, and vital functions might be impossible. The processes whereby cells interact and "communicate" through chemical messengers are of great interest and suggest parallels on other system levels. Sussman notes that many cells can do what a few cannot, if the accumulation of a threshold concentration of some compound that each can produce in small amounts is essential to a given process. A different form of interaction is the production by one kind of tissue of a substance essential for development of a different tissue; or, in contrast, inhibition of development by competition for material or by production in one tissue of material that blocks growth in another.[14]

Such a field perspective drastically qualifies the usefulness of any sharp distinction between heredity and environment. Lewin's dictum that there are no dichotomies in science applies even here. The sex of an infant today is "genetically determined." Does it become environmentally determined tomorrow if the process is brought under human control? Perhaps a wiser approach is to realize that sex is determined by the genetic endowment interacting with a particular situation. Operationally, we can define heredity as that part of the organism-environment field not yet subject to control; but we will be wiser to get rid of the polarity of terms.

THE FIELD VIEW IN BEHAVORIAL SCIENCE

Long-established ways of looking at the world, philosophical perspectives, and even the structure of language have imposed obstacles to the attainment of a field point of view in physics and biology. Additional problems occur when we attempt to apply the field view to human behavior. There is a serious moral question. A person *ought,* many believe, to be sharply distinguished from his environment, both to assign to him the necessary dignity and to ensure that he has a sense of responsibility.[15]

This is not an issue that can be handled satisfactorily even if treated at length, which in any event would take me too far from my purpose in this study. Yet I must risk a brief statement of my own view, either to inform the reader or to help him protect himself against it. I see no loss of human dignity in the unfolding discoveries of how deeply we as individuals are related to others and to the environment. Discovery and recognition of the laws of our being, of the limits and the possibilities of human life, far from destroying the sense of responsibility, are a necessary support for it. Certainly a world view that sets the individual apart as a unique and intrinsically separate person has proved to be no guarantee of responsible action (by whatever criteria one wishes to judge responsibility).

The principle of multiple possibilities. Related to this moral question, but capable of specification in neutral terms, is an objection to field theory based on a conception of the person as a selective, purposive being. Analogies from physics or biology, the argument runs, may hide the fact that man, as a conscious, remembering, goal-seeking creature, is far more than one of a group of interacting forces. I shall explore this question more fully in Chapter 7, but can profitably give it brief attention here.

Once formed, and however formed, the self acts upon the environment; it chooses, weighs, and avoids; it is not simply reactive or interactive, but proactive, to use a term employed by H. A. Murray, Gordon Allport, and others. Within limits, all but the more extreme behaviorists accept this idea. Insofar as the individual is a distinguishable system, he manifests the system maintenance, boundary-preserving processes that are essential to the very idea of system.

Within the broad limits of agreement, however, there is significant disagreement. "Personalists" among psychologists emphasize the person as "altogether central in the scheme of things," in Allport's words. A field theorist contends, however, that the sociocultural system within which individuals live also has system-maintaining processes that set limits on the action possible within it. The task of the sciences of man is to specify the results of the transactions between these systems.

Since the whole of this book is concerned with various dimensions of this problem, I want here only to indicate the field approach to it. Perhaps this can be introduced by looking once again at a biological process. I have noted that cells contain multiple possibilities, that the lines of their development are not fixed in their structure. Once a cell has taken its place in a system of cells and tissues, however, the potentialities for further change are narrowed. That is to say, at the present level of knowledge and in situations so far observed, most processes of cell development are irreversible after a certain length of time. Some de-differentiation, a partial return to flexibility, has been observed, usually under conditions of drastic change of environment; but that is not a common occurrence. (The loss of potential may not be an intracell loss, however; it may reflect reciprocal or similar losses in surrounding cells, in which case the "permanent" cell differentiation is a function of the larger system and not simply of the cell's internal properties.)

Undoubtedly a similar process of "loss of potential" takes place in the individual. At birth his tendency system might have developed in any number of different directions; but once certain paths are followed, other paths are, within the known range of conditions, blocked off.

This observation may seem to contradict the principle of multiple possibilities. Some persons interpret the maturation process as a series of irreversible decisions that produce an adult with a pattern of fixed responses or traits. But there is an important difference between what is true for cell or tissue or organ and what is true for the organism as a whole. In the exceedingly complex nervous system, a great many potentialities can be "stored." [16] Each one separately, we can assume (exaggerating the probable truth), is an irreversible pattern, but seen collectively they make up a repertoire of potentialities for behavior, only some of which can be expressed at any given time. So complex is the storage system that new patterns can be learned and old patterns can be extinguished throughout life.

For present purposes we need not be concerned with the various interpretations of the processes involved in extinction.[17] It can be defined, in terms of learning theory, as the decrease in strength of a conditioned response that occurs when a subject receives a conditioned stimulus without the usual reinforcement. But extinction does not mean the elimination of potential. Among the several interpretations of extinction, there is general agreement that a response, once learned, is more readily learned a second time even after extinction. The environmental change associated with extinction may inhibit the response, may interfere with its manifestation in behavior, or may fail to fulfill an expectancy associated with the response;[18] but the environmental change does not obliterate the tendency.

In short, a person has many tendencies to behave: some conscious, others unconscious; some strong, others weak. Which one will be acted upon cannot be predicted by knowledge of the individual alone, because each requires a facilitating environment. Behavior is never in an environmental vacuum.

The principle of multiple possibilities applies equally to situations. Their meaning for behavior cannot be defined independently of the individuals who experience them, for the same cue or the same force will affect persons with different tendencies differently. The implications of a given sociocultural situation for behavior may be strong or weak, that is, the range of possibilities may be wide or narrow; but only in the limiting case does a situation "determine" behavior, producing the same results among all persons regardless of their tendencies.

The term "multiple possibilities" expresses the fact that each system contains stresses and ambivalences. No sociocultural situation defines precisely what behavior is required or permitted: role designations have a range; behaving "others" set various contexts for interaction. No person has a fixed "program": he has incompatible inclinations; he experiences alternation in the strength of tendencies at different times, and often he lacks clear hierarchies at a given time; he is oriented to a variety of reference groups. The ambiguities can be resolved only when the facilities and the constraints of the individual and the situation are brought together. Parsons has emphasized that the tendency system of an individual who is ambivalent may express itself, depending upon the situation, in forms as various as ill health, criminality, religious sectarianism, or chauvinism.[19] One might add that a given situation can activate responses as various as high achievement, demoralization, or aggression, depending upon the tendencies of the receiving individuals. We have a problem of solving two simultaneous equations. Both the situation and the individual are "unknowns" that can be defined only when the other is also defined.

FROM A DISCIPLINARY TO AN INTERDISCIPLINARY FIELD VIEW

In general terms there is substantial agreement on this point of view among many behavioral scientists. Sociologists who have developed a "theory of action" or who stress social interaction, a large proportion of social psychologists, those psychologists who identify with the Gestalt and Lewinian traditions, anthropologists interested in behavior theory, and many psychoanalysts and psychiatrists share this frame of reference.[20] Beneath the agreements, however, are differences of interpretation that need to be made explicit and then reduced. This process will both aid and be aided by an increase in the present modest level of research designed to handle individual and structural variables simultaneously.

The difficulty in achieving an interdisciplinary perspective is shown even in the pioneering work of Lewin, whose interpretation of the field view did not entirely successfully incorporate personal and situational forces into the unit of analysis. In describing Lewin's work, Deutsch writes:

Psychology must take into account physical and social facts which obey nonpsychological laws and which determine the external events that will impinge upon the perceptual motor regions of the person....

The nonpsychological milieu cannot have direct effects upon behavior because its parts are alien to psychological environments, except as its parts get transformed into goals, barriers, and other psychological facts through peception. However, as Wright and Barker point out:

"It is nonetheless true that the nonpsychological milieu affects behavior indirectly. It provides the physical and social raw materials for psychological habitats; and by supplying these resources it goes far to determine just what behavior shall and shall not be possible for all who live within it." [21]

This statement well represents Lewin's dominant, if not his only, interpretation of the field approach. What is not said, however, and what prevents the Lewinian view from being fully field theoretical is that *the psychological environment cannot have direct effects on behavior either;* it must be conjoined with a facilitating nonpsychological milieu, as Deutsch calls it. And in the same sense, the system of psychological tendencies provides the raw materials capable of being influenced by the environment and thus "goes far to determine just what behavior shall and shall not be possible," to use the phrase from Wright and Barker. It is one thing to take account of environmental forces as limiting conditions, as most psychologically trained field theorists do. It is another thing to incorporate personality variables and environmental variables into the very unit of analysis, with full attention to the fact that neither by itself has "direct effects upon behavior"—that is, has effects which are not mediated through the other system of influences.

In Lewin's work, field means "psychological field"—that part of the total series of forces that is perceived by an individual. He is not entirely free of ambiguity on this question, however. Thus he writes: "The actual behavior of the child depends in every case both upon his individual characteristics and upon the momentary structure of the existing situation." But shortly thereafter he qualifies this: "Of course, in the description of the child's psychological environment one may not take as a basis the immediately objective social forces and relations as the sociologist or jurist, for example, would list them. One must rather describe the social facts as they affect the particular individual concerned." [22] The latter statement is subject to misinterpretation, in my judgment, unless one adds its counterpart: A field-relevant description of an individual's characteristics is not the "immediately objective" qualities as the psychologist or the psychiatrist might list them. One must rather describe the individual facts that are activated or polarized by the particular situation being encountered.

It seems reasonable to a psychologically trained person to say that an individual cannot be influenced by a force of which he is unaware. (I shall not explore here the several possible levels of perception.) "For all practical purposes," the author of a recent book writes, "this perceptual field is reality to the person doing the perceiving . . . ; it may not be in accord with the external observer's perceptions, but it and it alone determines behavior." [23] This kind of observation overlooks the fact that a person's perceptions are a function not only of his sensitivities but also of the available stimuli, many of them derived from culture and social structure. Priority in determining behavior can be assigned neither to the sensitivities of the person nor to the facilitating forces in the environment, because both are always involved in the equation.

CONCLUSION

Field theory is certainly not "true" in some ultimate sense. It is a parsimonious way of organizing much of what is known about behavior, particularly in societies where a great diversity of situations influences individuals with a wide variety of tendencies.

Field theory does not dismiss the significance of differences in individual tendency in favor of exclusive attention to situational forces. When Hartshorne and May reported their findings regarding the wide variation in honesty and self-control shown by children in various contexts, they were regarded as extremely situationalist. This is true, in my judgment, only because the perspective from which their evidence was examined was generally extremely traitist. From that perspective, the fact that a child is honest in one situation, dishonest in another seemed to remove the person from the equation entirely. The same evidence viewed from an extreme situationalist position, however, emphasizes that there were individual variations in the way the children responded to the various environmental changes.[24] The conception of a trait as something which one has or does not have is smashed by the kind of research done by Hartshorne and May; but this inadequate way of viewing the individual cannot, on the evidence, be replaced by the opposite extreme.

This is not to say, of course, that research designed to isolate the situational factors alone is undesirable. It is, in fact, essential. But we must not use the findings to build a general theory without reference to matching studies of individual factors.[25] There cannot be a social structure without any people in it. A culture cannot "exist" without individuals to express it, teach it to others, and leave their own stamp upon it in the process. Neither, however, can a theory of man be built on the Robinson Crusoe idea of the individual as a self-contained entity; ". . . no theoretical system constructed on the psychological level will be adequate until it has been embraced by and intermeshed with a cultural-sociological system." [26]

The field view carries a powerful moral and action implication. If one thinks in terms of authoritarian persons, mentally ill persons, delinquents, leaders, or achievers—that is, in terms of nouns and entities—certain kinds of actions seem appropriate to bring about some desired goal. If change is desired, for example, the task is to get "inside" the individual and to rearrange his tendencies, or to find those individuals who possess the desired characteristics. If one thinks, however, of authoritarian *behavior,* neurotic or psychotic behavior, deliquency, leadership, or achieving behavior—that is, in terms of adjectives and processes—his attention is directed toward a wider range of forces. The effort to discover and explain the anxieties of an individual by psychoanalysis is not given up; it is complemented by an examination of his contemporary interpersonal relationships, in his family, job, community, and hospital, which sustain and deepen or relieve those anxieties. The attempt to discover and give special training to children with high "test scores" is not set aside; it is complemented by attempts to replace "intelligence-inhibiting structures" with situations which facilitate the growth of potential. Where emphasis should be placed in specific therapeutic and action programs will partly be determined by strategic considerations. Inevitably we must ask where the largest gains can be made by the least expenditure of scarce resources. But the total effect of field theory on therapy will be to keep before us the full range of interacting factors that must be changed if desired goals are to be achieved.

Psychologists can doubtless reveal a bias in my thinking on this point, but I believe that under conditions of rapid social change, attention to social structure and process is more important for therapy or for guided change than attention to individual tendencies. This is true whether one is talking about increasing motivation in school, reducing discrimination, or participating in a process for making urban workers out of tribal villagers. Under such conditions, structural changes are the primary forces. For example, the massive piling up of poorly educated and semiunemployable young men in African cities is in the first instance a product of the drastic shifts in cultural and social patterns, not a result of personality changes. Personality changes are, of course, occurring and will feed back into the system; but when societies are undergoing upheaval, strategic considerations suggest attention to the structural origins of personality change. By such an emphasis one gives recognition to the fact that prevention is far more efficient than cure.

FOOTNOTES

Note: The bracketed number following an author's name refers to the footnote in which the source is cited in full.

1. The terms "psychology" and "sociology" are used here in their widest meaning to refer to the study of biopsychological tendencies and sociocultural structures. For some purposes, elaboration of a four-level model may be preferable. In fact, each of the levels is a *system* of multiple variables. Personality tendencies related to aspiration and motivation, for example, may converge or diverge, with very different results for behavior. For some studies of the interaction of two or more variables on the personality level see Bernard Rosen, "The Achievement Syndrome: A Psychocultural Dimension of Social Stratification," *American Sociological Review*, April, 1956, pp. 203–211, and his "Race, Ethnicity, and the Achievement Syndrome," *American Sociological Review*, February, 1959, pp. 47–60; and Loren Chapman and Donald Campbell, "The Effect of Acquiescence Response-set upon Relationships among the F Scale, Ethnocentrism, and Intelligence," *Sociometry*, June, 1959, pp. 153–161.

2. Kurt Lewin, *Field Theory in Social Science,* Harper & Row, Publishers, Incorporated, 1951, p. 240.

3. This analogy was suggested to me by Ralph H. Turner. Kenneth Burke once noted that a way of seeing is also a way of not seeing. Field theory does not eliminate this fact, but assimilates a presently defined figure-ground into a new figure. Epistemologists may have something to say about what the new ground is.

4. Walter Coutu, *Emergent Human Nature: A Symbolic Field Interpretation,* Alfred A. Knopf, Inc., 1949, p. 33.

5. Gordon W. Allport, *Personality,* Henry Holt and Company, Inc., 1937, p. 295. Note that social situations have a matching quality. A social movement, for example, may reduce a wide range of individual tendencies to functional equivalents, so far as the social processes are concerned. The motives of those who participate in a mass movement may vary widely, yet contribute to a common social process. Allport implies that one can often afford to disregard differences among situations, because a "trait" will make them functional equivalents. But if we add that one can often afford to disregard traits, because the situation will make them functional equivalents, the explanation becomes problematic again. As is so often true, the statement of one of these points of view without the other, in any attempt to develop a theory of behavior, is seriously misleading.

6. See Kurt Lewin, Ronald Lippitt, and Ralph White, "Patterns of Aggressive Behavior in Experimentally Created 'Social Climates,'" *Journal of Social Psychology*, vol. 10, 1939, pp. 271–299; and Lippitt and White, "An Experimental Study of Leadership and Group Life," in Theodore Newcomb and Eugene Hartley (eds.), *Readings in Social Psychology*, Holt, Rinehart and Winston, Inc., 1947, pp. 314–330.

7. Ralph K. White and Ronald Lippitt, *Autocracy and Democracy*, Harper & Row, Publishers, Incorporated, 1960, p. 198.

8. Gardner Murphy, *Personality: A Biosocial Approach to Origins and Structure*, Harper & Row, Publishers, Incorporated, 1947, p. 891.

9. R. Alexander Brink, "Basis of a Genetic Change which Invariably Occurs in Certain Maize Heterozygotes," *Science*, May 16, 1958, pp. 1182–1183.

10. Maurice Sussman, *Animal Growth and Development*, Prentice-Hall, Inc., 1960, p. 74.

11. Charles M. Child, *Physiological Foundations of Behavior*, Henry Holt and Company Inc., 1924, p. 247.

12. Sussman [10], pp. 76–77.

13. H. S. Jennings, *The Biological Basis of Human Nature*, W. W. Norton & Company, Inc., 1930, p. 122.

14. Sussman [10], chap. 7.

15. In some of the religiomoral systems of the East, no such problems would be raised. A blending of the person and the environment is wholly congenial to their world view. An exciting problem in the sociology of knowledge would be to study who, among those trained in the traditions of the West, with its sharper categorical lines, accepts the field perspective. I will leave it to others to explain how a touch of "Buddhism" seems to have got into the thinking of this somewhat heretical Midwestern Protestant.

16. Cells also have storage systems. But they are far less complex than those of the organism as a whole because of the greater stability of cell environment, and the unused capabilities of the cell are much less likely to be brought into play than those of the organism. Note also that societies have storage systems. Culture, in one possible definition, is the repository of learned adaptations available to a people. Only a small part of culture is brought into play in any one situation.

17. For an excellent discussion see Gregory A. Kimble, *Hilgard and Marquis' Conditioning and Learning*, 2d ed., Appleton-Century-Crofts, Inc., 1961, chap. 10.

18. See *ibid.* for evidence on such interpretations.

19. Talcott Parsons, *The Social System*, The Free Press of Glencoe, 1951, pp. 286–294.

20. See Harry S. Sullivan, *The Interpersonal Theory of Psychiatry*, W. W. Norton & Company, Inc., 1953; Clyde Kluckhohn, H. A. Murray, and David Schneider (eds.), *Personality in Nature, Culture, and Society*, Alfred A. Knopf, Inc., 1953; Helen Lynd, *On Shame and the Search for Identity*, Science Editions, Inc., 1961; Talcott Parsons in Sigmund Koch (ed.), *Psychology: A Study of a Science*, McGraw-Hill Book Company, 1959, vol. 3, pp. 612–711; Neil J. Smelser and William T. Smelser, *Personality and Social Systems*, John Wiley & Sons, Inc., 1963; Dorwin Cartwright, "Lewinian Theory as a Contemporary Framework," in Koch, *Psychology: A Study of a Science*, vol. 2, pp. 7–91; Lewin [2], and Kurt

Lewin, *A Dynamic Theory of Personality*, McGraw-Hill Book Company, 1935; Alfred R. Lindesmith and Anselm L. Strauss, *Social Psychology*, rev. ed., Holt, Rinehart and Winston, Inc., 1956; Murphy [8], Harper & Row, Publishers, Incorporated, 1947, chaps. 38 and 39; Talcott Parsons and Edward Shils (eds.), *Toward a General Theory of Action*, Harvard University Press, 1951; Alex Inkeles, "Personality and Social Structure," in Robert Merton, Leonard Broom, and Leonard Cottrell, Jr. (eds.), *Sociology Today*, Basic Books, Inc., 1959, chap. 11; Theodore M. Newcomb, *Social Psychology*, Holt, Rinehart and Winston, Inc., 1950; and Coutu [4].

21. Morton Deutsch in Gardner Lindzey (ed.), *Handbook of Social Psychology*, Addison-Wesley Publishing Company, Inc., 1954, vol. I, p. 193.

22. Kurt Lewin, *A Dynamic Theory of Personality* [20] pp. 71 and 75.

23. Otto Strunk, Jr., *Religion: A Psychological Interpretation*, Abingdon Press, 1962.

24. See Hugh Hartshorne and M. A. May, *Studies in Deceit, Studies in Service and Self-Control*, and *Studies in the Organization of Character*, The Macmillan Company, 1928, 1929, 1930.

25. See William Gnagey, "Effects on Classmates of a Deviant Student's Power and Response to a Teacher-exerted Control Technique," *Journal of Educational Psychology*, vol. 51, 1960, pp. 1–8 (reprinted in Smelser and Smelser [20], pp. 420–427); Solomon Goldberg, "Three Situational Determinants of Conformity to Social Norms," *Journal of Abnormal and Social Psychology*, July, 1954, pp. 325–329: Morris Rosenberg, "The Dissonant Religious Context and Emotional Disturbance," *American Journal of Sociology*, July, 1962, pp. 1–10.

26. H. A. Murray, in Koch [20], vol. 3, p. 45.

CHAPTER 4

Applications of Field Theory

In Part Three I shall explore in some detail the way three major research areas can be structured by application of a field perspective. Here I would like simply to sketch briefly a series of questions as seen from this perspective in an attempt to show how it can bring coordination to research on a wide variety of topics.

PERCEPTION

Perhaps in no other research area have the need for and the value of an interlevel theory been more clearly demonstrated than in the study of perception. Early studies, which were scarcely more than an application of physics or biology, have been extended first by a molar view (it is the person, not simply the eye or ear as a biophysical mechanism, who perceives), by a social-psychological view (perception is affected by processes of interaction in the group), and by an anthropological perspective (cultural norms and the structure of language influence the perception process).

I shall not undertake a review of the studies which have explored the neural, chemical, and physical aspects of sense perception. For my purposes it may suffice to say that inherited mechanisms, both on the species and on the individual levels, and many chemical and biological processes set limits within which the personality, group, and cultural influences on perception operate.[1] "We can only see and feel what our sense organs and nervous system let us sense."[2] The importance of the underlying structure is revealed when sensory or brain injury or a disturbance of chemical balance upsets normal processes of perception.

Studies in perspective readily show, however, that internal structure alone does not account for perception. Part-whole relationships, for example, affect what one sees: two parallel lines will seem to converge when seen in some settings, or an obtuse angle will appear to be a right angle in some contexts. These well-demonstrated observations began to contribute to personality theory when researchers asked, "How are various perceptions learned? [3] Do the needs, values, goals, and fears of individuals affect them?"

Hilgard notes that in the search for environmental stability, the whole person *achieves* his perceptions, that is, he regulates them in the service of need satisfaction. He may, for example, identify an object out of a partial clue, having learned that early recognition aids the avoidance of an undesirable situation or the pursuit of a desirable one.[4] The outside stimulus strikes a "tuned organism," one with established expectations or hypotheses of various strengths.[5] Perception is affected not only by what we may call ego functions, the effort to satisfy needs, but also by other personality tendencies; fears, prejudices, and inarticulate desires influence the highly selective process of responding to the potential stimuli around us.[6] Two groups of subjects were made "fearful" by receiving electric shocks and were then shown films of a man performing various tasks. They perceived the man to be fearful significantly more often than a control group did. Among the subjects, those who were told to forget or disregard their own fear were somewhat more likely to perceive the man as fearful than subjects who were encouraged to recognize and express their fear.[7] As a further illustration, perception of magnitude has been shown to be affected by the comparative value of perceived objects to the subjects.[8]

Research on perception as a molar process was an important step forward. Studies in this area have played a significant part in the accreditation of the personality level in psychology, with its emphasis on organization, as contrasted with studies that have been concerned with relatively isolated units of behavior in the familiar stimulus-response pattern. Some psychologists continue to insist that the construct "personality" (which, as an organized, boundary-maintaining system of tendencies, represents a new level of analysis) adds little or nothing to research on human behavior. If this group has declined since the days when Watson counseled against the use of the "mystery box," a major cause is the effectiveness of the molar view in explaining the facts of perception.

Social-psychological study of group influences on perception has served a similar function in strengthening the claim that research on human behavior must explore the systematic influences of interaction. The classic studies by Sherif, Asch, and others established that the group setting within which perception takes place affects that perception. Such variables as group size, ecological structure, degree of unanimity, and expressed norms of the group, interacting with personality tendencies (self-confidence, level of anxiety, authoritarianism, for example), clearly influence the process of perceiving.

In an interesting demonstration of the interaction of personality and group variables, Malof and Lott compared the responses of thirty students who rated high on the Berkeley E (ethnocentrism) scale with thirty whose scores were low. Out of 12 possible perceptions, the "high E" persons conformed to a unanimous group from 0 to 12 times; conformity among the "low E" person ranged from 0 to 4, a highly significant difference ($p < .001$). This is what one would expect from the emphasis, in "authoritarian personality" studies, on conformity needs of the highly ethnocentric. When those with high E scores were assigned a partner, however, their conformity scores dropped significantly, whether the partner was white or colored; their attitudes alone, in other words, were not predictive. This finding supports Rokeach's belief that rejection of a minority-group member is based in part on supposed incongruence of belief, not on prejudice alone.[9] When belief (or in this case, a similar perception) is shown to be congruent, the minority-group member is more likely to be accepted. Full explanation of the results of the Malof and Lott experiment requires attention both to the group setting (presence of a partner or unanimous perception opposed to that of the subject) and to the subjects' tendencies.[10]

Without undertaking to review further the extensive research concerning group influences on perception, I shall illustrate this level of analysis with an excellent study by Crutchfield.[11] The subjects were fifty men from an occupation that called for leadership. Most of them had had some college training; their average age was thirty-four. Working in groups of five each, they were asked to make several kinds of judgments. Each could see a panel of lights telling him the decisions of the other four persons, with the sequence of decision being rotated, so that sometimes an individual would make his judgment first, sometimes second, and so on, in order to permit measurement of the extent of group influence. What he saw on the panel of lights were not actually the choices of others in the group, but experimenter choices. Crutchfield was thus able to control the degree of perceived agreement in the group. Norms were established by using the actual judgments of a control group of forty men from the same occupation.

Out of a series of 21 judgments, only 2 were unaffected by the group. In judging the length of a line, for example, 15 subjects (30 per cent) accepted a presumed group false judgment. For an insoluble number series, 79 per cent accepted an irrational answer. Although none of the control group agreed with the following two statements, 31 per cent and 37 per cent, respectively, of the experimental group accepted them when they were presumed to be accepted by the rest of their group of five: "I believe we are made better by the trials and hardships of life," and "I doubt whether I would made a good leader." [12]

The latter tests are matters of perception only if the term is defined very broadly as "taking cognizance of." The study of perception shades off into the study of opinion, judgment, cognition, memory, and knowledge, for all of which attention to both individual and group factors is essential. In later studies, for example, Crutchfield added controversial opinion questions. The following statement was accepted by 21 per cent of a control group but by 58 per cent of the experimental group: "Free speech being a privilege rather than a right, it is proper for a society to suspend free speech whenever it feels itself threatened." [13]

It is important to note that the tendency to accept the group judgment was not uniform among the subjects. The range of conformity on 21 questions was wide, varying from 1 to 17, with a mean of 8. Thus it is not enough simply to know that a judgment is being made in a group context. The individuals who were more intelligent, higher in leadership qualities both on tests and by staff observers' ratings, more tolerant, more responsible, and less authoritarian, were more likely to be independent in their judgments. Such "independents" had more self-respect, were less compulsive about rules, showed a lower need for closure, were less anxious, showed more balanced judgments of parents, and were more permissive with children. They were not less neurotic; they came more often from broken homes.[14] Altogether, any attempt to predict or interpret their perceptions and their judgments must deal with the interaction between the group norm and the individual tendencies which affect the response to that norm.[15]

The extensive literature on interpersonal perception gives further support to the need for a field theoretical interpretation.[16] How another person is perceived (and thus, in one sense, what he "is" sociologically) is not simply a function of his characteristics, or of the characteristics of the perceiver, but also of the nature of their interaction. Jones and de Charms found that persons who failed in a contrived test were seen to be "less dependable" if that failure hurt the observer (cost him a one dollar prize) than if the objectively similar failure did not hurt the perceiver.[17]

What one remembers is also affected by factors from several levels; it varies with one's own needs and values, but it varies also with the group context.[18] When Bauer told subjects that they were going to report the contents of a speech on teachers' salaries to teachers, the subjects were more likely to remember the arguments in favor of salary increases than when he told them that their reports would be made to a citizens' committee interested in economizing.[19] Memory is thus in part a product of interaction and not simply a function of individual tendencies. The group influences memory, in the words of Bartlett, "First, by providing that setting of interest, excitement and emotion which favors the development of specific images, and secondly, by providing a persistent framework of institutions and customs which acts as a schematic basis for constructive memory." [20]

This statement suggests another level of influence on perception and other cognitive processes—cultural training. Frontiersmen, anthropologists, and others have reported the acute powers of observation characteristic of many of the peoples they have lived among or studied. Some Indians were able to detect and interpret the dust stirred up by a herd of buffalo many miles away. Native men of the Murray Islands were found to be "superior in being able to unmask the camouflage of coral fish against the background of their matching habitat. The natives had learned to use 'good' hypotheses, which served to utilize maximally what appropriate information was available. Their hypotheses were strong enough to maximize relevant conforming information, but not so strong as to be confirmed by what to the uninitiated might have been confirming information." [21] Had the Murray Islanders been reporting on their English visitors they might have marveled at the powers of Englishmen to distinguish among "imperceptible" variations of small black marks on white paper. Accumulating evidence from application of the Rorschach technique demonstrates wide differences in response on the basis of cultural experience.[22]

Cultural influences may inhibit as well as extend perceptual differentiation. Prejudice, which has a strong component of cultural learning, is expressed in part in the form of perceptual distortions. These prejudgments are not necessarily limited to minority groups. Malinowski reported that the Trobriand Islanders believe both that brothers do not look alike and that sons look very much like their fathers. This seems unreasonable on "logical" grounds, but the cultural norms served as screens that produced selective attention to the multitude of possible cues. When Bronfenbrenner showed a group of American schoolchildren some photographs of Russian roads lined with trees and asked them, "Why do you suppose they have trees?" he received such answers as these: "So that people won't be able to see what's going on beyond the road." "It's to make work for prisoners." When asked why our roads have trees, the children thought it was for shade or to keep the dust down.[23]

Cultural influences on perception are not identical for all members of a society. As will be discussed in Chapter 6, how the world looks depends in part upon the positions people occupy and the role privileges and requirements of those positions. Most persons have had the experience, upon shifting from one position to another, of perceiving things they never saw before. The change is not a function of a shift in individual perspective alone; it results also from interaction with different significant others and from the *shared* expectations that make up a role.

Cultural influences on perception are perhaps most strongly expressed in language and the value hierarchy. These reach the individual both directly, to the degree that he uses the language and has internalized the values, and indirectly, by affecting the social structures within which perception takes place. The fact that we see the world through lingual glasses is now well established. What Hallowell calls "the ubiquitous role of symbolic mediation of the world" [24] results from the way in which reality is defined by the concepts, categories, and descriptive terms of language. The words and structure of language are always less fluid than the reality with which they deal, and thus they arbitrarily highlight some aspects of the world and disregard others. One's language is learned in interaction; it is tested against the responses of others. As an inner forum, thinking permits the use of words as anticipatory of the acts of others; words prepare us for interactions. Thus language, as George Herbert Mead stressed, is inherently social.

This is not to say that language has no individualistic qualities. There is doubtless some autistic element in the language patterns of most persons, and it becomes dominant in a few. Language may float away from reality. It is one of the levels of response to experience, and if that experience is consistently punishing, an individual may attempt to restructure it by manipulating words. By the responses of other persons to our words, most of us are taught that words have a kind of independent reality. A child who has broken the cooky jar may discover that the words "No Mamma, I did not break the jar; it must have been the cat" have an almost magical quality in substituting one reality for another. This lesson having been learned, a person who faces continuous threat may to a large degree use words as a substitute for events rather than as a way of dealing with those events.

These brief comments on perception and related cognitive processes are merely an outline of the factors that must be taken into account in an adequate theory. Perception is simultaneously a biophysical, individual, group, and cultural process. To explain, for example, how an individual will perceive the size and intentions of a group of Negroes picketing a store, it is not enough to know his values, fears and prejudices. If we assume a normal and healthy organism, and thus disregard influences from the biophysical level, we still must ask. "With whom is he observing; what cues and stimuli from words and gestures come from others; and is he identified with those others?" Only some—probably a tiny proportion —of the potential cues will reach him. His own "prejudgments" will blot out many, but the actions of the police and the words and actions of others around him will also serve as perceptual screens. Shared vocabularies will furnish a vehicle or receptacle for some observations but not for others. A white crowd that knows only "niggers" is scarcely able to differentiate the wide variety of tendencies and actions that characterize the colored participants or to distinguish them from the stereotype built into the vocabulary. Or a white individual with a more complicated vocabulary will have only part of it brought into play in a context of shouts and actions from others.

THE SOURCES OF TALENT

Viewed historically, the development of a theory of talent has followed much the same course as the development of a theory of perception. There is no clear line of progression, but a series of overlapping stages. With the rapid development of biology after the middle of the nineteenth century, biological or presumed biological differences were often used to account for individual and group differences in talent. Status inequalities among races and classes were readily explained on the basis of inheritance, with little effort expended to control for culture or opportunity.[25] The clustering of success or failure in family lines was assumed to be proof of biological differences, with little attention paid to the fact that the family carries its influences on a sociocultural as well as a biological stream. This approach characterized not only the "racists," but outstanding scientists whose talent for seeing the full range of facts was obviously limited by their own cultural surroundings, despite their superior heredity.

Francis Galton, for example, in his study *Hereditary Genius,* argues essentially that a superior inheritance (which he "measured" by a person's reputation) is virtually the guarantor of superior performance.[26] According to him, serious obstacles seldom block the men of great reputations. Even if they were placed as infants in disadvantaged surroundings, most would achieve greatness, for they are "haunted and riven by an incessant craving for the intellectual work. If forcibly withdrawn from the path that leads towards eminence, they will find their way back to it, as surely as a lover to his mistress." Races and classes, Galton contended, can clearly be shown to have different biological capacities by the variation in the number of great men they produce.

In one of the earliest sociological discussions of the origin of talent, Cooley demonstrated that Galton's facts were insufficient to support his argument.[27] But Cooley's point of view received little attention for a quarter century.

The intelligence tests and various aptitude measures developed after 1908 were regarded by many persons as a highly objective and valid process for determining inherited differences. Since systematic group, as well as individual, differences appeared, there seemed to be support for the earlier more impressionistic accounts of the importance of heredity and of race. Only 12 per cent of the Negro recruits in the American Armed Forces during World War I, for example, achieved intelligence test scores above the median for white recruits.

I shall not describe here the process by which the cultural and subcultural biases and other environmental elements in intelligence tests were gradually revealed and to some degree reduced. Inherited influences cannot be isolated until environmental differences are controlled, but this is an exceedingly difficult if not impossible task. Variation in language facility, responses to the test situation, familiarity with the test content, attitudes toward the investigator, achievement motivation, cultural values, and other learned tendencies influence the measuring process. Comparisons of scores across major sociocultural lines are hazardous.

This is not to say that inheritance is not involved in differences in intelligence or other talents. Wide variation of scores within homogeneous groups strengthens the hypothesis that biological factors affect the result. Even in this instance, however, interpretation of the evidence is difficult. Homogeneity of experience within a group cannot be assumed; individual variation in health and motivation obscures the inherited factor. These

become major problems when comparisons are made across such significant social lines as those drawn by race. Despite continuing efforts to find
proof of racial differences in test scores,[28] the great weight of the evidence points to the conclusion that races differ little if at all in the
distribution of inherited intelligence.[29]

Some of the difficulty in arriving at an adequate formulation of the
sources of intelligence derives from a failure to make necessary distinctions. As a minimum one must distinguish inherited intelligence, or any
other inherited capacity, from knowledge or skill and from creativity. It is
especially important not to confuse the inherited capacity with behavior,
even the act of taking an intelligence test; for behavior is a product of the
whole field of individual and situational forces. Once these distinctions are
made, and the fact that the items do not vary directly with each other is
noted, we are led to a search for sources of their variation.

And adequate theory must account for such well-known facts as these:
An average high school student today knows more physics and mathematics than Aristotle did; creativity often comes in periods, such as the
Italian Renaissance, in such a way as to contradict expectations based on
a normal distribution of inherited capacity; persons from very similar
environments exhibit large differences in problem-solving ability and other
skills; Before July 8, 1954, no human being had ever run a mile in less
than four minutes, but since then over 70 such races have been run;
average IQ scores of Negroes in several Northern states are higher than
average IQ scores of white persons in several Southern states; there is
little IQ variation by race or class among very young children, but by age
12 or 14, such differences are fairly large, with contrasts up to 25 points in
group averages.

These miscellaneous facts take on a semblance of order in our causal
explanation when we add personality and sociocultural variables to inheritance. We might devise a Lewinian type of formula as follows: Effective problem-solving behavior or intelligence (I) is a function of capacity
(C), personality (P), group interaction (G), and level of culture (L); $I
= f(C,P,G,L)$. A similar formula could be stated for other talents.

We are getting valuable research on each of these factors. Getzels and
Jackson, for example, have found that the kind of problem-solving behavior they call *creativity* ("the ability to deal inventively with verbal and
numerical symbol systems and with object-space relations") [30] is not simply a manifestation of intellectual capacity, for it correlates only poorly
with various measures of IQ. It is an expression of other characteristics of
the individual that develop in certain family environments. Their line of
research is similar to that of McClelland and his associates, who have
sought to discover the sources of a tendency they call "achievement
motivation." [31] The numerous studies employing this concept have been
concerned not only with the achievement motive as a characteristic of the
person, but also with the cultural and subcultural environments and the
training experiences which promote or block its development.[32]

It is not enough, moreover, to see that such personality tendencies as creativity and achievement motivation are important *along with* inherited capacity in determining problem-solving ability. Other tendencies may work in the opposite direction, strongly inhibiting the full development of capacity. Roen found that fifty Negro and fifty white soldiers matched on ten demographic variables had average IQ differences of more than 10 points; but he also noted that they were significantly different on various anxiety and self-confidence measures. The Negroes had incorporated "intellectually defeating personality traits." [33]

From the point of view of field theory, it is important to emphasize that such "traits," whether of creativity or its opposite, are not situation-free. Not only are an individual's tendencies to aspire to high goals formed by sociocultural forces, but the manifestation of those tendencies in current behavior is situationally affected. With whom is one interacting? What norms of conformity, backed by what rewards and sanctions, press in on one? To return to our formula, we need to study the G, as well as C and P. The "level of aspiration" is not simply in the person, for the group aspiration level affects that of the individual, especially if he is strongly attracted to the group and believes the activities of the moment are relevant to its purposes. Stotland found that *individual* response to failure in an experimental group task was a function of the *group* level of aspiration. A personality factor was also involved, however. "Persons high in self-esteem protected themselves against unfavorable evaluations better than those low in self-esteem." [34]

Coleman has documented the fact that activity in a school cannot be understood if it is studied with reference simply to a series of individuals. Schools are social systems of closely interacting members; the teenagers are largely oriented to each other and together confront the adult world with something of a united front. Any attempt to account for the "problem-solving behavior" of each individual on the basis of his inherited capacity (if it could be measured) or his motives and aspirations, defined as inner forces, would be seriously incomplete.[35]

A field theory of talent must add to knowledge of capacity, personality, and interaction, an account of the cultural or subcultural resources on which individuals may draw. Peer-group influences in school are both interactional and cultural, that is, they are based both on the network of interpersonal relationships into which individuals are tied and on the norms which they agree upon to guide their interaction. The strictly cultural element in setting the level of ability has been emphasized by Faris. The richness of the social heritage and the breadth of its distribution are critical facts in determining the accomplishments of the members of a society. There is no reason to suppose that the average capacity of individuals in an industrial society is any higher than the average capacity of the members of a paleolithic band; but the former are supported by a "collective ability" that is carried in the stream of culture. ". . . in a literal sense, and to an important degree, a society generates its level of abil-

ity ... the upper limit is unknown and distant ... the processes of generation of ability are potentially subject to intentional control. But a half-
century or so ago a miniature Dark Age descended over the field of
human psychology and the doctrines of the mental testers convinced an
impressed public with a secular variant of an infant damnation doctrine." [36]

This last sentence puts the issue perhaps too strongly, for on a comparative basis, differences in inherited capacity remain. A social heritage
that can lift the performance of a person of average capacity a given
amount may lift the performance of a person of unusual capacity even
more. Yet Faris's point is of great importance: If a given sociocultural
situation is stimulating the use of only a tiny part of the potential ability,
because of inhibitory norms (isolation of "the brain" in high school) or
because much of the social heritage is inaccessible to many people, there
can be great gains in accomplishment within the limits set by capacity.
Perhaps the argument is best put mathematically. Let us assume that our
four variables are of equal importance (unless this is very far from the
truth, it does not affect the outcome appreciably), that each can have a
value on a range from 1 to 10, and that they are interactive, not simply
additive. In one situation we might find

$$I = f(8,2,2,2) = 64$$

while in another $\quad I = f(5,5,5,5) = 625$

In the first instance, we might have a lower-class Negro with high
capacity (8), but with "intellectually defeating personality traits"—
anger, frustration, a sense of hopelessness (2), interaction in a group that
is basically anti-intellectual (2), and life conditions that make the social
heritage inaccessible to him (2). The second instance might represent a
middle-class white person of average capacity (5) whose other tendencies,
group supports, and access to the social heritage are also average (5
each). Despite lower capacity, the problem-solving behavior of the second
person is considerably more effective than that of the first.

If the average level of the sources of talent discussed by McClelland,
Getzels and Jackson, Faris, and others were to be raised from 5 to 8, with
no change in capacity, the result would be startling:

$$I = f(5,8,8,8) = 2,560$$

This is simply to emphasize in pseudomathematical terms the enormous
shift in outlook that occurs when talent is studied field theoretically instead of biologically or individually.

OTHER APPLICATIONS OF THE FIELD APPROACH

The kind of interlevel statement I have applied to perception and talent
can bring system to observations on a wide variety of topics. Although I

shall not explore them here, I urge the reader to design a field-oriented study of *conflict* ("Do 'wars begin in the minds of men'; does aggression draw its force from repressed hostilities; is conflict a product of sociocultural structures and interpersonal relations?"), of *motivation* (to cite the full range of interpretations, "Is it instinctual, or an agreed-upon vocabulary of explanation?"), of *leadership,* or of such more limited and applied problems as *absenteeism* and *accidents.* On each of these subjects, current research points clearly to the need for a field interpretation.

In this chapter of procedural illustrations, I shall be content with brief statements on two other topics. The purpose is not to discuss them, but to note how the questions related to them can be raised most effectively.

Gerontology

Some areas of intensive contemporary research have become quite thoroughly field theoretical. Gerontology, for example, has developed a strong sociocultural emphasis to complement earlier attention to the physiological and psychological processes of aging. The quality of "being old" is not a matter simply of the inner diameter of the arteries or of oxygen supply to the brain. There are important questions related to self-conception, to role assignments, and to patterns of interaction. To be a widow with four married children who live on adjacent farms in a stable community is one fact; to be a widow with two married children who live in small apartments in widely separated cities is a different fact. Roles assigned to the aged and other cultural influences concerning old age vary widely from society to society.[37] Should one live with his married children? Is retirement a blessing or a curse? Are "golden age" homes and communities a good place to live? The answers to these questions rest in part on cultural and subcultural training. The meaning of old age varies with level of education, the quality and accessibility of geriatrics as a medical specialty, the number and significance of the role relationships that must be severed, the presence or absence of cultural bridges to new positions, and many other influences.

In a study of 500 recipients of old age pensions, C. M. Morgan found that those who could still do something useful for family or friends stayed happier and healthier; others disintegrated quickly.[38] Structural aspects of the environment influence the meaning of age. Do supporting friendship patterns decline with age? Yes, but not simply as a result of individual changes. Zena Blau discovered that the effects of widowhood or retirement varied with the prevalence of those positions in the age, sex, and class structure where the individuals were located.[39] To cite one illustration of this, Blau found that widowed men in their sixties had much lower friendship participation than married men in their sixties, but widowed men in their seventies had slightly higher friendship participation than married men in their seventies. In the younger group, widowers were "deviant"—in the minority; in the older group, married men were deviant. This social structural fact affected the meaning of "old age" for the individuals involved.

An excessively strong situational or structural interpretation of old age could not be defended, of course. Physiological and psychological facts of senescence press in, and the variations in their rates of influence cannot be explained solely by reference to different roles or other structural facts. But in a context where physiological facts must so obviously be taken into account, it is perhaps all the more significant to note that cultural and social-structural influences are also involved.[40]

Desire for Certainty

Field-oriented research frequently deals with the interaction of variables on two levels only, subsuming biological and psychological factors under "individual" and social and cultural factors under " situation." One might ask, for example: Is "desire for certainty" a trait of personality, a consistent motive that applies to different situations; or is it situationally governed; or is it both?

Many studies have shown that individuals vary in their fear of ambiguity, their degree of cognitive rigidity when faced with new problems, their tendency to acquiesce in test situations (that is, to answer "yes" or "agree" regardless of the question). Brim and Hoff found consistent personality differences in a similar tendency, the desire for certainty. They also found situational variation, however, The desire for certainty was operationally defined (1) by the tendency of respondents to check near the extreme ends of a scale (0–100) when asked to estimate the percentage of Americans who believed various statements, and (2) by the tendency to check "very certain" when they were asked how sure they were of their answer. There was some individual consistency across the range of answers, but this was far from complete.

Brim and Hoff introduced a situational variable by giving one group of subjects the Gottschaldt hidden-figure test while allowing them too little time to complete it. Another group of subjects was given sufficient time to complete the test. Both groups, plus a control group were then given the desire-for-certainty test. The frustrated subjects (those allowed too little time) had significantly higher desire-for-certainty scores than the satisfied group (at the 1 per cent level) and the control group (at the 5 per cent level). Thus the authors found both individual tendencies and situational variables involved, not simply one or the other.[41]

By the brief discussions of several topics in this chapter, I have sought to suggest the usefulness of field theory for a parsimonious statement of the issues involved in behavioral science. I have intended to illustrate the ways in which questions about human behavior can be posed most effec-

tively. The field perspective can go a long way toward reconciling conflicting interpretations and bringing them into a larger synthesis.[42]

Before examining several major research areas in detail, I shall explore
more carefully the key concepts of behavioral science—society, culture,
and personality—in an effort to relate each to the complex whole of
human life. On each of these topics there are significant disagreements in
conceptualization and interpretation to which we must give careful
attention.

FOOTNOTES

*Note: The bracketed number following an author's name refers to the
footnote in which the source is cited in full.*

1. See Sigmund Koch (ed.), *Psychology: A Study of a Science,*
McGraw-Hill Book Company, 1959, vol. 2, pp. 417–704, and vol. 5, 1963,
pp. 30–252, 365–487; Robert R. Blake and Glenn V. Ramsey (eds.), *Perception: An Approach to Personality,* The Ronald Press Company,
1951, esp. chaps. 2 and 3; for a review and appraisal of many approaches
to perception, see Floyd Allport, *Theories of Perception and the Concept
of Structure,* John Wiley & Sons, Inc., 1955. In these and other sources
one can, of course, find many different definitions of "perception." In its
most general sense it is an experience produced by an outside stimulation of the senses. But more specifically, "Perception refers to those
interactions between an organism and its (necessary) environment in
which the form of response is governed by the *signal* or *sign* significance as contrasted with the *energy strength* or *quality* or *pattern* of
the stimulus configuration itself." (Robert R. Blake, with Glenn V.
Ramsey and Louis J. Moran, in Blake and Ramsey, *Perception: An
Approach to Personality,* p. 5.) Use of the word "response" in this
statement raises a host of serious problems of definition. Some argue
that a clear distinction must be drawn between perception and response. (See W. R. Garner, H. W. Hake, and C. W. Eriksen, "Operation-
ism and the Concept of Perception," *Psychological Review,* vol. 63,
1956, pp. 149–159.) And on this basis they contend that many presumed
influences on perception are in fact simply influences on response. Many
complicated and important issues are involved here which I shall not
explore. More than one definition may prove to be useful. If, as Garner,
Hake, and Eriksen suggest, a distinct perceptual process can be inferred
by use of converging operations, even though only "responses" are
measured, the construct is doubtless of value. For our purposes, however, a behavioral definition is more appropriate. Perception as narrowly defined by many psychologists, then, can be viewed as *one* of the
elements in perceptual behavior. (Several aspects of the problem of
definition are discussed in a valuable way by Leo Postman, "Perception
and Learning," in Koch, *Psychology: A Study of a Science,* vol. 5, esp.
pp. 31–54.)

2. Clifford T. Morgan in Blake and Ramsey [1], p. 25.

3. Jean Piaget has contributed notably to this question. See *The
Language and Thought of the Child,* Harcourt, Brace, and Company,

Inc., 1926; and *The Child's Conception of the World,* Harcourt, Brace, and Company, Inc., 1929.

4. See Ernest Hilgard in Blake and Ramsey [1], chap. 4.

5. Jerome Bruner in *ibid.,* chap. 5.

6. See Walter Lippmann, *Public Opinion,* The Macmillan Company, 1922; Jerome Bruner, "On Perceptual Readiness," *Psychological Review,* vol. 64, 1957, pp. 123–152.

7. Seymour Feshbach and R. D. Singer, "The Effects of Fear Arousal and Suppression upon Social Perception," *Journal of Abnormal and Social Psychology,* November, 1957, pp. 283–288.

8. See Jerome Bruner and Leo Postman, "On the Perception of Incongruity: A Paradigm," *Journal of Personality,* vol. 18, 1949, pp. 206–223; H. G. McCurdy, "Coin Perception Studies and the Concept of Schemata," *Psychological Review,* vol. 63, 1956, pp. 160–168; H. Tajfel, "Value and the Perceptual Judgment of Magnitude," *Psychological Review,* vol. 64, 1957, pp. 192–204.

9. Milton Rokeach, *The Open and Closed Mind,* Basic Books, Inc., Publishers, 1960.

10. See Milton Malof and Albert J. Lott, "Ethnocentrism and the Acceptance of Negro Support in a Group Pressure Situation," *Journal of Abnormal and Social Psychology,* October, 1962, pp. 254–258; see also Ray R. Canning and James M. Baker, "Effect of the Group on Authoritarian and Non-authoritarian Persons," *American Journal of Sociology,* May, 1959, pp. 579–581. The importance of the unanimity of the group—a situation uncommon outside the laboratory—in affecting persons with authoritarian tendencies is further explored by Ivan D. Steiner and Homer H. Johnson, "Authoritarianism and Conformity," *Sociometry,* March, 1963, pp. 21–34.

11. Richard S. Crutchfield, "Conformity and Character," *American Psychologist,* May, 1955, pp. 191–198.

12. *Ibid.,* pp. 191–193.

13. *Ibid.,* p. 197.

14. *Ibid.,* pp. 193–197.

15. See George Moeller and Mortimer H. Applezweig, "A Motivational Factor in Conformity," *Journal of Abnormal and Social Psychology,* July, 1957, pp. 114–120.

16. See Jerome S. Bruner and Renato Tagiuri, "The Perception of People," in Gardner Lindzey (ed.), *Handbook of Social Psychology,* Addison-Wesley Publishing Company, Inc., 1954, vol. 2, chap. 17; and Renato Tagiuri and Luigi Petrullo (eds.), *Person Perception and Interpersonal Behavior,* Stanford University Press, 1958.

17. E. E. Jones and Richard deCharms, "Changes in Social Perception as a Function of the Personal Relevance of Behavior," *Sociometry,* March, 1957, pp. 75–85.

18. See Maurice Halbwachs, *Les Cadres sociaux de le mémoire.* Alcan, 1925; and Maurice Halbwachs, *Mémoire et Société, L'année Sociologique,* 3d series, vol. 1, 1949.

19. Raymond Bauer, "The Communicator and the Audience," *Conflict Resolution,* March, 1958, pp. 67–77.

20. F. C. Bartlett, *Remembering,* Cambridge University Press, 1932, from an excerpt in Eleanor E. Maccoby, Theodore M. Newcomb,

and Eugene L. Hartley (eds.), *Readings in Social Psychology,* Holt, Rinehart and Winston, Inc., 1958, p. 53.

21. Jerome Bruner in Blake and Ramsey [1], p. 135.

22. See Wayne Dennis in *ibid.,* chap. 6; A. I. Hallowell, "The Rorschach Technique in the Study of Personality and Culture," *American Anthropologist,* vol. 47, 1945, pp. 195–210; and Murray H. Sherman (ed.), *A Rorschach Reader,* International Universities Press, Inc., 1960, esp. part 3.

23. Urie Bronfenbrenner, *Saturday Review,* Jan. 5, 1963, p. 96.

24. A. I. Hallowell, "Cultural Factors in the Structuralization of Perception," in John Rohrer and Muzafer Sherif (eds.), *Social Psychology at the Crossroads,* Harper & Row, Publishers, Incorporated, 1951, pp. 164–195.

25. For a good summary, see Ruth Benedict, *Race: Science and Politics, Modern Age,* Inc., 1940.

26. Francis Galton, *Hereditary Genius,* rev. ed., D. Appleton and Company, 1879.

27. See Charles H. Cooley, "Genius, Fame, and the Comparison of Races," *Annals of the American Academy of Political and Social Science,* May, 1897, pp. 1–42.

28. See, for example, Audrey M. Shuey, *The Testing of Negro Intelligence,* J. P. Bell Company, 1958. For an examination of such recent emphasis on the importance of race, see Juan Comas, " 'Scientific' Racism Again?" *Current Anthropology,* vol. 2, 1961, pp. 303–340.

29. See R. M. Dreger and K. S. Miller, "Comparative Psychological Studies of Negroes and Whites in the United States," *Psychological Bulletin,* September, 1960, pp. 361–402; Kenneth Eells *et al., Intelligence and Cultural Differences,* The University of Chicago Press, 1951; Otto Klineberg (ed.), *Characteristics of the American Negro,* Harper & Row, Publishers, Incorporated, 1944; William McCord and N. J. Demerath III, "Negro vs. White Intelligence: A Continuing Controversy," *Harvard Educational Review,* Spring, 1958, pp. 120–135. For an interpretation of the effects of racial status on intelligence and other tendencies, see George E. Simpson and J. Milton Yinger, *Racial and Cultural Minorities,* 3d ed., Harper & Row, Publishers, Incorporated, 1965, chaps. 6 and 7.

30. Jacob W. Getzels and Philip W. Jackson, *Creativity and Intelligence,* John Wiley & Sons, Inc., 1962, p. 17.

31. See David C. McClelland, Alfred L. Baldwin, Urie Bronfenbrenner, and Fred L. Strodtbeck, *Talent and Society,* D. Van Nostrand Company, Inc., 1958; D. C. McClelland, J. W. Atkinson, R. A. Clark, and E. L. Lowell, *The Achievement Motive,* Appleton-Century-Crofts, Inc., 1953.

32. See Aaron Antonovsky and Melvin J. Lerner, "Occupational Aspirations of Lower Class Negro and White Youth," *Social Problems,* Fall, 1959, pp. 132–138; N. P. Gist and W. S. Bennett, Jr., "Aspirations of Negro and White Students," *Social Forces,* October, 1963, pp. 40–48; Bernard Rosen, "Race, Ethnicity, and the Achievement Syndrome," *American Sociological Review,* February, 1959, pp. 47–60; Bernard Rosen and Roy D'Andrade, "The Psychosocial Origins of Achievement Motivation," *Sociometry,* September, 1959, pp. 185–218; Jetse Sprey, "'Sex Differences in Occupational Choice Patterns among Negro Adolescents," *Social Problems,* Summer, 1962, pp. 11–23; Richard M. Ste-

phenson, "Mobility Orientation and Stratification of 1,000 Ninth Graders," *American Sociological Review,* April, 1957, pp. 204–212.

33. Sheldon R. Roen, "Personality and Negro-White Intelligence," *Journal of Abnormal and Social Psychology,* July, 1960, pp. 148–150.

34. Ezra Stotland *et al.,* "The Effects of Group Expectations and Self-esteem upon Self-evaluation," *Journal of Abnormal and Social Psychology,* January, 1957, pp. 55–63.

35. See James S. Coleman, *Adolescent Society,* The Free Press of Glencoe, 1961; Edward L. McDill and James S. Coleman, "High School Social Status, College Plans, and Interest in Academic Achievement: A Panel Analysis," *American Sociological Review,* December, 1963, pp. 905–918; Burton Clark, *Educating the Expert Society,* Chandler Publishing Company, 1962; Matilda Riley and S. H. Flowerman, "Group Relations as a Variable in Communications Research," *American Sociological Review,* April, 1951, pp. 174–180.

36. R. E. L. Faris, "Reflections on the Ability Dimension in Human Society," *American Sociological Review,* December, 1961, pp. 835–843.

37. See Ralph Linton, *Study of Man,* D. Appleton–Century Company, Inc., 1936, pp. 120–121.

38. C. M. Morgan, "The Attitudes and Adjustments of Recipients of Old Age Assistance in Upstate and Metropolitan New York," *Archives of Psychology,* 1937, no. 214 (cited in Gardner Murphy, *Personality: A Biosocial Approach to Origins and Structure,* Harper & Row, Publishers, Incorporated, 1947, p. 870).

39. Zena S. Blau, "Structural Constraints on Friendships in Old Age," *American Sociological Review,* June, 1961, pp. 429–439.

40. There is now an extensive literature on gerontology. See John E. Anderson, *Psychological Aspects of Aging,* American Psychological Association, Inc., 1956; Elaine Cumming and William E. Henry, *Growing Old: The Process of Disengagement,* Basic Books, Inc., Publishers, 1961; Talcott Parsons, "Age and Sex in the Social Structure of the United States," *American Sociological Review,* vol. 7, 1942, pp. 604–616; Clark Tibbitts and Wilma Donahue (eds.), *Aging in Today's Society,* Prentice-Hall, Inc., 1960; James Birren (ed.), *Handbook of Aging and the Individual: Psychological and Biological Aspects,* The University of Chicago Press, 1959; Clark Tibbitts (ed.), *Handbook of Social Gerontology: Societal Aspects of Aging,* The University of Chicago Press, 1960; Ernest W. Burgess (ed.), *Aging in Western Societies,* The University of Chicago Press, 1960; and the *Journal of Gerontology.*

41. Orville G. Brim, Jr. and David B. Hoff, "Individual and Situational Differences in Desire for Certainty," *Journal of Abnormal and Social Psychology,* March, 1957, pp. 225–229.

42. Systematic attention to individual and situational variables within a single research design is not the rarity it was even a decade ago. See Howard S. Becker and Blanche Geer, "The Fate of Idealism in Medical School," *American Sociological Review,* February, 1958, pp. 50–56; Doris C. Gilbert and Daniel J. Levinson, "Ideology, Personality, and Institutional Policy in the Mental Hospital," *Journal of Abnormal and Social Psychology,* vol. 53, 1956, pp. 263–271 (reprinted in Neil J. Smelser and William T. Smelser, *Personality and Social Systems,* John Wiley & Sons, Inc., 1963, pp. 619–629); Robert L. Hall and Ben Willerman, "The Educational Influence of Dormitory Roommates," *Sociometry,* September, 1963, pp. 294–318; A. O. Haller and I. W. Miller, "The Oc-

cupational Aspiration Scale: Theory, Structure and Correlates," tech. bull. 288, Michigan State University, Agricultural Experiment Station; A. Paul Hare and Robert F. Bales, "Seating Position and Small Group Interaction," *Sociometry,* December, 1963, pp. 480–486; Richard Jessor, Robert C. Hanson, Theodore D. Graves, and Lee Jessor, "Theory and Method in the Study of Deviance in a Tri-Ethnic Community," res. rept no. 25, Tri-Ethnic Research Project, University of Colorado; Leonard I. Pearlin, "Sources of Resistance to Change in a Mental Hospital," *American Journal of Sociology,* November, 1962, pp. 325–334; William T. Smelser, "Dominance as a Factor in Achievement and Perception in Cooperative Problem Solving Interactions," *Journal of Abnormal and Social Psychology,* vol. 62, 1961, pp. 535–542 (reprinted in Smelser and Smelser, *Personality and Social Systems,* pp. 531–540); Edward A. Suchman, "A Conceptual Analysis of the Accident Phenomenon," *Social Problems,* Winter,, 1960–1961, pp. 241–253; Larry Rosenberg, "Social Status and Participation among a Group of Chronic Schizophrenics," *Human Relations,* November, 1962, pp. 365–377.

Part TWO

ELEMENTS IN

THE FIELD THEORY OF BEHAVIOR

CHAPTER 5

The Relationship of Society and Culture to Personality

If it is held that the biological organism, the person, the interacting group, and the culture are separate systems—mutually influencing, yet separate—then any attempt to state their relationship must at the same time recognize their distinctiveness. The aim of the next several chapters is not to obliterate the lines of distinction nor to minimize the importance of each system, but to define a perspective that will permit each to be related to the larger behavioral system of which it is a part. Perhaps defining this perspective can be thought of as a second stage in the development of a science. In the first stage, major effort is given to isolating the properties of a system from the various "disturbing" forces of the empirical world in which that system is embedded. When this process has been reasonably successful, however, the task of relating the analytic system back to the larger complex of forces from which it has been abstracted must be undertaken. Regarding the development of a science, Hagen states:

As judged by the history of the physical, biological, and social sciences, study in any field is apt to begin with a none-too-ordered description of phenomena in the field, followed by a cataloguing of them on bases that seem to make sense. As understanding grows, the systems of classification become more closely related to the functioning of interacting elements. Gradually, generalizations about functioning are reached which are useful in predicting future events. As the generalizations gain rigor, they take the form of analytical models of the behavior of the elements being studied. An analytical model is a mental construct consisting of a set of elements in interrelation, the elements and their interrelations being precisely defined.[1]

To this process, further steps may be added. As knowledge grows, larger systems, with more interacting elements, can be constructed; but each of the analytically closed units must be redefined and opened so that their relationship to other units can be specified. In the process of doing this, we are likely to discover that the formerly separate units were not as closed as a formal definition might make them appear to be. Each unit almost always includes attention to other levels of influence; but as I have suggested, this attention is often included implicitly, by subtle extension of the scope of the "basic" level. Our task is to make this process explicit and thus to minimize the danger of absorption of one analytic system into another and to maximize attention to their mutual influence.

CULTURE AND PERSONALITY

Several generations of anthropological research have convinced almost all students of human behavior that personality is shaped in significant ways by culture. Long before the development of anthropology, of course, the importance of variation in cultural values was readily apparent to those who came in contact with persons from other societies. From Herodotus and Plato, from Ibn Khaldun, from Montesquieu, Hume, and Voltaire have come remarkable discussions of cultural diversity. Their information was sometimes sketchy, however, and their commentaries not always free from ethnocentrism. The first task of anthropology as a modern discipline was greatly to extend the range of observations and to improve the techniques for objective recording of events. (In this connection, it seems likely that "cultural relativism" is not only a description— sometimes exaggerated—of the actual range in cultural practices. Insofar as it also carries a value tone—an emphasis on the need for respect for the cultural systems of other peoples—it serves a methodological function, for it helps to control ethnocentrism and the influence of biased judgments.)

The second task of anthropology was to incorporate the vast range of observations into a theory of human behavior. The theories were held at first largely within the range of traditional anthropological interest, emphasizing questions of cultural origins, diffusion, kinship systems and terminology, and evolution. But in recent decades—one might arbitrarily say at least since Boas's *The Mind of Primitive Man*—anthropology has tended more and more to develop a behavioral science branch, generally under the topic of "culture and personality," and has contributed importantly to the theory of behavior with which this book is concerned. The persistent concern for wholeness and the tradition of complete and meticulous description strongly supported those tendencies in anthropology most closely related to behavioral science. The development of functionalism gave further impetus to these trends; for the basic question of functionalism is in a sense a field question: How does this item under examination fit into the larger scheme of things?

There were some barriers to the development of a theory of behavior in anthropology or, more accurately, to the achievement of anthropology's potential contribution to an interdisciplinary theory. Reaction to the sweeping generalizations of some early anthropologists led, among other results, to an emphasis on description that was often atheoretical if not antitheoretical. To describe each society in its full particularity became a prominent aim. Few attempts were made to work out common units of observation. With the development of comparative anthropology, this difficulty has been substantially reduced, but problems still remain in coding and transposing monographs that were prepared at a time when there were few agreed-upon categories for the recording of observations.

Despite its vast diversity of interests, anthropology has a special concern with the study of culture; and from this specialization arises its greatest contribution to a theory of personality. Paradoxically, the most serious limitation of anthropology may also rise from this focus of attention. The very centrality of culture as a concept encourages diffusion of its meaning, until its value as a scientific term has become seriously weakened.[2] Without attempting to discuss or to interpret the various meanings of culture, we can note the primary disagreement in usages. Starting from the basic idea that culture is "the way of life" of a people, some researchers think in terms of behavior—the way things are in fact done—and others in terms of norms—the way things ought to be done according to the standards of the group in question.

There is, in fact, a strong tendency to confuse or to equate these two meanings. This is a result, in part, of the common tendency for a discipline to spread out its central concepts to try to cover the full range of human activity—one manifestation of the fallacy of misplaced concreteness and the difficulty of maintaining a clear analytic focus. Anthropology, with its encyclopedic interests, has been particularly uncomfortable with any limitation to one analytic level; yet its central concepts have not been adequate to incorporate systematic attention to individual or structural factors. Although it may come as close as any other discipline, anthropology as a body of knowledge and as method is not the science of man.

So long as anthropology concentrated on full ideographic descriptions of relatively simple and relatively strange societies, researchers felt little pressure to examine carefully the implications for a behavioral science of their emphasis on culture. The relatively close meshing of individual tendency systems, structural patterns of interpersonal relations, and cultural norms made it possible for an anthropologist to concentrate on the last of these and still get fairly good *indexes* of the other two. (Fairly good, of course, is not good enough; and a disciplinary ideology that tended to overestimate the coherence, unity, and homogeneity of cultural systems led to underestimation of individual variations and, paradoxically, underestimation of universal similarities—as well as to neglect of the strains between the social structure and the culture.)

The growth of anthropology as a science; the increasing awareness of and criticism from related disciplines; and the extension of interest to rapidly changing societies, to comparative work, and to heterogeneous societies, all have helped to reveal the inadequacies of a science of man built in too limited a way around the study of culture. After 1940, "there was a growing consensus," Voget notes, "that the fit between the individuals of any society and their culture was far looser than formerly assumed." [3] How should theory be enlarged to take account of this fact? The necessary extension could be made by redefining, extending, and then subdividing the whole idea of culture, so that it included a broader range of factors. Or the job could be done by methodically adding subsystems which were concerned with individual and structural forces.

Linton, for example, who was one of the most sensitive students of this question and whose theoretical system was highly permeable and open to new elements, shows aspects of both these processes. Recognizing the range of individual behavior and the frequent contrasts between norms and actual behavior, he suggested three concepts: "Real culture" ("The real culture of any society consists of the actual behavior . . . of its members"), "cultural construct" (the mode of the real series, used as a necessary descriptive tool), and "ideal patterns" (the consensus of opinion on how people should behave in particular situations).[4]

Although this is a valuable recognition of difficulties in the use of the single term "culture," I think it is an unfortunate terminological "solution," for it does not make clear the multiple sources of behavior or precisely designate the place of normative influences. If "real culture" is "actual behavior," we scarcely need both terms; as synonyms they are confusing. Surely the minimum definition of culture is that it is learned and shared, while behavior clearly has biological and individual components as well as those deriving from groups.

For my purposes, then, culture will be thought of as the system of norms shared by the members of society, the prescriptions and proscriptions indicating how things should be done or should be appraised. Culture is a system of blueprints for action. In the words of Kluckhohn and Kelly: "By 'culture' we mean all those historically created designs for living, explicit and implicit, rational, irrational, and nonrational, that exist at any given time as potential guides for the behavior of men." [5] Although there is still some disagreement on this usage, the concept of culture as a shared system of normative patterns is now the dominant one. Kroeber and Parsons have noted that early definitions, the widely quoted one by Tylor for example,[6] were used when a major task was to designate the social and environmental facts separately from the biological. The analytic distinction between society, as a network of patterned social relationships among individuals and groups, and culture, as the system of normative guidelines to the interaction, was a later development. Many of the earlier definitions of society, those of Spencer and Durkheim, for example, were similar to Tylor's definition of culture.[7]

The designs for living which in total make up a culture refer to many different varieties of human activity; there are technical, aesthetic, moral, and religious norms. They share in common, however, the quality of group-supported "oughtness." In addition to classification by types of action, norms can be scaled along several dimensions. They vary, for example, in the degree to which they are explicit and clearly articulated. Linton observed that:

> Even in the most analytically minded and culture-conscious societies the investigator finds again and again that informants are quite unable to tell what the proper behavior in a particular situation would be and have to fall back on relating what happened on various occasions when this situation arose. This lack of ideal patterns is the more striking since comparison of the narratives usually reveals the presence of a real culture pattern with a recognizable mode of variation.[8]

Linton used this statement to contrast ideal patterns with behavior (real culture). If my proposed terminology is accepted, however, a more useful approach is to indicate that although some cultural norms are covert and poorly verbalized, they are not lacking in power to influence behavior. The nurses in a hospital may arrive at certain patterns of activity that become established as the proper way of doing things; new personnel may be socialized to these norms; sanctions may be exerted on those who deviate; yet the norm may be entirely implicit and scarcely identified with any "ideal culture" of the hospital on the explicit level. The inference by the scientific observer that a covert cultural norm "is there" in a sense not fully summed up in the behavior of individuals—that the norm exists in the stream of group communication and influence as a "collective representation"—is correct if patterns of sanctions and rewards are consistently emanating from the group to produce the desired behavior.

Cultural norms can also be classified in terms of the range of their acceptance. This is, of course, a critical dimension for a behavioral science. A society made up of persons who share to a high degree the same cultural blueprint is significantly different from one in which many interactions lack normative agreement. But how widely must a norm be shared before it is part of the culture? One might arbitrarily say that it must have majority support. We might be wiser, however, to think of a variable rather than of some decisive cutting point and to ask: What are the consequences for behavior of various levels of agreement? In addition to the number of supporters of a given norm, distinctions about it might be drawn on the basis of the sanctioning power or status of the supporters.

It is difficult to think of culture in this adjectival way—as a quality, not as a thing—but such a shift in our usual perspective is essential if we are to measure accurately the full range of normative influences. In thinking of extent of agreement as a variable and in seeking observations about it, we are led to record the possible clustering of agreement in certain parts of a society. Where a norm is widely shared among the members of a subsociety but lacks majority support in the total society, we can speak of a subcultural norm, of a groupway rather than a folkway. A subcultural system, by definition, is always incomplete. It furnishes normative guidelines for only part of the situations faced by those who hold it. It differentiates these people, in part, from other members of the society to which they belong. In a formal definition, a subculture is a differentiating system of norms of a group which does not have sufficient size or complexity to fulfill all the prerequisites of social life.[9]

If we accept the normative definition of culture, we cannot deal with the weaknesses of a purely cultural theory of human behavior simply by enlarging and subdividing the meaning of culture. In the last quarter century, anthropology has broadened its theoretical system in another—and more successful—way. There has been a significant increase in the reaching out toward other disciplines, particularly toward psychology (including psychiatry) and sociology. An oversimplified but perhaps useful statement of the case is that in the United States, anthropology has attempted to incorporate some of the methods and concepts of psychology,[10] while in Great Britain, anthropological interest in social structure has led toward sociology.[11] Exceptions come readily to mind, of course: In the United States, for example, Linton and Kluckhohn reached out toward both psychology and sociology and have thus been important in the development of a discipline—whether or not it should be called anthropology—which is concerned with the interaction of the individual, culture, and society. Some of the same tendencies are found in the work of Lloyd Warner and Margaret Mead. In England, Malinowski cast a wide theoretical net. And reversing the formula suggested above, Murdock in the United States has emphasized social structure while in England Gorer, a psychologist and anthropologist, has emphasized the relationship of culture and personality.

Granted the importance of such exceptions, the leaning of American anthropology toward psychology and of British toward sociology seems quite clear. Hints in the work of Boas and others about the relationship of culture and personality became the explicit focus in the work of Mead, Sapir, Linton (especially in his collaborative work with Kardiner), Benedict, Hallowell, Kluckhohn, and many others. In Great Britain, emphasis on the analytic distinction between culture and society and at the same time on their empirical unity is found particularly in the work of Evans-Pritchard, Nadel, and Radcliffe-Brown. Somewhat more loosely, Malinowski can be called one of this group. In France, a similar approach is generally labeled sociology, as in the work of Durkheim, Mauss, and Halbwachs.

I shall not undertake to describe the works of these various writers. They are mentioned here in order to indicate the strength of the pressures in anthropology, as in psychology and sociology, to enlarge its theoretical scheme, to move toward a behavioral science. My purpose is to ask how culture and personality studies can be incorporated into a field theoretical view of behavior. In examining this problem it is necessary to distinguish two questions:

1. Under what conditions does culture influence individual tendency systems, so that it enters into character?

2. In what ways does culture as a contemporary fact of the situation external to an individual affect behavior?

CULTURE AS EXTERNAL ENVIRONMENT

If we imagine a person placed in a strange society with whose culture he was unfamiliar, we realize that his behavior would be affected by the culture around him—through the stimuli he received, the nature of the opportunities and alternatives furnished, the sanctions imposed—even though he had not been socialized to its values. It is equally true but perhaps less obvious that a familiar surrounding culture brings stimuli, alternatives, and sanctions that affect behavior as external constraints and not only as the source of internal tendencies. Thus Durkheim noted that suicide rates were high in groups with high divorce rates (as an index of anomie) even among individuals who were not divorced.

This external cultural influence is brought to bear in the systems of social relationships that an individual experiences. It does not exist independently of those relationships. For this reason, the phrase "sociocultural environment" is a valuable, if awkward, expression. Society and culture, group and norm, can be defined separately as abstract concepts, but they are experienced together as normatively guided interaction. If one's interest is in a behavioral science, he must agree with Radcliffe-Brown: "Neither social structure nor culture can be scientifically dealt with in isolation from one another." [12]

Failure to distinguish between culture as external environment and culture as a source of individual tendencies has led to an exaggeration of the extent to which knowledge of culture means knowledge of character. Commenting on Benedict's characterization of the Kwakiutl as megalomaniacal, Linton notes:

It is quite certain that the behavior of the chiefs of this tribe is such that if it occurred in a European country...it would be characterized as megalomaniacal. [However]...in order to acquire the property which the chiefs used in competitive and self-aggrandizing potlatching—and potlatching was almost entirely the chief's business—it was necessary that the surplus created by all the non-chiefly members of the chief's sub-tribe be funnelled into the chief's hands...it is quite evident that the so-called megalomaniacal behavior of the chiefs required that there be also other individuals, making up about 85% of the population of the tribe, who not only were not megalomaniacal, but were actually a lot more cooperative than is the average individual in our society.[13]

This is not to say that the cultural pattern of the potlatch was unimportant in affecting the tendencies and behavior of the commoners. But the effects were indirect; customs surrounding the potlatch were part of the cultural environment within which behavior occurred.

Social Structure and Culture

Culture as a source of personality tendencies has received far more attention, and criticism, than culture as part of the external environment. Or to state this fact more generally, sociocultural factors in the *socialization* of individuals have been more fully observed and commented upon than have sociocultural factors in the *social control* of behavior. This has especially been true in the work of psychologists and anthropologists, but even among sociologists the Cooley-Mead emphasis on socialization has, until recently, prevailed over the Durkheim-Ross emphasis on sociocultural systems as external forces of facilitation and constraint. This trend has changed to some degree in the last several years. We have seen the rise of a special emphasis on social structure and personality to complement earlier emphasis on culture and personality.

Unfortunately, use of these and related terms is far from consistent or explicit. The result is theoretical confusion—a loss of both analytic clarity and synthesizing unity among related specialties. To some degree, "culture and personality" and "social structure and personality" are used as synonyms, each being a general label for studies of interactions among individual, cultural, and social forces. Whatever the label chosen, research monographs, collections of studies, and texts tend to examine all three sets of factors, and sometimes biological factors as well. Anthropologists tend to use culture and personality and sociologists to speak of social structure and personality, but seldom do any of them give explicit attention to analytically separated cultural and structural variables. Usage is more closely related to their familiarity with the terms, or perhaps to their wish to stake out a disciplinary claim, than to careful definition. Most work converges finally on the interactions of individuals and *sociocultural* systems.

There is an implicit division of labor, in my judgment, that is not based on the society-culture distinction but on the two questions noted at the end of the last section. The culture and personality studies are primarily concerned with socialization, with observation of the sociocultural factors involved in establishing certain individual tendencies. The social structure and personality studies are primarily concerned with social control, with analysis of the ways in which the external sociocultural environment, interacting with individual propensities, affects behavior. This difference in emphasis has scarcely been recognized and is difficult to maintain in research. It represents, however, an analytically important distinction that requires attention, whether within one discipline or as the basis of a division of labor.

This is not to imply that a clear analytic distinction between culture and social structure is either impossible or unnecessary. Indeed, a critical research task is to isolate the extent to which structural conditions influence behavior when the effects of culture and personality variation have been controlled. In a comparative study of "industrial man," for example, Inkeles demonstrates that the structure of relationships of the occupational world produces certain standard responses "despite the countervailing randomizing effects of persisting traditional patterns of culture," [14] and despite individual variation in personality. He does not deny the influence of culture and personality, of course, but shows how the networks of interpersonal relationships implicit in the structure of an industrial society have similar influences on behavior among persons with different personal tendencies and in different cultural contexts. (Part of his explanation of the influence of industrial environment, however, rests upon the emergence of a "subculture" supplementing the traditional cultures of the several industrial societies. To some degree, therefore, he is discussing the effects of norms as well as of structure.)

An analytically clear distinction between culture and structure is difficult to keep and perhaps even more difficult to apply in research; but I believe it must be done. There is now substantial evidence that behavior is affected by the channels and barriers to communication, the size of a group, the physical shape of the group and the individual's location in it, the degree of impersonality of the relationships, and other structural variables.[15] Thus the suicide rate of the elderly may be affected, not only by their personality tendencies (some of them a result of physiological processes) and the culture of their society (including such things as their role assignments and losses and the culture's degree of respect for the aged), but also by such facts as their comparative size as a group. If they make up a small proportion of a community, for example, this will affect the types and extent of interaction and the ease with which the elderly can be cared for.[16] Infielders and catchers may become baseball managers more often than pitchers and outfielders because their spatial location increases their rate of interaction with other players and therefore promotes the learning of various skills and attitudes.[17] The fact that a cab driver and his fare have a "fleeting relationship" affects the nature of their interaction at the same time that personality and cultural variables are affecting it.[18]

The concept of social structure is commonly used to refer not only to the contextual facts noted above but also to the normative system. Blau, for example, writes: "if we should find that, regardless of whether or not an individual has an authoritarian disposition, he is more apt to discriminate against minorities if he lives in a community where authoritarian values prevail than if he lives in one where they do not, we would have evidence that this social value exerts external constraints upon the tendency to discriminate—structural effects that are independent of the internalized value orientation of individuals." [19] Undoubtedly, shared systems of values are crucial "external" variables; they influence the rewards and punishments a person will experience for various actions, the cues he will receive, the prestige of his various reference groups, etc. But there are external influences in the situation Blau describes which are not normative: How large is the minority which is being discriminated against? Where are they located in the occupational system? What is the structure of economic opportunity for members of the majority? Such questions as these may suggest that among persons with given levels of "authoritarian disposition," living in communities with given levels of "authoritarian values," there may be wide variation in behavior as a result of variation in the social structure.

It is important, therefore, that we not blur the distinction between culture and social structure or subsume one under the other. I am not saying that use of "structure" as a construct which includes both levels of variables is unwarranted, but only that such use should be explicit so that one set of variables is not overlooked.

Sometimes confusion comes from an opposite tendency—apparent reference to culture or to structure, but examination of both. Titles may seem to indicate that a study or a commentary is specifically concerned with one or the other, while content and definition encompass both. Thus Barnouw writes that "Culture-and-personality is an area of research where anthropology and psychology come together. . . ." And then, "This book . . . will focus on the cultural and social determinants of personality." [20] Hsu, in seeking to differentiate "psychological anthropology" from "social psychology," suggests, among other differences, that the former "deals not only with the effect of society and culture on personality (a basic concern of social psychology) but also with the role of personality characteristics in the development, formation, and change of culture and society." [21] Cohen notes that his book, entitled *Social Structure and Personality,* is a quest for principles involved in "the relationships of personality to the social-structural arrangements of society," [22] which he thinks of as an effort distinct from that of its "progenitor"— culture and personality. Yet his definition of aims might readily be accepted by most students of culture and personality. Several of the topics, and also of the authors, found in his collection are also found in Kaplan's *Studying Personality Cross-culturally* [23] and Hsu's *Psychological Anthropology,* which identify with the culture-personality approach.

The pioneering collection of papers edited by Kluckhohn and Murray explicitly includes culture and society (as well as "nature"—biological factors) in its title and approach, which it designates a "field" approach.[24] It thus takes a broader perspective than the other works cited, although research on the influence of social structure is not well represented. Research in this area has expanded rapidly since publication of the volume. This expansion is shown in the collection edited by Smelser and Smelser.[25] They prefer the term "social systems," of which both social structures and norms are elements, but they give greater attention to structural influences and less to culture than do Kluckhohn, Murray, and Schneider.

Such explicitly interdisciplinary, if eclectic, work is far from the rule. Some anthropological monographs carry the strong implication that to know culture is to know personality,[26] while some psychological discussions of personality pay almost no attention to culture.[27] In the face of such wide differences of opinion, how can we incorporate the study of culture and social structure into a field theoretical statement? There can be no objection, of course, to focusing attention on part of a complex whole; but the criteria of selection must be explicit if we are to avoid terminological confusion and pseudo-arguments based on failures of communication. And what is in fact a specialized analytic study must not be offered or accepted as an explanation of behavior.

Almost all writing in this area contains laments over disciplinary boundaries, even if in the next sentence, subtle differences between the study at hand and similar material are emphasized. One way to give substance to the differences is to choose a different title for them; thus many of the same problems are dealt with under these various labels: culture and personality, social structure and personality, cultural psychology, psychological anthropology, and—to a substantial degree also—social psychology and the psychology of personality. This diversity would be harmless if it simply represented private enterprise in titles. Unfortunately it reflects and helps to perpetuate theoretical disarray. If one specializes, he should truly specialize and not seek to slip the whole science of human behavior under his preferred label. On what grounds, then, can distinctions be drawn? What are the possible differences in emphasis within the field of culture and personality (to use the most common title)? I believe there are three:

1. Is primary emphasis given to social structure (S), to culture (C), or to both?

2. Is primary emphasis given to individual personality or "traits" (P), to behavior (B), or to both?

3. Does the flow of causation which is being studied move from the sociocultural system to the individual, from the individual to the sociocultural system, or both?

INCORPORATING CULTURE AND PERSONALITY STUDIES INTO A FIELD VIEW

Having examined the relationship of culture and personality studies to associated work, we can return to a statement of the possible place of these studies in a field view. To make maximum use of culture and personality research, we must try to identify the kinds of questions it is equipped to answer.

The tendency by some investigators to employ this research as a complete theory of personality has served to increase its vulnerability to criticism and reduce its value as one of several approaches. Several careful reviews of it have noted unexpressed assumptions and methodological weaknesses.[28] For example, a tendency to assume the cultural patterning of and the importance of infant-training experiences has led to the neglect of adolescent and adult experience.[29] Subcultural variations have been disregarded. Specification of cultural norms has sometimes been used as a substitute for description of individual tendencies; the investigator has thereby assumed the very relationship which needs study.[30] Ethnocentrism has sometimes interfered with observation. Latent consequences of culture for personality—consequences that are often far removed from the manifest values and norms—have been overlooked.[31] Questions associated with culture change have been neglected, partly because some anthropologists assume a resilience and toughness in cultural systems even in the face of drastic changes in situation (an assumption similar to the assumption of stability in ego organization made by some psychologists). The differences between the cultural influences of literate, mobile, and heterogeneous societies and those of preliterate, relatively stable, and homogeneous societies have been insufficiently explored.[32] And finally, culture is often treated as a completely independent variable, rather than as the product in part of elaboration from individual interpretations and reinterpretations.[33]

If culture is to be seen as a causal influence on behavior, it must be shown to exist independently of the individuals whose behavior is being explained. Sometimes a norm is inferred from observation of regularities of behavior and then used to "explain" that behavior. Only by introducing a time dimension to the observation can the adequacy of such explanations be tested. Perhaps the reason for the frequency with which infant-training procedures are used in culture-personality studies lies not only in the theoretical emphasis on the importance of infancy, but also in the ease with which the time sequence can be established. Clearly the patterned methods of child training exist prior to and independently of the children. As a general methodological problem, however systematic efforts to establish culture as an independent factor are scarce.

Specialized study of the relationship of culture and behavior, in sum, needs a more careful specification of the questions it seeks to answer. Offhand references to "sociocultural systems" need to be turned into careful studies of the ways in which norms and structures affect each other. The influence of cultural emphasis on individualism and achievement, for example, is strongly affected by structured patterns of relationship between classes, and vice versa. To know "the culture" on this topic without relating it to relevant structures is to be poorly equipped to determine the cultural norm's significance for behavior.[34] Only as a cultural norm enters into and affects interaction does it become relevant for a science of behavior.

Similarly, the researcher needs to keep clearly in mind that a cultural norm is not an individual tendency, even though the operations by which the norm was isolated as an analytic fact required individual measurements. "Interest in automobiles," if the term "interest" is used in the sense employed by Linton, is part of American culture; this can be noted by observation of economic activities, conversation, and actions of many kinds. Such a cultural fact affects an individual whether or not he himself has internalized that interest. (The effects on those who share and those who do not share the interest are different, of course.) This is another way of calling attention to the distinction between socialization and social control. The sociocultural system is an important source of individual tendencies. It influences behavior "externally" also, however, by the way in which patterns of opportunity and sanction facilitate and inhibit the expression of various tendencies.

Field theoretical studies of culture and personality emphasize that the relationship is reciprocal, that an a priori assumption concerning the direction of influence is unwarranted, and that the research task is to specify the conditions under which an existing normative system is internalized without much change and the conditions under which individual responses to and interpretations of culture lead to normative variation. Chapter 10 will note that many interpretations of delinquency are of the culture → personality variety and will suggest that they need to be complemented by a personality → culture emphasis. In contrast, Chapter 11 will examine the personality → culture theory of prejudice (to give an overly simple label to the "authoritarian personality" thesis) and will indicate the need for strong correction by a culture → personality point of view. This does not mean that all is ceaseless flux, that "everything influences everything else," as the field theory viewpoint is sometimes characterized. It means that causal influences flow from many directions; that we should not be content with easy assumptions about priorities; and that we need careful specification of the conditions under which various factors are predominant.

Biology, culture, and social structure. In fact, to note the interaction between the cultural and the personality levels is not enough. Culture also influences and is influenced by the biological potentialities and limits of the human species. The effect of the Freudian tradition has been, in my judgment, to define these limits too narrowly; but the opposite assumption by some behavioristic psychologists and some anthropologists that the biological inheritance is almost infinitely malleable seems equally wide of the mark. If the character types developed by Freud in terms of psychosexual development [35] seem at once too biological and too universal (that is, too little affected by cultural variation), the remedy is not to forget that man has an inheritance.

In a stimulating hypothesis, Parsons has suggested that types of character emerge from the structure and function of the nuclear family. Power
differentiation occurs on a generational basis (the inevitable product of
the helplessness of the child and his lack of control over the techniques
that culture will furnish him); and differentiation on the basis of instrumental and expressive functions occurs between male and female. Agreeing with Freud about the strong erotic (not specifically sexual) impulses
of the child, Parsons suggests that these are used by the parents to socialize him to familial roles (which are, indeed, roles with counterparts in all
organizations).[36]

In another interesting attempt to relate biological forces to social and
cultural facts, Slater interprets the biological influences not only as forces
to be used in socialization, as Parsons does, but also as challenges to be
met if groups are to survive. He redefines Freud's life and death instincts
to speak in terms of "libidinal diffusion" and "libidinal contraction."
"Social systems are seen as ultimately dependent upon a biological tendency toward libidinal diffusion, and continually threatened by a contrary
biological contracting tendency, here equated with Freud's death instinct." [37] If libido is focused narrowly on self, the species would die out,
and it focused narrowly on a dyad or family, the society with its culture
could not survive. Many social structures, as Slater interprets them, are
designed to prevent or reduce the likelihood of narcissistic, dyadic, and
familial withdrawal from the larger society. (He agrees with Parsons, for
example, that this may be the source of the powerful and near-universal
incest taboos.) [38]

Slater, following Freud, sees man as narcissistic and ego-centered by
nature. Since ego centeredness endangers the group, many social control
mechanisms have been developed of necessity to reduce the tendency
toward withdrawal. Thus Slater poses an antithesis between self (or small
group) and society. But if one were to start from an opposite premise, the
relationship between biological forces and social structure would appear
different. There are reasons to affirm that man is by nature a group-
dominated animal: his long dependency, the relative lack of instinctual
answers to survival problems, and his reliance on language (group symbols) tend to pull him into group dependency. From this point of view, the
"danger" is not withdrawal to self or dyad but the failure to affirm self. A
dedicated Freudian might argue that this would prove how effectively
society had thwarted the individual in socializing the helpless infant; but
such an argument would assume the very problem under examination.

Better than either assumption, for an empirical science attempting to
measure the interaction of biological and sociocultural forces, is to ask,
"Under what conditions is cathexis concentrated on self, dyad, or family
(Slater's regression); under what conditions is it concentrated on larger
groups, on tribe, or class, or nation; and what combinations of these
tendencies occur?" It seems unwise to begin with assumptions about
either self or group being the starting point.

The interaction of biology and culture can be noted even in the process of biological evolution. The common assumption that cultural development began when human capacity, perhaps as a result of mutation, had reached a level which made possible the use of language and abstract thought overlooks "the role of culture itself as the determinant of man's capacity for culture." [39] Early culture yielded adaptive advantages; persons capable of it survived in higher ratio, so that the next generation was more capable of culture building, with its still further survival advantages. Although there is serious doubt about the operation of this interactive process today, it seems likely to have been important through most of the cultural history of man.[40]

The interaction of personality, culture, and social structure. Assuming a constant biological capacity, the basic questions for culture-personality research seen through a field perspective can be stated in this way: "How does a normative system, acting on persons of given tendencies (including some tendencies that have been shaped by that system), and expressed through a specified structure of interacting persons, affect behavior? And conversely, how is culture modified by the behavior of individuals of given tendencies interacting in a specified structure?"

Culture is perhaps too infrequently noted as a dependent variable under some conditions. There are evidences today of a "culture-building" process among some Negroes in the United States, for example. This is not simply cultural evolution; it springs from discriminatory interaction, and from the resulting personality tendencies, acting upon the received tradition. Voget notes that conditions of *anomie,* which we might for the moment think of as a cultural vacuum, often promote new cultural movements, not simply minor adaptations of traditional forms.[41]

Studies of culture and personality by anthropologists have not commonly developed such themes of interaction, but have asked a more limited question: "How are individuals shaped by their culture?" Approximations of field design, however, are by no means lacking. For example, in a series of publications on the Menomini, George and Louise Spindler have carefully studied the interrelationships of individual tendencies (obtained by Rorschach tests and interviews), native cultural values and their various modifications, and structural conditions (economic status and access to economic opportunities).[42] The breadth of the authors' theoretical orientation encourages them to ask not simply "How does Menomini culture affect personality?" or "How does culture change affect personality?" but also "How do individuals torn by culture conflict participate in cultural innovation and change (e.g., the Peyote Cult)?" and "How does the implication of culture conflict vary with the nature of contact with the dominant white society?"

I shall not undertake to summarize the authors' findings, which deserve careful study for their excellence as monographic work as well as for their methodological and theoretical range, but I shall comment briefly on the

last question above. The Spindlers observe that "basic personality structure" has often been shown to be quite stable over time, even when
individuals have accepted many values and objects from a culture different from their own. If this fact is observed without corresponding observations of the social structure, however—without study of the network of
interactions into which the individuals are tied—its significance may be
misinterpreted. Thus Scudder Mekeel noted that physical bravery, gen-
erosity, and fortitude, as the cultural essence of a good man, survived
among the Teton Dakota in a way that injured their ability to succeed
according to dominant American standards.[43] Before one reads this as
evidence for the resilience of both culture and personality, however, he
should note the situation of the Teton Dakota. There was no secure place
for them in the dominant society; maintenance of the old values meant
continuing identity with a group where they were accepted. The Spindlers
found a similar situation among the Menomini except for one group.
Those who, by their work in the Indian lumber industry, had obtained
economic and social positions equivalent to whites, and who therefore had
chances to identify with the dominant group and opportunities for interaction with them without suffering discrimination, developed values and
tendencies very similar to the white middle class.

This suggests that impressive continuity of personality and culture may
occur where opportunities to participate in the dominant society are
limited. In an open opportunity structure, however, individual tendencies
and cultural norms change more rapidly. The nature of the mutual
culture-personality influence is a function of the social structure.

MODAL CHARACTER

One further aspect of the culture-personality approach requires careful
examination. This branch of behavioral science is often identified by an
interest in "basic personality," "modal personality," or "national character." These terms, with their variations in meaning, have been strongly
criticized, particularly when applied to the members of large, heterogeneous, and changing societies. We need to inquire whether or not they
can be incorporated into a field view.[44]

Expressed in extreme form, in which it is rarely found but which may
be a useful point of departure here, the basic-personality concept can be
stated in this way: The influence of culture is so powerful and is experienced so uniformly by the members of a society that they have many
basic character traits in common. Know the culture to which an individual has been socialized, and you know how he will behave in many
situations.

As a common-sense idea, there is a great deal of stereotypy in this
notion. It becomes easy, as a substitute for knowledge, to speak of "the"
Frenchman, "the" Russian, or with reference to smaller, preliterate

groups, "the" Kwakiutl, or "the" Trobriand Islander. A moment's thought leads to qualifications, of course. Role differences are recognized; status variation and individual contrasts appear. But the idea that many important similarities underlie these differences is a pervasive one.

Specifying the opposite point of view will indicate the theoretical range of judgments, although this extreme would also rarely be defended: As a result of biological variation, role differentiation,[45] accidental experiences, the range of permissiveness in cultural requirements, and other factors, the amount of character shared by the members of a society is minimal; the impressive fact is the extent of the differences in character among persons socialized to the "same" culture.

Relying on "logic" and selective evidence, one can make a good case for either of these extremes. Such a fact indicates the need for more careful specification of the conditions under which shared tendencies are numerous and those under which they are few.

Before noting what appear to be such conditions, we need to make clear which of several possible meanings of "basic" or "modal" or "national" character is being used. *First,* it should be emphasized that even under maximum conditions of cultural influence, the tendencies shared by the members of a society make up only one "layer" of character. For a complete description of any individual, one must add those tendencies he shares with subsocietal groups and his unique characteristics as well.

Second, reference to character indicates that we are dealing with a property of individuals, not of cultures. The basic or modal patterns are not necessarily the culturally required or ideal patterns.[46]

Third, we make no a priori assumption that shared tendencies must be basic, in the sense that they are the product of early experience (infant training) and are at the foundation of personality development.[47] Shared tendencies as a result of common infant experiences, "basic personality structure" in the Kardiner-Linton sense, may be an outcome of life in a homogeneous, slowly changing society; but if so, they are only part of national or societal character. Later experiences in the occupational or educational world, or in the communication network, may be more widely shared and equally influential. This necessity for the separation of "shared" and "basic" tendencies is related to the need for a shift of attention from culture alone to the sociocultural complex. Norms can affect behavior only as they are factors that influence the patterns of interaction. Even highly patterned child-training norms reach the infant only through his interactions with adults; that is, social structure as well as culture is involved.

It is important to recognize this third distinction, because culture and structure may vary independently; persons may be involved in similar structures of interaction even though cultural guidelines vary, and vice versa. A large majority of persons in industrial societies, for example, are affected by bureaucracies. Such social structures bring certain common influences to bear on individuals despite variation in cultural content.

That is, there are *some* common elements in the interactions experienced in a hospital, a university, an industrial plant, an army base, the national office of a church—or, to change the base of comparison, in a Russian industry, a Japanese industry, and an American industry—despite the wide range in cultures. The division of labor, the impersonality, the size of the interacting group and the consequent complexity of the communication network, and the like, are structural elements of formal organizations that are not tied to specific cultural content.[48]

Fourth, "national character" must not be thought of as a system of almost identical tendencies found among almost all members of the society. Even in small and relatively homogeneous societies, there are significant variations around the shared qualities. This fact has led Inkeles and others to use the term "modal personality" and to suggest that in heterogeneous societies multimodal distributions may be the rule.

On the basis of these four criteria, one readily accepts the definition of Inkeles and Levinson: "National character refers to relatively enduring personality characteristics and patterns that are modal among the adult members of a society." [49] I would modify it only slightly by adding a *fifth* criterion essential to its use as a field construct: National character refers to shared tendencies, not to behavior. Since behavior is situational, knowledge of tendency does not suffice for prediction of behavior. The French proverb noted at the beginning of this essay suggests the idea: *Chacun prend à l'adversaire, qu'il le veuille ou non.* If we take on some of the appearance of the enemy, whether or not we wish to (and certainly our behavior may be affected much more by interaction with friends whom we wish to emulate), it is clear that explanations of behavior on the basis of character alone are inadequate. Therefore critics of the national-character concept cannot refute it by reference to changes, however drastic, in behavior (e.g., Japan, 1944, versus Japan, 1954). There is danger here, to be sure, of constructing an irrefutable concept. This can be avoided only by designing independent measures of tendencies that are applied at several periods of time, to discover the degree to which the tendencies are constant despite changing situations.

The need for distinguishing tendency from behavior is demonstrated by comparisons in space as well as time. It is possible, paradoxically, that behavior will be different *because of* similarities in tendencies. Insofar as American Negroes share the same values and aspirations as other members of the society but face discriminatory barriers to their achievement, any differences in behavior can be accounted for in part by reference to the shared qualities. (It is also true that there can be behavioral similarities in spite of differences in tendency—in values, motives, goals. Virtual unanimous support of a nation by its people in time of war is no proof of similarities of character. Modern societies require a great deal of cooperative and common behavior which does not demand identity of norms. Some core of agreement is implied—i.e., that in general, the given activity is worthwhile—but extensive dissimilarity is also possible.)

On the basis of these five criteria, I shall use the following modification of the Inkeles-Levinson definition: *National character refers to relatively enduring tendencies that are modal among the adult members of a society.*

We can return now to the attempt to specify the conditions under which shared tendencies are numerous and when they are few. There would be substantial agreement, I believe, on the following list. It is not made up of analytically distinct variables, for there is much interdependence among the items; but listing them in this way may help us to shift from the question "Does national character exist?" toward a scale which can be applied to any society.

VARIABLES RELATED TO NATIONAL CHARACTER

Conditions promoting many shared tendencies	Conditions associated with few shared tendencies
Few contacts with other societies	Many contacts
Slow rate of sociocultural change	Rapid sociocultural change
Small population	Large population
Slight status differentiation	Extensive status differentiation
Little division of labor	Extensive division of labor
Extensive social mobility	Closed class system
Extensive physical mobility within society	Little physical mobility
Few racial, religious, or national groups with distinctive subcultures	Many groups with subcultures
Communication system reaches all members	Gaps in communication network; many small networks
Homogeneity among major socializing institutions—family, school, church	Heterogeneity among major socializing institutions

If such a list has validity, it is clear that there are more shared tendencies in a small, preliterate group than in a contemporary nation. But the list should also warn us against assuming an inevitable reduction of shared tendencies in the modern world. Compared with a large feudal society, for example, an open-class, mobile society with an elaborate communication network may produce more "national character."

Unfortunately it is impossible to speak with any confidence on this question because, despite hundreds of commentaries, there are few rigorous measurements. Most of the methodological problems mentioned earlier in this chapter in connection with the general topic of culture and personality apply to the work on national character. Better samples and additional measuring instruments are needed. As Inkeles and Levinson note, the measurement of national character requires examination of large and representative samples studied individually.[50] But most research examines cultural products and norms, then infers character from them. More extensive comparisons are required to identify those tendencies that are panhuman (under equivalent conditions) or class-oriented ("Is there a 'poverty character' that shows the imprint of the culture of poverty?"), as well as those that are modal to the members of a society.

Empirical studies that apply techniques of public opinion research and even experimental designs are beginning to appear to supplement the anthropological field studies and the somewhat impressionistic commentaries on modern societies, commentaries based on cultural products (the link to character being assumed) or on samples of unknown representativeness. Such commentaries contain essential hypotheses; some of their descriptions may prove to be substantially correct. The need, however, is for more carefully controlled research that will test their validity, establish the modal tendencies and distributions around them for stated populations, and locate subcultural variations. Valuable beginnings along these lines include the work of Centers, who has measured the distribution of Riesman's inner- and other-directed character types among a cross section of 1,077 Los Angeles adults. Using a modified version of an "inner-other social preference scale" developed by Kassarjian, he found the scores to be normally distributed on the 50-point range, with a mean of 28 and a standard deviation of 6.9. Thus a large majority of the scores fell within a fairly narrow range. Middle-class persons were not more other-directed, as measured by this scale, as Riesman thought likely. The only consistently significant relationships (with other variables partialed out) were between education and inner-directedness and between age and inner-directedness. Without panel data, it is impossible to know whether the latter result demonstrates an increase in other-directedness in the population, or the effects of growing older.[51]

An earler study by McGranahan applied the methods of opinion research. He asked 1,600 American high school students and 191 German boys a series of questions. Since there were no tests of reliability or validity and the respondents were not samples of any designated universe, the results are difficult to evaluate; but significant differences did appear. The subjects were asked, for example, to indicate which of two boys they thought was worse: one who tyrannizes and beats up smaller children or one who disobeys his superiors. Of the American boys, 68 per cent chose the former, compared with 41 per cent of the German boys.[52] This is scarcely a demonstration of clear-cut national characters, but it is an interesting item that permits extension and correction by other empirical studies.

Milgram has devised a small-scale experimental study that suggests techniques for the measurement of modal tendencies. Students from several different parts of Norway and France were asked to discriminate between the lengths of two tones. Each was led to believe that there were five other persons present in other booths of the experimental room making similar judgments. The "others" were tape-recorded answers controlled by the experimenter. In each of several tests, the French students were more "independent," the Norwegian more "conformist" to the announced judgments of the "others"; but the differences were not large. When giving their judgment last, after hearing the others, 62 per cent of the Norwegians conformed to a unanimous erroneous statement by the others, compared with 50 per cent of the French students. When allowed to write their answers rather than announcing them, the conformist scores of both groups fell—to 50 per cent for the Norwegians, 34 per cent for the French. When subjected to criticism (over a tape recorder), (*Voulez-vous vous faire remarquer?*) conformist scores went up to 75 per cent and 59 per cent.[53]

This is the kind of ambiguous result one is likely to get from empirical studies of "national character": wide range within each group and overlap between groups, yet some systematic modal differences, in this case corresponding to the picture of the French as independent and the Norwegians as highly cohesive. Such findings are useful if they are interpreted with full caution as part of a large series of measures designed to indicate character profiles.

CONCLUSION

I have been primarily concerned in this chapter with an undifferentiated view of culture and social structure, reserving until the next chapter and elsewhere an examination of influences that are more specific—in particular, those associated with positions and roles. Thinking still in general terms, how can we summarize the relationships among culture, the individual, and the social structure?

In behavioral science the study of culture continues to occupy an important place. Because it is persistently examined in the context of structural and individual factors, however, it is seen in a somewhat different light from that of a specialized discipline. In the latter, the scientist tends to view the normative system always as the independent variable. He is also more inclined to assume that individual tendency systems are fully harmonious with culture (or at least, that they need to be for smooth human interaction)—that individual motives and social norms tend to be isomorphic in a viable society.

This conception may be adequate as a model in the limiting case of an isolated, homogeneous, stable society; but it would be difficult to approximate empirically. And in the urban world, individual motive and role requirements may get widely separated without disrupting interaction. The society says, in effect, "We don't care *why* you do what is required, so long as you do it." For example, men live up to the cultural requirements for service in the armed forces for widely different reasons. Behavior that is adequate according to the norms does not require identity of motivation. Nor do we need to assume that lack of normative agreement inevitably leads to personal disorganization. I suspect that the persistent confusion between anomie and alienation (see Chapter 9) is based in part on the unstated assumption that culture and personality are the same phenomenon seen from different perspectives.[54]

This chapter has noted the need for studying social structure in addition to culture as a source of individual tendencies. This is often done, particularly in attempts to discover the origins of modal character in modern societies, even though the terminology may be that of culture. Shared tendencies in the United States, for example, have been accounted for by the networks of relationship into which we are bound—peer groups replacing or supplementing family influences, large industrial work forces, the paradoxical combination of isolated independence and interdependence of the frontier, constant interaction with strangers in the mobile city, and the like. These are qualities of the social structure which do not imply particular cultural content.

It is also important to recognize that behavior expresses the influence of the situation as well as of the individual's tendencies. Messinger and Clark believe that Riesman, in failing to make this distinction, develops as a series of personality types what are better seen as patterns of conduct located in specific situations and institutional complexes. Their argument is not with the concept of "other-directedness," for example; but they look upon other-directedness as better explained by structural conditions (this is a latent theory in Riesman) than by reference to types of individuals (this is Riesman's manifest theory).[55] I believe that effective resolution of the question requires systematic observation, in varying situations, of the behavior of persons whose tendencies have been measured. I would only indicate that a priori, attention to both the structural and personality sources, and to their various patterns of interaction, seems desirable.

There are also cultural interpretations of American character, of course. The Puritan ethic, the value placed on the individual, orientation toward achievement and the future—these are among the cultural influences believed to be important in shaping modal character in the United States. Many diverse and even contradictory qualities in American culture, however, overlie the shared norms. Such modal tendencies as further study may document among the members of heterogeneous modern societies seem likely to be the product more of the members' co-participation in national institutions and of their similar experiences than of socialization to a common culture.

FOOTNOTES

Note: The bracketed number following an author's name refers to the footnote in which the source is cited in full.

1. Everett E. Hagen, "Analytic Models in the Study of Social Systems," *American Journal of Sociology*, September, 1961, p. 144.

2. A. L. Kroeber and Clyde Kluckhohn, *Culture: A Critical Review of Concepts and Definitions*, Peabody Museum Papers, vol. 47, no. 1, 1952.

3. Fred W. Voget, "Man and Culture: An Essay in Changing Anthropological Interpretation," *American Anthropologist*, December, 1960, p. 954. See also A. Irving Hallowell, *Culture and Experience*, University of Pennsylvania Press, 1955.

4. Ralph Linton, *The Cultural Background of Personality*, Appleton-Century-Crofts, Inc., 1945, pp. 43–53.

5. Clyde Kluckhohn, *Culture and Behavior*, The Free Press of Glencoe, 1962, p. 54.

6. "That complex whole which includes knowledge, belief, art, morals, law, custom, and any other capabilities and habits acquired by man as a member of society" E. B. Tylor, *Primitive Culture*, 1871, p. 1.

7. See A. L. Kroeber and Talcott Parsons, "The Concepts of Culture and of Social System," *American Sociological Review*, October, 1958, pp. 582–583.

8. Linton [4], pp. 52–53.

9. It would be inaccurate to say there is full agreement on what those prerequisites are, but a strong consensus does exist on those described by David Aberle *et al.*, "The Functional Prerequisites of a Society," *Ethics*, vol. 60, 1950, pp. 100–111.

10. Or sometimes, more narrowly, psychoanalysis, in the sense both of theory and of methods based upon psychoanalytic theory. It is a bit sobering, in this connection, to think how much of the work in "culture and personality" becomes problematic if the Rorschach technique is questioned.

11. Evans-Pritchard speaks of social anthropology "as a branch of sociological studies" chiefly devoted to primitive societies (*Social Anthropology*, The Free Press of Glencoe, 1952). "...the modern anthropologist tends to think more in terms of society than of culture—of social systems and values and their interrelations. He asks not so much whether people have rules of exogamy but, for example, what is the significance of these rules for the study of their intercommunity relations" (*Ibid.*, p. 92).

12. A. R. Radcliffe-Brown, *A Natural Science of Society*, The Free Press of Glencoe, 1957, p. 107. The interpenetration of culture and social structure is shown in Florence Kluckhohn and Fred Strodtbeck, *Variations in Value Orientations*, Harper & Row, Publishers, Incorporated, 1961.

13. Ralph Linton, *Culture and Mental Disorders*, Charles C Thomas, 1956, p. 18.

14. Alex Inkeles, "Industrial Man: The Relation of Status to Experience, Perception, and Value," *American Journal of Sociology*, July, 1960, p. 1.

15. For numerous studies exploring these and other structural influences, see Dorwin Cartwright and Alvin Zander (eds.), *Group Dynamics*, Harper & Row, Publishers, Incorporated, 1960; Paul Hare, Edgar F. Borgatta, and Robert F. Bales, *Small Groups*, Alfred A. Knopf, Inc., 1955; and Paul Hare, *Handbook of Small Group Research*, The Free Press of Glencoe, 1962.

16. See Jacqueline H. Straus and Murray A. Straus,, "Suicide, Homicide, and Social Structure in Ceylon," *American Journal of Sociology*,

March, 1953, pp. 461–469. [Reprinted in Neil J. Smelser and William T. Smelser, (eds.), *Personality and Social Systems,* John Wiley & Sons, Inc., 1963, pp. 578–587.]

17. Oscar Grusky, "The Effects of Formal Structure on Managerial Recruitment: A Study of Baseball Organization," *Sociometry,* September, 1963, pp. 345–353. Grusky notes that personality factors involved in initial selection of positions were not controlled.

18. Fred Davis, "The Cabdriver and His Fare: Facets of a Fleeting Relationship," *American Journal of Sociology,* September, 1959, pp. 158–165.

19. Peter Blau, "Structural Effects," *American Sociological Review,* April, 1960, pp. 178–193.

20. Victor Barnouw, *Culture and Personality,* The Dorsey Press, 1963, pp. 1 and 27.

21. Francis L. K. Hsu, *Psychological Anthropology,* The Dorsey Press, 1963, pp. 12–13.

22. Yehudi A. Cohen (ed.), *Social Structure and Personality,* Holt, Rinehart and Winston, Inc., 1961, p. vii.

23. Bert Kaplan (ed.), *Studying Personality Cross-culturally,* Harper & Row, Publishers, Incorporated, 1961.

24. Clyde Kluckhohn and H. A. Murray (eds.), *Personality in Nature, Society, and Culture,* Alfred A. Knopf, Inc., 1948; 2d ed. with David M. Schneider, 1953.

25. Smelser and Smelser [16].

26. See Ruth Benedict, *Patterns of Culture,* Houghton Mifflin Company, 1934.

27. Thus the lengthy review of theories of personality by Calvin Hall and Gardner Lindzey (*Theories of Personality,* John Wiley & Sons, Inc., 1957) has little reference to sociocultural influences. The interactional or social-psychological theories that are dealt with—Adler, Fromm, Horney, Sullivan, Lewin, and Murphy—are all those of psychlogists or psychiatrists, albeit writers with broad-gauged interests. Neither culture nor society appears in the index. Role theory is undiscussed. This volume "provides . . . summaries of the major contemporary theories of personality." A student reading that and then examining *Studying Personality Cross-culturally,* edited by Bert Kaplan (also a psychologist), or *Personality and Social Systems,* edited by Neil J. Smelser and William T. Smelser (a sociologist and a psychologist), might well be puzzled about the usage of terms.

28. See Harold Orlansky, "Infant Care and Personality," *Psychological Bulletin,* January, 1949, pp. 1–48; A. R. Lindesmith and A. L. Strauss, "A Critique of Culture-Personality Writings," *American Sociological Review,* October, 1950, pp. 587–600; Alex Inkeles, "Some Sociological Observations on Culture and Personality Studies," in Kluckhohn, Murray, and Schneider [24], pp. 577–592; Alex Inkeles and Daniel J. Levinson, "National Character: The Study of Modal Personality and Sociocultural Systems," in Gardner Lindzey (ed.), *Handbook of Social Psychology,* Addison-Wesley Publishing Company, Inc., 1954, vol. 2, chap. 26; Anthony F. C.. Wallace, "Individual Differences and Cultural Uniformities," *American Sociological Review,* December, 1952, pp. 747–750.

29. For critiques of this view, see Esther Goldfrank, "Socialization, Personality, and the Structure of Pueblo Society," *American Anthro-*

pologist, vol. 47, 1945, pp. 516–539; and Edward M. Bruner, "Cultural Transmission and Cultural Change," *Southwestern Journal of Anthropology*, vol. 12, 1956, pp. 191–199.

30. See John W. Bennett, "The Interpretation of Pueblo Culture," in Douglas Haring (ed.), *Personal Character and Cultural Milieu*, 3d ed., Syracuse University Press, 1956, pp. 203–216 (first published in *Southwestern Journal of Anthropology*, vol. 24, 1946, pp. 361–374).

31. See Dorothy Eggan, "The General Problem of Hopi Adjustment," *American Anthropologist*, vol. 45, 1943, pp. 357–373.

32. See Howard Becker in Harry E. Barnes, Howard Becker, and Frances B. Becker (eds.), *Contemporary Social Theory*, D. Appleton-Century Company, Inc., 1940, pp. 502–505; and Robert Bierstedt, "The Limitations of Anthrological Methods in Sociology," *American Journal of Sociology*, July, 1948, pp. 22–30.

33. For valuable comments on the interaction, see M. Brewster Smith, "Anthropology and Psychology," in John Gillin (ed.), *For a Science of Social Man*, The Macmillan Company, 1954, chap. 3; Kluckhohn [5], pp. 34–35; and Clyde Kluckhohn, "Culture and Behavior," in Lindzey [28], pp. 921–976.

34. See, for example, Harold Wilensky and Hugh Edwards, "The Skidder: Ideological Adjustments of Downward Mobile Workers," *American Sociological Review*, April, 1959, pp. 215–231; Albert K. Cohen and Harold M. Hodges, Jr., "Characteristics of the Lower-blue-collar-class," *Social Problems*, Spring, 1963, pp. 303–334; Peter M. Blau, "Social Mobility and Interpersonal Relations," *American Sociological Review*, June, 1956, pp. 290–295; and Richard L. Simpson, "Parental Influence, Anticipatory Socialization, and Social Mobility," *American Sociological Review*, August, 1962, pp. 517–522.

35. See Sigmund Freud, *New Introductory Lectures on Psychoanalysis*, W. W. Norton & Company, Inc., 1933, esp. chap. 4.

36. See Talcott Parsons, "The Incest Taboo in Relation to Social Structure and the Socialization of the Child," *British Journal of Sociology*, vol. 5, 1954, pp. 101–117; reprinted in Smelser and Smelser [16], pp. 136–149. See also Talcott Parsons and Robert F. Bales, in collaboration with James Olds, Morris Zelditch, Jr., and Philip Slater, *Family, Socialization and Interaction Process*, The Free Press of Glencoe, 1955; and Guy E. Swanson, "Mead and Freud: Their Relevance for Social Psychology," *Sociometry*, December, 1961, pp. 319–339.

37. Philip E. Slater, "On Social Regression," *American Sociological Review*, June, 1963, p. 339.

38. See *ibid.*, pp. 339–364.

39. Anthony F. C. Wallace, *Culture and Personality*, Random House, Inc., 1961, p. 55.

40. See *ibid.*, pp. 45–83; J. N. Spuhler (ed.), *The Evolution of Man's Capacity for Culture*, Wayne State University Press, 1959; S. L. Washburn and F. C. Howell, "Human Evolution and Culture," in Sol Tax (ed.), *The Evolution of Man*, The University of Chicago Press, 1960, pp. 33–56.

41. Voget [3]; see also A. F. C. Wallace, "Revitalization Movements," *American Anthropologist*, vol. 58, 1956, pp. 264–281.

42. See George D. Spindler, "Personality and Peyotism in Menomini Indian Acculturation," *Psychiatry*, vol. 15, 1952, pp. 151–159; George D. Spindler, *Sociocultural and Psychological Processes in Menomini Acculturation*, University of California Publications in Cul-

ture and Society, vol. 5, 1955; George D. Spindler and Louise S. Spindler, "American Indian Personality Types, and Their Sociocultural Roots," *Annals of the American Academy of Political and Social Science*, May, 1957, pp. 147–157; Louis S. Spindler and George D. Spindler, "Male and Female Adaptations in Culture Change," *American Anthropologist*, vol. 60, 1958, pp. 217–233.

43. See H. S. Mekeel, *The Economy of a Modern Teton Dakota Community*, Yale University Publications in Anthropology, no. 6, 1936.

44. There is an enormous literature on this subject. Among the commentaries I have found valuable are D. G. Mandelbaum, "On the Study of National Character," *American Anthropologist*, vol. 52, 1953, pp. 174–187; Otto Klineberg, *Tensions Affecting International Understanding*, Social Science Research Council, 1950; Inkeles [28]; Inkeles and Levinson [28]; Reinhard Bendix, "Compliant Behavior and Individual Personality," *American Journal of Sociology*, November, 1952, pp. 292–303 (reprinted in Smelser and Smelser [16], pp. 55–67); Talcott Parsons, *Essays in Sociological Theory Pure and Applied*, rev. ed., The Free Press of Glencoe, 1954, esp. pp. 104–123, 238–274; and Seymour M. Lipset and Leo Lowenthal (eds.), *Culture and Social Character: The Work of David Riesman Reviewed*, The Free Press of Glencoe, 1961. The monographic literature is even more extensive. See Abram Kardiner with Ralph Linton, *The Individual and His Society*, Columbia University Press, 1939; Abram Kardiner with the collaboration of Ralph Linton, Cora DuBois, and James West, *The Psychological Frontiers of Society*, Columbia University Press, 1945; Benedict [26], and *The Chrysanthemum and the Sword*, Houghton Mifflin Company, 1946; Jean Stoetzel, *Without the Chrysanthemum and the Sword: A Study of the Attitudes of Youth in Post-war Japan*, UNESCO, 1955; Goeffrey Gorer, *The American People*, W. W. Norton & Company, Inc., 1948; Goeffrey Gorer, *Exploring English Character*, The Cresset Press, 1955; Margaret Mead, *From the South Seas*, William Morrow and Company, Inc., 1939; Margaret Mead, *And Keep Your Powder Dry*, William Morrow and Company, Inc., 1942; Margaret Mead and Martha Wolfenstein (eds.), *Childhood in Contemporary Cultures*, The University of Chicago Press, 1955; E. H. Erikson, *Childhood and Society*, 2d ed., W. W. Norton & Company, Inc., 1963; David Riesman with Reuel Denney and Nathan Glazer, *The Lonely Crowd: A Study of the Changing American Character*, Yale University Press, 1950.

45. I shall discuss role theory in the next chapter.

46. This is to disagree with Emily M. Nett, "An Evaluation of the National Character Concept in Sociological Theory," *Social Forces*, May, 1958, pp. 297–303.

47. For an empirical study of some of the effects of infant experiences, see William H. Sewell, "Infant Training and the Personality of the Child," *American Journal of Sociology*, September, 1952, pp. 150–159.

48. See Inkeles [28].

49. Inkeles and Levinson [28], p. 983.

50. *Ibid.*, p. 981.

51. Richard Centers, "An Examination of the Riesman Social Character Typology: A Metropolitan Survey," *Sociometry*, September, 1962, pp. 231–240. For a description of the scale and an account of tests of reliability and validity, see W. M. Kassarjian, "A Study of Riesman's Theory of Social Character," *Sociometry*, September, 1962, pp. 213–230.

See also Elaine G. Sofer, "Inner-direction, Other-direction, and Autonomy: A Study of College Students," in Lipset and Lowenthal [44], chap. 14; and Matilda White Riley, John W. Riley, Jr., and Mary Moore, "Adolescent Values and the Riesman Typology: An Empirical Analysis," in *ibid.*, chap. 16.

52. D. G. McGranahan, "A Comparison of Social Attitudes among American and German Youth," *Journal of Abnormal and Social Psychology*, vol. 41, 1946, pp. 245–257.

53. Stanley Milgram, "Nationality and Conformity," *Scientific American*, December, 1961, pp. 45–51.

54. For commentary along this line, see Kaplan [23], especially chaps. 2, 3, 6, and the epilogue, which are by Melford Spiro, Anthony Wallace, George Devereux, and Bert Kaplan, respectively.

55. Sheldon L. Messinger and Burton R. Clark, "Individual Character and Social Constraint: A Critique of David Riesman's Theory of Social Conduct," in Lipset and Lowenthal [44], chap. 5. While agreeing with their emphasis on the need to study structure, I do not share their view that an interdisciplinary approach is misdirected.

Position, Role, and Internalized Role

Few terms in the lexicon of the social scientist promise as much for the development of cross-disciplinary research as the concept of role. It has been fruitfully used by anthropologists (e.g., Linton, Nadel), sociologists (e.g., Parsons, Merton, Gross, Cottrell, Brim, Bates, Turner, Goode), and psychologists (e.g., Newcomb, Sarbin, Levinson, Maccoby, Sargent). The very attractiveness of role theory to several disciplines, however, has disadvantages. Although it deals with issues at the point of articulation of personality, culture, and social structure, specialists are sometimes tempted to develop it in such a way that this interdisciplinary quality is lost. With slight bows toward the related fields, they interpret the basic issues in terms of the "primary" field. This is seldom done explicitly. In fact, the general, not the specialized, usefulness of role concepts is widely heralded. But our thought processes, particularly as they are shown in the way we use words, tend to reflect our special perspectives and to obscure the several levels of analysis required.

Reacting against the resulting confusion, some social scientists have suggested that we ought to dispense entirely with the concept of role and its related terms. This seems to me, however, to be unwise. The terms refer to important aspects of social reality. If we set them aside, the same problems with which we now struggle will only slip in under other labels. Our present difficulties spring both from the inherent difficulty of abstracting for observation separate portions of a complex empirical world, and from the limited theoretical perspectives we bring to the task. Important gains have been made in the last several years, however; and by relating the study of positions and roles to field theory, perhaps we can consolidate those gains and contribute to the orientation of future research.

It is my hope in this chapter to clarify the terms employed in role theory and to outline the basic questions faced by research in this area. If we are to make headway in answering those questions, we need an explicit, shared vocabulary of terms that apply unambiguously to social structure, to culture, and to character. I shall not attempt to survey or evaluate research on roles except where that may prove desirable to illustrate the central questions as they appear at this stage of development.

TERMINOLOGY: POSITION, ROLE, AND INTERNALIZED ROLE

Following a number of recent authors,[1] but departing to some degree from each of them, I shall use the term *position* to refer to a unit of social structure. It can be defined as a "location . . . in a system of social relationships." [2] Implied in this definition is the concept of structure, with connotations both of recurrence or some degree of permanence and of relatedness to other positions.[3] A characteristic of structured relationships is that the participants have expectations concerning their own and others' behavior.

"We propose then to define role as a structured behavioral model relating to a certain position of an individual in an interactional setting." [4] *Role* is a unit of culture; it refers to the rights and duties, the normatively approved patterns of behavior for the occupants of a given position. Since both position and role can be defined independently of reference to any person, a personality term is also needed to refer to the internalization of the role by a given occupant of a position. The terms "self" and "ego" are sometimes used in this way,[5] but not appropriately so, for they refer to larger constructs than position and role. We need a coordinate concept. I shall use the term *internalized role* to refer to that part of the self which represents a given individual's tendencies to perform a role in a given way. This is clearly different from the role itself, which is a culture construct. Internalized role has a particular person's mark or style imprinted on it, for it is affected by all the positions he occupies, by the ways in which he learned the role, and by the total personality system in which it is embedded.

Each of these terms—position, role, and internalized role—must be distinguished from behavior. Knowing the position a person is occupying at a given moment, knowing the culturally prescribed obligations and privileges of that position (its role), and knowing how a person has internalized the role, one still cannot, except in the limiting case, predict his behavior. The actual process of carrying out the role will be influenced not only by the internalized role, but by the self and the total personality of which it is a part. It will also be affected by the situation within which the activity occurs, including the actions of persons occupying reciprocal positions, and by the larger setting within which the interaction takes place.[6]

Why has it proved so extraordinarily difficult to get agreement on these important concepts? Disciplinary perspectives are certainly involved: the psychologist's concern for the individual, the anthropologist's for culture, and the sociologist's for society—to put the matter overly simply. But there are additional reasons. The distinctions drawn above require a level of abstraction that is difficult to maintain. Our definitions tend always to be pulled in the direction of behavior—that is, to lose their analytic clarity. The distinction between position and role, for example, is often lost because defining position independently of its role specifications is a difficult task. There can be no position without a role, no role without a position (just as, with their "parent" terms, there can be no social structure, in the sense of a system of social relationships, without a culture, a normative system influencing but not determining those relationships).

Intuitively we can distinguish the position "teacher" from the rights and duties implied by that term, but a full definition is likely to include a specification of role characteristics. The problem can be reduced by thinking of position in cross-cultural and in functional terms. The *position* "teacher," for example, designates a person who possesses socially desired knowledge and skills and interacts with others not thus qualified in order to transmit the knowledge and skills. *What* is transmitted and *how* (that is, the role specifications) vary in time and place. The role of the teacher in the Soviet Union is not identical with the role of the teacher in the United States. The role of a teacher in a rural high school a century ago is not the same as the role in a metropolitan school today.

Thus position thought of as a location in a system of social relationships can be defined, at least in part, independently of role. And to do this is important. Not only does a clear analytic distinction between position and role facilitate cross-cultural and cross-temporal comparisons of the *various* roles of one position, but it also contributes to the study of consensus. There may be high agreement among the members of a society on the designation of the position "father" in the system of social relationships, but less consensus on the rights and duties—the role.

Distinguishing clearly between role, internalized role, and role behavior entails similar difficulties. The culture construct "role" can only be inferred from how various persons behave in particular positions, how others behave toward them, and how they all describe the rights and duties in verbal behavior. Since there may be disagreements among these various designations, a serious problem of what the role "really is" may arise. Role sometimes becomes a matter of a "least common denominator." There may be consensus on a few central cultural norms, but disagreement on others.

Deferring this question of consensus for the moment, we can say that a role is the list of what most members of a social group believe a position occupant should and should not, may and may not, do. It is not a list of what most occupants of a position in fact do. An important series of empirical questions arises in connection with the relationship of the culturally approved role and the statistically normal behaviors of position occupants.[7] Under what conditions will a role persist when it is not behaviorally validated by most persons? If 90 per cent of a group believe that a given behavior is required but only 30 per cent fulfill this norm, does the requirement itself (the role specification) soon change? What are the causes and consequences of wide deviation between role designations and *average* role behavior? These questions will be lost if we fail, through lack of adequate measurement, to distinguish between the culturally designated rights and duties and role behavior, either average or individual.

The concept of internalized role draws our attention to subcultural and individual variation in role definitions. Because the cultural norm may be imprecise in its designation of role characteristics, and because each person learns the role under somewhat idiosyncratic conditions, individual conceptions of a role vary. This is part of the question of role consensus. The internalized role is not behavior; but it may prove to be a significant intervening variable between position occupancy and behavior.

For the student of the interplay among personality, culture, and social structure, the central question from role theory is this: Knowing the positions that a person occupies, and knowing the roles of those positions and his internalized versions of them, to what degree can we predict his behavior? The answer depends upon many conditions which we must explore carefully. First, however, it may be useful to state the conditions under which prediction would be at a maximum from knowledge of nothing else but a person's positions and their roles. This can be thought of as the limiting case against which the expected departures can be measured. Prediction of behavior from knowledge of positions and roles alone is at a maximum when there is perfect role consensus, when there is complete and uniform role internalization, when there has been perfect role internalization by others occupying reciprocal positions, and when there has been no internalization of contradictory tendencies in the personality system (or when such tendencies are not induced by the situation under study).

Such qualifications may seem to make role research almost useless, for surely the conditions stated are seldom achieved or even approximated. Yet one must make the observation that all men do, in fact, predict behavior of others from common-sense knowledge of roles alone. This point is often overlooked in statements that emphasize individuality, heterogeneity, and change. Moreover, current research is beginning to document more precisely the conditions under which position occupancy affects behavior.

In summary, an easy assumption that knowledge of roles yields direct prediction of behavior is clearly inadequate. It is also inadequate, however, to disregard the extent to which we count on and receive certain patterns of behavior from others—many of whom we know only as position occupants. The task is to explore, without rigid presuppositions, the factors that affect the extent of role influence on behavior.

The Internal Structure of Roles

To speak of a series of rights and duties is perhaps to make a role seem to be a collection of undifferentiated cultural norms. In fact, role requirements range from those that are mandatory—in the absence of which one would say that the role was not being performed at all—to those that are optional. The optional norms may be "alternatives," in the sense that Linton used the term: ways of behavior for a position occupant which are permissible but not required and which are no more permissible than other possible ways of dealing with the same situation.[8]

This concept of a continuum of norms raises serious problems in defining the limits of a role. Particularly difficult to decide is which of the various permitted activities, as contrasted with the mandatory ones, should be included. Two questions are involved here that are not always distinguished. One is: Do most people believe that a given activity is required of the occupants of a position? Another is: Granted that most people agree that a given activity is appropriate to a position, is this activity mandatory, desirable, or permissible (to suggest three words to mark points along a continuum)? The fact that the members of a group may designate many norms as permissible does not mean lack of consensus. Permissibility of that norm can be precisely part of the consensus.

Internal structure of a role, then, refers to the mandatory, desirable, and permissible rights and duties that most members of a group believe appropriate to the occupants of a position. Here the degree of consensus, which I shall discuss below, has been assumed by the use of the phrase "most members." High consensus may prove empirically to be associated with the tendency to assign many rights and duties to the mandatory list and few to the permissible list, and the reverse may hold true under conditions of low consensus. But this remains to be documented, the conditions under which it is true explored, and exceptional cases studied.

If the definition of a role includes many norms that are simply permissible, the cultural boundaries of the role are difficult to specify. This is a common problem in research on human behavior: the terms refer to phenomena that are matters of more or less. Role shades off into nonrole by imperceptible gradations; only by some arbitrary decision do we say that from a given point on, in degree of precision of normative requirements, no role will be said to "exist." We would be nearer to the nature we seek to describe if we used adjectives rather than nouns in this kind of situation. Interactions could be compared on the degree to which they possess rolelike qualities—that is, on the degree to which the behavior of the participants is guided by culturally designated norms.

But nouns have their use if we do not reify them, if we recognize them as convenient ways of designating certain parts of a continuum. Nadel, for example, distinguishes between "class" and "role." Class implies only one shared property, whereas role implies a series of culturally prescribed behaviors as well. Thus "old man" might simply specify a class (in this case designating two common properties of age and sex); but when a series of privileges and obligations is associated with these properties, the term specifies a role. (In my terminology, "old man" would be a position, with role norms associated; but Nadel does not use this distinction.)

Nadel notes that it is not always clear whether we are dealing with a class or a role. Perhaps presumed roles will prove, on analysis, to be mere classes, with no culturally designated behavior associated with them. This may be a result of culture change in which a former role has "decayed" although the role name is still in use, being employed now to refer to a class. For example, the rights and duties of an English "gentleman" may have been quite distinct a century ago. Knowledge that a person occupied this position could yield modest prediction of how he would behave. Now, Nadel suggests, gentleman may be no more than a class term associated with few other distinguishing characteristics. An opposite process is the crystallization of a role out of a former class—an event which may receive little public recognition while it takes place, but which can be of some importance to social process.[9]

How definite should the norms be before one speaks of a role? The requirements of research rather than of theory are likely to give the answer. Those clusters of rights and duties that contain a relatively high proportion of mandatory and desirable behavior (often with matching proscriptions) and a low proportion of permissible behavior are more readily studied. This quality of the internal structure of roles I shall call *role flexibility*—low flexibility being characteristic of roles with many mandatory norms, high flexibility meaning the presence of many permissive norms. It is well to note again that the degree of flexibility is not synonymous with degree of consensus.

Dimensions of Positions and Roles

Implicit in the discussion so far is the idea that positions and roles can be compared and contrasted along a number of dimensions that are related to the direction and strength of the position and role influence. Among the most important dimensions are these:

1. The degree of specificity or diffuseness of the obligations and privileges. The role norms associated with the position "mother" are exceedingly diffuse; those associated with the position "clerk" are highly specific.

2. The size of the position network. There may be dozens of counterpositions in the network of a company president, but presumably there is only one counterposition to "best friend." The larger networks are likely to have quite indistinct boundaries, so that a difficult research task is to determine where the network shall be presumed to end.

3. The extent of a network's connectedness. If position *A* is related in a network to positions *B, C,* and *D,* but the latter are only minimally related to each other, the structure is quite different from one where all the possible relationships among positions *A, B, C,* and *D* obtain. Following Gross, Mason, and McEachern,[10] we can call the former a position-centric model and the latter a system model. Although careful research is lacking, much common-sense knowledge indicates that these models are associated with different kinds of role behavior. They create different contexts for settling the role bargain. Thus a child may go to some pains to make sure that his parents do or do not know, depending on the situation, something that his sibling has done. A foreman who works in a shop where the superintendent and the workers seldom meet occupies a different kind of position from one where worker-superintendent communication is frequent. Some college presidents have gone to great lengths, or so the faculty may believe, to ensure a minimum of contact between the trustees and the faculty. The intended consequence of this may be to give him greater freedom in defining his role; the unintended consequences are perhaps not known.

4. Symmetrical or asymmetrical quality of reciprocal roles. The rights and duties of friend as ego and friend as alter are generally symmetrical; what ego grants to and expects from alter is, in turn, granted to and expected from ego by alter. The roles of a mother and a child, however, are asymmetrical.

5. Equality or inequality in the relationship. This is related to but not identical with symmetry. Symmetrical role relationships are necessarily equal, but asymmetrical ones are not necessarily unequal. *Vive la différence* between husband and wife, but this need not preclude equality.

6. The length of occupancy of a position. Since this can vary from a moment to a lifetime, the significance for behavior has a wide range.

7. The group within which the position has relevance. Some positions are recognized in a whole society or a subsociety, but others are pertinent only to a much smaller system.[11]

8. Ascription and achievement. This contrast, discussed so meaningfully by Linton, should not be thought of as a dichotomy. Some positions may be almost entirely ascriptive (child), but others that are open to achievement may have negative ascriptive aspects, as Linton points out.[12]

9. The range of knowledge, skill, and attitudinal requirements. To become a shaman may require years of training; also, one achieves the position doctor of philosophy, "with all the rights and privileges thereunto appertaining" only after a long period of study. But one may acquire or be assigned the position "church member," in many instances, with a minimum of preparation. This dimension is perhaps correlated with length of occupancy, but is not identical with it. It is important particularly because the strength of the influence of self on role and role on self varies with the range of personality tendencies required for the position occupant.

10. Extent of prestige and power related to a position. This variable may be associated not only with the degree to which a position occupant can influence others, but also with the extent to which its norms affect him. That is, the extent of his prestige and power affects the degree to which, in the self-role interaction, self is the independent variable, influencing his role perception and performance, and the degree to which his rights and duties are the independent variable, shaping his personality. Although we lack solid research knowledge, it is possible to test the hypothesis that the more powerful and prestige-filled the role, the more it affects behavior of the role performer (that is, the less his role behavior is subject to influence from his total personality). He has more to gain by approved role performance in a powerful or prestigious position; and others in the network may be eager to secure correct role activity because of the importance of the position.[13]

Role Consensus

Early work on the role concept, much of it based on studies of relatively small and homogeneous societies, took for granted that there was a great deal of agreement on role requirements. Such requirements were, in Linton's phrase, "ascribed by society." Contemporary studies, however, emphasize the extent to which different members of a society may disagree on role specifications. What are the rights and duties associated with the position "wife" in contemporary America? There is wide variation in the answers; the role "ascribed by society" is far from clear.[14] When Sherwood asked fifty-one Bantu clerks and fifty-three white supervisors to write essays on the topic "What I expect from a Bantu clerk . . ." he found a great deal of consensus on work requirements in the limited sense, but great disagreement on appropriate interpersonal relations (which the clerks themselves thought most important).[15] Coleman's study *The Adolescent Society* makes abundantly clear that the role of a high school student as seen by the students is incongruent in many ways with that role as viewed by teachers and parents. There is, in fact, substantial lack of consensus among the students themselves.[16]

Undoubtedly the usefulness of the role concept to the student of personality and social structure is small until the question of consensus has been carefully explored. Gross, Mason, and McEachern note a number of broad questions raised by the problem of consensus:

How much consensus on what behaviors is required for a society to maintain itself? How much disagreement can a society tolerate in what areas? To what extent do different sets of role definers hold the same role definitions of key positions in a society? On what aspects of role definition do members of different "subcultures" in a society agree and disagree? To what extent is deviant behavior a function of deviant role definitions? [17]

Several of these questions imply the need, when studying consensus, to ask, "Consensus among the members of what group?" For some purposes, a total society may be the appropriate unit; for others, an interacting pair. In investigating questions of institutional change or social mobility, the extent of consensus within society is a crucial variable. For example, if lower-class men typically think of the role of father in terms different from those of middle-class men, and if there are matching behavioral differences, barriers to social mobility may be present. If the research task, however, involves a smaller universe—urban middle-class white families, let us say—the unit of reference in the study of consensus would be much smaller. The fact that agricultural migrants from Mexico disagreed on these role designations, while an important fact for some purposes, would be of little significance for others.

I make this obvious point because there has been some tendency to swing from a position where consensus was not explored at all in research and commentary on the topic of role, to a position where lack of society-wide consensus is seen as a severe blow to the usefulness of the concept. Complex societies have many ways of reducing lack of consensus and controlling its effects on social and personal systems.

Consensus, of course, is a variable, not an attribute that is present or absent. If 75 per cent of the members of a group, to pick a wholly arbitrary number, agreed on the ten most important obligations and privileges of a physician, we might call this substantial role consensus. (The measure could be refined by having the respondents rank the characteristics by importance or centrality to the role.) If 50 per cent of a group agreed on the role description and the other 50 per cent of responses were scattered through a variety of other descriptions, we could speak of partial role consensus. But a different situation would be one where half of the measured population tended to accept one picture of a role while the other half accepted a different picture. This would be a case of substantial *subcultural* role consensus. If the largest plurality for any one list of rights and duties was 25 per cent, we could describe this group as having slight role consensus. As measures were refined, these common-sense descriptive terms could appropriately be replaced with a larger number of numerical classes.

A great deal could be learned about the relationship of personality and the social structure by a more complete plotting of the "role map" of a society—the extent and areas of consensus and dissensus, the location of consensual groups.[18]

Position and Role Networks

The significance of the extent of role consensus is best seen by studying the process of role performance. For the moment, I shall disregard the fact that it is a person, not an abstract position occupant, who carries out a role. Aspects of self other than those related to the position affect the performance, but we are interested here in the fact that the behavior of others influences role enactment.

The influence of self and the influence of others in the role-taking process are two major emphases in the social interaction, or Mead, tradition. To some degree this complements and to some degree contradicts the approach based on an anthropological, or Linton, tradition. It represents a shift away from structure to an emphasis on process—a reduction in attention to culture and an increase in attention to society. This point of view is well expressed by Turner:

The idea of role-taking shifts emphasis away from the simple process of enacting a prescribed role to devising a performance on the basis of an imputed other-role. The actor is not the occupant of a position for which there is a neat set of rules—a culture or set of norms—but a person who must act in the perspective supplied in part by his relationship to others whose actions reflect roles that he must identify. Since the role of alter can only be inferred rather than directly known by ego, testing inferences about the role of alter is a continuing element in interaction. Hence the tentative character of the individual's own role definition and performance is never wholly suspended.[19]

The social interaction approach underlines the fact that a cultural blueprint is not behavior and thus helps to correct for any tendency in an anthropological approach to equate role with behavior. Unhappily, in making this correction interactionists sometimes make the opposite error: they equate behavior with role. They think of roles as the repetitive patterns of behavior that emerge from interaction. We shall continue to have such disagreements and terminological differences as long as we persist in trying to get a complex series of meanings into one word. If we define "role" as the more or less agreed-upon blueprint for action, we can then study the range of its influence in affecting behavior, the extent to which the role is modified in the process of being carried out, the effect of differences in role definition, and other empirical questions. It is one thing to say that cultural *pre*scriptions are unimportant in guiding most interaction, at least in a mobile and heterogeneous world, that the regularity of behavior is primarily an *emergent* of interaction. This is an empirical question, capable of proof or refutation by research. It is something else to say: Therefore I shall call these regularities roles. Different phenomena, even those that strongly affect each other, require different names.

Newcomb, Turner, and Converse define role as "one person's end of a behavioral relationship . . . characterized by regularity." They include both those regularities that are unique to the relationship of two or more persons and those associated with a position.[20] I see no problem in conceptual clarity related to the use of role to refer to small social systems as well as to large. (I shall not go so far as to suggest that we add "subrole" as a phrase coordinate with subsociety and subculture, although strict logic might require this.) I do see difficulty, however, in speaking of a role as a "behavioral relationship" and two or more roles as a "behavioral system." In our concepts we need to distinguish between that which individuals have come to expect of one another when they are in a particular relationship and the behavioral relationship itself, even if it is "characterized by regularity." If we try to make one term do double duty, we obscure the *various* forces that may be involved in the production of regularities of relationship: personality tendencies and situational pressures, as well as mutual expectations. Since these may vary independently of one another, we need separate terms to be able to describe their various combinations.

The need is to study *both* the cultural or subcultural norms associated with a position *and* the processes of interaction involved in role taking (imagining how one looks from another's standpoint), role playing (behavior associated with position occupancy), and role making (normative modifications that result from interaction).[21] The importance of the symbolic interaction approach to field theory is the emphasis it gives to behavior as cause as well as effect. To think of behavior simply as a result of the interaction of individual, cultural, and social forces is far too static a picture of human action. Whatever combination of forces produces behavior, we must recognize that it in turn affects personality, social structure, and culture (including roles). It feeds back into the system that produced it. If one acts in a nondiscriminatory way, perhaps because of situational pressures which counteract personal prejudices, his own attitudes are likely to be modified. In carrying out a role one is involved in a continual process of validation and modification—he leaves some mark, however faint, upon the cultural definition.

We need, then, to define role clearly as a distinctively cultural term but to recognize it as an abstraction. It becomes "visible" only when it enters into action, which implies the actions of others. Since a position, by definition, is a location in a system of social relationships, it always involves one or more counterpositions, each with role specifications vis-à-vis the position in question. "Dealing with human behavior in terms of roles . . . requires that any given item of behavior must always be placed in some specified self-other context." [22] I shall use the term "position network" to refer to a focal position plus all the other positions linked to it in a system of social relationships. Thus the network of the position "foreman" would normally involve other foremen, workers, and the plant superintendent. There is seldom a sharp line designating the boundaries of a network; but one is assisted in setting its limits if he remembers that it is a network of positions, not of persons. Only those other positions are included which relate to the focal person as a position holder. A role network, by extension, is the interlocking system of rights and duties of position holders thus linked into a system.

If a person has internalized a role that fits the role expectations of others in a position network, and these others agree among themselves, behavior tends to follow the role specifications. But this is something of a limiting case, especially in a mobile, changing society. More commonly, a person has the task of balancing the claims of one network member against those of another, of negotiating among differing and perhaps even contradictory expectations. Mother and father may not agree on what the child should do; schoolmates and teachers often expect different activities.

Lack of consensus among the members of a position network makes it impossible to explain behavior by simple reference to the position's role. As Merton has pointed out, for example, in the case of teachers, what one person believes to be essential to the role, another may think subversive.[23] In a later section I shall examine the significance of lack of consensus for role behavior and role change.

ROLES, THE SELF, AND ROLE BEHAVIOR

A dynamic conception of roles leads naturally to an examination of the influence of the self on role bargaining and performance. This requires that one view the situation, not only from the point of view of a position network, but also from what might be called the personality network in which the internalized role is embedded.

Postponing until the next chapter a full definition of "self," I shall think of it here as the organizing, regulating aspect of personality. This is close to Mangus's definition: "Once it is well established, the social self becomes the chief executive for the organization and direction of the conduct of the person. The social self becomes the chief instrument by which a person's conduct is ordered and directed toward motive satisfaction." [24] The difficulty with Mangus's definition is that it suggests more power for the self in controlling behavior than may be warranted. The self is influenced from "below" by the total personality, including many unconscious forces that can block or change processes initiated by the self. And it is affected from "above" by the external situation that sets limits within which the self must work. The behavior of other persons is a significant part of the external situation. This "below-above" formulation is, of course, close to Freud's description of the ego constrained by the demands of the id, on one hand, and circumscribed by the requirements of the superego on the other. These terms, however, seem to me too narrow to encompass the range of forces at work.

For some research it may be useful to introduce the concept of internalized role as an intervening variable between the self (and the whole personality of which self is a part) on one hand and role behavior on the other. I have defined internalized role as the individual's personal role definition, the way in which he has learned to view the rights and duties of a position which he, or someone with whom he is interacting, occupies. Internalized roles are part of self, but only part; conflict between an internalized role and other self-tendencies presents an important problem for study.

Brim has suggested that "the major sources of variation between individuals in roles . . . involve different degrees of ignorance of what is expected, different degrees of ability to learn and perform what is expected, and different degrees of role-appropriate motivation." [25] These factors can be thought of as aspects of internalized role. By noting them, Brim encourages us to ask what the sources of variation are. Why does one person emphasize some dimensions of a role while another stresses different dimensions? He comments on variation in the social structure within which a child is socialized ("the presence or absence of the father, the presence or absence of sibs of the same or opposite sex. . . .") and on cultural and subcultural differences in the content of the role. Brim includes in role content the idiosyncratic interpretations of roles by persons with whom a child interacts; but it seems to me wiser to record this as a third source of variation in internalized roles. His emphasis is on the structural sources of socialization to particular role patterns: e.g., if a wife acts toward her husband as if he were her father, this may be an expression, not of unconscious motives, but of the fact that she had no opportunity to learn other kinds of intimate female-to-male interaction.[26] Such structural factors are undoubtedly important. Attention to the role-learning process, however, leads one also to explore other sources of variation in internalized roles (differences in talent or capacity, for example).

Variation in role behavior results not only from differences in internalized roles, but also from the fact that the occupants of a given position do not necessarily occupy similar other positions. When studying behavior associated with one role, we can regard the tendencies based on other identities as part of the total self. Although these tendencies are to some degree inhibited in "inappropriate" settings, they are rarely completely inhibited. An important problem for research, in fact, is the study of the conditions under which role performance is affected by the various other role obligations and privileges that a person has. Does a college professor who is also a church member carry out his professorial role differently from the nonmember? How does the fact that some wives are also mothers, secretaries, bridge club members, or PTA presidents influence role performance? I shall refer to some aspects of this problem under the topic "role conflict," but unless this phrase is defined very broadly, it does not include all the effects of multiple roles.

Gouldner has developed some aspects of this question by suggesting the need for distinguishing between manifest and latent roles. Two college professors, to use his example, may carry on their activities quite differently because one has a latent identity with the local college community as a whole, while the other feels more closely identified with fellow specialists elsewhere.[27] In a sense, they perform their role before different audiences and are influenced by the difference.

To some degree, the distinction developed by Gouldner can be expressed in terms of variation in internalized roles: the local and the cosmopolitan, to use his terms, are persons who define the same role differently. But this need not be the case. As he notes: "Neither the similarities nor the differences . . . need be due to the intrusion of 'personality' factors or other individual attributes. They may derive from the nature of the latent roles, that is, from the responses to the latent identities of group members, which yield culturally unprescribed yet structured interactions and orientations with others." [28] A nice problem of research would be to distinguish between variation in internalized roles and variation in the influence of latent roles. Beginnings of a distinction can be made by asking "Is there a position with which the latent role can be identified?"

Note that "latent" role, in this usage, is not one which is held in abeyance while the person engages in another role. Since virtually everyone is associated with several positions, shifts in role performance are a fact of everyday life. We can distinguish, then, between active and "passive" roles—the latter being all those which one has learned but which are not now being carried out. Latent roles, on the other hand, are active but "inappropriate" roles—they intrude into the performance of the manifest role, affecting the way it is played. One way of saying this is to indicate that "pure role performance" is rare; one tends to act, not as a total person, perhaps, but as something more than the occupant of a given position. The "researcher" leans over the shoulder of the "teacher" while he does his job, affecting him in one way or another. The public official who is also a party member may be influenced in his public acts by the latent responsibilities of party membership.

This is not a moral distinction, of course. Whether or not latent roles *should* be allowed to influence the performance of manifest roles can be meaningfully explored only by measuring all the long-run consequences against a stated series of values.

In the study of self-role interaction, three major problems appear: What are the effects of self (that is, nonrole aspects of self) on role behavior? What are the effects of position occupancy on self and on behavior? What are the effects of role conflict?

Effects of Self on Role Behavior

Virtually no one disagrees with the observation that role performance is affected by personality.[29] Even those who emphasize most strongly the ways in which a role network and other external forces control behavior are ready to grant that there are important individual variations in role enactment. The research task is to isolate the variables that produce relatively similar and relatively dissimilar role behavior.

Perhaps the following self-related variables affect role behavior.

1. Differences in internalized role. We are unlikely to be successful in predicting role performance until we know, among other things, how the individuals involved define the rights and duties.

2. The significance of the position to the individual's self-identification. This affects his readiness to accept the role definition of others. If the position is relatively unimportant, few other personality forces are drawn into the performance; if the position is at the center of the individual's identity, however, other personality tendencies, not related to the role, will influence the performance.

3. Other positions being occupied. If the selection process draws persons into position A who have highly dissimilar position constellations (one occupying B, C, and D; another occupying E, F, and G, etc.), role performance is likely to vary more widely than if all those in position A share positions B, C, and D as well.

4. The degree of similarity in personality tendencies not related to the role. Individuals who vary in authoritarianism, intelligence, level of energy, and values, for example, are likely to perform the same role in different ways.

Although the influence of many of these variables has not been systematically explored, there have been careful observations of differences in role performance related to some of them. For example, Gilbert and Levinson classified nurses' aides as "custodial" or "humanistic" in their treatment of patients on the basis of supervisor ratings. Although assigned the same tasks, the custodial aides made more threats to patients and were primarily interested in keeping the wards quiet, whereas the humanistic aides acted in more therapeutic ways and showed more friendliness to the patients.[30]

Effects of Position Occupancy on Self and on Behavior

We commonly observe, to our delight or our dismay, that persons who enter new positions soon begin to act like other persons in those positions. This is scarcely surprising insofar as it simply involves the performance of the functions appropriate to the new location, but there are sometimes hints of more subtle and permanent value and attitude changes. The range of judgments concerning the extent to which roles affect the personality is wide. Researchers who emphasize the continuity of personality and the resilience of the self-system contend that, although a new position may require some new behavior and may even remake some surface attitudes and values, it scarcely touches the "deeper" layers of personality. When a person becomes a physician, for example, his new rights and duties will obviously permit and require new behavior; his attitudes toward illness will be different from those he held when he was a student or a patient; but the extent of his authoritarian or democratic tendencies, the degree of his self-confidence, and the ranking of his basic values in life will scarcely be affected.

On the other side are researchers who argue that a position, especially one long occupied, deeply affects the personality. Working within a

bureaucratic structure, Merton contends in a well-known paper,[31] produces general, not simply role-specific, personality tendencies that affect
behavior in other positions as well.

Arguing this question in general terms is of little value. Since there is
evidence both that position occupancy affects personality and that personality affects role performance, the task is to state as clearly as possible the
variables instrumental in fixing the extent of a role's influence. Consensus,
degree of specificity, and significance of the position to those involved are
likely to affect the interaction. The recruitment process is also important.
Some positions may be occupied largely by those for whom the role
requirements are highly congenial. Others may be filled on grounds quite
irrelevant to the role requirements, increasing the possibility of personality-
role conflicts or the chance for personality change.

There are two important distinctions to make in a discussion of the
effects of positions on the self. First is the contrast between the intended
or expected effects of a position (the acquisition of tendencies necessary
to perform the role) and the unintended effects. To say that a person who
takes on a new position acquires certain attitudes, skills, and values related to it is simply to say that he learns the role. But to say that certain
unintended personality changes occur as well—changes that are not intrinsic to the role performance—is something else. When Lord Acton
declared that power corrupts, he offered a hypothesis (although with him
it was a bold assertion, no conditions specified) that acquisition of a position of power has nonrole as well as role consequences for the personality. The student of bureaucracy suggests, in the concept of goal
displacement, that bureaucratic positions produce shifts in attitudes and
behavior that not only are unrelated to role performance but actually
hinder it. Thus we must distinguish between the direct personality effects
of learning a role and the indirect personality effects of its performance.

A corollary to this proposition is that we need to distinguish between
differences in behavior which occur when one enters a new position and
the possible effects of one position which become embedded in the
personality system and thus influence all role performances. When a
person becomes a father, he is likely to acquire tendencies and values
related to the new position that are to some degree different from those in
other positions he occupies. If, as a result of becoming a father, he
becomes somewhat more future-oriented, more family-oriented, more
tender, more irritable, or whatever, *and these inclinations affect his behavior in other positions as well,* the position father has had general as
well as specific personality consequences. I shall call these two influences
"role-specific" and "general personality" effects.

Although many perceptive observations can be found concerning possible general personality effects of a position, firm knowledge is difficult to
arrive at. When a young seminary student in a university setting shifts to
the pastorate of a middle-class church in a small town, his rights and
duties as a religious professional change, but so also may his attitudes and

behavior with respect to politics, civil liberties, or economic matters. The struggling young management interne who wins a regular position on the staff acquires new obligations and privileges, and he also may experience a shift in his aesthetic tastes, his recreation, his political beliefs, or his religious allegiance.

Convincing research on general personality effects is difficult to carry through because of the long time sequence and the number of variables involved. Role-specific influences can be studied much more definitively, however; and from such study we may be able to isolate many of the factors that produce general personality effects as well.

Lieberman, for example, compared the attitudes of 23 workers who had been promoted to the rank of foreman with those of 35 workers who had been elected shop steward by their unions. Before these changes, he had asked the workers in the factory to express their attitudes toward management, unions, a management-sponsored incentive system, and the union-sponsored seniority system. As a control group he used 81 workers matched with the others on several demographic, motivational, and attitudinal measures.

Several months after their selection, the new foremen and stewards were tested again. The foremen had moved significantly ($p = .05$ or less) in the pro-management direction on 8 out of 16 questions. On 2 additional questions a probability level of .10 was reached. The foremen had become both more pro-management and more anti-union. The stewards changed significantly on only 3 out of 16 questions, having become more pro-union but no more anti-management. The greater influence on the foremen can be accounted for by the facts that they made a more permanent shift in jobs. They assumed a new full-time job, while the stewards served only a few hours a week; and the foremen had to leave the union, whereas the stewards simply became spokesmen for the union. Thus the shift to foreman involved more basic role changes.

In the course of the next two years, 8 of the 23 foremen were returned to the rank of worker due to cutbacks in production, 12 remained foremen, and 3 left the plant. Although 14 stewards returned to the worker position, only 6 were still in the plant when the third measurement took place. On the whole, the ex-foremen returned to their old attitudes (partly, perhaps, as a result of bitterness as well as role change); the continuing foremen became even more pro-management. Contrasts in the steward group were less sharp, because the original shift in attitudes had been smaller. In summary, in 1951 the mean answers of the future foremen and future stewards differed by 0.1 per cent on the 16 questions. In 1952, after the two groups had occupied their new positions for several months, they differed by 47.8 per cent; and by 1954 those still in these positions differed by 62.4 per cent.

How can one account for these developments? Lieberman offers two explanations: First, the shift in reference groups, particularly for the foremen, meant a new source of standards and of rewards. Secondly, the personality may exert pressure to encourage attitudes consistent with actions. The chain of events, according to this argument, would lead from role change to function change to action change to attitude change.[32]

Questions concerning the relationship of self to role are not easily subjected to experimental measurement, but valuable approximations can be made if one accepts laboratory assignments of appropriate behavior as roles. (The extent to which brief and "artificial" role assignments express the same factors as long-lasting and "natural" designations remains problematic. This is, of course, a critical question for behavioral science in general.) Borgatta designed a role-playing setting in which the members of three-person groups were asked to play assertive, submissive, or emotional roles. Activity during a series of twenty-minute scenes was recorded in a revised version of Bales's interaction process categories. A year earlier an "assertiveness" score for the subjects had been obtained by rating of peers. Borgatta found that assertiveness in interaction was a function in part of the assertiveness score obtained a year earlier. It was also partly a function of the role assignment: highly assertive persons placed in submissive roles, for example, received lower scores than did submissive persons playing assertive roles.[33]

Role Conflict

The interaction of self and role is nowhere more clearly shown than in the analysis of role conflict. Unhappily, the failure to distinguish a social fact from a personality fact is sometimes found in discussion of this question and obscures the study of role conflict. We need at the outset, therefore, to distinguish between internal and external role conflict.

Internal role conflict occurs when an individual has internalized a role that includes contradictory expectations or when he occupies two or more positions that carry incompatible role expectations. These incompatibilities may or may not be perceived or recognized by the individual. The assumption that only if they are perceived do they have behavioral consequences is false. In fact, many personality processes may be set in motion precisely to block such perception; unrecognized conflicts may be more important than the recognized ones.

External role conflict occurs when an individual is confronted with incompatible expectations from two or more persons in his position network or networks. Again, the incompatibility may or may not be perceived. Thus the definition offered here is broader than that of Gross, Mason, and McEachern, who refer only to perceived incompatibilities.[34] Such a limitation excludes important aspects of role conflict, because unperceived conflicts in the expectations of others affect *their* behavior and thus the whole interaction. Moreover, an individual may be motivated not to perceive contradictory expectations from others just as he seeks to avoid recognition of internal conflicts. And this motivation affects his role behavior.

The distinction between internal and external role conflict is analytic; empirically they are often found together. Contradictory expectations of others are, in fact, an important source of internal conflict. Yet the distinction is necessary. External role conflict may be unimportant in the behavior of one person whose internalized roles do not reflect the conflict or who has devised ways of managing the contradictory requirements; external role conflict may, however, have great significance for the behavior of another person toward him. Conversely, external consensus is no proof of lack of internal conflict. Consensual demands may *seem* incompatible to some individuals, or they may conflict with other tendencies related to other roles or personality forces.

Thus external role conflict is only an inadequate index of internal role conflict. Seeman makes this point well, although he uses the phrase "role conflict" to refer to external conflict only, when he writes: "The term 'role conflict' may be somewhat misleading, carrying implications of necessary personal conflict. This refers, however, only to situations in which *the observer notes what appear to be* conflicting sets of expectations—i.e., to *potential* sources of difficulty for the actor." [35]

Role conflict can rest on expectations that are legitimate or illegitimate. Gross, Mason, and McEachern define these as expectations which the incumbent of a position believes others do or do not have a right to hold. "An expectation which is felt to be legitimate will be called a *perceived obligation*. One which is felt to be illegitimate will be called a *perceived pressure*." [36] Although the distinction between legitimate and illegitimate expectations is valuable, I think it should be developed separately from the question of perception. One can define as illegitimate a claim made by some members of a position network on a role participant that is not accepted by most members of the network or is not part of the definition of that role found in the culture. Perception or nonperception of this fact is then an additional variable to study. The social fact of legitimacy must be defined and measured independently of the personality fact of its perception. If an expectation that is perceived to be legitimate by an actor is actually, as defined above, illegitimate, his misperception does not remove its illegitimacy and the consequences thereof in the actions of others.

Sometimes a college professor will perceive it to be a legitimate part of his role to show a great deal of personal interest in his students, to be friendly outside of academic situations, to converse with students over coffee, or to invite them to his home for supper. Some students and colleagues, however, may define this as illegitimate. Questions of favoritism, loss of dignity, undue courting of student enrollments, or reduction in effectiveness as a teacher and scholar may be involved. If these are the prevailing views, his actions are illegitimate by a cultural definition even though he perceives them to be a desirable and perhaps necessary part of his internalized role.

All sorts of things then begin to happen to the professor *regardless of the perceived legitimacy of his role performance*. Some kinds of students are attracted to him—perhaps those who need emotional support—while others are alienated—perhaps those most academically inclined. Or his popularity with students increases only to be followed by loss of contact with his colleagues, who resent his popularity, or resist "unfair competition," or look with sorrow on his declining scholarly activity.

The teacher may then be delighted, puzzled, and hurt, all at the same time, by what is taking place, without his recognizing the situation as one of role conflict. If his relationships with his colleagues or his prospects for promotion are injured by the situation, he may believe that there has been favoritism or that he is the target of personal attack. If his internalized role, which I have described here as socially illegitimate in some aspects, is firmly believed in (i.e., if it is congruent with other personality tendencies which anchor it), he may be quite unable to recognize the source of the problem. Needless to say, if his perception of legitimacy—that is, his internalized role—had corresponded with the views of significant others, they would have responded to him differently, with rewards instead of sanctions.

One other distinction is if value: "An individual is confronted with an *intrarole conflict* if he perceives that others hold different expectations for him as the incumbent of a single position. . . . In *interrole conflict,* an individual perceives that others hold different expectations for him as the incumbent of two or more positions." [37] I would modify this only by suggesting again that these aspects of role conflict may or may not be perceived. The intrarole-interrole distinction is significant because the processes of making the role bargain and of staying in or leaving a position are different when one position is involved in the conflict from what they are when two or more positions are involved.

On the basis of the four variables discussed here, sixteen possible types of role conflict can be designated.[38] Not all of them are likely to be important empirically, but some of the varieties can profitably be illustrated.

Internal role conflict. Perry and Wynne discuss methods of role conflict resolution employed by psychiatrists at a research hospital. The psychiatrists' obligations as clinicians sometimes collided with their research tasks, in what we can call, on the basis of the list above, an internal, perceived, legitimate, interrole conflict. When a schizophrenic patient was seriously frightened and disoriented by an experimental drug, the psychiatrist had either to discontinue use of the drug, thus losing the time spent on this patient as part of a research study, or to continue a treatment that was clinically unwise.

How do physician-researchers handle such a dilemma? Perry and Wynne suggest that they work out one or the other of two types of role redefinition. The first is an integrative redefinition in which the person experiencing interrole conflict attempts to combine the roles, compromising differences between them and establishing a hierarchy of obligations. The physician-researcher role might come to include the responsibility to pull back from clinically harmful research tests of a certain order of risk. The second redefinition Perry and Wynne call the split-relationship type, in which "the physician establishes a relationship with one patient for purely therapeutic purposes; he establishes another relationship with a different patient for purely research purposes." [39]

In a changing society, such role redefinitions are a continuing fact. Role research must deal with them as fully as with stable role definitions. Redefinitions demonstrate in a particularly important way the interaction among personality, role, and social structural forces. The redefinition process discussed above is affected by the kinds of persons, in terms of general personality tendencies, who become physician-researchers. It is influenced by hospital structure and by the values of the supporting community.

A useful approach to role conflict resolution is to hypothesize a *tendency toward* the reduction of conflict, both on the part of individuals who experience it and on the part of the social systems within which it takes place. By establishing a hierarchy of values or by segregating (in time and circumstance) contradictory expectations, as Perry and Wynne suggest, or by other mechanisms, individual and group processes move in the direction of role conflict resolution. These processes may be slower than other processes tending to increase role conflict, of course, with resulting strains for the individual and social systems.

External role conflict. Whether or not a person is confronted with role dilemmas and contradictions as a result of his own definitions, he may face incompatible expectations from others. As I have noted, these may be perceived or unperceived by the individual; they may be legitimate or illegitimate expectations; and they may have reference to one position or more than one. Perhaps the most important cases of external role conflict are perceived, partially legitimate–partially illegitimate, intrarole conflicts. The individual is under cross pressures from various members of a position network; he is aware of these cross pressures; and some of them push him toward behavior that violates the role norms. The basic element in such role conflict is lack of consensus.

Under other conditions a person can experience external role conflict when there is no lack of consensus and no illegitimate demand made upon him. This type of conflict occurs when a person occupies two or more positions which have fully consensual role definitions, but either the roles cannot be performed simultaneously or they make mutually limiting demands upon his resources. (This situation can, of course, be called lack of consensus even though role obligations are agreed upon, because the ordering of behavior when the roles compete for time or resources is not agreed upon.)

It is one thing for a school superintendent to work in a situation where pupils, teachers, principals, school board members, and taxpayers define his role in different ways and make contradictory demands upon him (intrarole conflict). It is another thing for him to experience contradictory or mutually exclusive demands as the result of the fact that he is a husband, father, church deacon, and member of the Rotary Club as well as school superintendent (interrole conflict). This distinction is important because the process of selecting the obligations of one position over another is not necessarily the same as the process of conforming to one expectation rather than another within a position.[40] Nor are the personality and social consequences of interrole and intrarole conflict identical.[41]

Role conflict resolution. Perhaps the most useful way to study external role conflict in its various manifestations is to examine the processes of conflict resolution. In what ways do individuals and groups seek to mitigate the effects of role conflict?

With reference to the *intra*role situation, Merton discusses a number of processes by which a person may seek to reduce the difficulties in performing his role in the face of contradictory expectations. First, some of the counterpositions will be on the periphery of the network and the occupants only marginally involved in role performance. Any contradictory requirements from them can be played down or disregarded. A school board member may devote five or six hours a month to his duties in that position, while his major interests involve his family, business, church, and golf club. A person who occupies the position of superintendent, however, may regard that as his central concern. Insofar as there is lack of consensus between board member and superintendent regarding the teacher's role, the teacher will minimize his difficulties by following the role expectations of the superintendent. Obviously this statement needs qualification, however, because we are dealing with a system, not a series of dyadic relationships. The board member influences the teacher in part through his relationship to the superintendent. And on certain issues the salience of his membership on the board may be high.

Second, lack of consensus can partly be controlled by playing one network member off against another. Merton suggests that the position occupant thus wins more autonomy, which we can take to mean, wins a greater chance to make manifest his internalized role.

Third, the fact that not all role activities are observable, or that they are observable by only some members of the position network, allows a person to reduce the difficulties related to lack of consensus. There are structural arrangements connected with many positions that permit the occupant to perform the role free in part from direct observation. The physician has privileged information; the university classroom is to some degree insulated. As Merton observes, such mechanisms may be necessary for the performance of a role, but may also be used to hide its malperformance.[42] Our concern here is with the function of these mechanisms in modifying the effects of lack of role consensus. Occupational roles, for example, often involve privileges, or *licenses* to perform acts which are deviant and forbidden outside those roles.[43] The surgeon may cut and the teacher may explore controversial questions objectively. But licenses vary in the degree to which they are accepted by all the persons involved; and acceptance depends in part on the relative nonobservability of the activities which are licensed. In Coser's words, "The determination of who can hide from whom may be as essential to the workings of a social system as determination of who has power over whom." [44]

Fourth, Merton observes that difficulties connected with conflicting demands on a position occupant can be reduced by confronting one person in the network with the demands of another, asking, in effect, "How can I satisfy you both?" This action may help him to explain his role performance or may lead to compromise or reconciliation among the disagreeing members of the position network. Rather than reducing the effects of lack of role consensus, this process may increase the consensus or help to redefine the role.

Fifth, individuals occupying similar positions may respond to a lack of consensus by collective bargaining—by efforts to get their definition of the rights and duties accepted. In a heterogeneous and changing society, where traditional definitions of roles are constantly being altered and persons with differing role conceptions frequently interact, this is an important mechanism. It can be thought of as leading to *temporary role consensus*, sufficient to allow the role to be performed, yet responsive to changing forces. Urban cultures are doubtless characterized better by an image of temporary and fluid role bargains [45] than by a static picture of traditional roles or the opposite, a chaotic picture of role confusion and utter lack of consensus.

Collective bargaining is widely used in the role-defining process. The children in a family, who themselves are often exuberantly lacking in role consensus, may on occasion join together to win a definition of rights and duties from their parents that none could win alone. Bargaining may be quite subtle, as when the pupils in a school, by the rewards and punishments they are able to use with their teachers, by their activities and the lacks thereof, by pressures on one another, and the like, are able to influence the role definition.

Lack of consensus on a role may be so severe that no combination of the mechanisms discussed here can produce a workable definition. Sometimes an individual can simply leave a position whose role performance seems difficult. But leaving is often impossible, and if a temporary working consensus cannot be devised, the role performance will have disruptive effects on the social and the personality systems involved.[46] This disruption, however, is not *ipso facto* a good or bad thing. Perhaps role malperformance will initiate change in a social system that has been blocking the achievement of stated values. Malperformance may help to promote role severance, or a search for consistency, or other processes within an individual that contribute to personal or group values.

To the degree that role consensus is treated as a variable, research on roles must go beyond a simple model that asks such questions as "What is the role? To what degree is X able and willing to perform that role? How well has he been socialized to the role—i.e., is the internalized role close to the cultural definition? Are those in reciprocal positions well socialized to their roles?" The questions must be rephrased: "What is the extent of role consensus? What mechanisms are present for handling dissensus among persons in the network? What are the effects of those mechanisms on the role, on the social system, and on the personalities involved?"

To explore such questions requires a dynamic view of roles in action, not a static role map. Doubtless a useful point of departure is a model of an interacting group of people trained to give certain role performances expected by others and to expect certain performances from others. Positive and negative sanctions of each to the others produce conformity with the role patterns. (In the learning process, these are administered sanctions, but increasingly they become simply expected sanctions.) [47] In a setting where role consensus is low, however, the situation is more complicated. The prevailing, but nonuniversal, role definition can be thought of as the starting point for temporary role bargains. These bargains will also be a function, however, of the individual's internalized role, of other personality influences, and of the total situation.

I shall use the term *role clarity* to refer to the extent to which an internalized role lacks contradictions; thus role clarity is to the individual what consensus is to the group.[48] By *role congruity* I shall refer to the extent to which an individual's various roles are mutually consistent and harmonious. And by *situation congruity*, I shall mean the degree to which a situation permits the performance of a role.

Goode makes the interesting suggestion that "In general, the individual's total role obligations are over-demanding." [49] Thus the individual experiences "role strain" and seeks a role bargain to reduce it. The bargain he makes varies with his own role commitment, his judgment of the behavior expected by those in reciprocal positions, the rewards and punishments they will employ, and the responses of others in the position network to the bargains being worked out.[50] One might add that the bargain varies also with situational influences—forces outside the network. Thus we have, not a neatly intermeshed series of behaviors—each person performing a role that he has learned—but an emergent role bargain only part of which can be understood by knowledge of the culturally defined roles.

We can think of a teacher before a new class somewhat tentatively seeking a modus vivendi. If there were substantial role consensus, he would have no problem. But he is not sure what it is to "be a teacher" (lack of role clarity); his students do not entirely agree with his rough model, nor does he agree with their equally vague notions of what it is to "be a student" (lack of consensus); other teachers and students, the principal, the parents, and others in the network are not fully ready to accept any definition worked out in the classroom (further lack of consensus); and shortage of time, equipment, and money reduces the chances of carrying out any emerging consensus (lack of situational congruity).

One can imagine several possible processes in such a context: If the teacher overdemands, the students may complain or avoid the role requirements as he defines them; yet they are constrained by sanctions, by some degree of consensus, and by the desire to enter other positions later. If he underdemands, other teachers may employ sanctions, because his actions affect how they can perform their roles. If he explores a controversial issue too frankly, the principal may mention the bond issue about to come before the voters. And if he concludes that the adequate performance of his role requires new laboratory equipment, others may agree, but shortage of funds may prevent its acquisition. As the result of such interacting forces as these, a working model of the rights and duties of the teacher emerges. Even though consensus is not substantial, acceptable role performance from the point of view of both the individual and the group is often possible by the use of the various techniques of intrarole conflict resolution.

External *inter*role conflicts confront an individual with somewhat different kinds of problems. His difficulties stem not from contradictory expectations of the members of one position network, but from the fact that he occupies two or more positions for which the role requirements are incompatible. For a number of reasons, these problems may seem to the individual easier to handle than those connected with intrarole conflict, although the process of handling them may have equally strong effects on him and the social system.

In fact, interrole contradictions may be sharper than intrarole contradictions, because the persons involved in the latter are parts of the same system. As such, they have at least some shared expectations and a mutual interest in the functioning of the network. But the persons in two or more networks to which an individual belongs may have little mutual interest in his successful role performances. They may indeed be competitive for his time and energy. A hard-driving boss may have little concern for the impact of his demands on the family life of a young executive in his firm. He is likely to have some concern, however, for the contradictions between his requirements and the assignments of the division superintendent under whose immediate supervision the young executive works.

Thus we can hypothesize that external interrole conflicts are likely to be sharper than intrarole conflicts; but at the same time—and perhaps because of that fact—there are more techniques for dealing with interrole conflict. For example, the value scheme of the culture often furnishes a hierarchy of obligations that helps a person decide which of the contradictory requirements takes precedence. The value scheme leads others to accept his decision also.

The degree to which one's behavior is observable is perhaps even more important in interrole than in intrarole conflict resolution. At least, in the short run incompatible behavior is easier to hide from the members of two networks than from the members of one. (Since this has the effect of permitting more incompatible behavior to continue, its long-run significance for the individual and the larger social system may be great, and may finally lead to more observability.)

Most of the mechanisms of intrarole conflict resolution apply to interrole conflict as well. Just as some members of a network may be on the periphery, and thus more easily disregarded, so some networks may be less powerful or important and thus their role demands may be more readily overlooked or modified. In addition, one can play off the members of one network against these of another and so may win a measure of control over their mutually contradictory expectations. Other techniques of role conflict resolution have been discussed by Toby: Stalling in hopes that the issue will subside; becoming ill or using other kinds of escape from the field; and repudiating the obligations of one position.[51]

Variables affecting role conflict resolution. Doubtless the primary research task, as Toby notes, is to discover the conditions under which various styles of role conflict resolution will be employed. Several variables are involved. In their valuable chapter on role conflict resolution [52] Gross, Mason, and McEachern discuss the effects of legitimacy, sanctions, and personality predispositions in determining the behavior of an individual who experiences contradictory role expectations. These apply to both intra- and interrole conflict situations. Some of the people making demands upon an individual are better able to enforce those demands by use of the rewards and sanctions at their disposal. The demands vary in legitimacy—that is, in the extent to which others agree that a given expectation is appropriately associated with a position.

Other things being equal, expectations that are backed by strong sanctions and by legitimacy are more likely to be accepted by ego and to become part of his role behavior than expectations with weak sanctions and low legitimacy. When the force of sanctions and legitimacy coincide, the outcome, other things being equal, is clear; but when they work in opposite directions, role behavior is problematic. The issue is complicated by the fact that each of these influences is a variable with many possible scale values. A nice problem for research is to determine at what point, for a given individual, sanctions outweigh legitimacy.[53] Common sense tells us that every man has his price—that at some point sanctions will prevail over legitimacy. Perhaps common-sense knowledge is overly cynical and needs to be supplemented by the statement that every man has his morality. (This phrase has to be invented, but equivalents are not lacking. There is honor among thieves, which is to say that legitimacy may prevail over sanctions even among unlikely persons.)

A third variable, or cluster of variables, affecting role conflict resolution is the predispositions of individuals. For simplicity we can distinguish between predispositions associated with the internalized role and more general personality tendencies. If one individual defines a role differently from another, he will respond differently to the same set of sanctions and legitimacies. A person's internalized role may be among the most important forces affecting his perceptions of the sanctions and legitimacies of conflicting role requirements.

On the more general personality level, there may be a tendency, as shown by the research of Stouffer and Toby, for individuals to vary in the degree to which they resolve role conflicts in a particularistic or universalistic direction. In a series of imagined conflicts between obligations to friends and to society, Stouffer and Toby's subjects could be ranged along a scale from universalistic (putting societal obligations first) to particularistic (putting the obligations of friendship first).[54] How stable a tendency this is (i.e., to what degree it would hold under varying conditions) can be determined only by further research.

Gross, Mason, and McEachern suggest an additional personality variable (or perhaps another way of looking at the same variable). Individuals may vary in their tendencies to give primacy to the legitimacy and the sanctions elements in conflict situations. One person may place emphasis on the right of others to hold certain expectations for him in a given position (the moral orientation); another may give priority to the *power* of others to punish or reward him for following their expectations (the expedient orientation). Still others may respond equally to right and power and act in terms of the net balance between them (the moral-expedient orientation.) [55]

By putting the three variables we have discussed (power, legitimacy, and orientation) into quasi scales, we can see how they might interact to produce role behavior (if we disregard for the moment the influence of other forces). We shall have to make certain assumptions. Assume that each variable ranges along a scale from 1 to 9. Assume further that when an individual experiences two contradictory expectations, their total value on each scale equals 10—that is, if one expectation carries a sanctioning force of 8, the other must carry the force of 2. Applying these to imaginary situations, we can see what behavior might occur.

Situation A:

Expectation 1 has power of 9   Expectation 2 has power of 1
Expectation 1 has legitimacy of 9   Expectation 2 has legitimacy of 1

Under these conditions, whether an individual is oriented primarily to power, to legitimacy, or to a balance between them makes no difference:

he will always follow expectation 1. In simple mathematical terms, assuming a 5-5 orientation:

Expectation 1		Expectation 2	
power = 9 × 5:	45	power = 1 × 5:	5
legitimacy = 9 × 5:	45	legitimacy = 1 × 5:	5
	90		10

If the individual is oriented primarily toward power (responds more to sanctions than to legitimacy) the result is nevertheless the same. Assume an 8-2 orientation toward power:

Expectation 1		Expectation 2	
power = 9 × 8:	72	power = 1 × 8:	8
legitimacy = 9 × 2:	18	legitimacy = 1 × 2:	2
	90		10

No other outcome is possible, whatever the individual's personal orientation.

Situation B:

Assume now a situation where expectation 1 carries stronger sanctions, but expectation 2 carries stronger legitimacy. Here the personal orientation can make a difference. Suppose it to be 6-4 in favor of power.

Expectation 1		Expectation 2	
power = 8 × 6:	48	power = 2 × 6:	12
legitimacy = 2 × 4:	8	legitimacy = 8 × 4:	32
	56		44

Even though the second expectation is perceived to be more legitimate, the individual is more likely to follow the first.

Situation C:

If a person is strongly oriented toward the power dimension (9-1), a small differential in sanctioning power (6-4) would overweigh a large differential in legitimacy running in the opposite direction (1-9).

Expectation 1		Expectation 2	
power = 6 ×9 :	54	power = 4 × 9:	36
legitimacy = 1 × 1:	1	legitimacy = 9 × 1:	9
	55		45

These pseudomathematical operations can only suggest some of the ways in which three variables can combine to determine choice in a role conflict situation. The outcome might, of course, be a stalemate (50-50), resulting in apathy or withdrawal (as has been found in somewhat similar situations in political behavior). Or an additional variable not accounted for in this simple model might be the decisive factor. Undoubtedly research for some time to come will have to be content with dichotomies or trichotomies for these variables rather than more complete scales.[56] But the logic of their interaction will be the same.

Simultaneous and successional role conflict.   The discussion of both internal and external role conflict has assumed that we are dealing with a given moment in time. Some aspects of role conflict can be understood, however, only if we consider a time dimension. In the course of life, an individual moves through a series of positions, and some tendencies acquired in one position are not necessarily unlearned even though they are inappropriate to a new position. This continuity of personality is influenced by the possibility that some associates may continue to respond to the individual as if he were still an occupant of an earlier position, encouraging him to play a pseudorole. I shall speak of *successional role conflict* when an individual's performance in a contemporary position is interfered with by continuing personality tendencies, or continuing expectations of others, or both.

Successional role conflict is one aspect of self-role interaction, since much of self has been formed out of earlier role experiences; but it requires some special mention. Societies differ in the amount of simultaneous role conflict they create, since they vary in the degree to which their members occupy positions that carry contradictory expectations. In the same way, societies differ in the extent to which they make successional role conflicts likely. It is often assumed that a highly mobile society in all the meanings of mobility—a society in which one's future roles are only poorly prefigured by the people ahead of one on the age ladder—makes it difficult to step from position to position. Yet there may be adaptive social mechanisms that facilitate position change and help to create individuals capable of such change without major conflict. The implications of "other-directedness" or styles of child rearing for this problem are getting attention from anthropologists, psychologists, and sociologists.[57]

In her well-known paper on "Continuities and Discontinuities in Cultural Conditioning," [58] Ruth Benedict developed the thesis that in America the position "child" permits a number of tendencies that are a hindrance to successful performance of the role of the adult. She believed that many societies, particularly preliterate ones, handle the problems connected with the cycle of growth more skillfully. The child in America is expected to be nonresponsible, submissive, and asexual, and then to become rather abruptly a responsible, dominant, and sexual adult. In some primitive societies, however, responsibility is required early, submissiveness is not expected, and childhood sexuality is recognized—a situation that allows an easy transition into adulthood. Without exploring the validity of the specific illustration used by Benedict, we can at least recognize the significance of the question. In general terms, the problem is to specify the conditions under which successional role conflict is most likely to occur; or somewhat differently, to discover the social mechanisms that may be devised to help an individual bridge the gap between one position and another.

Role transitions are of two kinds, for which the problems of analysis are different. In some shifts a person moves from one position of a network into a reciprocal position with which he has long interacted. For example, the son becomes a father. Other changes, however, imply no such linkage, at least in so full a sense. (The dichotomous formulation of this question is arbitrary, of course.) For example, the nonemployed boy enters the adult occupational world. Any discontinuities involved in this shift would concern general tendencies learned in various positions, not the kind of role-specific tendencies which are part of the son-to-father transition. From the point of view of role conflict, the linked transitions have both advantages and disadvantages. In playing the role of son, one learns also some of the necessary reciprocal tendencies of father; thus the break may not be so sharp as Benedict suggests. By the same token, however, one may mislearn the reciprocal role or learn opposition to it, thus making the transition more difficult. Societies vary in the proportion of role transitions that are linked and that are relatively independent (that involve transfer into new networks). Such variation is very important in the comparative study of role conflicts.

There are related differences in the likelihood that a society will have a definite cultural bridge marking and assisting the process of role transition. *Rites de passage* clearly define the end of childhood and the beginning of adulthood, both for the individual involved and for others who interact with him. Such a definitive line is difficult to draw in a society where an individual may be sexually mature at sixteen, militarily mature at eighteen, politically mature at twenty-one, and occupationally mature at twenty-five. It is perhaps the ambiguity of the timing of the transition from one position to another more than the discontinuous tendencies that produces role conflict.

The function of *rites de passage,* which range from long and painful initiation ceremonies to commencement exercises (the distinction is not always clear), is to facilitate the learning of new tendencies and the unlearning of old. This is a problem of motivation. How are tendencies to perform the new role promoted and the old tendencies inhibited? Shifts in the system of rewards and sanctions used by significant others are involved; reference groups are changed; and motive may follow function— being structurally required to perform a role influences an individual's motives in the direction of consistency.

Perhaps the clearest illustration of this process in the contemporary world is the making of a soldier out of a civilian. The new position carries obligations often strongly opposed to earlier tendencies: the obligation to give or accept orders that violate moral norms, the obligation to subordinate the self, and the like. The initiation ceremony may involve weeks of tiring and ego-shattering activity in "boot camp" or a year-long "gigging" at a service academy. One of the functions of such initiations is to push aside earlier role expectations, to clear the field for new definitions of duties and rights.[59]

The inhibition of earlier tendencies is not a uniform phenomenon. The distinction must be drawn between unlearning (the extinction of a motive) and repression (the blocking of a continuing motive). The extent to which one or the other of these prevails may be of great importance to behavior in the new role and also to general behavior.

Not only are there societal differences in the frequency of successional role conflict and the cultural mechanisms related to them, but there are individual differences as well. In complex societies particularly, one individual may experience a large number of role discontinuities while another experiences relatively few. There are also differences in difficulty or ease of transition related to the self rather than to the specific role. One person may find it relatively easy to shift from the role of nonresponsible child to responsible adult, whereas another finds it difficult. In this area, as in most of social science, common-sense knowledge on the question is plentiful. (And as in most of social science, many of the common-sense propositions may be true; the difficulty is that we are not sure which ones.) The common-sense knowledge tends to emphasize the problems associated with role transition—the tribulations of the *nouveaux riches,* the gaucheries of the bridegroom, the excessive zeal of the newly commissioned lieutenant. It is more than language alone that distinguishes a servant girl from a duchess.

There are large research tasks related to the question of successional role conflicts: In which kinds of societies and cultural systems are they most likely to occur? What social mechanisms are associated with efforts to reduce the conflicts, and what is their comparative success? Can individuals who are particularly vulnerable to the strains of successional role conflict be identified? What are the comparative results of extinction and repression of tendencies appropriate to the role being left? Many theoretical and practical questions are related to this issue.

THE STRUCTURAL SETTING OF POSITIONS AND ROLES

To understand the influence of a position on behavior, we need to relate it not only to the personalities of the occupants and to the network of reciprocal positions with which it is connected, but also to the larger community and society structures within which it operates.[60] Generations of social scientists and moral philosophers have dealt with the significance of "the division of labor" for human life. One of the most useful ways of studying the division of labor and the social change which has accompanied its growth is in terms of the effects on positions and roles. Although there may be exceptions to these propositions, it seems generally true that with the growth of modern society, the number of positions has increased; their role specifications have become narrower; consensus may have declined; the number of positions that can be achieved has increased; the size of position networks has tended to grow; and positions that formerly clustered in one person have been broken apart.

These changes are of great importance to the student of the personality-culture–social structure unit. A few illustrations will indicate how the total social setting within which positions are located affects them—and doubtless is affected by them. In some societies, there is a strong tendency for positions to cluster: the occupant of one is likely to be the occupant of all others in the cluster. In fact, as Nadel makes clear, a nice problem of definition is to determine whether, under these circumstances, we are dealing with one position that has highly diffuse obligations and privileges, or with several positions that are closely related. As a normal result of the sociocultural system, one man may be family head, manager of the economic unit, elder of the political system, and priest. Another may be family dependent, worker, common citizen, and worshipper. In such a situation, the replacement of a family head will tend to be followed by a continuation of the role performances in all the various aspects of the position cluster.

Compare that pattern with a situation where these positions had been combined in one man fortuitously:

On his replacement a number of changes are apt to happen: one or the other concomitant role may disappear, at least temporarily, until a separate, new actor is recruited; or the roles, though not disappearing, will be redistributed, so that the former congruence no longer holds; or finally, the successor may bring with him some new role (say that of a leader in warfare or dancing), not formerly linked with that of family head, again disturbing the previous pattern of roles and relationships.[61]

In modern society, position clusters tend to be broken apart. Persons who occupy position *A* will not necessarily, as a matter of social structural influence, occupy positions *B, C,* and *D* as well. As a result, different position occupants will be subject to different cross pressures that will affect their role performances. Such a situation doubtless reflects and contributes to social change.

The mutual influence of role, network, and larger social structure is well shown in Bott's study of twenty families in Greater London.[62] She started with the question: How can one explain the wide variation in the ways husbands and wives perform their roles? The families in her study were all English, urban, Protestant families with young children, yet the internalized roles and the role performances varied widely. The range is from a situation where husband and wife maintain a strict division of labor, engage in few joint activities, operate on separate budgets (the wife is assigned an allowance for the household)—a "segregated role relationship"—to a situation in which they share many activities, have an indistinct division of labor, and make decisions together—a "joint conjugal role relationship."

Several factors influence the type of relationship. Segregated role relationships are more likely to be found where the husband is a manual worker than where he is a white-collar worker. They occur more frequently in homogeneous city neighborhoods of low mobility than in heterogeneous areas where family mobility is higher. Personality factors are also involved. In Bott's paper, however, the structural setting of the role relationships is the factor under study. She distinguishes between a highly connected network, where one's associates are also friends of each other, and a dispersed network, in which the family associates with several other families but the latter have little contact with each other.[63] There was a close connection between the role relationship of husband and wife and the type of network they were involved in. Couples with highly segregated role relations had highly connected networks; these might be different networks for husband and for wife, as expressed in the saying that men have friends, women have relatives. Joint role relationships were associated with dispersed networks, usually shared by husband and wife.

This study suggests in an interesting way the mutual influences of personality, role, network, and social structure. Although the direction of causal influence cannot be specified with confidence from the data, probably each level of influence has some independent effect, that is, can explain some of the variance in behavior. One could hypothesize, for example, that personality tendencies were the independent variable. Thus in a culturally flexible situation where there was a good deal of "play" for individual interpretations, persons with certain inclinations would define their family role relationships in a certain way. This would impose limits on the network pattern. And although by this time the causal force would be largely spent, the individual interpretations might to some degree influence the larger social structure—by affecting the degree of readiness for mobility, for example.

Perhaps a more tenable hypothesis would start at the other end of the chain and move from social structure "down." The occupational system (with its effects on working hours, values, the ecological patterns of cities, mobility, and the like) and other social structures strongly influence the type of network to which families will be tied. These networks, in turn, set limiting conditions for the kinds of role relationships to be found within a family. And the structurally supported roles influence the personalities of the persons involved, although by this time, again, the causal force would be largely dissipated. Undoubtedly one could start with either the role relationships or the type of network as the independent variable and, moving both up toward social structure and down toward personality, explain some of the variation in these variables.

In Bott's view, however, a social influence—mobility—is of prime importance in affecting type of network and role. Connected networks develop where husband, wife, friends, and relatives grow up and live in the same neighborhood. Each comes to marriage with connected networks already built. Although the marriage will require some change in these networks, it can largely be superimposed on them. In such a situation, both husband and wife have a limited emotional investment in the marriage relationship; they can, in a sense, "afford" the segregated role relationship.

Those who have moved about all their lives, however, already are parts of dispersed networks when they marry. If mobility is the norm, they will meet new persons continually. Under these conditions, high standards of conjugal compatibility and joint conjugal role relationships become the source of stability and continuity.[64] One need scarcely emphasize the significance of this pattern for family structure, stability, and the socialization of children. Altogether, Bott's study demonstrates the great importance of locating roles in larger social contexts; it helps to see roles in dynamic terms.

CONCLUSION

Despite the widespread use of the terms "position" and "role," current sociological and interdisciplinary research is not, in my judgment, employing them adequately. Disagreement on their definition and failure to draw various necessary distinctions have reduced their value. Yet the research area to which they are relevant holds great promise, particularly for the analysis of problems that relate social structure, culture, and personality. My aim in this conceptual analysis has been to contribute to the systematic definition of position, role, and internalized role and to note how their use can improve our understanding, not only of changeless and conflictless (and therefore imaginary) societies, but also of the dynamic equilibrium that the word "society" must denote in the world today.

FOOTNOTES

Note: The bracketed number following an author's name refers to the footnote in which the source is cited in full.

1. See especially T. M. Newcomb, *Social Psychology*, Holt, Rinehart and Winston, Inc., 1950; Talcott Parsons, *The Social System*, The Free Press of Glencoe, 1951; T. R. Sarbin, "Role Theory," in Gardner Lindzey (ed.), *Handbook of Social Psychology*, Addison-Wesley Publishing Company, Inc., 1954, vol. 1, chap. 6; F. L. Bates, "Position, Role, and Status: A Reformulation of Concepts," *Social Forces*, May, 1956, pp. 313–321; Neal Gross, Ward Mason, and Alexander McEachern, *Explorations in Role Analysis: Studies of the School Superintendent's Role,*

John Wiley & Sons, Inc., 1958; Anne-Marie Rocheblave-Spenlé, *La Notion du Rôle en Psychologie Sociale: Étude Historico-critique,* Presses Universitaires de France, 1962; S. F. Nadel, *The Theory of Social Structure,* The Free Press of Glencoe, 1957; O. A. Oeser and Frank Harary, "A Mathematical Model for Structural Role Theory, I," *Human Relations,* May, 1962, pp. 89–109. The last is an interesting mathematical graphing of role ideas.

2. Gross, Mason, and McEachern [1], p. 67.

3. "In any field of inquiry a 'structure' is a relatively fixed relationship between elements, parts, or entities (as, e.g., the structure of a house, an animal, or a plant) containing gross, observable parts that maintain a fixed relationship to one another for an appreciable time" (Robin M. Williams, Jr., *American Society,* rev. ed., Alfred A. Knopf, Inc., 1960, p. 20).

4. "Nous proposons donc de définir le rôle comme un modèle organisé de conduite, relatif à une certaine position de l'individu dans un ensemble interactionnel." Rocheblave-Spenlé [1], p. 153, my translation.

5. See S. Stansfeld Sargent, "Concepts of Role and Ego in Contemporary Psychology," in John H. Rohrer and Muzafer Sherif (eds.), *Social Psychology at the Crossroads,* Harper & Row, Publishers, Incorporated, 1951, chap. 15; and Sarbin [1].

6. Levinson has noted that "role" has been defined as "structurally given demands," as an individual's conception of the part he is to play, and as the action of an individual playing a given part. "Many writers use a definition that embraces all of the above meanings without systematic distinction, and then shift, explicitly or implicitly, from one meaning to another" (Daniel J. Levinson, "Role, Personality, and Social Structure in the Organizational Setting," *Journal of Abnormal and Social Psychology,* vol. 58, 1959, pp. 170–180. Reprinted in Neil J. Smelser and William T. Smelser, *Personality and Social Systems,* John Wiley & Sons, Inc., 1963, pp. 428–441. Quote is from p. 431 of the latter). The confusion rests in part on the tendency to assume a high degree of congruence among the three dimensions noted—an assumption that seems dubious under many conditions. Although Levinson does not develop the concept of position, he discusses "personal role-definition" (equivalent to what I have called internalized role) as an important link between the total personality and the behavioral situation.

The distinctions he draws, and others as well, are often overlooked. Considering the widespread agreement on the need for societal, cultural, and personality levels of analysis, it is remarkable, and unfortunate, that few writers have defined terms for the three levels unambiguously, or, having defined them, have used the terms consistently. Ralph Linton's classic chapter in *The Study of Man* (D. Appleton–Century, Company, Inc., 1936), despite its major contribution to role theory, is not without difficulties. Linton does not make clear the distinction between status (position) and role, or between role and role behavior. His choice of the term "status" was also not an entirely happy one, for the connotations of status as a ranking term obscure its use in the nonhierarchical sense that he intended. I join those who enthusiastically, but without a great deal of hope (note the recent usages of Merton and Goode, for example), assign the term "status" to stratification theory.

Even Talcott Parsons, whose work is so important in the effort to develop a systematic theory of society, culture, and personality, does not always clearly differentiate between role and role behavior, or between role as a cultural fact and its personality manifestation (Parsons [1], pp. 25–26 and 38–39).

Sarbin, after indicating that role is a unit of culture, position a unit of society, and self a unit of personality, proceeds to define positions as "collections of rights and duties," or sets of "expectations or acquired anticipatory reactions" with reference to others. Or again, "A position in a social structure is equivalent to an organized system of role expectations" (Sarbin [1], p. 226). These statements blur the distinction between role and position. Role is then defined as "a patterned sequence of learned *actions* or deeds performed by a person in an interaction situation" (*ibid.*, p. 225), which tends to blur the distinction between role and role behavior.

Newcomb offers no formal definition of position, but states that one position can be distinguished from another in terms of the functions performed for the group. He clearly separates position from role: "The ways of behaving which are expected of any individual who occupies a certain position constitute the *role*...associated with that position" (Newcomb [1], p. 280). This would seem also to prepare the way for a clear distinction between role and role behavior, a distinction that Newcomb generally maintains with great clarity. He allows it to become somewhat blurred, however, when he writes that a role "refers to the *behavior* of the occupants of a position—not to all their behavior, as persons, but to what they do *as occupants of the position*" (*ibid.*). On this question of definition, see Gross, Mason, and McEachern [1], chap. 2.

7. See Leon Festinger, "An Analysis of Compliant Behavior," in Muzafer Sherif and M. O. Wilson (eds.), *Group Relations at the Crossroads,* Harper & Row, Publishers, Incorporated, 1953, pp. 232–256.

8. See S. F. Nadel [1], pp. 31–35; and Newcomb [1], pp. 281–282.

9. S. F. Nadel [1], pp. 20–47.

10. Gross, Mason, and McEachern [1], pp. 51–53.

11. Robert F. Bales has described a process of role differentiation in groups that are both small and temporary. Although he uses the term "role" more nearly to mean specialized function and behavior than a normative pattern, it appears from his research that roles in the normative sense begin to appear as part of a "culture-building process" even in temporary groups. See Talcott Parsons and R. F. Bales, *Family, Socialization and Interaction Process,* The Free Press of Glencoe, 1955, chap. 5. See also Alan P. Bates and Jerry Cloyd, "Toward the Development of Operations for Defining Group Norms and Member Roles," *Sociometry,* March, 1956, pp. 26–39.

12. Whether or not a position is assigned can affect the nature and extent of its influence. For an interesting attempt to study this experimentally, see Ivan D. Steiner and William L. Field, "Role Assignment and Interpersonal Influence," *Journal of Abnormal and Social Psychology,* September, 1960, pp. 239–245.   ,,

13. For discussions of dimensions of positions and roles, see Aidan Southall, "An Operational Theory of Role," *Human Relations,* vol. 12, 1959, pp. 17–34; Sargent [5]; Gross, Mason, and McEachern [1].

14. Mirra Komarovsky, *Women in the Modern World,* Little, Brown and Company, 1953; Talcott Parsons, "Age and Sex in the Social Structure of the United States," *American Sociological Review,* vol. 7, 1942, pp. 604–616.

15. Rae Sherwood, "The Bantu Clerk: A Study of Role Expectations," *Journal of Social Psychology*, May, 1958, pp. 285–316.

16. James Coleman, *The Adolescent Society*, The Free Press of Glencoe, 1961.

17. Gross, Mason, and McEachern [1], p. 31.

18. These comments on role consensus can be put in schematic form in the following way:

Substantial consensus

		Role characteristics of position X (ranked from 1 to 10)									
		a	b	c	d	e	f	g	h	i	j
Rating groups	I	1	2	3	4	5	6	7	8	9	10
or individuals	II	1	2	4	3	5	7	6	8	9	10
	III	2	1	3	4	5	6	8	7	9	10
	IV	1	2	3	4	6	5	7	9	10	9
	V	1	3	2	4	5	6	7	8	9	10

Subcultural consensus

		Role characteristics of position X									
Rating groups	I	1	2	3	4	5	6	7	8	9	10
	II	2	3	1	4	5	6	7	8	9	10
	III	1	2	3	5	4	6	7	8	10	9
	IV	8	9	10	x*	x	x	1	2	3	4
	V	8	10	9	x	x	x	2	1	3	4

* Not considered part of role

Slight consensus

		Role characteristics of position X									
Rating groups	I	1	2	3	4	5	6	7	8	9	10
or individuals	II	6	5	8	9	1	3	2	10	7	4
	III	2	1	3	4	7	8	6	5	10	9
	IV	1	2	4	3	7	6	5	9	8	10
	V	2	1	4	5	3	7	6	8	9	10

19. Ralph Herbert Turner, "Role-taking: Process versus Conformity," in Arnold Rose (ed.), *Human Behavior and Social Process*, Houghton Mifflin Company, 1962, p. 23.

20. Theodore M. Newcomb, Ralph Harold Turner, and Philip E. Converse, *Social Psychology: The Study of Human Interaction*, Holt, Rinehart and Winston, Inc., forthcoming.

21. See Walter Coutu, "Role-playing vs. Role-taking," *American Sociological Review*, April, 1951, pp. 180–187; Turner [19], pp. 20–40; Eleanor E. Maccoby, "Role-taking in Childhood and Its Consequences for Social Learning," *Child Development*, June, 1959, pp. 239–252; and Sheldon Stryker, "Conditions of Accurate Role-taking: A Test of Mead's Theory," in Rose [19], pp. 41–62.

22. Leonard S. Cottrell, Jr., "The Adjustment of the Individual to His Age and Sex Roles," *American Sociological Review*, vol. 7, 1942, p. 617.

23. Robert K. Merton, "The Role-set: Problems in Sociological Theory," *British Journal of Sociology,* June, 1957, pp. 106–120. Merton uses the term "role-set" in approximately the same way I am using position network. Despite the convenient brevity and wide currency of the phrase role set, I believe it obscures certain necessary distinctions; therefore I shall translate Merton's terms into mine. Where he employs "status" in the Linton sense, I shall speak of position. Where Merton uses role set to refer both to the clusters of positions (statuses) and to the interlocking obligations and expectancies (roles), I shall use two terms.

24. A. R. Mangus, "Role Theory and Marriage Counselling," *Social Forces,* March, 1957, pp. 200–209.

25. Orville E. Brim, Jr., "Personality Development as Role-learning," in Ira Iscoe and Harold W. Stevenson (eds.), *Personality Development in Children,* University of Texas Press, 1960, p. 144.

26. For his paper, see *ibid.,* pp. 127–159.

27. Alvin W. Gouldner, "Cosmopolitans and Locals: Toward an Analysis of Latent Social Roles, I," *Administrative Science Quarterly,* December, 1957, pp. 281–306; and "Cosmopolitans and Locals: Toward an Analysis of Latent Social Roles, II," *Administrative Science Quarterly,* March, 1958, pp. 444–480.

28. *Administrative Science Quarterly,* December, 1957, pp. 286–287.

29. Deviations from role performance, in fact, may be used as clues to "true self"—to tendencies that are likely to be expressed regardless of role. Edward E. Jones, Keith E. Davis, and Kenneth J. Gergen found that persons rating others felt confident about their judgments of those who had departed from experimentally assigned roles. See "Role Playing Variations and Their Informational Value for Person Perception," *Journal of Abnormal and Social Psychology,* September, 1961, pp. 302–310.

30. Doris Gilbert and D. J. Levinson, "Role Performance, Ideology, and Personality in Mental Hospital Aides," in Milton Greenblatt, D. J. Levinson, and R. H. Williams, eds., *The Patient and the Mental Hospital,* The Free Press of Glencoe, 1957, pp. 197–208.

31. Robert K. Merton, "Bureaucratic Structure and Personality," *Social Forces,* vol. 18, 1940, pp. 560–568.

32. Seymore Lieberman, "The Effects of Changes in Roles on the Attitudes of Role Occupants," *Human Relations,* vol. 9, 1956, pp. 385–402. See also Leon Festinger, *Theory of Cognitive Dissonance,* Harper & Row, Publishers, Incorporated, 1957.

33. Edgar F. Borgatta, "Role-playing Specification, Personality, and Performance," *Sociometry,* September, 1961, pp. 218–233. See also Richard Videnbach and Alan P. Bates, "An Experimental Study of Conformity to Role Expectations," *Sociometry,* March, 1959, pp. 1–11; and John H. Mann, "Experimental Evaluations of Role Playing," *Psychological Bulletin,* May, 1956, pp. 227–234. With regard to this last reference, and to much of the experimental work in "role playing," I should note that knowledge of role is often assumed or is only slightly built up experimentally. It may be wiser to speak of "position occupancy" rather than role playing, unless the research shows that the subjects are acting in terms of a knowledge of the rights and duties of a position.

34. Gross, Mason, and McEachern [1], p. 248.

35. Melvin Seeman, "Role Conflict and Ambivalence in Leadership," *American Sociological Review,* August, 1953, p. 373. Note the valuable discussion of role conflict, especially as a source of deviance, in Parsons [1], pp. 280–283.

36. Gross, Mason, and McEachern [1], p. 248.

37. *Ibid.,* pp. 248–249.

38. Listing them in a formal system may help to emphasize the necessity for the distinctions drawn here. Types of role conflict:

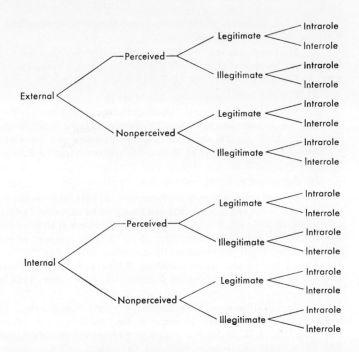

39. Stewart Perry and Lyman Wynne, "Role Conflict, Role Definition, and Social Change in a Clinical Research Organization," *Social Forces,* October, 1959, pp. 62–65. See also Mark G. Field, "Structured Strain in the Role of the Soviet Physician," *American Journal of Sociology,* March, 1953, pp. 493–502.

40. Gross, Mason, and McEachern [1], pp. 5–6.

41. For further discussions of role conflict, see Robert Hanson, "The Systematic Linkage Hypothesis and Role Consensus Patterns in Hospital-Community Relations," *American Sociological Review,* June, 1962, pp. 304–313; Alvin L. Bertrand, "The Stress-Strain Element of Social Systems: A Micro Theory of Conflict and Change," *Social Forces,* October, 1963, pp. 1–9; Alver Jacobson, "Conflict of Attitude toward the Roles of the Husband and Wife in Marriage," *American Sociological Review,* April, 1952, pp. 146–150; John P. Spiegel, "The Resolution of Role Conflict within the Family," *Psychiatry,* February, 1957, pp. 1–16; and Frederick L. Bates, "Some Observations Concerning the Structural Aspect of Role Conflict," *Pacific Sociological Review,* Fall, 1962, pp. 76–82.

42. Merton [23], pp. 115–116.

43. Everett C. Hughes, "The Study of Occupations," in Robert Merton, Leonard Broom, and Leonard Cottrell, Jr. (eds.), *Sociology Today,* Basic Books, Inc., Publishers, 1959; Lee Braude, "Professional Autonomy and the Role of the Layman," *Social Forces,* May, 1961, pp. 297–301.

44. Rose Laub Coser, "Insulation from Observability and Types of Social Conformity," *American Sociological Review,* February, 1961, pp. 28–39.

45. William J. Goode, "A Theory of Role Strain," *American Sociological Review,* August, 1960, pp. 483–496; see also his "Norm Commitment and Conformity to Role-status Obligations," *American Journal of Sociology,* November, 1960, pp. 246–258.

46. On all of this, see Merton [23].

47. See Parsons [1], pp. 36–42; Nadel [1], pp. 50–62.

48. Harold B. Gerard has shown that role clarity affects self-perception of effectiveness and concern over the quality of one's performance (concern is high if clarity is low), especially among those who have been assigned low status in an experiment. See "Some Effects of Status, Role Clarity, and Group Goal Clarity upon the Individual's Relations to Group Processes," *Journal of Personality,* June, 1957, pp. 475–488.

49. Goode [45], p. 485.

50. *Ibid.,* p. 489. Some astute observations along this line, although role terminology is not used, are found in Erving Goffman, *The Presentation of Self in Everyday Life,* University of Edinburgh Social Sciences Research Center, Monograph no. 2, 1956.

51. Jackson Toby, "Some Variables in Role Conflict Analysis," *Social Forces,* March, 1952, pp. 323–327. Toby also discusses culturally supported explanations ("It was an accident, I couldn't help it"); etiquette; and legitimate deception (the use of white lies). However, these seem more nearly to be attempts to handle nonperformance of role than to negotiate among conflicting role requirements.

52. Gross, Mason, and McEachern [1], chap. 17.

53. Gross, Mason, and McEachern treat these two variables in terms of the perceptions of an actor. Let me emphasize again that these forces can affect behavior whether or not they are perceived. Perception of a force, to be sure, affects the ways in which it will influence behavior, but it does not determine the influence of that variable.

54. Samuel Stouffer and Jackson Toby, "Role Conflict and Personality," *American Journal of Sociology,* March, 1951, pp. 395–406.

55. Gross, Mason, and McEachern [1], pp. 289–295. See also Howard J. Ehrlich, James W. Rinehart, and John C. Howell, "The Study of Role Conflict: Explorations in Methodology," *Sociometry,* March, 1962, pp. 85–97.

56. Gross, Mason, and McEachern [1], pp. 306–307

57. See Ruth Benedict, "Continuities and Discontinuities in Cultural Conditioning," *Psychiatry,* vol. 1, 1938, pp. 161–167; David Riesman, in collaboration with Reuel Denney and Nathan Glazer, *The Lonely Crowd,* Yale University Press, 1950; Daniel Miller and Guy E. Swanson. *The Changing American Parent,* John Wiley & Sons, Inc., 1958; Margaret Mead, *From the South Seas,* William Morrow and Company, Inc., 1939; Robert R. Sears, Eleanor E. Maccoby, and Harry Levin, *Patterns*

of Child Rearing, Harper & Row, Publishers, Incorporated, 1957, especially pp. 368–376; J. Milton Yinger, "The Changing Family in a Changing Society," *Social Casework,* October, 1959, pp. 419–428; Albert Bandura and Richard H. Walters, *Social Learning and Personality Development,* Holt, Rinehart and Winston, Inc., 1963; Eleanor E. Maccoby, "The Choice of Variables in the Study of Socialization," *Sociometry,* December, 1961, pp. 357–371; Beatrice B. Whiting (ed.), *Six Cultures: Studies of Child Rearing,* John Wiley & Sons, Inc., 1963.

58. Benedict [57].

59. See Samuel A. Stouffer *et al., The American Soldier,* Princeton University Press, 1949, vol. 1, pp. 389–390; Morris Janowitz, *Sociology and the Military Establishment,* Russell Sage Foundation, 1959, pp. 44–63 and 88–92; Charles E. Bidwell, "The Young Professional in the Army: A Study of Occupational Identity," *American Sociological Review,* June, 1961, pp. 360–372; and Sanford M. Dornbusch, "The Military Academy as an Assimilating Institution," *Social Forces,* May, 1955, pp. 316–321. Erving Goffman makes a number of interesting observations on the interactions of self and system when new roles are being learned in *Asylums,* Doubleday & Company, Inc., 1961. Many processes far more severe than those involved in "making a soldier" have functionally similar steps of weakening or destroying one role relationship and establishing another. Some of the results, both intended and unintended, of concentration and prisoner-of-war camps, for example, can be interpreted in this way. I shall discuss them in Chapter 8.

60. Southall [13].

61. Nadel [1], p. 69.

62. Elizabeth Bott, "Urban Families: Conjugal Roles and Social Networks," *Human Relations,* vol. 8, 1955, pp. 345–384.

63. *Ibid.,* pp. 347–348. Note that Bott is using the term "network" differently from the way I have used it above. She is dealing with a network of persons, not of positions.

64. *Ibid.,* pp. 371–372.

7

Personality, Character, and the Self

No concept is more important to a behavioral science than that of personality. And none is more difficult to develop in field theoretical terms. Personality can well be thought of as the central concept, the area where all the sciences of man meet; but if this point of view is adopted, personality must be defined in such a way that the several factors studied by the various disciplines are brought to bear upon it.

One can readily find hundreds of definitions of personality,[1] and these vary so widely that classification is difficult. Disregarding most of the variations for the moment, however, we can roughly divide the definitions into those which refer to processes and structures inside the individual and those which refer to behavior. Valuable use can be made of either of these types of definition, provided the limitations imposed by a given concept are accepted. But many theorists have been unwilling to do this.

For example, the point of departure for many psychologists is personality as the internal tendency system: that which "lies *behind* specific acts and *within* the individual" (Allport), "the more or less stable and enduring organization of a person's character, temperament, intellect, and physique" (Eysenck). Yet Allport says in another place: "The systems that constitute personality are in every sense *determining tendencies*" (his italics); and the last phrase of the sentence from Eysenck states, ". . . which determines his unique adjustment to his environment." [2] It is exceedingly difficult, after adopting an internal definition, to hold to an abstract conception and to avoid the temptation to think of behavior as being determined by personality. Thus Child states: "For the present discussion, personality will be defined as comprising consistencies of individual differences in behavior which are internally determined. In substance, this agrees with much recent usage, such as that of Allport and Eysenck." [3]

Other students of personality prefer a behavioral definition: "Personality is considered here as a flowing continuum of organism-environment events." [4] It is the totality of behavior during a lifetime.[5] ". . . personality is the relatively enduring pattern of recurrent interpersonal situations which characterize a human life." [6] The problem in this kind of definition is the tendency, on the part of some who use it, to blur the *analytic* distinction between individual and situation, rather than simply to emphasize their empirical interaction. There is an inclination to assume a one-to-one relationship between individual tendency and social norms, or to infer the structure of the inner tendency system directly from observation of behavior. Sanford believes these difficulties have characterized many developments in field theory:

Lewin's field theory started out as a purely psychological theory. Behavior was to be understood as a result of the interplay among factors in the person and in the psychological environment. But much of the experimental work that has proceeded from this orientation has tended to smudge over the boundaries between the psychological and the objective or nonpsychological environments or to assume that the relations between them were one to one. In addition, since factors in the objective environment were much easier to get hold of than those in the person, the experimental work has tended to accent the former and neglect the latter, sometimes even reducing the person to a "point region." [7]

This is a useful warning from a writer whose own work and perspective have made him particularly alert to the inner structure of the person. It is perhaps more useful when field theorists themselves demonstrate their awareness of the requirements of a field perspective. Thus Murphy notes that the child slowly achieves an inner organization that enters into the field as one of the causal forces, and throughout his book he emphasizes the significance of the tendency system.[8] And Parsons, who defines personality analytically but stresses its constant interaction with the environment, writes:

My view will be that, while the main content of the structure of the personality is derived from social systems and culture through socialization, the personality becomes an independent system through its relations to its own organism and through the uniqueness of its own life experiences; it is not a mere epiphenomenon of the structure of the society. There is, however, not merely interdependence between the two, but what I call *interpenetration*.[9]

Different definitions of personality are possible, but one must accept the implications of his own definition. If one prefers an intraindividual definition, then personality cannot be used as a direct explanation of behavior, but only as one component in behavior determination. If personality is defined as behavior, it must be treated as a field construct, with full awareness of the facilitating and inhibiting influences of the situation, the tendencies of the individual, and the patterned results of their interaction. If both types of definition are used, whichever one is

intended should be clear beyond doubt in each context. Only confusion
has come both from the tendency to define personality in intraindividual
terms while using it to account directly for behavior, and from the opposite tendency to define it as behavior while using it to infer, or to
minimize the importance of, inner structure.

No one who has read this far will be surprised to learn that I prefer, for
what I believe are sound theoretical reasons, a behavioral definition of
personality. Personality is the totality of the behavior of an individual with
a given tendency system, interacting with a sequence of situations. This is
scarcely more than a restatement of Murphy's definition given above. It
suggests the range, the variation in behavior, and the extent of the personality's involvement with the environment, thus calling attention to part
of the common-sense meaning of the term. When we say, "That is his
personality," our judgment is based on observed behavior in certain
settings. If we see the same person in an unaccustomed setting and behaving differently, we are likely to say, "That's a side of his personality I was
not familiar with." As personae we do not wear the same masks continuously.

The common-sense meaning, however, has another side which is not
covered by a behavioral definition: Individuals have characteristic ways of
behaving that appear over some range of situations; there is continuity as
well as variation. We have all exclaimed at one time or another, "Now
isn't that just like John!" when we have witnessed activity that seems to
demonstrate a persistent tendency even in the face of an apparently unsupporting environment. This is the emphasis in such definitions of
personality as Hilgard's, which refers to the "total of individual characteristics and ways of behaving which in their organization or patterning
describe an individual's unique adjustment to his environment." [10]

Few behavioral scientists deny the importance of the individual tendency system, however they may account for it. If we use the term "personality" for the flow of behavior, therefore, we need another term to
designate what Newcomb calls "the individual's organization of predispositions to behavior." For this I shall use the word "character." The
character of a person is what he brings into the behavioral situation.

Now these are only words, and we can assign them the meanings we
find useful; but they can serve as scientific concepts only if they are used
in a way that clarifies our understanding of nature. There is such a strong
tendency for personality to take on behavioral connotations that it seems
wise to accept this factor in the definition. If we define personality wholly
in intraindividual terms, we tend to reify it, to make it more "real" than
the group or the setting; we tend to assume or to exaggerate consistency,
and to treat personality simply as an independent variable—as the cause
of behavior.

We shall not avoid these difficulties, of course, simply by calling "the
individual's organization of predispositions to behavior" character instead
of personality. But by giving attention to the need for both concepts, we

may avoid more successfully the tendency to "smudge over boundaries," to use Sanford's phrase. The need for both an intraindividual term and a behavioral term is what requires emphasis, not the particular choice of words. There is no difficulty in such a definition as that of Sears: "personality is a description of those properties of a person that specify his potentialities for action," [11] if one holds consistently to its level of abstraction. Many times here I have used and shall use personality in this sense as a synonym for character, where the context permits or where quotation makes it desirable. If the context does not make this clear, however, I shall use personality to mean the flow of behavior. Unlike "character," "personality" has become a central word for all the behavioral sciences. Anthropologists and sociologists as well as psychologists and psychiatrists are deeply involved in personality studies. The word has become in some uses, in fact, almost the symbol of holistic and unified field research; "an adequate personality theory must be a thoroughgoing behavior theory and all theories of behavior must be personality theories." [12]

THE SELF

Character as I have defined it is a complex system, not a homogeneous unit. Full examination of its significance for the student of human behavior requires a description of its internal structure and of its several functions.[13] I shall do that here only with reference to what is perhaps the central unit of character, the self; but this will permit discussion of many issues related to questions of inner structure and function.

No concept dealt with by the sciences of human behavior touches upon more significant issues, yet entails more ambiguities, than that of the self. It is a concept of interest to many philosophers, theologians, and humanists, as well as to social scientists; [14] yet to others in the same fields it is useless or misleading. Psychologists with strong behavioristic leanings believe the whole concept to be at best an unnecessary construct, and at worst a source of pseudo "explanations" of behavior that are purely tautological. Yet other psychologists regard it as an essential, even if slippery, concept and focus their attention upon it. Some sociologists believe that study of the self is wholly outside their discipline, while others in the *Mind, Self, and Society* tradition consider such study to be fundamental. One might hope that the cross-cutting of disciplines with regard to interest in self would lead to helpful confrontation and eventual clarification of concepts; but for the most part the separate groups have moved along in dignified isolation, so far as theory is concerned. Some of the recent research, however, overrides disciplinary boundaries and can help us to explore the value of the self concept for a behavioral science.

Among contemporary psychologists, Skinner is perhaps most vigorous in his assertion that nothing is gained by positing a self (or other inferred characteristics of the individual) as a causal or intervening variable in the study of behavior. He believes that self, or some state of the self (e.g., anxiety) is often used as an "explanation" of behavior when we know no other explanation, but that such concepts melt away when we try to define them operationally. To insert an O (organism) in the $S \rightarrow R$ formula ($S \rightarrow O \rightarrow R$) is to add what Watson called a mystery box, the content of which is "put there" by inferences based on observations of behavior. "The alternative to the use of the concept [of self] is simply to deal with demonstrated covariations in the strength of responses." [15]

The dangers of tautological reasoning that Skinner emphasizes are widely recognized today. The weaknesses in the explanations of behavior that were based on the simple process of assigning a series of instincts to man are not always avoided by those assigning him a self (or an unstable triumvirate of id-ego-superego). The emphasis has shifted, to be sure, from universally shared instincts to partially learned qualities that are to a high degree unique with each individual. But explanation by something "in there" which has been inferred from examination of the very behavior which is then explained thereby is no more satisfactory when the presumed trait is "ego" than when it is "instinct."

The inferences are not wholly arbitrary, of course. They may be based on a wide range of behavior observed over a period of time. Some would add that various projective techniques have enabled us to get "inside" in order to measure; and these techniques do yield tantalizing shadows of inner life that can be shown to have some power of prediction. Response to projective tests, however, is still behavior. It is a mistake, I believe, to think that in using them we have escaped the need for inferring inner structure and can now measure it directly. The proper question is "What can we do with the inferences derived from various processes?" This qualifies Skinner's objections as much as it does users' enthusiasms, for it suggests that the appropriate question is not "Are such concepts as "self" necessary?" but "If one successfully avoids reification, can he use them to improve his power of prediction and understanding?"

Despite the force of the behaviorist argument against self-constructs carelessly used, most of us have an intuitive concept of self that is not easily set aside. Man the language-using animal carries on an almost continuous inner conversation with "himself." The present is filled with past and future, brought there by language. The continuity of our bodies and of many of our roles reinforces our identity. That amazing computer the human brain can store so many "instructions," and produce them on demand, that it is difficult to escape the notion that "somebody" has programmed them very effectively. The concept of a simple recording instrument fails to make sense out of these observations and feelings.

In discussing this question, Gordon Allport contrasts the tradition of Locke with that of Leibnitz—the view that nature is passive (and the individual a *tabula rasa* on which experience writes) with the belief that nature is active. There is nothing in intellect, said Locke, that was not first in the senses. Nothing, Leibnitz replied, except the intellect itself.[16] The first tradition, pressed to an extreme, becomes a mechanistic view of man that makes light of the importance of language as an inner forum, finds the idea of purposive, goal-directed behavior difficult, and in general looks upon the human being in any unitary sense of the term as a dependent variable. The second tradition, pressed to an extreme, so emphasizes the unique qualities of each person and the importance of his purposes in shaping perceptions and selecting among alternatives that cause is seen to reside almost wholly "in" the person.

For half a century or more, the great weight of experimental psychology supported the view that "self" and "ego" and the many smaller motivational concepts associated with them were of little value. The point was more often made by complete disregard than by direct critical attack. In recent years, however, the theoretical influence of psychoanalysis (both Freudian and other versions), the rise of an "ego psychology," and the increasing interest in using the findings of the science of man for clinical purposes, indicate changes in emphasis.

Although the social scientists involved in this new wave of interest in the person are more aware of the scientific dangers of relying heavily on constructs of inferred properties or processes, they have not avoided all such difficulties. In a development which brings the study of personality close to the humanities, research interest in the self shades off into a partially valuative interest in defining or discovering the "real self," "identity," "self-actualization," the "mature" or "autonomous" person. (One thinks readily of Erich Fromm, Kurt Goldstein, Carl Rogers, Gordon Allport, Erik Erikson, Carl Jung, A. H. Maslow, and Alfred Adler in this connection.) Since I share the values from which this concern springs, I do not mean to suggest that this is an unhappy development. Risks are involved, however, in the failure to define scientific and value questions separately.

Some of the work in personality psychology is so closely tied to the existential search for meaning, to the affirmation of the individual in the face of the presumed depersonalizing forces of industrial society, that barriers are imposed on the ways in which questions can be raised. If questions cannot be asked in such a way that we are alerted to the forces at work, they cannot be answered satisfactorily. Yet the deep lament over the crushing of the individual, from Marx and earlier philosophers to those thinkers particularly sensitive to the tragedies of the twentieth century, can easily lead to assumptions about the individual *versus* society. In a day of totalitarian powers, it is not difficult to accept the belief, variously expressed and interpreted by Thoreau, Nietzsche, Freud, Camus, and many others, that society is the enemy of man.

The affirmation by Cooley, for example, that social life can be the source of freedom and expression sounds almost Pollyannaish. In our time, the liberals and the intellectuals typically fight the structures around them as the "cause" of man's difficulties. One of the ways this tendency

expresses itself among many humanists and psychologists is an antisocio-
logical bias, for it is sociology's professional task to call attention to and
study those structures. (People who study a phenomenon are often
blamed for its existence.)

The mixing of evaluation and analysis in some of the writings on the
"self" tends to retard both moral and scientific development of the subject. The propensity to set self against social structures sometimes leads to
utopian rejection of structure. But the state does not wither away; or
traditional structures are broken only to be replaced by peer-group structures scarcely less limiting; or the burden of freedom leads to many efforts
to escape it. An adequate formulation of the relationship of the individual
to society can scarcely be developed on the basis on an a priori assumption
of their essential antipathy. The need, rather, is to ask the prosaic but
central scientific question: What are the conditions under which various
consequences flow from the range of interactions between self and
society?

If the self has been rediscovered by some psychologists, it has never
been lost from sociology, at least among the large number of sociologists
influenced by the Cooley-Mead-Dewey-Thomas approach to the field.
Certainly since *Human Nature and the Social Order* it has been a major
concept. The referent for the word, however, is sometimes quite different
in sociology from what it is in psychology. Not surprisingly, just as a
social dimension often disappears from the meaning of "self" when the
term is used in psychology, so the individual dimension is obscured in
some sociological uses. For these the self appears only as the inner dimension of roles, incapable of being specified independently of relationships
with others. Brim, for example, in stating a basically sociological view of
personality, writes:

> The learned repertoire of roles is the personality. There is nothing
> else. There is no "core" personality underneath the behavior and
> feelings; there is no "central" monolithic self which lies beneath its
> various external manifestations ... the "self" is a composite of many
> selves, each of them consisting of a set of self-perceptions which are
> specific to one or another major role, specific to the expectations of
> one or another significant reference group.[17]

I agree with much in this statement, particularly its opposition to
explanations of behavior on the basis of qualities of individuals alone.
There is, however, a blurring of distinctions among personality, role,
and self that seems to me unfortunate. This point of view emphasizes the
importance of interaction in the determination of self-perceptions, but
Brim fails to make an important distinction: It is one thing to say that the
self *has been built out of* an individual's responses to the actions of others
toward him (an idea so nicely protrayed by Cooley's description of the
"looking-glass self"). It is something else to say that the self *as a contemporary fact* has no organization, no powers of hierarchization of po-

tential experience, no independent influence on behavior. Mead is sometimes ambiguous on this point, but generally he recognized a distinction
between origin and contemporary function. For example:

> The self, as that which can be an object to itself, is essentially a
> social structure, and it arises in social experience. After a self has
> arisen, it in a certain sense provides for itself its social experiences,
> and so we can conceive of an absolutely solitary self. But it is im-
> possible to conceive of a self arising outside of social experience.[18]

This brief commentary may have indicated the range of interpretations
of the concept of the self. Removing the qualifications that most scholars
would use, we can describe three basic approaches in these terms:

1. The concept of a self is unnecessary and harmful to the development of a science of human behavior. It is based on inferences that
cannot be measured. It generally becomes tautological, because it is used
to explain behavior which has already been employed to ascertain the
existence and the presumed qualities of the self. A more parsimonious
approach is to measure behavior directly.

2. The concept of the self is essential to a science of man. It corresponds with our intuitive grasp of experience. It explains consistency of
behavior more readily than alternative concepts. It gives adequate recognition to the unique qualities in each person and to the basic human
capacity for continuous inner activity through thought. In many situations, self is the independent variable that accounts for the sequence of
events.

3. The concept of the self is a valuable link between the individual and
the significant others who surround him. It appears, develops, and expresses itself only in social interaction and cannot be defined or understood, therefore, independently of that interaction. Its major components
are the various role specifications learned in interaction with the significant others in one's experience.

While these conceptions are, to an important degree, mutually incompatible, elements can be drawn from each to design a fourth construct of
self that is harmonious with the field approach of this book and is, in my
judgment, theoretically more adequate than most current usages. From
the first point of view expressed above, we can draw the emphasis on self
as a construct to be used on the basis of its contribution to research. We
can also be alerted to the dangers of circular reasoning in the use of such
a concept.

A strictly psychological approach, as in the second point of view above,
brings recognition of the system properties at the individual level. The
paradoxical fact is that a field view, which in one sense obscures boundaries by designing a multilevel system, at the same time demands analytic
clarity in the specification of separate systems. The self, as I shall use the
term, is an individual fact. It is not, however, the behavior of an indi-

vidual, or the independent cause of his behavior; it is the name for certain qualities of the individual. This distinction is lost in some psychological work. The significance of those qualities for behavior cannot be measured independently of the total field in which they are located.

A strictly sociological approach, as in the third point of view, emphasizes the social origin of those qualities of the individual called self. The self as agent is primarily a role performer and is deeply affected, therefore, by the structure of relationships into which he is bound. These are essential elements in a field view, although the field researcher would also warn against disregarding that which an individual brings into an interaction. Such disregard may spring from a failure to distinguish between the social origin of self and the social context with which self, once formed (or partially formed, since this is a continuing process), interacts.

It is difficult to write a brief definition of self that carries the full range of meanings implied in this discussion. The definition used by Murphy and Newcomb violates none of the criteria of a field term and is a good starting point: "Self . . . refers to the individual as perceived by that individual in a socially determined frame of reference." [19] This is expressed somewhat more fully by Deutsch and Solomon. They define self as the symbolic representations one makes of his various biological, psychological, ethical, and social characteristics.[20]

Lindesmith and Strauss emphasize a different point when they designate self" as (1) a set of more or less consistent and stable responses on a conceptual level, which (2) exercise a regulatory function over other responses of the same organization at lower levels." [21] Thus they introduce the idea of structure into self and suggest the processes whereby some order is imposed on the multiplicity of tendencies that might be brought into a given interaction. Many resources valued by the individual —time, energy, money, etc.—are scarce; selections must be made among alternative ways of spending those resources. One aspect of self, then, is the organizing, regulating process of hierarchization of values. The order of preference is continually being redefined as a result of cyclical and other changes in needs and as a result of the opportunities furnished and costs imposed by others.

The strict behaviorist is not happy with such comments. He is likely to say, "Why not merely indicate that when certain measurable conditions prevail, an observable individual behaves in stated way?" Somewhat uncomfortably—for the danger of reification is great—I would reply that the *construct* of self is a useful shorthand description of consistent orientations toward behavior.

The social behaviorist of the Mead tradition is likely to say that the inferred consistency of self is based on observations of behavior under conditions where continuity of social positions, with their roles, is also an outstanding fact. Unless the "manager of scarce resources" can be shown to produce consistency over and beyond that which one would expect from position continuity, no self concept is needed. This is a valid criticism, or source of redefinition, of the self idea. I shall comment below on some of the efforts to measure possible gains in prediction that come from positing a self construct as one of a series of interacting variables. It is probably more on intuitive than on experimental grounds, however, that I find the concept of self useful in the study of man, the conscious, remembering, valuing, future-planning creature.

Although terminology is highly inconsistent in the literature, I shall use the term "ego" to refer to those "managing" processes of self which attempt to shape events toward maximum need satisfaction in a given physical and social "reality." This is, of course, close to Freud,[22] although I would emphasize the degree to which the managing processes are affected by the context in which they are expressed. For this reason I would modify somewhat Murphy's definition of ego as a "group of activities concerned with enhancement and defense of self." [23] Ego is a group of inner tendencies the outcome of which depends upon a transaction with the outer world.

Ego thus defined is not synonymous with self. The self includes also the ways in which an individual answers to himself the questions "Who am I?" (self concept) and "What do I want to be?" (self ideal). There are numerous demonstrations that the answers to these questions are social products, closely related to the positions one occupies and the "others" with whom one interacts.[24] Nevertheless, as aspects of self, they are individual tendencies, not social facts.

Just as ego, self concept, and self ideal are aspects of self, self is an aspect of character, that total system of tendencies and capabilities of an individual. There is more to character than the reflexive "individual as known to the individual." The self is embedded in a character, and the three processes I have identified with the term "self" are influenced by the system of which they are a part. Tendencies and potentialities of which an individual is completely unaware characterize him no less than the qualities which he can articulate.

On the basis of this discussion, can self be defined in a way that harmonizes with field theory? Self often has antifield connotations (e.g., the self, as an independent force, determines behavior). Full "explanation" by reference to individual motives and decisions is a commonplace of everyday speech and thought: "He dropped out of basketball because he was falling behind in his lab work." I.e., an individual, weighing comparative values, independently arrives at a decision which causes behavior. Nonself values and tendencies that influenced the decision—significant others who helped to determine motivation, for example—are absent from this explanation. No harm may come from such common-sense formulations of the kind of statement illustrated here; but the reification of self as an independent cause can be a great barrier to scientific understanding and clinical work. If we continue to be content, for example, with explanations that our enemies do what they do because of what they "are," or "because" of various motives which they express, we shall neither understand them nor be effective in changing our interactions with them.

In short, self concepts and related motivational concepts are incorporated into a field view only with difficulty. Nevertheless they seem to me to be valuable when properly conceived. By "self" I shall mean those processes by which an individual internally answers the questions: "Who am I?" "What do I want to be?" and "How shall I rank my various desires?" Self, so conceived, is an individual construct; it refers to tendencies; it is largely the product of interaction with others and continues to be closely associated with the positions one occupies; and it has structure, including a hierarchy of desires. It is known only in behavior, and therefore can never be perceived "by itself" but must be inferred from patterns of behavior in different contexts. In research it can be treated as both an independent and a dependent variable; a priori assumptions that it is one or the other are unwarranted.

Basic Questions in a Theory of Self

I shall not undertake a review of the large body of literature dealing with the self, but brief reference to a few studies and commentaries may furnish opportunity for clarifying further the ways in which the concept can be brought within the field view.

The origin of self. On the basis of Mead's insightful formulations, Freud's fundamental work, Piaget's detailed and rich observational studies, and a growing empirical literature,[25] there has developed a picture of the process of the origin of self on which there is substantial agreement. The nature of the process is too well known to require more than minimal statement here. It is not simply that a child can *discover* himself only in the actions of others toward him, much as he can see his face only in a mirror. More than that, the self is *formed* out of the actions of others, which become part of the individual as a result of his having identified with these others and responded to himself in their terms. Retrospectively, one can ask "Who am I?" *But in practice, the answer has come before the question.* The answer has come from all the definitions of one's roles, values, and goals that others begin to furnish at the moment of birth. "You are a boy; you are my son; you are French"; "You are a good boy and fully a part of this group" (with rewards confirming the words); or "You are a bad boy" (with significant others driving the point home by the sanctions they administer). Sometimes one receives highly ambivalent messages about who he is. On one level he is taught that certain goals are evil, while on another level of influence he is encouraged to pursue those very goals. In words, he may be told how good he is and how much he is wanted, although the actions of the speakers may convey more convincingly the idea that he is an unmitigated nuisance.

Simply to state that the self-image is shaped out of the messages sent by others is not enough, however. We need also to ask "What motivates an infant to identify with others?" Traditional learning theory does not raise this question, or raises it in a wholly different fashion. Traditional theory is uncomfortable with the concept of motivation (although the require-ment of some kind of "starter" concept is shown by the introduction of need or drive terms when motive is left out). And such theory's heavy reliance on animal experimentation and the study of single individuals leaves unexplored many critical aspects of the human learning situa-tion.[26] Some of these aspects are the focus of attention in contemporary "social learning" research, however.[27] And much of the vast literature on the family and socialization is relevant to this topic.[28]

The influence of others is vital to the learning process, including the acquisition of a sense of self, because others are essential to survival and need satisfaction or, in Whiting's useful phrase, they are "resource mediators." He uses this concept as a link between learning theory and a social theory of self by showing the concept's implication for identifica-tion. To a child, and to all persons to some degree, resources are available only through the mediation of others. One envies those who have such resources. Identification is not based on this perception alone, however, for so long as the other furnishes him the desired resource, one has the envied status himself; there is no pressure to identify with the other.

It is only when the mother begins to socialize the child, however, and for purposes of controlling him and training him begins to withhold or deprive him of resources, that the process of identification begins. It is then that he perceives that she has more efficient control of re-sources, begins to envy her status, attempts unsuccessfully to perform her role, and ends up with a new kind of fantasy in which he sees himself as the mother, rather than as the child.[29]

By being mother, he can control the resource. Later on, when the child has learned to distinguish between self and other, there is a shift from being mother to pleasing mother, but both desires are part of a continuous process of looking at one's self from the perspective of "resource mediators."

This way of describing the origin of the self fits readily into a field view, although it requires two further ideas, both of which were touched upon but not fully developed by Mead. First, a social theory of mind and self should not lead us to overlook differences in biological starting points. That the structure of self is built in a social process seems highly plausi-ble. This does not mean, however, that variations in intelligence, in other capacities, in biologically influenced thresholds of response do not affect the process. At the present time the possible importance of such individual variations in inheritance for self-formation are as unresearchable as Mead's basic idea. But it seems likely that biological factors are involved. They are given some ambiguous recognition in Mead's concept of the "I," as the emergent aspect of self.

Second, we must recognize that self, as a system of tendencies that have arisen in an individual with certain biological potentialities in interaction with various other people, is not wholly a dependent variable. As the self is formed it begins to act back upon the situation from which it came and upon new situations into which the individual enters. Mead noted this relationship at several points, but did not systematically explore it. Speaking both of mind and self, he wrote:

Once mind has arisen in the social process it makes possible the development of that process into much more complex forms of social interaction among the component individuals than was possible before it had arisen. But there is nothing odd about a product of a given process contributing to, or becoming an essential factor in, the further development of that process.[30]

This point has been carefully developed by Gerth and Mills. Once the self is formed out of the series of previous appraisals and expectations from others, it attains some autonomy. "For the adult, it is more accurate to say that the attitudes and expectations of others facilitate or restrain the self-image." [31] They also note that as a person grows older, there is usually an increase in the "others" who are significant to him and some power to select which others he will interact with. "The image of self which a person already possesses and which he prizes leads him to select and pay attention to those others who confirm this self-image, or who offer him a self-conception which is even more favorable and attractive than the one he possesses." [32] There are important limits to this process, of course. Children can seldom decide in favor of different parents and siblings; jobs, residence, and positions limit the choices of adults. "One avoids as best he can the enemies of the self-images one prizes." And if he cannot avoid them, he defines their significance downward: their opinions do not matter; only the peer group or the close friend counts—"the confirming use of the intimate other," in the words of Gerth and Mills. Or he distorts their opinions in a favorable direction.[33]

Contemporary sources of self-processes. When we shift from questions relating to the origin of self to problems concerning the interaction of self and situation, we come to an area more readily subjected to empirical study. Under what conditions does one downgrade the evaluations of others, for example, if they contradict self-appraisal (operationally defined by some test), and when does one downgrade self-appraisal? Is the alternative one selects a function of the situation (e.g., success or failure), the prestige of the other, or the nature of the original self-image and the total character of which it is a part?

Much of the research on such questions grows out of problems suggested by the concepts of cognitive dissonance, balance, strain toward symmetry, and similar ideas.[34] When self is seen as the independent variable, the researcher hypothesizes that perceptions which produce "imbalance" will be redefined in such a way as to restore balance. Harvey and his associates suggest that the self, along with other systems, has a "tendency toward self-maintenance," [35] as well as a tendency to think less well of one's self when negatively appraised. The former response is shown by the way in which these investigators' subjects protected a given self-image by errors of recall and by downgrading the source of a negative appraisal. The subjects thought less well of the persons who were experimentally made to appear to have rated them poorly; they believed the raters careless or lacking sensitivity; or if the rater was a friend, they believed him angry "for some reason" or less well acquainted with them than the subjects had thought. Persons who had received high "authoritarian" scores were more disposed to protect their self-image.[36]

Under some conditions, initial self-appraisal does not seem to affect the interaction significantly. In a study of 132 women telephone operators, for example, Deutsch and Solomon tested this hypothesis: "If an individual evaluates some aspect of himself (as positive or negative) and another evaluates it similarly, the individual will tend to evaluate the other person favorably; if their evaluations are dissimilar, the individual will tend to evaluate the other unfavorably." [37] This study goes beyond a common tendency to deal only with positive self-evaluation. If the possibility of negative self-evaluation is hypothesized, then dissonance or balance theory can be used to explain such otherwise awkward facts as feelings of discomfort in victory, continuation of practices known to be injurious to health, or the "seeking" of punishment by a child.

Deutsch and Solomon asked their subjects to fill out a self concept scale and then to work on a Gottschaldt concealed-figures test in teams. Some of the subjects were experimentally made to fail, and their group also was failed. Others were made to do better than their failing team, to do poorer than their winning team, or to do well on their winning team. The results showed that self-rating on the test was not a function of initial self-esteem; it rested, rather, on the information given the subjects concerning their presumed comparative performance scores. Those who thought they had succeeded evaluated negative note writers, who were judging their work, negatively; but those who believed they had done poorly rated negative note writers favorably. Those who received positive notes evaluated the rater positively, especially if they had been led to think well of their own performance. Thus a "strain toward symmetry" was involved in the judgments, and self-appraisal was influenced by the experimentally controlled pattern of success or failure; but the initial level of self-esteem did not operate as an independent variable.[38]

Backman and Secord have brought this type of research more fully into a field context by studying the ways in which the interaction process, among individuals with given tendencies, affects the appraisals of self and others. Pressures to eliminate cognitive dissonance, in their view, are best understood not as intraindividual forces but as interpersonal ones.[39] The behavioral outcome of a situation, with respect to stability or change in self-appraisal, is a product first of the interaction between the tendency of self to select confirming others and to perceive their actions as supportive of the existing self-regard, and second of the influence of others (varying with their number, significance, and frequency of support). If dissonance exists between one's self-appraisal and the regard offered by others, harmony can be reestablished by changing self-regard, by disregarding or misperceiving the behavior of others, or by some combination of these two processes. Which process or combination is likely to occur? If the two variables are recorded simply as high or low, there are four possibilities, each with a probable outcome:

Stability of self-regard	Significance of defining others	Probable outcome
High	Low	Dissonance reduced by misperception of others.
Low	High	Dissonance reduced by change in self-regard.
Low	Low	Dissonance disregarded.
High	High	Dissonance unresolvable. Anxiety, withdrawal may result.

For example, a student entering college with an all-A high school record may experience severe incongruity when his college scores begin to come in. If he thinks of himself as a top scholar, and if the number and significance of the persons responsible for the incongruity are low as far as he is concerned, his self-appraisal may change very little: the tests were poor, favorites were rewarded, and the professors are dull anyway. If he is less certain of his scholarly abilities and tends to feel pretty small in the new environment, and if he values the opinions of those who are judging him, he may reduce dissonance by lowering his self-regard. If little of "self" is involved in the scholarly enterprise and the academic part of college life is unimportant, he can shrug off incongruence. The fourth possibility is most problematic: If the picture of his self as a scholar is important and the judgment of others significant, he can neither change the self-image nor disregard the dissonance. There may be efforts to get reassurance that the appraisal is tentative, perhaps even an error; or anxiety, ill-health, or withdrawal may result; but most common, perhaps, is more intense activity along the lines that in the past have been the source of the self-appraisal and of confirmation by others.

Self-appraisal and confirmation by others are not attributes, of course, but variables, and the range of possibilities may better be noted by plotting them on a graph.

Along line AB there is no dissonance; there is a "sale" because both self and others say that they are willing to "buy" such levels of appraisal. At point I, however, the self is asking too much and others are offering too little. Balance can be reestablished by misperception (the causes and long-run consequences of which require careful investigation), as indicated by the arrow pointing from I to C. Or balance can be obtained by the lowering of self-appraisal, as symbolized by the arrow pointing from I to D, or by a mixture of the two processes (I to E).

RELATIONSHIP BETWEEN SELF-REGARD
AND APPRAISAL BY OTHERS

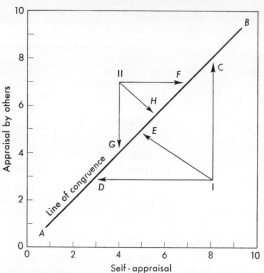

Perhaps we assume too readily that most situations of strain, to use Newcomb's term, fall below the line of congruence; that is, that self-appraisal exceeds the appraisal of others. One does not need to be a psychiatrist of Adlerian persuasion, however, to recognize how often an "inferiority complex" enters into human interaction. Point II symbolizes such a situation of incongruence. Again incongruence can be eliminated by change toward point *F* (increase in self-appraisal, "living up to" the appraisals of others), by a shift to point *G* (lowering the appraisal of others, "seeking punishment"), or by a mixture of the two. The critical task is to specify clearly the conditions under which these various possibilities obtain.

We also need to examine situations in which incongruence persists over a significant period of time and to study the various possible consequences of such persistence. Even though we have good reason to posit *a tendency toward* balance, there is also evidence of persisting imbalance, of incongruence lived with. The danger, in particular, is that students of self may exaggerate the power of "psychological gerrymandering," as Harvey calls it,[40] as a process by which the existing self continually gets "reelected."

The "presentation of self in everyday life" may clash, as Goffman notes, with the definitions of others; "the interaction itself may come to a confused and embarrassed halt." [41] But circumstances may require that the interaction continue despite the clash. I believe that psychosis, for example, *defined interpersonally,* is a process in which persistent self-other differences in appraisal disrupt interaction. The self "cannot" yield (his experience with others having been so capricious and disturbing that only his own definitions, however painful, seem to offer security), and others will not yield (and probably equally cannot) and will not accept his definition of self and the behavior that is related to it.

The problem of identity. Study of the close interaction of self-regard and the appraisals of others leads us readily to the question of identity. The self deals with others, who may support or contradict one's self-image and assist or hinder one's pursuit of goals; and it deals also with nonself tendencies of the individual and with its own lack of coherence. We are multiple selves—not only, as William James long ago noted, because of the different pictures of us that others have (on which they act), but also perhaps because of a lack of clear hierarchization of our own desires.

Probably all persons have had experience with complex choices where the costs and gains are not clearly predictable. (This situation is chronic with the neurotic.) Activity directed toward one goal encounters internal resistance from tendencies toward other goals—a self-splitting experience based on previous caprice, on conflict in definitions, and on other inconsistencies arising from actions of significant others. One cannot be certain of the costs or gains that follow from a choice, because the signals from others are confused or the charges they will make are unpredictable.

If this experience is generalized, if it is continuous, it becomes part of the problem of identity. The term "identity," used so frequently in contemporary thought, has a wide variety of meanings. Perhaps its substance can be suggested by two questions: "What is my social location?" and "What is my dominant self?" These are the outer and inner dimensions of the identity question. "How do others place me?" and "How do I want to be placed?" Because these questions have been asked primarily in connection with examinations of anxiety and alienation, I shall postpone further discussion of them until Part Three. But here let me remark that identity has normal as well as pathological forms. Significant others may agree on one's placement; an individual may feel comfortable with his own answer to the question "Who am I?" And these social and personal statements of identity may be harmonious with each other.

SOCIALIZATION AND SOCIAL CONTROL

At several points I have referred briefly to the concept of socialization, the process whereby those "polymorphous, perverse" little apes are shaped into group members. A detailed examination of the literature on this subject or of the many important questons related to it would take me too far from my central purpose; [42] yet it is essential that socialization be related to a field perspective.

From the point of view of the individual, socialization is the process of learning what will satisfy his needs—what patterns bring rewards or punishments. Since others are deeply involved in the answers to these questions, socialization means learning to view the world as powerful others do. In Freudian terms, it means shifting from a pleasure principle—the search for immediate gratification—to a reality principle in which costs and consequences are weighed. This requires that the child learn to accept many of the definitions of "the good" from those around him. He is nearly helpless and they are powerful; many of his satisfactions are dependent upon them; and in time their very presence and approval become values in themselves.

From the point of view of the group, socialization is the process whereby predictable and acceptable behavior is built into the characters of its members. Group goals cannot be achieved nor interaction guided by mutual expectations unless there are provisions for training new members in the group's values, skills, and standards.

Beginning in the nursery, the process of socialization continues throughout life. Among other things, what must be learned are: the power to inhibit, or to moderate, the expression of unacceptable needs; the ability to transfer cathexis from a prohibited goal-object to an acceptable substitute; the habitual and automatic use of a large number of approved action patterns (methods, manners, and emotional attitudes); and the ability to adapt to schedules (to do things at the proper time, keep appointments, etc.).[43]

On the topic of socialization, as on so many others, one sees a great increase in interdisciplinary work. The highly individualized "child psychology" of an earlier period is now developed with considerable attention to cross-cultural, class, and structural variables.[44] For some time, anthropological discussions of socialization have had psychological and psychoanalytic dimensions; anthropologists are beginning to give attention to structural factors as well. In this connection, Aberle observes: "The task ahead is that of tracing the impact not only of ecological and technological factors, but of economic and political factors on units in which the bulk of childhood socialization occurs—the family in almost all societies, age groups where they are present, and schools in literate societies." [45]

This task is being carried out by such studies as those of Miller and Swanson, who have explored the relationship of socialization practices to the "entrepreneurial" or "bureaucratic" occupational experiences of the parents; Brim's investigation of the effects of family structure on sex-role learning; and Inkeles's examination of the influence of revolutionary change on parent-child interaction.[46] Parsons and his associates have contributed extensively to a field perspective on socialization by systematically relating Freud's interpretation of personality development to patterns of interaction in the family.[47]

I believe that in the last two decades. four isolated traditions of research on questions of socialization have been brought into close interaction. The psychoanalytic account of personality development, child psychology, cultural and cross-cultural studies, and investigations of structural influences on socialization have affected each other in many ways. Although there are gaps and contradictions, something approaching a single theory of socialization is now imaginable.

Perhaps the next major step will be a more adequate formulation of the relationship of socialization to social control. By social control I mean those processes used by society (or a smaller group) in an attempt to ensure normative action even in the absence of conviction on the part of an individual. Social control is a second line of defense.[48] From a field perspective it is important to observe the connections between, as well as the analytic separation of, socialization and social control. Societies may vary in the emphasis given to one or the other, some stressing guilt and others shame, as anthropologists have put it; some depending upon inner-direction, others on other-direction, which is a related distinction.

Every empirical situation, however, exhibits aspects of both socialization and social control. They are best understood in interaction with each other. Which socialized tendencies are expressed in behavior in a given situation depend upon the prevailing reference group in that situation, on the significant others with whom one is interacting, and on the controls these others use to inhibit and facilitate various activities. Conversely, which social controls will be effective depend upon the socialized tendencies of the individuals experiencing them. Only in the limiting case can one predict behavior by knowledge of socialized tendencies alone or means of social control alone.

The interaction of tendency and situation (in the present case, expressed in terms of socialization and social control) is the basic theme of this book and need not, therefore, be discussed at length in this section. But an example of research which explores the problem may be useful here, even though the mutual influence of socialization and social control is not often made the topic of research. In a study of the social control networks among 2,500 high school students, Riley and Cohn noted interaction among the factors of status, individual tendency, and control processes. They discovered a conformity-approving relationship among friends and a deviation-disapproving relationship among "enemies," and emphasized how these two processes worked together in the control network.

In Riley and Cohn's study the effect of group influence on high-status persons was different from the effect on those of low status. the former were in the spotlight and were relatively rigidly controlled. Their tendencies toward conformity were reinforced and their tendencies toward deviation constrained by the responses of others. But low-status persons, who had a higher *ratio* (not a higher absolute number) of "enemies," were treated differently. Their conformity went unnoticed, while their deviation was emphasized. This fact motivated them, among other things, to disidentify with the group, perhaps to identify with an outside group which would reward their deviation. Only by the study of the interaction of group controls and individual tendencies can this full range of events be interpreted.[49]

In summary, the impact of the social controls is a function of the individuals who experience them, and the importance of individual tendencies is a function of the setting in which they are expressed. This interaction raises a number of problems concerning continuity and change of character, problems that permit a further examination of the relationship of socialization to social control. I shall turn to them in the next chapter.

FOOTNOTES

Note: The bracketed number following an author's name refers to the footnote in which the source is cited in full.

1. See Gordon Allport, *Personality,* Henry Holt and Company, Inc., 1937; and Nevitt Sanford, "Personality: Its Place in Psychology," in Sigmund Koch (ed.), *Psychology: A Study of a Science,* vol. 5, *The Process Areas, The Person, and Some Applied Fields: Their Place in Psychology and in Science,* McGraw-Hill Book Company, 1963, pp. 488–592.

2. Allport [1], pp. 218 and 49; H. J. Eysenck, *The Structure of Human Personality,* John Wiley & Sons, Inc., 1953, p. 2.

3. Irvin L. Child, in Koch [1], p. 593.

4. Gardner Murphy, *Personality: A Biosocial Approach to Origins and Structure,* Harper & Row, Publishers, Incorporated, 1947, p. 21.

5. Franz Adler, "A Unit Concept for Sociology," *American Journal of Sociology,* January, 1960, pp. 356–364.

6. Harry Stack Sullivan, *The Interpersonal Theory of Psychiatry,* W. W. Norton & Company, Inc., 1953, pp. 110–111.

7. Nevitt Sanford in Koch [1], p. 529.

8. Murphy [4], pp. 884–885.

9. Talcott Parsons, "Social Structure and the Development of Personality: Freud's Contribution to the Integration of Psychology and Sociology," *Psychiatry,* vol. 21, 1958, pp. 321–340; reprinted in Neil J. Smelser and William T. Smelser, *Personality and Social Systems,* John Wiley & Sons, Inc., 1963, pp. 33–54; quote from p. 35 of latter.

10. E. R. Hilgard, *Introduction to Psychology,* Harcourt, Brace & World, Inc., 1953, p. 407.

11. Robert R. Sears, "A Theoretical Framework for Personality and Social Behavior," *American Psychologist,* August, 1951, p. 480.

12. G. S. Klein and David Krech, "The Problem of Personality and Its Theory," *Journal of Personality,* vol. 20, 1951, p. 11; quoted by Sanford [1], p. 569.

13. Among the many discussions of this question, see Sigmund

Freud, *The Ego and the Id*, The Hogarth Press, Ltd., 1957; Sigmund Freud, *New Introductory Lectures on Psycho-analysis*, W. W. Norton & Company, Inc., 1933, especially chap. 3; Henry A. Murray and Clyde Kluckhohn, "Outline of a Conception of Personality," in Clyde Kluckhohn, Henry A. Murray, and David M. Schneider (eds.), *Personality in Nature, Society, and Culture*, Alfred A. Knopf, Inc., 1953, pp. 3–49; Sanford [1], especially pp. 498–547; Alex Inkeles and Daniel J. Levinson, "The Personal System and the Sociocultural System in Large-scale Organizations," *Sociometry*, June, 1963, pp. 217–299; Smelser and Smelser, [9], pp. 4–8.

14. See John MacMurray, *The Self as Agent*, Faber & Faber, Ltd., 1957; John MacMurray, *Persons in Relation*, Harper & Row, Publishers, Incorporated, 1961; Paul E. Pfuetze, *The Social Self*, Bookman Associates, 1954; and Martin Buber, *I and Thou*, 2d ed., Charles Scribner's Sons, 1958.

15. B. F. Skinner, *Science and Human Behavior*, The Macmillan Company, 1953, p. 286.

16. See Gordon W. Allport, *Becoming: Basic Considerations for a Psychology of Personality*, Yale University Press, 1955, pp. 1–17.

17. Orville E. Brim, Jr., "Personality Development as Role-learning," in Ira Iscoe and H. W. Stevenson (eds.), *Personality Development in Children*, University of Texas Press, 1960, p. 141.

18. Anselm Strauss (ed.), *The Social Psychology of George Herbert Mead*, The University of Chicago Press, 1956, p. 217.

19. Theodore M. Newcomb, *Social Psychology*, Holt, Rinehart and Winston, Inc., 1950, p. 328; based on Murphy [4], p. 996.

20. Morton Deutsch and Leonard Solomon, "Reactions to Evaluations by Others as Influenced by Self-evaluations," *Sociometry*, June, 1959, pp. 93–112.

21. Alfred Lindesmith and Anselm Strauss, *Social Psychology*, rev. ed., Holt, Rinehart and Winston, Inc., 1956, p. 416.

22. "One can hardly go wrong in regarding the ego as that part of the id which has been modified by its proximity to the external world and the influence that the latter has had on it, and which serves the purpose of receiving stimuli and protecting the organism from them...." (Freud, *New Introductory Lectures* [13], p. 106.) For an excellent discussion of this and other Freudian concepts see Philip Rieff, *Freud: The Mind of the Moralist*, The Viking Press, Inc., 1959.

23. Murphy [4], p. 984.

24. See Manford H. Kuhn and Thomas S. McPartland, "An Empirical Investigation of Self Attitudes," *American Sociological Review*, February, 1954, pp. 68–74; Manford H. Kuhn, "Self-attitudes by Age, Sex and Professional Training," *Sociological Quarterly*, January, 1960, pp. 39–56. See also Daniel R. Miller, "The Study of Social Relationships," in Koch [1], especially pp. 670–698; and Leo G. Reeder, George A. Donohue, and Arturo Biblarz, "Conceptions of Self and Others," *American Journal of Sociology*, September, 1960, pp. 153–159.

25. See David A. Goslin, "Accuracy of Self Perception and Social Acceptance," *Sociometry*, September, 1962, pp. 283–296; Martin L. Maehr, Josef Mensing, and Samuel Nafzger, "Concept of Self and the Reaction of Others," *Sociometry*, December, 1962, pp. 353–357; and Morris Rosenberg, "Parental Interest and Children's Self-conceptions," *Sociometry*, March, 1963, pp. 35–49. See also T. R. Sarbin in Gardner

Lindzey (ed.), *Handbook of Social Psychology,* Addison-Wesley Publishing Company, Inc., 1954, vol. I, pp. 238–244.

26. See Skinner [15]; and C. L. Hull, *Principles of Behavior,* Appleton-Century-Crofts, Inc., 1953.

27. See R. R. Sears, E. E. Maccoby, and Harry Levin, *Patterns of Child Rearing,* Harper & Row, Publishers, Incorporated, 1957; Edward C. Tolman in Talcott Parsons and Edward A. Shils (eds.), *Toward a General Theory of Action,* Harvard University Press, 1951 (reprinted as a Harper Torchbook, 1962), part 3; James Olds, *The Growth and Structure of Motives,* The Free Press of Glencoe, 1956; J. W. M. Whiting and I. L. Child, *Child Training and Personality,* Yale University Press, 1953; J. W. M. Whiting, "Resource Mediation and Learning by Identification," in Iscoe and Stevenson [17], pp. 112–126; Allison W. Davis and Robert J. Havighurst, *Father of the Man: How Your Child Gets His Personality,* Houghton Mifflin Company, 1947; and John Dollard and Neal E. Miller, *Personality and Psychotherapy,* McGraw-Hill Book Company, 1950.

28. For value commentaries, see Talcott Parsons and Robert F. Bales, in collaboration with James Olds, Morris Zelditch, Jr. and Philip E. Slater, *Family, Socialization and Interaction Process,* The Free Press of Glencoe, 1955; Eleanor E. Maccoby, "The Choice of Variables in the Study of Socialization," *Sociometry,* December, 1961, pp. 357–371; Urie Bronfenbrenner, "Socialization and Social Class through Time and Space," in Eleanor E. Maccoby, Theodore M. Newcomb, and E. L. Hartley (eds.), *Readings in Social Psychology,* Holt, Rinehart and Winston, Inc., 1958, pp. 400–425; and Urie Bronfenbrenner, "The Changing American Child: A Speculative Analysis," *Journal of Social Issues,* vol. 17, 1961, pp. 6–18.

29. Whiting in Iscoe and Stevenson [17], pp. 119–120.

30. George H. Mead in the Strauss edition [18], p. 259.

31. Hans Gerth and C. Wright Mills, *Character and Social Structure,* Harcourt, Brace & World, Inc., 1953, p. 85.

32. *Ibid.,* p. 86.

33. See Carl W. Backman and Paul F. Secord, "Liking, Selective Interaction, and Misperception in Congruent Interpersonal Relations," *Sociometry,* December, 1962, pp. 321–335; Carl W. Backman, Paul F. Secord, and Jerry R. Pierce, "Resistance to Change in the Self-concept as a Function of Consensus among Significant Others," *Sociometry,* March, 1963, pp. 102–111; and Deutsch and Solomon [20], who, however, note situational influences on self-evaluation. Gordon Allport has expressed something of the same idea in his concept of the "functional autonomy of adult motives" [1], chap. 7; and *Personality and Social Encounter,* Beacon Press, 1960, pp. 140–145). He provides a valuable correction of the belief that the biological "roots" of action account for the final "flowering." But he does not sufficiently take into account the social sources of motivational development, the shared vocabularies which are mutually acceptable in a group as designations of cause and intention, and the situational forces which influence whether one or another motive will be acted upon. See Max Weber, *Theory of Social and Economic Organization,* Oxford University Press, 1947, pp. 98–99. Gerth and Mills [31], chap. 5, have made excellent use of Weber's concept of shared vocabularies in their discussion of motivation.

34. See Leon Festinger, *A Theory of Cognitive Dissonance,* Harper

& Row, Publishers, Incorporated, 1957; Fritz Heider, *The Psychology of Interpersonal Relations,* John Wiley & Sons, Inc., 1958; Theodore M. Newcomb, *The Acquaintance Process,* Holt, Rinehart and Winston, Inc., 1961; and Edward E. Sampson, "Status Congruence and Cognitive Consistency," *Sociometry,* June, 1963, pp. 146–162.

35. O. J. Harvey, "Personality Factors in Resolution of Conceptual Incongruities," *Sociometry,* December, 1962, p. 336. This does not mean, of course, that behavior can be predicted by knowledge of self alone; a physical system can also be thought of as having a tendency toward self-maintenance, and its present action will continue "unless acted upon by some outside force"—that is, unless outside forces are presently acting change. See also O. J. Harvey, Harold H. Kelley, and Martin M. Shapiro, "Reactions to Unfavorable Evaluations of the Self Made by Other Persons," *Journal of Personality,* June, 1957, pp. 393–411; and Thomas S. McPartland, John H. Cumming, and Wynona S. Garretson, "Self-conception and Ward Behavior in Two Psychiatric Hospitals," *Sociometry,* June, 1961, pp. 111–124.

36. Harvey [35].

37. Deutsch and Solomon [20], p. 97.

38. See *ibid.,* pp. 93–112; for other studies of self-regard as a dependent variable affected by the responses of significant others, see Richard Videbeck, "Self-conception and the Reaction of Others," *Sociometry,* December, 1960, pp. 351–359; and Maehr, Mensing, and Nafzger [25].

39. See Paul F. Secord and Carl W. Backman, "Personality Theory and the Problem of Stability and Change in Individual Behavior: An Interpersonal Approach," *Psychological Review,* January, 1961, pp. 21–32; Backman and Secord, [33]; and Backman, Secord, and Pierce [33].

40. Harvey [35], p. 337.

41. Erving Goffman, *The Presentation of Self in Everyday Life,* University of Edinburgh Social Sciences Research Center, Monograph No. 2, 1956, p. 6.

42. For a useful brief summary and bibliography, see William H. Sewell, "Some Recent Developments in Socialization Theory and Research," *Annals of The American Academy of Political and Social Science,* September, 1963, pp. 163–181.

43. Murray and Kluckhohn [13], p. 45.

44. See Sears, Maccoby, and Levin [27]; Eleanor E. Maccoby, "The Choice of Variables in the Study of Socialization," *Sociometry,* December, 1961, pp. 357–371; Irwin L. Child, "Socialization," in Lindzey [25], vol. 2, chap. 18; and Bronfenbrenner, "The Changing American Child: A Speculative Analysis," [28].

45. David Aberle, "Culture and Socialization," in F. L. K. Hsu (ed.), *Psychological Anthropology,* The Dorsey Press, 1961, p. 383. Aberle's essay contains a number of observations on the interaction of structure, socialization, and personality. For extensive use of psychoanalytic and cultural concepts in the study of socialization, see Whiting and Child [27]; and Beatrice B. Whiting (ed.), *Six Cultures: Studies of Child Rearing,* John Wiley & Sons, Inc., 1963.

46. See Daniel R. Miller and Guy E. Swanson, *The Changing American Parent: A Study in the Detroit Area,* John Wiley & Sons, Inc., 1958; Orville G. Brim, Jr., "Family Structure and Sex Role Learning by Chil-

dren: A Further Analysis of Helen Koch's Data," *Sociometry*, March, 1958, pp. 1–16; and Alex Inkeles, "Social Change and Social Character: The Role of Parental Mediation," *Journal of Social Issues*, vol. 11, 1955, pp. 12–23.

47. See Parsons and Bales [28].

48. See Talcott Parsons, *The Social System*, The Free Press of Glencoe, 1950, pp. 297–321; and Parsons and Shils [27], pp. 228–229.

49. See Matilda W. Riley and Richard Cohn, "Control Networks in Informal Groups," *Sociometry*, March, 1958, pp. 30–49.

CHAPTER 8

Continuity
of Character

The preceding chapter noted that the self system emerges out of interaction but that, once formed, it is to some degree an independent influence on behavior. There are evidences of "steady state" processes,
analogous to homeostatic processes in the body, that are designed to
maintain or restore desired situations. To accept the idea of continuity as
essential to the very concept of "system" on the individual level, however,
is not to make it the one overriding principle. It is qualified as a guide to
the understanding of behavior, in contrast to its validity as an analytic
statement, by the application of other principles. The most important
other principle for the purpose here can be suggested in the form of a few
questions: To what degree does the self-system continue to change as a
result of the continuous succession of new experiences, new roles, new
problems that are the stuff of human biography? Is there some decisive
cutting point—at three years of age, at ten, at twenty-one—after which
no "basic" changes occur? Is the self an open system or a closed system?

In exploring these questions from a field perspective, I shall enlarge
them beyond reference to self and return to the more encompassing term
"character," which includes not only "the individual as known to the
individual," but also many inarticulate tendencies beyond awareness that
affect behavior.

Both opponents and proponents of field theory sometimes suppose that
it eliminates or minimizes the idea that character has continuity. They
interpret field attention to the importance of situational influences to
mean that the individual is a creature of all the outside forces playing
upon him at a given moment. His tendencies are so numerous and so
lacking in structure that the facilitating and inhibiting forces of the environment become the crucial variables. In emphasizing the ahistorical
nature of science, for example (only those influences at work in the
contemporary field can affect behavior; their histories are not directly
relevant), Lewin challenged the importance of a genetic approach to

personality and thus seemed to minimize the importance of continuity. A careful statement of field theory, however, does not in fact deny continuity. Such a formulation does require a reinterpretation of the concept.

Certainly field theory challenges the supreme importance of experiences in infancy and childhood as determining forces in behavior. Whether it be William James's idea of individual habit as "the enormous fly-wheel of society," Freud's conception of basic character structure, or the emphasis of much contemporary learning theory on the canalization of response through reward and punishment—presumably to the end of stable response patterns—any theory that focuses on internal forces operating independently of the present context seems inadequate. Yet each of these points of view can be made consonant with a field approach. When habits, character structure, or canalized responses are interpreted as a readiness to act, not as behavior, they need not clash with a field view. If it is true that an individual never behaves in a vacuum, it is equally true that the sociocultural and physical environments never call out behavior in a tendency-free individual. But in making this observation, we need to remember that in each person's tendency system there are multiple possibilities, only some of which a given situation will promote. One tendency may have greater salience than another and yet be expressed in behavior less often because of the balance of barriers and facilities in the situation.

When he described the ahistorical quality of science, Lewin did not deny the significance of past events. He simply noted that they could be significant for behavior only insofar as there were precipitates of these events in present tendencies.[1] Stated in this way, the extent of tendency continuity becomes an empirical problem for investigation. Surely there are good grounds for hypothesizing substantial continuity of character. The bringing of the past into the present through memory, the continuity of the body, the very meaning of "self" and the insightful if not definitive construct of self-consistency—all suggest the usefulness of the idea that there is continuity. This is not the same thing as hypothesizing continuity of behavior. A consistent character can have diverse tendencies (it is consistent in its diversity); and because of changing situations, behavior may vary even when there is a great deal of individual continuity. (Conversely, behavior may remain quite consistent, owing to continuity of roles and situational influences, even if the tendency system of an individual has changed extensively.)

Clinical insight into the way a person with neurotic tendencies clings to his symptoms, evidence that prejudices often persist even in the face of powerful challenging facts, knowledge that propaganda messages can be twisted by a perceiver to support his established views, and the vivid impression that most persons have of a strong lifeline connecting them with their own past, all support the idea of continuity. For each such supporting item, however, contrary evidence also exists: neurotic symptoms sometimes change or disappear, prejudices shift or are eliminated, communications may change attitudes, and individuals sometimes have the pleasant or unpleasant sense of drastic changes in themselves.

Slowly we are learning some of the conditions which produce these various outcomes. Most of the research on this problem, however, deals with comparatively short-run processes that are subject to some experimental controls. The relatively few efforts to measure personality consistency over long periods of time face the great difficulty of sorting out the effects of situational continuity or change operating on the individual during the same period. Strong, for example, has reported a correlation of .75 for vocational interests of college seniors after twenty-two years.[2] Since most of the persons tested were probably participants in relatively stable occupational structures during those years, however, the significance of his finding for a theory of personality continuity is not clear. It is possible that persistent vocational interests are simply a dependent variable reflecting the influence of occupational structure. It is also possible, of course, that occupational choice and continuity are the dependent variable, reflecting the influence of the individual variable. Or both of these things may be true.

Perhaps the most extensive study of consistency of adult character has been reported by Kelly. The first data were secured from 300 engaged couples between 1935 and 1938, with complete test-retest data on 176 men and 192 women between 1952 and 1954. The following statistically significant changes occurred on the various personality measures: [3]

	Men	Women
Allport-Vernon scale of values (6 measures)	3	2
Remmers's generalized attitude scale (6)	5	4
Strong vocational interest scores (11)	3	2
Various Bernreuter and Strong personality measures (5)	1	2
Self-ratings (10)	4	4

Thus out of the total of 38 measures, there were significant shifts for one or both sexes in 18. The magnitude of the shifts was small, with men and women generally changing in the same directions. Looking at the same data from a different perspective, we find that the various test-retest correlations (coefficient of determination) after twenty years were: Values, 48 per cent; vocational interests, 45 per cent; self-rating, 31 per cent; other personality variables, 30 per cent; and attitudes, 8 per cent. (Short-term reliability measures for the various tests had ranged from 70 to 80 per cent.)

As Kelly notes, these results can be used to support many different theories of personality. They do not argue for an impressive continuity; yet they do give evidence of stability. In Kelly's judgment, "the potentiality, yes even the probability of this amount of change during adulthood is considerably greater than would be assumed from any of the current theories of personality." [4] Difficult questions of reliability are, of course, involved in the use of tests after the passage of a long period of time, but Kelly's judgment seems well supported by the facts.

Many would argue, however, that in addition to the problem of the reliability of the instruments, the degree of change revealed in Kelly's research is a result of the fact that he was measuring easily verbalized aspects of character and missing the "deeper" layers. In their study "Personality under Social Catastrophe," Allport, Bruner, and Jandorf observe:

Very rarely does catastrophic social change produce catastrophic alterations in personality. Neither our cases nor such statistics as are available reflect any such number of regressions, hysterias, or other traumatic neuroses as the gravity of the social crisis might lead one to expect. On the contrary, perhaps the most vivid impression gained by our analysts from this case-history material is of the extraordinary continuity and sameness in the individual personality.[5]

The data presented by Allport, Bruner, and Jandorf can scarcely be said to support this conclusion unambiguously. They themselves report changes in political views, great increases in anxiety and feelings of insecurity, many expressions of resignation, heightened in-group feelings, shifts in levels of aspiration, changes in philosophy of life, and other modifications. The authors tend, however, to explain such behavioral changes as ways of making character change unnecessary—a theory-protecting interpretation that requires more independent evidence than it gets. From the data presented, one might as readily conclude that the very process of protecting some aspects of character from change in a drastically changed setting seems to require that other character tendencies be modified. In some instances, moreover, the subjects in the study experienced heightened family and other group support (which is a structural condition promoting continuity of character), and not simply catastrophic social change.

Granted these problems of interpretation, Allport, Bruner, and Jandorf's evaluation of "the extraordinary continuity and sameness in the individual personality" seems difficult to accept. Moreover, their case material was drawn from 90 life-history documents out of over 200 that were submitted in response to an announcement of a prize competition. It would seem pertinent, before speaking confidently about the effects of catastrophe on personality, to know something about the 110 or more unanalyzed documents, the life stories of the thousands of other escapees from Nazism who did not enter the contest, and the millions more who opposed or accepted Nazism within Germany. An examination of the full range, from martyr to Storm Trooper, would reveal not only continuity in the face of crisis but also some deep-going changes.

In summary, it is necessary to speak tentatively on the question of continuity, because a definitive test of character continuity is difficult to design. But persons of widely differing theoretical perspectives may agree substantially on these propositions: Individuals vary in the extent to which they experience character change as adults; some are "chameleons" and some are "beavers," to use Eugene Lerner's terms, and most are in between. Societies vary in the proportions of chameleons and beavers they produce, or in the extent to which they promote inner- and other-directedness, in Riesman's terminology. Some aspects of character are more malleable than others; judgments may change more readily than opinions, opinions more readily than attitudes, attitudes than values, and values than self-image—to put the issue in overly simple terms. Character changes are least likely to occur when the group structures in which the individual is involved remain stable.

CONTROL OF BEHAVIOR AND CHANGE OF CHARACTER

These last sentences suggest a field orientation to the question of continuity and change; but we need a body of evidence on which they can be tested. Perhaps the most stringent test can be found in the study of the efforts in recent years to manipulate human beings. These efforts have ranged from verbal communications designed to change opinions and closely linked actions, to major campaigns to "brainwash" military captives and to transform their basic values, allegiances, and self-identity. While most branches of the psychology of personality and of psychoanalysis stress continuity of character, some recent interpretations of propaganda and manipulation emphasize the power of outside agencies to control the individual. Looking at "turncoats" and "unduly cooperative prisoners of war" from a perspective shaped by such commentaries as *Brave New World, Animal Farm,* and *The Hidden Persuaders,* many persons are convinced that human beings are quite easily manipulated. There is an implication of "lack of" character (i.e., little continuity), or lack of a hidden resister to counter the persuader.

With this problem, as with so many issues, assumptions and limiting theoretical positions can prevent us from asking the critical question in the most fruitful way. On the most general level, this question is: What are the conditions which determine the extent to which efforts at manipulation will produce character change and/or behavioral change? An adequate theoretical formulation must be relevant to the extreme cases, from the benevolent manipulations of the psychiatrist to the malevolent manipulations of an enemy commander. But a theory based on such cases alone will almost certainly miss key variables and thus cannot be parsimoniously extended to account for less extreme situations. A good starting point for study is with the ordinary efforts at control through symbolic means which we call propaganda. These have an additional advantage in that they can be experimentally tested in a more rigorous fashion than extreme control efforts.

It is not always clear whether measurement of the effectiveness of control through symbolic manipulation is concerned simply with behavioral changes, or whether some character changes—attitudes and values, for example—are also under study. A commercial propagandist is primarily interested in behavior, in the purchase of goods; even negative opinions, if they become the subject of conversation ("Did you ever see such an awful ad?"), may support the desired behavior. This is probably an unusual situation, however. More commonly, propagandists attempt to influence character as well as behavior. A politician wants to persuade his hearers not only to vote correctly, but to develop the values and attitudes that will make his task easier the next time. Certainly the student of propaganda must be keenly aware of the relationships of behavioral change to character change. Unfortunately, most research designs make this difficult. The effect of a brief stimulus—a movie to reduce prejudice, for example—is often measured by changes in verbal behavior, with opinion change inferred. If changes persist over a fairly long period of time, the inference is strengthened; but design problems (sensitization to the experimental variable by the pretest, consistency responses, and the like) [6] associated with the measuring process reduce confidence in the findings.

I am concerned at this point, however, not with specifically methodological problems, but with a designation of the variables that require attention. They are more numerous than is apparent from theories which emphasize either continuity or persuasibility. For example, some early research showed that a communication which aroused fear was more effective than a rational appeal. The implication was, of course, that all other things were equal. But for such an analytic statement to be helpful in explaining behavior, the qualifying conditions need to be specified. Some of those conditions can be stated in propositional form:

Fear-arousing messages increase anxiety and lead to their acceptance more readily than rational messages.

> Except that, if anxiety is already high, such messages may reduce it by making it more specific, thus reducing their effectiveness.

>> Except that a communicator believed to be ill-informed or biased will not reduce anxiety and will be believed less than an expert or neutral source.

>>> Except that, when subjects are tested four weeks later on their recall of the messages, the message of the biased source may prove to be as effective as the expert source.

This is far from a complete listing of the necessary propositions,[7] but it illustrates the required addition of variables to the original "message" variable. Who is sending the message and who is receiving it must also be investigated.

In field theoretical terms, the basic question in communication research can be stated briefly: How effective is a given *message,* conveyed by a designated *communicator,* received in a specified *situation,* by an *individual* with certain tendencies, interacting in a particular *group?* As Schramm, Klapper, and others have pointed out, most communicators control only one or two of these factors and thus are far from controlling the result.[8] Neither the behavioral outcome nor possible changes in tendencies of the individual can be fully understood without reference to all the factors. The organization of the message (degree of repetitiveness, presence or absence of counterarguments, location of strongest arguments, etc.), the qualities of the communicator ("Is he an expert? A stranger? Is he skilled?"), the nature of the situation ("Is there a war? Do surrounding experiences confirm the message?"), the tendencies of the individual ("What are his values, fears, condition of health, prejudices?"), and the group context ("Is the message received among peers? Is it received by opinion leaders who pass it out horizontally through the group?")—all of these affect the outcome.[9]

A field approach to questions of communication and persuasion does not contradict analytic research aimed at isolating separate factors. Field theory calls attention to the level of abstraction on which such research works, however, and emphasizes its incompleteness as a source of behavioral predictions. This limitation is sometimes overlooked. In *Personality and Persuasibility,* for example, Janis and Hovland report on a series of studies designed to locate the quality of "persuasibility" in a person, presumably regardless of the content of messages, the media of communication, the communicators, or any other situational factor. They are looking for what they call the "unbound" trait of persuasibility:

> Unbound persuasibility factors, on which this volume is primarily focused, involve a person's general susceptibility to many different types of persuasion and social influence. We assume that these factors operate whenever a person is exposed to a persuasive communication and that they do not depend upon the presence or absence of any given type of content or on any other specifiable feature of the communication situation. Thus unbound factors are communication-free, and this differentiates them from even the most general of the bound factors.[10]

High persuasibility seems to be related to low self-esteem, a need for social approval, and a tendency toward projection.

For the most part the editors and the authors of the research reported on in the volume are alert to the qualifications needed in the use of a construct of an "unbound" trait. They think of it as one factor which, when carefully measured, may aid prediction of behavior under some conditions. Arthur Cohen notes, for example, that "social conditions within which pressure is strong might move everyone in the direction of intended influence, regardless of differences in personality; where pressure is weak and few explicit demands are made on the person, relevant personality characteristics might make for greater differences in behavior." [11]

The very search for an "unbound" trait, however, makes it difficult to hold to this perspective. Such a construct is not readily made part of a general theory of behavior concerned, as in the present case, with the question: Who will accept which messages from whom in what context? Research dealing with high school students responding to communicators from a relatively familiar range in an accustomed setting may isolate apparent individual differences; from these may come inferences of trait variation. Attempts to use the trait variable to predict behavior in more diverse situations, however, are likely to prove inadequate. How "persuasible" is the person with a high score if the message comes, for example, from his little brother or a sixth grader? How unpersuasible are the low scorers when they know that persons with strong powers of reward and punishment will see the responses? Some of the hypotheses in *Personality and Persuasibility* are borne out only because conditions in the studies varied over a narrow part of the imaginable range of messages, media, and communicators, and because the authors isolated those persons for study who tend to be persuaded by a wide variety of communicators or messages.

Let me put the argument in mathematical terms. Assume that a score of 24 or more will produce persuasion of a given individual by a given message in a particular situation. Assume further that individuals vary from 0 to 10 in persuasibility tendency (not an "unbound" trait) and that situations (the message-communicator complex) also vary from 0 to 10 in possible influence. Persons with a persuasibility score of 8 will be persuaded by all situations with a score of 3 or higher, but those with a score of 3 will be persuaded only by communications with an influence score of 8 or higher.[12]

Hovland, Janis, and their associates, by discovering persons with a high tendency score, could afford to disregard message content, medium of communication, and other situational aspects, and still get good prediction, because a large proportion of situations would have the requisite influence. A fairly simple concept often seems quite good when applied to extreme cases. (Paradoxically, a simple opposite theory may seem equally good. I suspect a Durkheim could develop a usable theory of "situation and persuasion," disregarding individual differences entirely.) A sterner test of a theory's adequacy, however, is whether it can be used to interpret the behavior of persons along the whole range of tendencies toward persuasibility. For such a task, what is needed is not the isolation of presumed traits, but the specification of the conditions under which various tendencies are expressed.

Persuasibility or conformity on one hand and independence on the other do not constitute a simple dichotomy. The two qualities, to be sure, can be defined separately: Independence is the persistence of a tendency over a wide range of differing situations; conformity is behavior that corresponds to group influences rather than to the individual's previously expressed preferences. Any given action, however, is likely to have qualities both of conforming and of independence. Lionel Trilling has remarked that many of us admire both nonconformity and community, so that we decide "we are all nonconformists together." This is reminiscent of Sapir's comment that fashion is the result of the effort to satisfy two opposite desires: one wishes to stand out, to be unique and independent; yet one wishes also to belong, to share the security of group identity. The variations in fashion which carry the impression of individual choice, but are kept within the bounds of group definitions, allow one to pursue these contradictory desires with a feeling of "adventurous safety." [13]

Virtually every action is simultaneously independent and conformist when viewed against the multiple standards and group memberships affecting an individual. By behaving in accordance with the standards of one group, we express independence of another. Jahoda has suggested that we should not speak of independent persons, but only of independent actions. I would go one step further and say we should speak only of independent actions with reference to stated groups and standards. The question then becomes: Under what conditions will a particular pattern of independence-conformity prevail instead of some other pattern? The size and authority position of the group, the reference groups salient for an individual in a given context, and the issues involved will all affect the outcome. There are individual variables as well—the level of self-confidence, degree of anxiety, and feelings of acceptance, for example. Jahoda believes that the "degree of investment" in a problem may be a critical variable. What does an individual care about; what is most important for his self-esteem? Issues that one cares a great deal about are likely to be interconnected with many other issues and to involve a long time span. The research task is to scale the several variables, isolate those with greatest explanatory power, and study their mutual influence.[14]

MANIPULATION UNDER "TOTAL" CONDITIONS

In the last several decades, there have been many attempts to control human beings that have gone far beyond the symbolic techniques of persuasion. Systematic efforts to crush resistance and to remake the value hierarchies of individuals in concentration camps and prisoner of war camps provide a severe, and abhorrent, test of the degree to which persons can be manipulated.[15] Difficult problems are involved in the interpretation of the evidence, for it can be viewed in several different ways. An observer who is convinced that the character of an individual is a fairly stable organization of traits, the result of early experience acting upon a unique inheritance, will see drastic changes as temporary products of unusual situations. The "real" personality will reappear when conditions return to "normal." From the perspective of field theory, this is an inadequate formulation. If earlier tendencies manifest themselves again when an agency of manipulation is removed, the reason is not only because they have remained in the person, but also because the situation that encourages them has returned. To say, "It seldom snows here," is fundamentally different from saying, perhaps with the local chamber of commerce, "Our H_2O will return to its natural state as soon as this unusual weather disappears." Crystals *are* the natural state of H_2O under low-temperature conditions. This is not a radical situationalist statement, for the potentialities of H_2O are as thoroughly involved in the outcome as the environmental conditions are. Glycerine, for example, does not form into white crystals when the temperature drops.

The influence of factors from every level is nowhere more clearly shown than in the efforts to manipulate human behavior. Biochemical, characterological, cultural, and interactional forces, in various combinations, are involved. Each of these, in their extreme manifestations, can account for great changes in behavior. Under conditions of extreme sleep deprivation, fatigue, illness, and hunger, for example, a person may confess to "germ warfare" even if the forces of character, culture, and group structure are largely opposed to such confession. Or, under conditions of extreme group deprivation—when patterns of mutual support are broken up by removal of opinion leaders, by limiting "information" to that furnished by the captors, by arousal of in-group suspicion, by the manipulation of rewards for "informing," and the like—even persons in good physical health, with clear values and normal "ego functioning," may waver. In most circumstances, however, no one factor is of sufficient power to produce major shifts in behavior.

Substantial evidence is available indicating the importance of each level of influence. Brain function can be seriously impaired by disturbance of the balance of organic and inorganic substances necessary to its working.[16] Isolation, fatigue, and loss of sleep have been experimentally, as well as observationally, shown to be capable of drastic effect on brain function.[17] There are, of course, important individual variations in susceptibility as a result of constitutional or character differences, or both; but overwhelming deprivation overrides these differences. As Hinkel says: "Disordered brain function is indeed easily produced in any man. No amount of 'will power' can prevent its occurrence. It can be produced without using any physical means, that is, by fatigue or sleep deprivation. Since it may be associated with mental clouding, confusion, lack of discrimination, impaired judgment, and increased suggestibility, it is probably true that most men can be brought to a state where they will agree to statements that are dubious, incomplete, or quite inaccurate." [18]

In all but the most extreme situations, the biochemical influences on behavior are mediated by the character of the individual and the interpersonal setting. The effect of drugs, for example, is influenced by the status of the administering person, the motivations and other tendencies of the recipients, and the definitions and interpretations of significant others.[19] Hill and his associates found that the effects of morphine and pentobarbital on visual reaction time could actually be reversed by manipulating the incentives; thus an explanation of their effects based on biochemical concepts alone would have been misleading.

Viewing the individual as a system, we can note that resistance or susceptibility to influence varies with his knowledge of the issues, reactions to pain, level of anxiety, degree of commitment, extent of self-confidence, and other characteristics.[20] But these characteristics do not operate independently. The level of self-confidence, for example, is doubtless a function of the group with whom one is interacting, on one hand, and the state of the organism on the other.

Sociocultural factors also influence the extent to which individuals can be persuaded or manipulated. There is some evidence that Turkish soldiers captured during the Korean War were less easily influenced than American captives. This may have been due to more intensive efforts on the part of the Chinese to control their American captives, but it may also indicate greater consensus among the Turks on the role "soldier," the greater value placed on "toughness" in their culture, and their greater acceptance of the war. Structural factors were intertwined with such cultural influences. The Chinese Communists in some camps systematically destroyed the group structure among prisoners: leaders were removed, informers rewarded, and a sense of alienation from home support promoted by allowing only unhappy letters to come through. Individuals who are cut off from the sustaining influence of familiar groups are more easily manipulated.[21] Here again, however, both character and organism influenced the impact of the group factor. Loss of group support for a person with strong mental imagery, strong convictions, and reasonably good health has different consequences from loss of support for an individual who lacks self-confidence and suffers from serious fatigue or hunger.

To put the field perspective on this question in mathematical terms, imagine three scales, ranging from 0 to 10, representing the biochemical, individual, and group forces. (Culture is represented both by internalized norms and by its influence on group structures.) Assume that no one of these forces is sufficient by itself to produce major changes in behavior, although each may be dominant under some circumstances. Assume further that a "score" of 50 indicates a situation where major change is likely, e.g., accepting the rules and even the legitimacy of the guards in a concentration camp or confessing to bacteriological warfare. Assume finally that the factors are multiplicative, not additive—a mathematical expression of their interaction. They could then be put together as shown in the following chart.

Several types of situation might occur as a result of various combinations of these three forces. In situation *A*, relatively stable persons with their group structures intact experience the "normal" hunger, fatigue, and sleeplessness attendant upon life as a captive and undergo no significant character change. (Their score is only 20—5 × 2 × 2.) In situation *B*, the same individuals experience some loss of group support and a major increase in disturbance of biochemical processes, perhaps as a result of semistarvation or administration of drugs. Under such conditions, the score of 72 (9 × 2 × 4) is above the critical point of 50. Among particularly vulnerable individuals, major changes may occur under less severe conditions of deprivation even if group supports remain strong, as suggested in situation *C* (5 × 8 × 3). And finally, there may be circumstances in which relatively stable persons are subjected to medium-severe conditions of hunger and sleeplessness but face a major attack on the supports derived from their usual groups, as indicated in situation *D* (4 × 2 × 8).

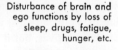
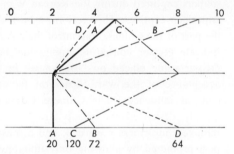

These arbitrary figures are at best rough approximations, of course. The various relationships may be curvilinear, not linear; and the variables may require different ranges, rather than equal maximums of 10. Present knowledge of behavior under conditions of severe deprivation, however, makes these seem to be reasonable assessments.

Collaboration or Conviction

I shall not survey here the extensive literature bearing on the question of conformity and manipulation. It ranges from experimental studies of the effects of loss of group support, isolation, or sleep deprivation to intensive interviewing and participant observation. There remain major problems of distinguishing between long-lasting changes in character and behavioral changes that represent an adjustment to new circumstances without changes in inner tendency. Such a distinction requires reliable observations at different times, with situational influences controlled—a difficult design to achieve.

My own inclination—or theoretical bias—would be to assume that every behavioral adjustment has *some* effect on tendency, that motive follows action as well as action following motive. The task is to discover the conditions under which the residue of action in the tendency system is slight or great. Duration or frequency of a response—even if at first it is purely collaborative—seems likely to be important. The degree to which a pattern of action ties an individual into new structures, with their systems of reinforcement, is involved.

A prisoner of war who agrees to participate in a discussion group out of boredom or in an effort to escape punishment may find himself drawn in more and more deeply and reciprocally more cut off from his original group.[22] Although the evidence is somewhat contradictory, the extent of individual involvement—through discussion, seeking out information on one's own, presenting a point of view in oral form, etc.—appears to affect the extent to which a new influence survives the original situation.[23] Once established, a new tendency, can have cumulative effect even if the individual returns to his former situation, because he will be sensitive to stimuli which he had earlier disregarded. "Sleeper" effects in propaganda or other attempts to manipulate behavior derive from the fact that under some conditions an original stimulus leads to additional reading, to choice of different friends, to association with different groups than would have been the case without the original message. The effect may be more than a "sleeper" (that is, delayed); it may also be multiplied. A young person influenced by attendance at a conference on "race relations" to take one step can be drawn into groups and sensitized to literature that make further steps likely. Thus action and motive become reciprocally reinforcing.

In the study of the distinction between surface conformity and character change, we must recognize the need for measurement of unintended as well as of intended consequences. The Chinese Communists during the Korean War were notably unsuccessful in their manifest intent—to win converts to their cause among their captives.[24] This is by no means the same thing as saying, however, that the prolonged and intense experiences associated with capture and life in the prison camps had no long-lasting effects on the values, motives, and inclinations of the men involved. Evidence on such effects is lacking,[25] but the latent consequences of life in the somewhat similar circumstances of prisons or racial segregation have been much observed. Racial segregation, of course, begins to influence a child as a socially perceived fact before he has formed a stable system of tendencies, so that the perception affects the very process of self-formation and not simply the processes of re-formation.[26] But this complication does not enter into the study of prisoners, who become skilled at minimum collaboration while resisting character change in the officially designated ways, although they often change extensively in unintended ways. They may become bitter, revengeful, or more intent upon crime than they were before they were sent to prison.[27]

We can also gain insight into the question from study of more limited efforts to break down the self-system and to build a more compliant person with different values. These range from fraternity hazing, to the stripping of individuality from recruits in a military unit, to the coercions of some hospitals.[28] In some of these situations, the newcomers are more or less willing participants in the self-changing process. One can argue, in fact, that various changes in behavior result not from character changes, but from the reinforcement of some tendencies and the inhibition of others that are already there. It seems more reasonable to hold, however, that change in comparative salience *is* character change, for the hierarchy of interests and values is one of the important characteristics of a person.

In most of these situations, it is difficult to distinguish between character change and collaboration in an effort to avoid punishment or win a favor. Strongly cooperative behavior with military captors in the camp situation does not prove ideological change. But what is perhaps less readily noted, a return to earlier patterns of behavior upon repatriation—that is, when earlier group influences and other situational influences return—does not demonstrate that character change had been slight. The effects of efforts to manipulate range along a scale from heightened resistance, to outer conformity, to conformity in depth.

Schein classifies the prisoners of war in Korea into "get-alongers," "resisters," and "cooperators," but he notes that many shifted in different situations and even fell into different categories without situation changes.[29] In *The Captive Mind*, Czeslaw Milosz describes some of the processes of survival among persons in the Soviet satellite countries who oppose the regime. Since direct opposition is impossible or fatal, patterns of overt conformity without inner commitment develop. Milosz explains several varieties of the doctrine of *Ketman*—a belief in the wisdom of a kind of calculating other-directedness (one might say an inner other-directedness) that helps one to avoid exposure of self or family to unavailing persecution.To carry out such a belief requires a skill at playing a role which contradicts important aspects of self. In time, the self is influenced by the role playing; outer conformity becomes, at least in part, inner conformity. "After long acquaintance with his role, a man grows into it so closely that he can no longer differentiate his true self from the self he simulates, so that even the most intimate of individuals speak to each other in Party slogans. To identify one's self with the role one is obliged to play brings relief and permits a relaxation of one's vigilance. Proper reflexes at the moment become truly automatic." [30]

A coercing power may be willing to overlook, if it is aware of, some discrepancy between role performance and conviction. If the discrepancy does not interfere with behavior, coercion may actually be made easier when individuals are allowed their inner convictions. They may find it easier to rationalize acceptance of a repugnant role if their inner convictions are not interfered with. And if these deeper feelings tend to break through and disrupt role performance, Milosz notes, a totalitarian force can increase the sanctions which will push the compromise deeper.

Limits to this arrangement are, of course, set by the inner strain produced by the contradiction and by the risk of poor role performance. For
in the last analysis, role performance is "best" (nearest the model) when
self-role contradictions are at a minimum.[31] Strictly speaking, one should
always specify the conflict as one between the role requirements and *some*
aspects of self, aspects that might be dominant under more usual circumstances. The manipulator would not be successful if he did not engage a
tendency or series of tendencies which are already part of self or of total
character. By his coercions he may raise the desire for survival, for food,
or for freedom from pain to the top of the tendency system. In this sense,
there is always inner conformity with role behavior. The manipulator does
not block the stronger tendency; he maneuvers the situation in such a way
that other tendencies become stronger still. But this is a tautology which,
while true, is not very helpful. Viewed in a time dimension, one can say
that what is at this moment the stronger tendency may be inhibited and a
weaker tendency brought to the fore.

Under some conditions, then, major transformations of character have
been produced by manipulation. It is one thing to carry on under a highly
repressive regime in which, nevertheless, the individual is allowed to continue in his job, live with family, and maintain a few of his accustomed
associations. It is another thing to come under the absolute power of the
guard in a concentration camp. Perhaps 10 per cent of the prisoners in
the Nazi camps survived. Many of them did so only with major character
changes; indeed, some of these changes seem to have been necessary for
survival. The rigidity of the rules, the brutal punishment for tiny infrac-
tions, chronic hunger, the complete inability to make any plans for the
future—all made the usual patterns of behavior useless as forms of
adaptation. One of the consequences was the development of a sense of
detachment, even from self: These things are not happening to me, but
only to "him"—an object, not a subject.[32] Since any effort at self-
advancement was bound to fail, survival became the chief concern; and
this required the protective coloration of anonymity. Anything that made
one stand out from his fellows was a danger. Perhaps most significant of
the character changes was the reappearance of childlike behavior and
patterns of dependence. This went so far in many cases that the prisoners
identified with the guards and the values of the Gestapo.[33]

Such drastic changes are difficult to explain by a theory of self-
consistency or a declaration that "the basic pattern of personality tends to
be quite set in early life." [34] It seems more meaningful to state that under
conditions of slight situational variability and low external coercion,
presently dominating tendencies of the individual continue, with only
small changes. Under conditions of major situational change and massive
coercion, however, more basic changes occur. New tendencies are learned
and others that lie dormant under almost all conditions are brought into
behavior when conditions are extreme (i.e., when they are both highly
unusual and exceedingly powerful). This does not mean that character

differences are unimportant, for individuals vary, even under extreme conditions, in the extent and direction of behavioral changes.

The shift in perspective required by this kind of field interpretation is well stated by Leo Alexander:

The psychiatrist stands in amazement before the thoroughness and completeness with which this perversion of essential superego values was accomplished in adults ... it may be that the decisive importance of childhood and youth in the formation of [these] values may have been overrated by psychiatrists in a society in which allegiance to these values in normal adult life was taken too much for granted because of the stability, religiousness, legality, and security of the 19th Century and early 20th Century society.[35]

CONCLUSION

In summary, how does field theory deal with the question of the continuity of character and the opposite question of the extent to which manipulation is possible? The answer is drawn from several points of view. Elkins observes, for example, that several different theories might account for the drastic changes in behavior in concentration camps. The orthodox Freudian view, with its "assumption that the content and character of the superego is laid down in childhood and undergoes relatively little basic alteration thereafter," [36] cannot easily explain the dramatic changes that sometimes take place in adult behavior. In the orthodox Freudian view, the old values are pushed into the background by the shocks which produced the "acute depersonalization" of which Cohen and Bettelheim have written. Drives of hunger and survival are brought to the fore. They can be handled only by identification with the all-powerful "father"—the SS guards. "It could simply be said that under great stress the superego, like a bucket, is violently emptied of content and acquires, in a radically changed setting, new content." [37] Such an interpretation, although keeping the Freudian terminology, seems to be a more drastic revision of Freudian theory than Elkins implies. It requires a recognition that situational change is not simply a limiting condition which calls up various defense mechanisms from an essentially stable self. Instead, the situation becomes an interdependent variable to be studied along with character in terms of *mutually limiting* influence.

Sullivan's interpersonal theory may err on the other side, for it has little place for self-initiating activity. The expectations and sanctioning power of significant others—those who hold the key to one's security—are the major forces in determining behavior. The prisoner in a concentration camp, like the child, has little power of selectivity over significant others and thus becomes utterly involved with the dominating power. The camp "focused the prisoner's attention constantly on the moods, attitudes, and standards of the only man who mattered. A truly childlike situation was thus created: utter and abject dependency on one, or on a rigidly limited few significant others." [38]

This rather extreme situationalism, which is theoretically more acceptable with reference to children in the process of building a self-system than to adults with established tendency patterns, requires some qualification. It is more capable of explaining extreme cases than the full range of actual behavior, including behavior of those who consciously accepted the norms of the camp as the only chance for survival [39] and those who refused even such a shift in "significant others" and were killed. Nor can one explain who took these various positions—identification, adaptation, and resistance—simply by reference to individual variation. There were differences in the severity of the situation and the length of exposure to it. These and other variables interacted with character variables.

The great value of the interpersonal approach is that it alerts us to the *continuing* process of character formation and the social interactional forces involved in it. The general principle of this approach can be stated as follows: Other things being equal, behavior will vary with the extent to which a situation controls the values and sanctioning power of the significant others with whom a person interacts. The main "other thing" which must be equal would be the tendency systems of the individuals at the start of the interaction. Not everyone will respond to a tightly closed social situation in the same way.

Role theory, Elkins suggests, offers a third possible interpretation of the drastic changes in behavior in concentration camps. The prisoner is assigned what for him is a new role, one similar to the dependent, obedient child. Specifications of the role are clear and rigidly enforced, with death the likely outcome for poor performance. Elkins believes that role theory may be the best of the three interpretations of behavior in the prison camps; but it seems to me to require extensive supplementation. By itself it does not help to answer the questions: How deeply are the role norms internalized? How wide is the variation in interpretation and acceptance of the role by different persons? "Role" is a cultural term. It can explain behavior only when it is related to concepts of social interaction and personality in a larger system of constructs. [40]

Schein, Schneier, and Barker also examine several different perspectives in their study of "coercive persuasion." In a careful review of the evidence they distinguish between the forces that "unfreeze" an individual—opening him to new influences—and those that cause him to accept new patterns of behavior. Psychophysiological exhaustion and deprivation of group support for accustomed behavior may unfreeze him. But what is the source of new tendencies? The answer must be given from several perspectives.

From the point of view of learning theory, efforts to coerce an individual in the direction of beliefs and actions which conflict with his dominant views arouse anxiety and guilt. These serve as drive states which lead to a search for their reduction. "However, the only response which can reduce the anxiety and guilt is a cognitive change in the prisoner, namely, the adoption of beliefs and values which justify the elicited behavior. Changes in beliefs and values in the direction of those of the captor are reinforced because they reduce anxiety and guilt, and because they lead to extrinsic rewards in the form of praise and improved material conditions from the captor." [41]

This is a helpful view of the problem of continuity and change, but it leaves important questions unanswered. ". . . most learning theorists are willing to become circular in their definitions and rely on an empirical criterion of what sorts of stimuli constitute reinforcements for a given individual, and what kinds of motivational states are of particular importance to him. There is nothing in the theory itself, however, which would offer to predict what would be motivating and what would be reinforcing." [42]

At this point, psychoanalytic and sociological theories offer interpretations complementary to learning theory. Moloney's version of a psychoanalytic interpretation, for example, is based on the belief that some individuals are characterized by an authoritarian, heavily demanding superego with which the ego always deals only with difficulty. Under conditions of physical and emotional stress, when a decisive authority figure is present (the captor or the prison authorities), such individuals will attempt to deal with their anxiety by giving in to the demands of those who dominate them.[43] This view introduces guilt and anxiety as motive forces, stresses individual variation in the learning process, suggests the operation of unconscious and other nonself influences, and otherwise extends an explanation based on learning theory alone.

Further extensions are necessary, however. Continuity and change in character are vitally influenced by the responses of others. Persistent refusal by others to accept one's definitions of a situation or to respond to one in accustomed ways deprives the self of the social confirmation essential to its functioning. ". . . we know ourselves largely through what we do; when we are prevented from doing what we are accustomed to, our self-knowledge begins to be undermined. For example, it may be difficult for a doctor to continue to see himself as a doctor if he is prevented from practicing. The denial of role, then, is one way in which the prison environment operated to undermine sense of identity. . . . A second and perhaps more fundamental threat resided in the fact that the prisoner's cellmates typically refused to confirm *any* of his self-perceptions which were in any way predicated on assumptions of innocence or blamelessness." [44]

The extent of character continuity, in short, is a function both of self and of others, of tendencies already laid down in the individual and of situational influences that reinforce or block those tendencies. While there is evidence to suggest that the concept of system-maintaining processes is of particular value in understanding human behavior, it must be used with full recognition of certain qualifying ideas:

The character system being maintained is a *moving equilibrium,* constantly incorporating new experience which modifies the existing tendencies. It is an open system.

Character is a complex structure with many tendencies, only some of which are brought into play in any given situation. The degree of continuity and change, therefore, cannot be understood independently of the contexts of behavior; for what appears to be change may simply indicate the facilitation of existing, but previously inhibited, tendencies by a changed situation; or what appears to be continuity may be an expression of the influence of continuing external structures.

And finally, the system-maintaining processes of character have developed in connection with a certain range of conditions. When experience goes well beyond that range, there may be a "dropping back" to simpler adjustments (that of the helpless child in some concentration camps, e.g.) and, at the extremes of experience, a loss of system-maintaining or homeostatic processes entirely. Character then is completely "unfrozen." A new character- and self-building process is begun.

FOOTNOTES

Note: The bracketed number following an author's name refers to the footnote in which the source is cited in full.

1. An interesting application of this point is found in the criticisms of Freud made by Horney, Boss, and others, for his tendency to assume that the past is the present. See Karen Horney, *New Ways in Psychoanalysis,* W. W. Norton & Company, Inc., 1939, especially chap. 8; and Medard Boss, *Psychoanalysis and Daseinsanalysis,* Basic Books, Inc., Publishers, 1963.

2. E. K. Strong, Jr., "Permanence of Interest Scores over 22 Years," *Journal of Applied Psychology,* vol. 35, 1951, pp. 89–91.

3. E. Lowell Kelly, "Consistency of the Adult Personality," *American Psychologist,* November, 1955, pp. 659–681.

4. *Ibid.,* p. 676. For other studies that make valuable use of measures through time, see William McCord and Joan McCord, *Origins of Crime: A New Evaluation of the Cambridge-Somerville Youth Study,* Columbia University Press, 1959; Sheldon Glueck and Eleanor Glueck, *Predicting Delinquency and Crime,* Harvard University Press, 1959; Lee N. Robins, Harry Gyman, and Patricia O'Neal, "The Interaction of Social Class and Deviant Behavior," *American Sociological Review,* August, 1962, pp. 480–492; and Lee N. Robins and Patricia O'Neal, "Mortality, Mobility, and Crime: Problem Children Thirty Years Later," *American Sociological Review,* April, 1958, pp. 162–170.

5. Gordon W. Allport, J. S. Bruner, and E. M. Jandorf, "Personality under Social Catastrophe," in Clyde Kluckhohn and Henry A. Murray, with the collaboration of David M. Schneider (eds.), *Personality in Nature, Society, And Culture,* rev. ed., Alfred A. Knopf, Inc., 1953, pp. 442–443. For a sharply contradictory interpretation, emphasizing change of personality when situation and role change, see Howard S.

Becker, "Personal Change in Adult Life," *Sociometry*, March, 1964, pp. 40–53.

6. See Carl Hovland, A. A. Lumsdaine, and F. D. Sheffield, *Studies in Social Psychology in World War II*, vol. III, *Experiments on Mass Communication*, Princeton University Press, 1949.

7. See Carl Hovland, I. L. Janis, and Harold H. Kelley, *Communication and Persuasion: Psychological Studies of Opinion Change*, Yale University Press, 1953.

8. Wilbur Schramm (ed.), *The Process and Effects of Mass Communication*, University of Illinois Press, 1954; and J. T. Klapper, "What We Know about the Effects of Mass Communication: The Brink of Hope," *Public Opinion Quarterly*, vol. 31, Winter, 1957–1958, pp. 453–474.

9. See Hovland, Janis, and Kelley [7]; Elihu Katz and Paul Lazarsfeld, *Personal Influence: The Part Played by People in the Flow of Mass Communications*, The Free Press of Glencoe, 1955; and M. W. Riley and S. H. Flowerman, "Group Relations as a Variable in Communications Research," *American Sociological Review*, April, 1951, pp. 174–180.

10. Irving L. Janis and Carl I. Hovland, *Personality and Persuasibility*, Yale University Press, 1959, pp. 13–14.

11. In *ibid.*, p. 120.

12. The simple product model used here is doubtless inadequate. It is quite possible that a 24 produced by a 3 × 8 combination has a different meaning from one produced by a 6 × 4 combination.

13. Edward Sapir, "Fashion," *Encyclopedia of the Social Sciences*, The Macmillan Company, 1931, vol. 6. pp. 139–144.

14. See Marie Jahoda, "Conformity and Independence," *Human Relations*, vol. 12, 1959, pp. 99–120; Richard H. Willis, "Two Dimensions of Conformity-Nonconformity," *Sociometry*, December, 1963, pp. 499–513; Robert R. Blake and Jane S. Mouton, "The Experimental Investigation of Interpersonal Influence," in Albert Biderman and Herbert Zimmer (eds.), *The Manipulation of Human Behavior*, John Wiley & Sons, Inc., 1961, pp. 216–276; Irwin Berg and Bernard Bass (eds.), *Conformity and Deviation*, Harper & Row, Publishers, Incorporated, 1961; and A. Paul Hare, Edgar F. Borgatta, and Robert F. Bales (eds.), *Small Groups: Studies in Social Interaction*, Alfred A. Knopf, Inc., 1955, chap. 6 and elsewhere.

15. For evidence on this question see Bruno Bettelheim, "Individual and Mass Behavior in Extreme Situations," *Journal of Abnormal and Social Psychology*, October, 1943, pp. 417–452; Biderman and Zimmer [14]; E. A. Cohen, *Human Behavior in the Concentration Camp*, W. W. Norton & Company, Inc., 1953; I. E. Farber, Harry F. Harlow, and Louis J. West, "Brainwashing, Conditioning and DDD (Debility, Dependency, Dread)," *Sociometry*, December, 1957, pp. 271–285; Czeslaw Milosz, *The Captive Mind*, Alfred A. Knopf, Inc., 1953; Edgar H. Schein, "The Chinese Indoctrination Program for Prisoners of War: A Study of Attempted 'Brainwashing.'" *Psychiatry*, May, 1956, pp. 149–172; and Edgar H. Schein, with Inge Schneier and Curtis H. Barker, *Coercive Persuasion*, W. W. Norton & Company, Inc., 1961.

16. See Lawrence E Hinkle, Jr., "The Psychological State of the Interrogation Subject as It Affects Brain Function," in Biderman and Zimmer [14], pp. 19–50.

17. See P. Solomon, P. H. Leiderman, J. Mendelson, and D. Wexler, "Sensory Deprivation: A Review," *American Journal of Psychiatry*, vol. 114, 1957, pp. 357–363; P. E. Kubzansky, "The Effects of Reduced Environmental Stimulation on Human Behavior: A Review," in Biderman and Zimmer [14], pp. 51–95; W. Heron, W. H. Bexton, and D. O. Hebb, "Cognitive Effects of Decreased Variation to Sensory Environment," *American Psychologist*, vol. 8, 1953, p. 366; Kingsley Davis, "Final Note on a Case of Extreme Isolation," *American Journal of Sociology*, vol. 52, 1947, pp. 432–437; E. Ziskind, "Isolation Stress in Medical and Mental Illness," *Journal of the American Medical Association*, vol. 168, 1958, pp. 1427–1431; and A. S. Edwards, "Effects of Loss of 100 Hours' Sleep," *American Journal of Psychology*, vol. 54, 1941, pp. 80–91.

18. Hinkle in Biderman and Zimmer [14], p. 44.

19. See H. E. Hill, R. E. Belleville, and A. Wilker, "Motivational Determinants in the Modification of Behavior by Morphine and Pentobarbital," *American Medical Association Archives of Neurological Psychiatry*, vol. 77, 1957, pp. 28–35; Howard S. Becker, "Becoming a Marihuana User," *American Journal of Sociology*, November, 1953, pp. 235–242; Louis A. Gottschalk, "The Use of Drugs in Interrogation," in Biderman and Zimmer [14], pp. 96–141; Isidor Chein *et al.*, *The Road to H: Narcotics, Delinquency, and Social Policy*, Basic Books, Inc., Publishers, 1964; John A. Clausen, "Social Patterns, Personality, and Adolescent Drug Use," in Alexander Leighton, John A. Clausen, and Robert Wilson (eds.), *Explorations in Social Psychiatry*, Basic Books, Inc., Publishers, 1957, pp. 230–277.

20. See H. C. Kelman, "Effects of Success and Failure on 'Suggestibility' in the Autokinetic Situation," *Journal of Abnormal and Social Psychology*, vol. 45, 1950, pp. 267–285; P. H. Mussen and J. Kagan, "Group Conformity and Perceptions of Parents," *Child Development*, vol. 29, 1958, pp. 57–60.

21. Schein, "The Chinese Indoctrination Program for Prisoners of War," [15].

22. See *ibid.*

23. See, for example, Kurt Lewin, "Group Decision and Social Change," in Eleanor Maccoby, Theodore Newcomb, and Eugene Hartley (eds.), *Readings in Social Psychology*, 3d ed., Holt, Rinehart and Winston, Inc., 1958, pp. 197–211, and the somewhat qualifying articles reprinted there: Edith Bennett Pelz, "Some Factors in 'Group Decision,'" pp. 212–219, and Lester Coch and John R. P. French, Jr., "Overcoming Resistance to Change," pp. 233–250.

24. Perhaps 15 per cent of American captives were "unduly cooperative"; this refers to action ranging from giving more information than required by Red Cross convention to signing confessions of bacteriological warfare. But only twenty-one were persuaded to defect, and several of these have since returned to the United States. See H. A. Segal, "Initial Psychiatric Findings of Recently Repatriated Prisoners of War, *American Journal of Psychiatry*, vol. 111, 1954, pp. 358–363.

25. But note Theodore Newcomb's discussion of the interaction of role and self changes among returned British prisoners of war, in *Social Psychology*, Holt, Rinehart and Winston, Inc., 1950, pp. 476–477.

26. Of the extensive literature on this question, see Abram Kardiner and Lionel Ovesey, *The Mark of Oppression: A Psychological*

Study of the American Negro, W. W. Norton & Company, Inc., 1951;
Charles S. Johnson, *Growing up in the Black Belt,* American Council on
Education, 1941; John H. Rohrer and Munro S. Edmonson (eds.), *The
Eighth Generation: Cultures and Personalities of New Orleans Negroes,*
Harper & Row, Publishers, Incorporated, 1960; Stanley M. Elkins,
Slavery: A Problem in American Institutional and Intellectual Life,
The University of Chicago Press, 1959; Robert Coles: *The Desegre-
gation of Southern Schools: A Psychiatric Study,* Anti-Defamation
League and Southern Regional Council, July, 1963; Thomas Pettigrew,
A Profile of the Negro American, D. Van Nostrand Company, Inc., 1964;
and George E. Simpson and J. Milton Yinger, *Racial and Cultural Mi-
norities: An Analysis of Prejudice and Discrimination,* 3d ed., Harper
& Row, Publishers, Incorporated, 1965, especially chaps. 6 and 7.

27. See Gresham M. Sykes, *The Society of Captives,* Princeton
University Press, 1958.

28. See the references cited in note 59, Chapter 6.

29. Edgar H. Schein [15].

30. Czeslaw Milosz [15], p. 55.

31. See William J. Goode, "Norm Commitment and Conformity to
Role-status Obligations," *American Journal of Sociology,* November,
1960, pp. 256–257.

32. Bruno Bettelheim [15], p. 431.

33. *Ibid.;* and E. A. Cohen [15], p. 177.

34. Kluckhohn, Murray, and Schneider [5], p. 436.

35. Leo Alexander, "War Crimes: Their Social-Psychological
Aspects," *American Journal of Psychiatry,* September, 1948, p. 173.

36. Stanley Elkins, "Slavery and Personality," in Bert Kaplan (ed.),
Studying Personality Cross-culturally, Harper & Row, Publishers, Incorporated, 1961, p. 254.

37. *Ibid.,* p. 235.

38. *Ibid.,* p. 257.

39. See Schein, Schneier, and Barker [15], p. 226.

40. For Elkins' full paper, see "Slavery and Personality" [36], pp.
243–267. See also his book *Slavery* [26], pp. 81–139.

41. Schein, Schneier, and Barker [15], pp. 205–206.

42. *Ibid.,* p. 208.

43. J. C. Moloney, "Psychic Self-abandon and Extortion of Confession," *International Journal of Psycho-analysis,* vol. 35, 1955, pp. 53–
60. See the useful discussion of this and other psychoanalytic interpretations in Schein, Schneier, and Barker [15], p. 211 ff.

44. *Ibid.,* p. 222. See also Robert J. Lifton, *Thought Reform and the
Psychology of Totalism,* W. W. Norton & Company, Inc., 1963.

Part THREE

DEVIATION AND ABNORMALITY IN FIELD PERSPECTIVE

CHAPTER 9

Anomie
and Alienation

Among the wide range of topics of concern to behavioral scientists, those dealing with "deviation" and "abnormality" offer particularly valuable areas for the development of a field perspective. Interest in delinquency, discrimination, and mental illness, to list the three subjects which I shall explore in Chapters 10, 11, and 12, is strongly behavioral and clinical. That is, most students of these topics are not primarily concerned with isolating one abstract relationship which, however accurately described, cannot account for the behavior of the persons being observed. On issues of such importance, the social scientist's almost irresistible desire is to interpret *behavior,* not to state an analytic relationship. To this is added his desire to cure or prevent, not simply to understand. Through decades of specialization and of mutual disregard among disciplines, these desires have led investigators repeatedly to attempt to stretch propositions derived from one level of analysis into total theories. Research has constantly ignored the principle that the more one is interested in the full range of "natural" behavior, the less adequate are the "if-then" statements of specialized disciplines.

From the point of view of field theory, there are no delinquents, there is only delinquent behavior; there are no prejudiced persons or "authoritarian personalities," there is only discriminatory behavior; there are no psychotics, there is only behavior pathology. This does not mean, of course, that there are no tendencies toward these various deviations or that such tendencies do not vary in strength from individual to individual. But by using nouns ("delinquent," "authoritarian," "psychotic"), we run the risk of placing the cause of behavior within the individual regardless of the other facilitating or inhibiting forces in the total field which accounts for behavior. Once again the structure of our language coerces and limits our observations. The search for the "is-ness" (essence) of things comes naturally. Yet "The boy *is* delinquent" can only mean that he has a tendency to violate certain laws under particular conditions. The same boy "is" also nondelinquent: he has tendencies not to violate certain laws under particular conditions. By using nouns, we risk obscuring the very core of the scientific problem, the specification of the total range of forces producing a given act.

There is a similar danger of reifying the situational influences. Insofar as we are concerned with them as factors influencing behavior, delinquent subculture, mass society, anomie, and the like do not exist independently of experiencing individuals. Yet such terms are frequently used to explain behavior directly, in contradiction to the principle of multiple possibilities. The significance of these structural influences for behavior cannot be measured adequately unless we recognize that "the same" situation can produce different results among persons with different tendencies. (Combine hydrogen with oxygen and one gets water; combine it with chlorine and one gets hydrochloric acid.)

I shall introduce Part Three's discussion of the field approach to deviation and abnormality by examining two concepts of great general interest and importance: anomie and alienation. Since the various forms of deviation and abnormality are functional alternatives to some degree, we may be better prepared to understand them if we see their common sources in social and individual conditions. A review of anomie and alienation, with all the ambiguities and insights these concepts carry, reveals the issues involved in the study of situations in which the relationships among society, culture, and personality have become disturbed or problematic.

ANOMIE

Anomie is a word to conjure with. From its Greek root we might define it as "broken limits." Durkheim thought of it in these terms, adding the connotations of deregulation and normlessness. In the state of anomie, he wrote, "the most reprehensible acts are . . . frequently rendered pure by success. . . . The limits are unknown between the possible and the impossible, what is just and what is unjust, legitimate claims and hopes and those which are immoderate. Consequently there is no restraint upon aspirations." [1] What is anarchy in government is anomie in society.

I shall use the term in two closely related ways. In its largest meaning, anomie refers to a state of deregulation in which social norms—mutually agreed-upon goals and means—do not control men's actions. The individual participants may be clear in their own minds what the appropriate means and goals are, but if they are interacting with others who accept different norms, the social situation which they jointly share is normless.

Robert Merton has given the term a slightly narrower meaning. Building on Durkheim's usage, he notes that industrial societies particularly have opened up new opportunities and have encouraged their members to strive for these new goals. At the same time, less attention is often paid to teaching respect for, or furnishing opportunities for, culturally approved means. Anomie in this sense exists when there is little agreement on appropriate means to approved goals, or when many persons are caught in circumstances where appropriate means are inaccessible, or when institutional crises—business cycles or group conflict—block the road to expected satisfactions by approved means. What one is supposed to do under these conditions is unclear, for the pursuit of culturally approved goals may be possible only by illegitimate means, or the refusal to employ illegitimate means may entail repudiation of goals.[2]

The normless condition—not individual responses to it—constitutes anomie. It cannot be defined independently of a group. Anomie represents a loss of pattern in the *mutual* expectations for social action. The various ways in which individuals react to loss of pattern require different terms, although different terms are not always used. It is one thing to say that the players in a football game disagree on the rules; it is another thing to describe their different feelings and actions as a result of that disagreement. Some may seek to win by any method in which they believe they have an advantage; some may withdraw from the game. Others may attempt to impose their rules, may accept those of another, or may call for a conference; still others may cling so fixedly to the ways they have learned to play the game that they forego any chance of winning.

Although the distinction between the group condition, anomie, and individual causes and effects of that condition is clear, it is not difficult to understand why the two should sometimes be confused. Anomie is hard to measure directly; we therefore use as indexes various rates which are calculated from a series of individual measures. Suicides, crimes, or individual responses to questions designed to measure normative agreement —that is, a series of individual facts—are aggregated into a rate, a social fact. We follow this process in many patterns of thought without confusion: To say that one lives in a wealthy society is not the same as saying one is wealthy, even though the phrase "wealthy society" refers simply to the aggregation of individual facts. It is one thing to be poor in a wealthy society and something else to be poor in a poor society. That is to say, the group rate is a fact important in its own right. We must remember, however, that the individual measures are used simply as an index of the group property. "Lack of agreement on norms" is a quality that resides inherently in the *interaction* of two or more persons. In this sense, an individual cannot be said to have anomie or to be anomic.

Anomie should not carry a moral connotation. This is not said out of indifference to moral questions. Quite the contrary, it is an effort to get moral thinking where it belongs: in the study of goals and consequences, not in the processes of definition and observation. Anomie is not necessarily a "bad" state of affairs. Before making this judgment, one must know what the alternatives to anomie are. There was probably a high level of anomie in the American Colonies in 1775—a necessary aspect of the disengagement from the British Empire. Perhaps increase in anomie is an inevitable part of the process whereby old tyrannies are broken and new values given a field for growth. This point needs to be made because a strong ideological quality runs through many discussions of anomie and related discussions of "mass society." Durkheim himself linked anomie to the "pathological forms" of the division of labor, for he saw his beloved France torn apart by value conflicts. But if we attempt to have the term do double duty as a moral and descriptive concept, the danger is that our ability to observe the true state of affairs will be reduced—as, in the long run, our moral effectiveness will.

The point can perhaps best be made by trying to define the opposite of an anomic situation. Is it a completely stable society where everyone agrees on both goals and appropriate means? Such a society is unimaginable in the modern world, where social change is chronic, diverse ethnic and religious groups live within the same society, and individual choice and freedom are ranked high as values. Anomie is a variable that can range from little to much. Any attempt to *eliminate* it—often based on the feeling that since "my" norms are being threatened, normlessness is upon us—tends toward tyranny. But this is not to say that efforts to *reduce* anomie tend toward tyranny. The search for value agreements in a heterogeneous society, and particularly the effort to create situations where all have access to legitimate means for the pursuit of cultural goals, reduces the threat of tyranny.

But this does not completely solve the problem. Are heterogeneous and pluralistic societies by definition anomic? Their members may disagree sharply on both means and goals. Each individual looking out at the social world is likely to see standards and behavior that contradict his sense of rightness. What he defines as good and necessary, others disregard or oppose. To be sure, by definition there is agreement in every society on broad principles and procedures; but from the point of view of normative integration these often seem to be symbolic more than operative—a thin veneer of unity covering deep splits. Some Americans believe that racial segregation is essential to harmony and justice; others are convinced that it destroys those very values. Some believe that gambling is an instrument of the devil; others play bingo in the church basement. Some look with dismay at changing sex patterns, while others are dismayed at the survival of what they believe are uncivilized codes. The list could be extended almost indefinitely.

A person strongly committed to his own values and thoroughly aware of the extent of value disagreement is likely to declare that society is dissolving in chaos, that anomie is upon us. But if anomie is not an individual moral term but a concept referring to the operations of a group, we need some way of distinguishing anomic value disagreements from what I shall call pluralistic value disagreements. A pluralistic disagreement does not disrupt the workings of the society—does not dis-organize the interactions of members that require the fulfillment of shared expectations. If you prefer sugar in your coffee but I prefer it black, this need not disturb our tête-à-tête—unless, by chance, the sugar must be put in while the coffee is being made, in which case our mutual expecta-tions would surely be disturbed.

In a less trivial example, if Mississippi disfranchises her Negro citizens and otherwise deprives them of opportunities, she can claim the rights of pluralism—and demand that the outside agitators stay home—only if her actions do not affect the national system. But as it happens, such dis-franchisement affects the quality of congressmen sent to Washington, who vote for laws that apply to citizens of New York as well as of Missis-sippi. Also, many citizens of the state migrate elsewhere, carrying the results of their various privileges and disprivileges with them. The segrega-tion crisis in the United States is clearly anomic by what I shall call the *interaction test*.

This test is easy to state but difficult to apply, for it is far from self-evident that a given value disagreement does or does not disrupt a society. Judgment can often be based only on technical knowledge of the work-ings of the society, although this may not be necessary in extreme cases —whether on the pluralistic or the anomic end of the range. If citizens of Philippine descent prefer to dance in the manner of their ancestors, we applaud and encourage them; if Mormons prefer polygyny, we condemn and prosecute them. The Mormon practice, we readily agree, strikes at a cluster of shared values that are both symbolically and functionally im-portant for our society. Our opposition may also involve some projection: we attack a custom that, if allowed to exist, might weaken our own somewhat precarious repression of tendencies toward polygyny.

Although extreme cases are fairly easy to classify—variation in artistic styles is pluralism, variation in marriage customs within a society is anomie—by what operations can we judge the ambiguous middle ground? Is the wide disagreement on the question of divorce a sign of normless-ness, of pluralistic variation—or even of a cultural alternative in the Linton sense? I have suggested that segregation in Mississippi disrupts the workings of an interdependent society. Does the divorce law of Nevada, so different from most other states, have the same effect? The answer is not quite so clear. We need information about the long-run consequences.

Merton has suggested that under some conditions anomie spreads and intensifies as a result of the "success" of deviant behavior, and this sug-gests a second test. If some people manage to avoid paying their full income tax and thus retain a higher share of their income, others hearing of this will feel more justified in underreporting their own earnings. "The process thus enlarges the extent of anomie within the system so that others, who did not respond in the form of deviant behavior to the relatively slight anomie which first obtained, come to do so as anomie spreads and is intensified. This, in turn, creates a more acutely anomic situation for still other and initially less vulnerable individuals in the social system." 3

I shall call this the *cyclic test* of anomie: value disagreements that tend to spread through the social system are anomic; those that have no tendency to spread are pluralistic. Disagreements over the desirability of paying one's legally defined income tax are undoubtedly anomic by this test and also by the interaction test. If I avoid paying my full tax, you must pay more to maintain the same level of services; while Philippine folk dancers in no way interfere with your freedom to dance the Twist.

Note again that this is not a moral distinction. Perhaps one ought *not* to pay his income tax: for some people, a government dollar is an evil dollar, while a private dollar is good; or in the view of some, to help support a fifty billion dollar defense establishment is evil. Both the cyclic and the interaction tests of anomie refer to the consequences of value disagreement for the workings of a stated system; if one dislikes that system, he should applaud and seek to increase anomie.

Here again, to state the cyclic test is easier than to apply it. We do not know a great deal about the conditions under which the spiraling of deviance takes place, or about the conditions that promote reverse processes which help to reestablish value agreement. If deviators belong to an esteemed group, their actions are more likely to spread. (The lack of publicity given to bankers' thefts, as compared with those of "thieves," may reflect this fact as well as the bankers' greater power.) Deviant responses will spiral if many persons are blocked from legitimate means to approved goals. And deviant responses are more likely to accumulate if substitute modes of response—culturally and individually available alternatives—are lacking.

But this is only one side of the equation. If it were the whole story, anomie would not only be the chronic state of man, but we would have to think in terms of a social parallel to the second law of thermodynamics —with normative systems inevitably "running down." On this basis their origin, their perpetuation, and their renewal would be impossible to explain.

Social patterns for reinforcing a value code, for preventing anomie or stopping it at a given level, have been much discussed in terms of the concepts of socialization and social control, and I shall not deal with them here. I am interested rather in the *new* structures that appear under conditions of spiraling anomie, structures which seem to be designed to halt the demoralization and establish a new basis for the mutual expectations that are essential to social life. Seldom—and certainly not in the contemporary world—are these structures likely to be revivals, returns to old forms. In his first discussion of anomie, Durkheim observed that its reduction depends on the building of a new moral order appropriate to the existing situation, not on an effort to reestablish a traditional order.

Perhaps the various distinctions I have suggested can be made clearer by a chart that shows the different levels of value disagreement and the types of social situations that result from their several combinations:

Type of social situation	Value disagree- ments are present	Value disagree- ments disrupt interaction	Value disagree- ments are cumulative
1. Cultural unity	No	No	No
2. Pluralism	Yes	No	No
3. Subcultural anomie	Yes	Yes	No
4. Full anomie	Yes	Yes	Yes

This quasi scale is meant to suggest a range from a situation in which normative agreement (in the sense both of harmony among goals and availability of means for achieving those goals) is high and governs most interactions to one in which normative agreement is low and, because of that very fact, tends to fall ever lower. In situation 1, interactions are effectively governed by the system of shared expectations. In situation 2, which I have called pluralism, there are some value disagreements, but these are accepted as legitimate or perhaps even desirable; they are at least tolerated. Ethnic differences in food customs, for example, or even religious differences under some circumstances, would fall in this category.

Situation 3 represents the beginning of anomie. Here value disagreements disrupt the pattern of mutual expectations; the differences make a difference. Each individual may "know how to behave," because he is a member of a subsociety with clear normative standards. Because there is important interaction among persons from different subsocieties, however, none can act in the expected ways. Even if they agree on goals, their disagreement over means retards or prevents the pursuit of the goals. When others do not play by the rules of the game—"my" rules—there is likely to be more argument and conflict than playing. Many of the activities at the United Nations are anomic in this sense. Within this country, race relations are often characterized by "demoralization"—the lack of widely shared norms to control the interaction.

In situation 4, full anomie, demoralization has gone further. Value confusion now characterizes not only interactions among individuals, but the inner lives of many individuals as well. Can a person honorably accept payment for simulating knowledge on a TV quiz program? It's only a game. Or is it only a game? Should a military officer responsible for contract determination accept expensive hospitality from a firm contending for a contract? This is a normal part of business procedure. Or is it? In a context of doubt about legitimate means—and in a society that encourages unlimited aspirations—there is likely to be, in Merton's term, a great deal of innovation. If innovation is successful, other individuals who are in doubt about the range of permissible means will be encouraged to innovate also, with the cyclical results described above.

All the types of social situation are found in the patterns of American race relations, in continuously changing proportion. When most Negroes were Southern, rural, and poor, the distribution of Negro-white contacts, according to the scheme suggested above, might have been somewhat as follows:

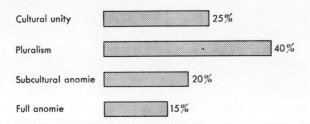

Thus contacts might have entailed some sharing of norms between the races, more pluralistic isolation, a little value confusion because of conflict-laden association, and at least a small amount of accumulation or spiraling of anomie.

In the present situation, with well over half of all Negroes living in cities, nearly half of them living in the North and West, most of them literate, and most well aware of the promises and potentialities of a democratic and affluent society, the patterns of interaction are quite different. Perhaps they would be distributed in these proportions:

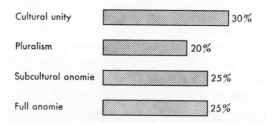

In this imaginary scale, I have added a little to the bar representing situations in which normative agreement prevails, sharply reduced the pluralistic situations (isolated disagreement), and increased the proportion of situations characterized by disrupting value disagreements and by full anomie. Whether or not these guesses are near the mark, the trend, I believe, is unmistakable: there has been a great increase in anomie, both in the sense of normlessness (disagreement on norms in an interacting group) and in the sense of the use of illegitimate means in the pursuit of culturally learned goals.

The present situation is far from stable, however. Suppose one of three movements were to achieve substantial success. The foes of desegregation, seeking to reestablish the plantation pattern in an urban society, could only succeed in reducing situations 1 and 2 and building up situations 3 and 4. To the degree that the Black Muslims grow in influence, however, they will reduce situations 1 and 4 and increase 2 and 3 (depending upon the extent to which they succeed in establishing separate economic activities and schools). They may well help to reduce full anomie, the spiraling of normlessness, but may increase normative conflict at the same time. If, as a third possibility, the civil rights movement grows in strength, it will tend to increase social interactions of type 1 and decrease or prevent further growth of types 2, 3, and 4.

If we were to assign numbers arbitrarily to these various estimates for, let us say, 1985, they might appear thus:

HYPOTHETICAL DISTRIBUTIONS OF RACE RELATIONS IN VARIOUS CONTEXTS, BY DEGREE OF VALUE AGREEMENT (PER CENT)

	1915	1965	Segregationist (1985)	Black Muslims (1985)	Civil rights (1985)
1. Cultural unity	25	30	10	10	45
2. Pluralism	40	20	15	30	20
3. Subcultural anomie	20	25	30	45	25
4. Full anomie	15	25	45	15	10

In each context, all four types are found. To emphasize this fact, I have assigned no value over 45 per cent, which represents the estimated strength of the modal situation for each of the three possible lines of development.

This exercise in imagination is designed to emphasize the complexity of modern societies. They are neither "riddled with anomie" nor likely to eliminate it in the foreseeable future. If one starts from a strongly ideological position, he is apt to mistake pluralism for anomie: "Since so many people do not behave according to my norms, there is normlessness." In a heterogeneous society it is not easy, as Robin Williams says, to distinguish deviation from the norms from (1) subcultural variation, (2) a permissible alternative interpretation of general norms, or (3) patterned evasions of "heroic" norms that are so common that the evasions themselves are normative.[4] Such normative complexity may be unfortunate from various value perspectives, but it is not all anomie.

I do not want to imply that all societies are equally anomic or that normlessness has not increased in the modern urban world. There are good reasons, as I shall discuss, for expecting that it has increased; but the data for definitive comparisons are lacking. The cynic may not be entirely wrong when he remarks that things are not as good as they used to be—and they never were. Efforts to measure trends in mental illness and crime, to name two possible indexes of anomie, yield highly contradictory results. It is not at all clear that rates have increased in the last several decades. Students of social stratification differ widely in their interpretation of evidence regarding opportunities for social mobility today com-

pared with earlier generations. Without undertaking here to survey the
evidence or the arguments, I would estimate that the forces promoting an
open society (increase in public education, increase in proportion of jobs
on higher status levels, expansion of universalistic criteria for advancement—civil service, seniority, open bidding for contracts—and the
like) approximately balance the increase in forces that block social mobility (automation that weakens the opportunities of the least skilled, oli-
gopoly in large segments of the economy, reduction of birth-rate differentials, etc.).

Anomie in field perspective. Anomie is a social fact; it is "the absence
of structured complementarity," in Parsons' nice phrase. Its implications
for behavior, however, are a function of the tendencies of the persons
who experience it, as well as of the "absolute" size of the gap between
socially established goals and the availability of culturally approved
means. One can define the temperature range in a given locality independently of the persons who live there; but understanding its full significance
requires knowledge of the distribution of fur coats and air-conditioned
houses. A 30-degree drop in the temperature may be a matter of indifference to some persons but a catastrophe for others.

In the same way, anomie can be marked off in both relative and
absolute units. Measurement in relative units requires knowledge of the
individuals who are involved. In this sense, to state that legitimate means
for pursuit of scarce goals are as prevalent now as formerly, as I have
done above, is not to say that the level of anomie has remained stable.
One has to introduce the level of aspiration into the formula.

I think there can be little doubt that the urbanization of American
society, the increase in education, the diffusion of media of communication, the enormous visibility of the goods and services that are available,
among other influences, have raised the levels of expectation enormously.
Opportunity structures have probably not kept pace with opportunities
envisaged—a phenomenon which is the very essence of anomie as Merton
sees it. The increase in the gap between aspiration and opportunity is
probably greatest among the nonwhite population of our large cities; but
even so apparently self-evident a statement should be treated cautiously.
The gap may increase not only because opportunities are structurally
lacking, but because widespread personality tendencies block their use.

There is no doubt that the ambitions of some Negroes exceed their
training; but it may also be true that the training of some middle- and
upper-class white young people exceeds their ambition. Having been
brought up in other-directed affluence (to condense a long story), many
may lack the discipline to work hard for that which they have come to
expect and take for granted. Some of the white-collar delinquencies and
crimes, as well as the ritualism and retreatism among the semisuccessful,
may be partly explicable in these terms. The disjunction between the
cultural system and the social system, that is to say, cannot be fully

measured without attention to personality tendencies which represent responses to that disjunction. I shall return to this problem in a later section.

ANOMIE AND MASS SOCIETY

I have suggested that anomie is difficult to define and even more difficult to measure. When such difficulties exist in an area of great human concern, ideological factors are almost certain to enter into the observation and interpretation of events. This is seen particularly in the literature on "mass society," a term that overlaps the meaning of anomie in most uses. In mass society traditional norms have been weakened or destroyed. What shared expectations there are derive less from a coherent culture than from the superficial unities created by "mass media." Or the patterns of mutual expectations are imposed from above by totalitarian power, in what might be thought of as a "postanomic" setting. A useful composite picture of the various meanings of mass society is drawn by Daniel Bell:

> The revolutions in transport and communications have brought men into closer contact with each other and bound them in new ways; the division of labor has made them more interdependent; tremors in one part of society affect all others. Despite this greater interdependence, however, individuals have grown more estranged from one another. The old primary group ties of family and local community have been shattered; ancient parochial faiths are questioned; few unifying values have taken their place. Most important, the critical standards of an educated élite no longer shape opinion or taste. As a result, mores and morals are in constant flux, relations between individuals are tangential or compartmentalized rather than organic. At the same time greater mobility, spatial and social, intensifies concern over status. Instead of a fixed or known status symbolized by dress or title, each person assumes a multiplicity of roles and constantly has to prove himself in a succession of new situations. Because of all this, the individual loses a coherent sense of self. His anxieties increase. There ensues a search for new faiths. The stage is thus set for the charismatic leader, the secular messiah, who, by bestowing upon each person the semblance of necessary grace and fullness of personality, supplies a substitute for the older unifying belief that the mass society has destroyed.[5]

This summary of the meanings of mass society suggests, among many things, that it is a situation in which people no longer interact on the basis of a system of shared values. Interpretations and evaluations of this situation vary widely. Many scholars would agree with Durkheim's statement (and might draw political conclusions that Durkheim himself would not accept): "At the very moment when traditional rules have lost their authority, the richer prize offered these appetites stimulates them and makes them more exigent and impatient of control. The stage of deregulation or anomy is thus further heightened by passions being less disciplined precisely when they need more disciplining." [6]

As the last phrase indicates, Durkheim was disturbed by the "every man for himself" effect of deregulation. Many students of the urban industrial world, however, are more disturbed by what they see as the opposite consequence: The loss of shared values and the destruction of stable group identities and individual positions have made individuals easily accessible to everything from peer-group influences to totalitarian movements. Thus two contrasting styles of interpretation of the consequences of anomie and mass society—sometimes blended or blurred in the writings of the same man—can be distinguished.

There are those who say that to remove the efficacy of a traditional set of norms is to get "the war of each against all" (Hobbes), "the sovereignty of the unqualified" (Ortega), the "era of crowds" (LeBon)— various expressions of a point of view that reaches back in some measure to Aristotle's fear of the *hoi polloi*. An anomic situation allows the welling up of presocial impulses and their coalescence in crowd control.

Then there are the critics of mass society who take an almost opposite view: that the breakup of old community structures and value systems has left man alone and afraid. He is more at the mercy of concentrated economic, political, and military power. The mass media bombard him endlessly with stimuli. Thus much of the freedom that the modern world has sought is endangered by concentrated power on the one hand and the individual's sense of fear and loneliness on the other. In such a setting, people have powerful tendencies to seek to "escape from the freedom of the lonely crowd" (if I may blur two well-known titles). As Kornhauser has said, the sequence of developments in mass society might run as follows: "(a) growing atomization (loss of community); (b) widespread readiness to embrace new ideologies (quest for community); (c) totalitarianism (total domination by pseudocommunity)." [7]

These interpretations imply that anomie is a social and cultural vacuum which, according to the aristocratic critics, is filled by the inferior values and standards of the masses and the rule of the crowd or, according to the democratic critics, is filled by the manipulated values and standards of the powerful and the rule of totalitarians.

These interpretations are mutually limiting but not mutually contradictory. There is no reason why both sets of processes could not be at work in the same setting—the balance between them being determined by many social and cultural variables. Each requires careful qualification, however. Paradoxically, both the aristocratic and the democratic critiques of mass society tend to view the present against a similar idealized picture of the past. They picture the stable, peaceful, homogeneous society in which man felt at home, at ease with his neighbors, content with his lot, interested in his work, and confident in his standards of right and wrong. Against a background of generations of turmoil, the validity of the contrast between moral *gemeinschaft* and anomic *gesellschaft* is difficult to doubt; but I believe we should be somewhat tentative in our views. Convincing evidence of the clash of values within and between people and of occasions when people showed greater interest in goals than in following culturally approved means can be found in the Old and New Testaments, in Greek drama, and in the writings of Luther, Dante, and Shakespeare.

When critiques of mass society, anomie, and alienation become ideological weapons, the tendency is to overlook signs of consensus and integration. Taking a second and third look at urban-industrial society, social scientists are finding more stable old patterns than were at first apparent. In addition, such societies are developing new norms and procedures (and personalities able and willing to accept them). Without attempting to discuss or even document the points, I might list several of the corrections which seem necessary in the picture of modern societies as anomic, atomized collections of individuals.

Old forms of primary groups, both the nuclear and the consanguine families, for example, now appear more resilient and adaptable than was at first thought. In addition, primary relations develop and prosper in many secondary situations—in the factory, the army, the street-corner gang—to give pattern to social life.

Excessive attention to anomie may cause us to overlook the signs of increasing value consensus in many areas of life. I would guess that there are greater (not less) consensus on race relations today than a generation ago, more agreement on legitimate political procedures, both national and international, and fuller acceptance of the values underlying social welfare (social security, minimum wages, unemployment compensation, and the like). This observation is not disproved by the existence of sharp conflict, because the conflict is often caused by those who see the rising consensus, dislike its implications, and make a last-ditch stand.

Good evidence suggests that any picture of the mass media simply as agencies of manipulation in a sociocultural vacuum is oversimplified and misleading. In some measure the mass media are a unifying force; to some degree they are dependent, not independent, forces—reflecting the values of audiences and filtered through the existing group structures in a "two-step," or three- or four step, process that shapes their messages.

Under some conditions, new social unities appear that counteract spreading anomie by offering new norms—or a mixture of old and new. Religious movements led by charismatic prophets or political movements can often be interpreted in this way. That some of these "normative reactions to normlessness," as Becker called them,[8] are repugnant by one's own standards should suggest again that anomie is not necessarily worse than the alternatives to anomie.

It would be a mistake to minimize the unifying effects of some of the large, formal structures so characteristic of the modern world. Political parties furnish unifying symbols and expectations (often reflecting negotiated compromise, of course) that are the basis for normatively guided interaction. Bureaucratic structures, seen in common-sense terms as instruments for frustrating individual desires, are perhaps more fully viewed as sources of procedural agreement and goal specification. The paradoxical mixture of chaos and rigidity by which large formal structures are often described is more likely to be the result of imperfect or incomplete bureaucratization than of its excessive development.

I do not mean to imply, of course, that anomie would disappear if all our associations were carried on within bureaucratic structures. As "artificially" designed sociocultural systems, they carry many imperfections; and since almost no one invests more than part of self in them, their interactions are affected by various competing values and interests. In my judgment, however, their net influence—granted the presence of a complex division of labor, heterogeneity of interests and values, and the mobility of the modern world—is to reduce anomie, both in the sense of lack of normative agreement among interacting individuals and in the sense of scarcity of culturally approved means for achieving approved goals.

As a final indication that anomie may not be as prevalent in the urban world as we sometimes suppose, one can point to the paradoxical fact that some of the presumed signs of normlessness—the "rebellious" behavior of youth, for example—are in part expressions of widely held norms. They appear to be violations because they are "second-level," or as David Matza and Gresham Sykes call them, "subterranean values." [9] For most persons they occupy a secondary position in the scheme of things; they are, in fact, at least partly in contradiction to basic values and are therefore frowned upon, especially if given prominence. Yet the search for thrills, the hope for a job where one gets maximum returns for a minimum of effort, aggression, and bohemianism all find their support in the dominant culture. One may not like some of these expressions, but that does not indicate they are not part of the culture. Some of the strong opposition to what is sometimes called the youth subculture can, in fact, be interpreted as projection: adults are having a difficult time repressing some of their own tendencies in similar directions. The vigor of the opposition is as much an effort to persuade themselves as the adolescents to hold fast to the primary values.

We should not exaggerate the point about subterranean values, for we need to explain why some persons should give major emphasis to what are for others muted themes. Anomie in the Merton sense is doubtless involved: unable to satisfy their aspirations by the most approved methods, some adolescents exalt into primary values those subterranean values for which means are available.

NORMATIVE COMPLEXITY AND ANOMIE

There is another approach to the question of the extent of anomie in modern societies. Many of the judgments are based on a model of a small, homogeneous, relatively slowly changing society. Against such a model, value complexity and even value conflict, numerous subcultures, and the breakup of traditional norms present a picture of apparent normlessness. But this is perhaps to ask the question in the wrong way. If we take for granted a great deal of social and physical mobility and social change— and I scarcely see how we can escape them—we then need to ask "What new structures are necessary for reasonably smooth running of such a system? Have such structures been developed?" The choice is not between cultural unity and full anomie, as I have used these terms above. Modern societies are made up of various combinations of the four normative situations I have discussed, with the two "middle" ones—pluralism and subcultural anomie—often of great importance. Such societies, if they are not to be torn apart by intolerant subsocieties within them or to fall apart as a result of full anomie, require certain values and structures, but they do not require full cultural unity.

What then are some of the requirements? There has to be substantial agreement on procedures, on the rules of the game; this implies a readiness to accept defeat. Such readiness depends upon a belief that most others accept the same rules and also upon a belief that defeat, if it comes, is only temporary (however long "temporary" may be in different perspectives). As part of its minimum cultural unity a heterogeneous society also requires tolerance, which in turn probably depends upon the sharing of several broad goals or core values; for it is doubtless true that we are never tolerant of values that seem to us to be fundamentally in error. Complex societies need a number of positions whose role is to negotiate between disagreeing and competing groups and individuals. Politicians, mediators, arbitrators, communication specialists, personnel officers, and some clergymen occupy such positions.

Since the urban-industrial world is generally characterized by high aspirations, it requires social processes to assist those who fail. Of course, this is one of the primordial functions of religion, which can be thought of (in a limited sense) as a group of beliefs and practices whereby a group struggles with its ultimate failures. The more exuberant varieties of nationalism and prejudice may be functionally connected with the fact or the fear of failure. (I scarcely need to note that such responses to the anomic gap between aspirations and achievements may be quite dysfunctional for the system within which they grow.) Identification with the heroes of the sports world, motion pictures, or fiction may add glamor and power to life, thus helping to close the gap. Projection of our hopes onto the next generation helps us to prolong the length of time we are willing to accept "temporary" failure (and for this reason, the disjunction between means and ends is least likely to lead to various deviant responses among groups with strong family systems).

Beyond these are a large number of other social processes which are designed to serve what Erving Goffman nicely calls the "cooling-out" function. The "failure" is offered a different position—one with less prestige perhaps, but not without its compensations; new chances to requalify are kept open; timing of announcement of the failure is designed to permit the individual to make it appear that he resigned; or he is eased out with a consolation prize—a pension, a paid vacation, or a letter of commendation.[10]

Burton Clark has described the elaborate cooling-out mechanisms in American higher education. In a society that stresses the need for college education and suggests that it is readily available to everyone, the abrupt flunking of those who did not measure up to minimum standards would produce a large amount of resentment, with tendencies toward deviation, apathetic withdrawal, and other socially disruptive responses. These may in fact be common responses (in view of the millions who have flunked out, it is unfortunate that we know little about the consequences), but they are reduced by means of probationary periods, counseling services, soft courses, nonacademic colleges (if that is not a contradiction in terms), and other devices for giving ill-prepared and ill-motivated students a college degree or easing them gently off the campus.[11]

These various processes can be thought of as the means by which a heterogeneous society prevents pluralism from developing into subcultural anomie and subcultural anomie from spiraling into full anomie. Underlying them all is the powerful bond of interdependence. However much the members of a complex society may disagree with one another, they cannot avoid the fact that they need one another. This interdependence is sometimes obscured (when defeat threatens to be permanent, when the value of tolerance has been insufficiently emphasized, when mediators are few, when core values are inadequate, when cooling-out mechanisms are lacking—to refer to our previous list). Then only a dramatic demonstration will make it clear again—clear to the Southern merchant that he needs Negro customers, to the industrialist that he needs well-motivated workers, to the Negro pupil that he needs teachers. Other things being equal, however, the growth of functional interdependence helps to integrate a society even when there are serious, if not absolute, value disagreements.

This general line of reasoning, which suggests that the criteria for judging the integration and strength of a small, homogeneous society are not wholly appropriate to the study of complex societies, can be carried one step further. Complex societies may *need* some value differences beyond those required to take advantage of the division of labor. On the surface it seems unfortunate that the trustees and the faculties of universities almost universally disagree on a number of questions. Their interaction often seems quite anomic. But such clashes of perspective, when limited by the devices I have discussed above, may be essential to facilitate the flexibility and inventiveness that are essential under conditions of rapid change of circumstance.

Moreover, insofar as different groups have different functions to perform, some value disagreement may promote effective coordination. In

Herman Turk's words: "Specialized values are seen not only as supports for the activities of specialized parts but also as deterrents against the entry of one part into the activity domain of another." [12] He was discussing the usefulness of the different values of student physicians and nurses in a hospital, but one can think of other instances: Value clashes between adults and adolescents may support the declaration of independence that the child finally has to make. In a rapidly changing society so obviously in need—to express my own opinion—of new patterns, a lack of discomfort among young people with the culture they were being handed would be a most unfortunate situation. Even religious leaders have been known to suggest that they bring not peace but a sword and are come to set son against father.[13]

Many of these observations concerning the integration of heterogeneous societies can be summed up by saying that clashes of values need not weaken a society and may indeed strengthen it if they do not run so deep that they cut through the agreement on procedures, tolerance, and the core values—and if they are not cumulative. By the last phrase I refer to the fact that in the modern world we often agree with a person on one thing and disagree on a second, while with another person we disagree on the first thing and agree on the second. This pattern is supported by the cross-cutting group memberships that characterize some societies, particularly the United States. We work on a committee of the PTA with political opponents and bowl with persons from another church. The people with whom we work often do not live in our neighborhood. Under such conditions, value disagreements do not reinforce one another. Political sociologists have shown that cross-cutting memberships are associated with the two-party system and stable democratic governments. If one's political opponents win, the fact does not seem disastrous, because they are members of one's church, occupational group, or association.

The stabilizing effect of this pattern has definite limits. Americans are members of fewer groups than the stereotype suggests—which means that there are fewer opportunities for cross-cutting memberships. Strong tendencies exist, moreover, toward the cumulation of differences. This is most obvious when races are compared, for differences of class, education, religion, residence, and other factors may be added to the racial difference. But cumulation occurs elsewhere also, as a small-town businessman knows when he talks to a college professor or as a wealthy farmer realizes when he meets an unemployed industrial worker.

We are led back, then, to the realization that modern society—despite the many "offsets" that I have referred to—has strong tendencies toward anomie. When individuals with different cultural training interact, as they do so frequently today, there are bound to be situations of normlessness —a lack of *mutually agreed-upon* goals and methods. When new elements, affecting various persons at different speeds, are introduced into a more or less coherent system at a rate as rapid as we have seen in the twentieth century, normative vacuums inevitably arise. The appearance of a money economy, as Simmel, Marx, Tönnies, and others have shown, predisposes a society to anomie. Money permits the development of an impersonal market, the substitution of a "cash nexus" for the face-to-face relationships of a self-sufficient or barter economy. For the most part, money is morally neutral. Once obtained, a stolen dollar buys the same goods and services as an earned dollar, a fact that weakens the social controls over legitimate means that characterize face-to-face economic exchanges.

Aspirations and expectations are more easily made available to the members of a society than are opportunities for their realization. An open society allows more climbing, but at the same time may promote more lowering of status. And the frustrations of those who do not climb, or who fall, are doubtless more severe in open than in closed societies. The result of the gap between desires and opportunities, as Merton has carefully shown, is to increase deviant behavior.

Democratic, industrial societies tend to lack value leaders, respected embodiments of the superego who can reaffirm shared values and help to form required new ones. Such a function can be performed only poorly by political leaders, who in a democratic society must be followers to an important degree. (This is not to suggest, of course, that oligarchy is better; it has its own problems in winning value allegiance. And even if it is more effective, one still must ask, "Effective in achieving what goals?") Students of the church, in the sociological meaning of the term, will note the dilemma faced by religious leaders—not unlike the dilemma faced by democratic politicians—in their attempts to serve as value leaders. Professors in our open and heterogeneous society seek objectivity and balance; few profess. The trained incapacity to ask policy and value questions is apparent in most scientists. Public schools are dependent institutions to a large degree, unable to depart far from their constituencies in exploring normative issues. There are, of course, important exceptions to each of these statements; but I believe the exceptions qualify without disproving the point that such societies as the United States are relatively lacking in positions whose role is to renew the value system.

ANOMIE AND ALIENATION

I have emphasized that anomie, as an analytic concept, is a property of groups. Interactions among individuals can be anomic, that is, lacking in consensus on goals or means or both, but in my use of the term, an individual cannot be anomic. Tendencies in the individual which contribute to or result from deregulation in the structures within which he acts are empirically associated with anomie in significant ways. To fail to conceptualize them separately, however, is to reduce our ability to understand the *variety* of relationships between anomic situations and the persons interacting therein. The individual fact is not the mirror image of the social fact or its simple cause or effect. We need terms which refer unambiguously to the individual as well as the social level.

This in no way implies that the levels lack mutual influence. Indeed, any full understanding requires that we explore further both the responses of individuals to anomie (including the conditions under which the responses are made) and the sources of anomie in various patterns of individual behavior. Merton's discussion of spiraling anomie referred to earlier is just such a statement of the mutual influence of anomie and individual behavior. And I have noted that the behaviorally significant dimension of anomie cannot be measured without reference to the tendencies of individuals who experience it.

The need for analytically distinct terms as well as for examination of empirical relationships is not always satisfied. The understandable but perhaps unfortunate propensity in some of the literature is to refer to anomie as an individual tendency. Thus Riesman speaks of anomic individuals who are, in his words, "virtually synonymous with maladjusted." [14] They are ruleless and ungoverned (which, he notes, is not necessarily an unhappy state of affairs). Seeman thinks of anomie as one of the forms of alienation, although he is careful to distinguish it from anomie in the sociological sense.[15] Srole has devised a scale for what he calls "self-to-others alienation" that he labels an "anomia" scale, thereby suggesting its relationship to the normlessness of Durkheim's term, yet calling attention to the individual referent by the Anglicized spelling. Anomia, as Srole defines it, is compounded of an individual's feeling "that community leaders are detached from and indifferent to his needs," that the social order is fickle and unpredictable, that his lot is getting worse, that life has lost meaning (which Srole regards as closest to Durkheim's use of anomie), and that even close personal relationships are unsupportive— "These days a person doesn't really know whom he can count on." [16]

Ample evidence now exists that individual tendencies measured by Srole's scale, and by various elaborations of it, are significantly related to class position and mobility experience, residence, race, religion, level of prejudice, and other individual attributes. Although it is not usually clear whether "anomia" is an independent or a dependent variable, one can at least affirm that when an individual's score on the Srole scale is known, other characteristics and tendencies can be inferred to a useful degree.

Strangely enough, however, none of the research on anomia as an individual fact examines its relationship to anomie as a property of the group. To measure individual responses to a brief test is relatively easy; to devise independent measures of normlessness as a property of a social system is exceedingly difficult. Thus the vast majority of studies of anomia, even though most of them have been carried out by sociologists, have almost no sociology in them. They relate one individual measure to one or more other individual measures (class status, religion, residence, authoritarian tendencies, etc.). Such items as class status are sometimes treated as structural variables, but not appropriately so when they refer to an individual's placement. The class pattern of one's neighborhood or community, on the other hand, is a structural variable; and it may independently affect anomia score. Thus Bell found in a probability sample of 701 San Francisco residents that what he called anomie scores, which could range from 0 to 10, varied significantly between areas of different economic standing, as well as between families of different economic standing when area was controlled.[17]

	Anomie score
High individual status in area of low average status	3.4
Low individual status in area of low average status	4.6
High individual status in area of high average status	2.7
Low individual status in area of high average status	3.6

These are simply statistical relationships, of course, and can be interpreted only by the introduction of various test variables or by other methodological procedures. But they do indicate the need for attention to structural influences on individual tendencies toward "anomia."

While Bell made use of a structural variable (economic status of the area) in his study of correlates of individual attitudes, he did not measure anomie as a group fact. Indeed, he kept the Durkheim spelling to refer to the measure of personal disorganization and demoralization, as do many others.[18] Perhaps a larger number of researchers have followed Srole's lead by using anomia as the term designating an individual's self-to-other alienation.[19]

Thus in the literature on this question one is confronted with a constant problem of translation. Keeping the terms straight would be no particular burden if it were not associated with risks of confusion and theoretical inadequacy. Virtually none of the research is interested in the problems raised by Durkheim: the implications of normlessness as a structural fact for individual behavior (self-centeredness, suicide, unrestrained ambition), and to some degree the implications of individual behavior for the spread of normlessness through the structure. Why then should we use the same term, "anomie," or a similar one, "anomia," to refer to an individual property? In my judgment, this use both reflects and perpetuates theoretical confusion. It indicates the difficulty of maintaining a sharp analytic distinction between the structural and the individual levels while yet exploring their mutual influences. To an important degree, the way these terms are used represents the psychologizing of sociology—the very process Durkheim fought against. It is ironic that a term which he brought into current use should prove to be one of the agents of the process.

I do not in any way imply that the analysis of demoralization as an individual fact is unimportant, but only suggest that its substitution for or confusion with the analysis of the deregulation of interaction is unfortunate. Unless both processes are kept before us, we are likely to disregard one or to assume an overly close causal connection between the two: deregulation causes demoralization, or vice versa. In fact, some persons in anomic settings are not demoralized, and some persons express high levels of "anomia" in a normatively coherent situation.

Perhaps we can learn to make the necessary distinction between anomie and anomia. I believe we would be wise, however, to use a different term for the latter. "Alienation" is often employed today to refer to some of the same individual tendencies that Srole included under anomia, although the connotations of alienation tend to be wider. The more impressionistic discussions are not free from the tendency to assume a uniform relationship between the individual and the group measurement. But research on the topic of alienation has tended to be much more concerned than the anomia studies with the influence of social structure, independently defined.[20]

On examination, alienation proves to be a highly complex concept. In a careful review of its many uses, Seeman separates five quite distinct meanings: powerlessness, meaninglessness, normlessness, isolation, and self-estrangement.[21] Further study is required to discover whether additional dimensions are needed or whether, on the contrary, these forms of alienation can be expressed in fewer dimensions or scaled as points along a single continuum. In his study of a random sample of the adult residents of a city in Florida, Middleton found interesting evidence of a Guttman scale formed from five of the six "types of alienation" which he had used. The coefficient of reproducibility was .90. Thus, he suggests, there may be a unity underlying the various expressions of alienation capable of measurement by a single scale.[22] In fact, we may need more, rather than fewer, measures of individual tendencies toward alienation; and we may need several measures of anomie in a social system. For purposes of simplicity, however, we can think in terms of two scales and can note that from a field theoretical perspective, behavior is a function of their interaction.

I have suggested above that the extent of normative agreement as a group variable might be scaled in four steps ranging from cultural unity to full anomie. Extending Middleton's suggested scale, which included only the "negative" end, we might speak of an integration-estrangement variable on the individual level, ranging from full identification with society to "normlessness," which was the most extreme expression of alienation in his measurements. (Preferably, of course, the two ranges would be described in numerical, not descriptive, terms.) Behavior, then, is not the result of contact with a situation at a given level of anomie, or the consequence of tendencies at a particular level of alienation. A highly anomic setting is experienced very differently by a person who is also deeply alienated than by a person who is low in alienation. The need is for systematic study of the consequences of various combinations of anomie and alienation. In addition, we require study of the effects of behavior on anomie and alienation. At a given moment in time, the prevailing levels of anomie and alienation can be regarded as causes of behavior; but seen in process, they must also be regarded as results.

In his classic papers on the subject, Merton carefully distinguishes anomie from individual responses thereto. He emphasizes the form of anomie characterized by scarcity of, or insufficient regard for, approved means to culturally taught goals. Thus he notes that under various circumstances, individuals may conform to both goals and means, strive for the goals by any available means (innovation), give up the goals in favor of maintaining approved means (ritualism), withdraw from allegiance to both goals and means (retreatism), or develop ambivalent attitudes toward both (rebellion).[23] The sociological task is to take such a paradigm, and such revisions as that of Robert Dubin,[24] and to specify the conditions under which the various individual responses are made. The task further is to note the ways in which the individual responses feed back into the social system, deepening or reducing the anomie which promoted them.

A full behavioral science takes an additional step. By including the study of individuals—of the presence or absence of alienation in various forms—it leads us to explore the *range* of effects of an anomic setting. Empirically we see such variant behavior as individual disintegration, withdrawal into some form of privatism, attempts to renew the normative order, attempts to establish new norms, and the shift of identity to a nonanomic subsociety. For example, among American Negroes, most of whom probably confront an anomic world, one finds a range from alcoholism and mental illness, to crime, to support for the Black Muslims, to Freedom Rides, to full yet critical participation in society. Doubtless this expresses in part the wide variation in the nature of their social experience; but since individuals from similar contexts respond differently, the range also suggests the need for study of the various tendencies they bring into the situation.

CONCLUSION

In the chapters that follow, I hope to contribute to a reformulation of the approach to three vitally significant areas of research: the study of criminal, discriminatory, and abnormal behavior. I shall discuss them from the perspective of this chapter by emphasizing the need for simultaneous attention to the structures and stresses both in the individual and in the social systems of which he is a part. This selection of topics does not imply that field theory is primarily designed to deal with the conflict-laden or abnormal forms of human behavior. I have chosen the topics for another reason: structures and processes that are difficult to see under relatively stable conditions are more clearly revealed under conditions of stress and change. The underlying principles which I seek to identify, however, should apply to the full range of human behavior.

FOOTNOTES

Note: The bracketed number following an author's name refers to the footnote in which the source is cited in full.

1. Emile Durkheim, *Suicide,* The Free Press of Glencoe, 1951, p. 253.

2. Robert K. Merton, *Social Theory and Social Structure,* rev. ed., The Free Press of Glencoe, 1957, chaps. 4 and 5.

3. *Ibid.,* p. 180.

4. Robin M. Williams, Jr., *American Society,* 2d ed., Alfred A. Knopf, Inc., 1960, chap. 10.

5. Daniel Bell, *The End of Ideology,* The Free Press of Glencoe, 1960, pp. 21–22.

6. Durkheim [1], p. 253.

7. William Kornhauser, *The Politics of Mass Society,* The Free Press of Glencoe, 1959 p. 33.

8. Howard Becker, "Normative Reactions to Normlessness," *American Sociological Review,* December, 1960, pp. 803–810.

9. David Matza, "Subterranean Traditions of Youth," *The Annals of the American Academy of Political and Social Science,* November, 1961, pp. 102–118; David Matza and Gresham Sykes, "Juvenile Delinquency and Subterranean Values," *American Sociological Review,* October, 1961, pp. 712–719.

10. Erving Goffman, "Cooling the Mark Out: Some Aspects of Adaptation to Failure," *Psychiatry,* November, 1952, pp. 451–463.

11. Burton Clark, "The 'Cooling-out' Function in Higher Education," *American Journal of Sociology,* May, 1960, pp. 569–576.

12. Herman Turk, "Social Cohesion through Variant Values: Evidence from Medical Role Relations," *American Sociological Review,* February, 1963, p. 28.

13. Were there time, the theme of this paragraph could be extended by explorations of such topics as the functions of conflict (Georg Simmel, *Conflict,* The Free Press of Glencoe, 1955; Lewis Coser, *The Functions of Social Conflict,* The Free Press of Glencoe, 1956), the functions of ignorance (Louis Schneider, "The Role of the Category of Ignorance in Sociological Theory," *American Sociological Review,* August, 1962, pp. 492–508; Wilbert E. Moore and Melvin M. Tumin, "Some Social Functions of Ignorance," *American Sociological Review,* December, 1949, pp. 787–795), and the functions of insulation (Rose L. Coser, "Insulation from Observability and Types of Social Conformity," *American Sociological Review,* February, 1961, pp. 28–39).

14. See David Riesman, *The Lonely Crowd,* Yale University Press, 1961, pp. 240–245.

15. Melvin Seeman, "On the Meaning of Alienation," *American Sociological Review,* December, 1959, pp. 783–791.

16. Leo Srole, "Social Integration and Certain Corollaries: An Exploratory Study," *American Sociological Review,* December, 1956, pp. 709–716.

17. Wendell Bell, "Anomie, Social Isolation, and the Class Structure," *Sociometry*, June, 1957, pp. 105–116.

18. A. H. Roberts and Milton Rokeach, "Anomie, Authoritarianism, and Prejudice: A Replication," *American Journal of Sociology*, January, 1956, pp. 355–358; Edward L. McDill, "Anomie, Authoritarianism, Prejudice, and Socioeconomic Status: An Attempt at Clarification," *Social Forces*, March, 1961, pp. 239–245; Dwight G. Dean and Jon A. Reeves, "Anomie: A Comparison of a Catholic and a Protestant Sample," *Sociometry*, June, 1962, pp. 209–212; and H. M. Blalock, Jr., "Correlated Independent Variables: The Problem of Multicollinearity," *Social Forces*, December, 1963, pp. 233–237. On the other hand, several recent studies have made effective use of anomie as a structural concept. See Robin Williams [4]; Alan C. Kerckhoff, "Anomie and Achievement Motivation: A Study of Personality Development within Cultural Disorganization," *Social Forces*, March, 1959, pp. 196–202; Richard A. Cloward and Lloyd E. Ohlin, *Delinquency and Opportunity*, The Free Press of Glencoe, 1960; William J. Goode, "Illegitimacy, Anomie, and Cultural Penetration," *American Sociological Review*, December, 1961, pp. 910–925; and Jetse Sprey, "Sex Differences in Occupational Choice Patterns among Negro Adolescents," *Social Problems*, Summer, 1962, pp. 11–23.

19. See Dorothy L. Meier and Wendell Bell, "Anomia and Differential Access to the Achievement of Life Goals," *American Sociological Review*, April, 1959, pp. 189–202; E. H. Mizruchi, "Social Structure and Anomia in a Small City," *American Sociological Review*, October, 1960, pp. 645–654; Robert C. Angell, "Preference for Moral Norms in Three Problem Areas," *American Journal of Sociology*, May, 1962, pp. 650–660; Robert L. Hamblin, "The Dynamics of Racial Discrimination," *Social Problems*, Fall, 1962, pp. 103–121; Lewis M. Killian and Charles M. Grigg, "Urbanism, Race, and Anomia," *American Journal of Sociology*, May, 1962, pp. 661–665; John D. Photiadis and Jeanne Biggar, "Religiosity, Education, and Social Distance," *American Journal of Sociology*, May, 1962, pp. 666–672; and Richard L. Simpson and H. Max Miller, "Social Status and Anomia," *Social Problems*, Winter, 1963, pp. 256–264.

20. See Gwynn Nettler, "A Measure of Alienation," *American Sociological Review*, December, 1957, pp. 670–677; Jan Hajda, "Alienation and Integration of Student Intellectuals," *American Sociological Review*, October, 1961, pp. 758–777; Leonard Pearlin, "Alienation from Work: A Study of Nursing Personnel," *American Sociological Review*, June, 1962, pp. 314–326; Melvin Seeman and John W. Evans, "Alienation and Learning in a Hospital Setting," *American Sociological Review*, December, 1962, pp. 772–782; and Russell Middleton, "Alienation, Race, and Education," *American Sociological Review*, December, 1963, pp. 973–977.

21. See Melvin Seeman [15]; see also Dwight G. Dean, "Alienation: Its Meaning and Measurement," *American Sociological Review*, October, 1961, pp. 753–758; and Arthur G. Neal and Salomon Rettig, "Dimensions of Alienation among Manual and Non-manual Workers," *American Sociological Review*, August, 1963, pp. 599–608.

22. Russell Middleton [20], p. 975; see also Nettler [20].

23. Robert Merton [2], chap. 4.

24. Robert Dubin, "Deviant Behavior and Social Structure," *American Sociological Review*, April, 1959, pp. 147–164.

CHAPTER 10

The Field View
of Delinquency

Law violation by juveniles has received a great deal of careful observation and theoretical interpretation in the last several decades. Although hampered by difficulties of definition and by inadequacy and noncomparability of data, researchers have been drawn to the subject both by its great practical importance and by its significance for a general theory of behavior.[1] The quality of the research is often very high.

Clear formulation of a theory of delinquency has been obstructed, however, by a tendency to overlook the complexity of the phenomenon. This tendency reflects not only the narrowing effects of disciplinary perspectives on some students of delinquency, but also a failure sometimes to recognize that delinquency may take many forms. To state a "theory of illness"—that is, to specify the broad range of variables which must be measured in the study of illness, is one thing; to state a theory of smallpox or influenza is something else. Propositions regarding the latter must, of course, be derived from the former. One seeks as powerful a general theory as he can devise, in order to explain the maximum number of observations with the fewest possible concepts. But the variables to which one's attention is directed by the theory may combine in exceedingly diverse ways. The task of research is to seek out the conditions under which the full range of combinations can occur.

Social scientists have always given some attention to types of delinquency, and this attention has grown, to the benefit of contemporary studies. But effective delineation of types has been retarded by the tendency to formulate them in fairly narrow terms. Few specialists today define problems of research in delinquency in strictly psychological or sociocultural terms. There is too much evidence that both inner tendencies and external situations are involved to permit a narrow statement of the questions. Researchers have a persistent tendency, however, to downgrade one or the other of these sets of forces to a minority position as a kind of nuisance that must be given some attention, but that actually obscures the fundamental causes.

Thus Sheldon Glueck writes: ". . . whatever be the element of social disintegration we are concerned with, its influence makes itself felt only on a *selected group of individuals*. It must therefore be the physical and mental make-up of offenders, as compared with nonoffenders, that pre-sents the crucial and practical issue in the study of crime causation." [2] The *non sequitur* in this last sentence is matched on the other side by some sociologists who emphasize cultural norms, the influence of the group, and community patterns as "the crucial and practical issues." They tend to overlook the problem associated with the fact that only some of those exposed to the crime-supporting situation engage in crime.

Cohen and Short have noted that much of the controversy concerning delinquency theory "turns out to be pointless . . . if we think of sociologi-cal theories and psychological theories as concerned with answering different questions." [3] This is certainly true. The attempt to identify indi-viduals who are delinquency-prone and the effort to describe situations which are delinquency-supporting are complementary. One frequent diffi-culty in such studies, however, has been to remember that one is abstract-ing from a complicated field of interacting forces. The temptation to try to explain behavior in terms of an analytic variable is very strong; it is encouraged, no doubt, by the inability of persons who seek to explain behavior by a different analytic variable to present a convincing case.

Even when a researcher recognizes the analytic quality of his state-ments and emphasizes the proviso "all other things being equal," the design of his study may cause him to overlook the principle of multiple possibilities. For example, suppose Sheldon and Eleanor Glueck estab-lished that delinquents differ from a matched group of "normal boys" in the factors presented in their prediction tables. (This supposes a great deal, but I will not explore here the question of sampling, the problems associated with dealing only with "committed" delinquents, the difficulty in establishing the time sequence of the variables measured, etc.) The Gluecks' findings do not establish these factors as independent causes. One needs to ask: Will overstrict and erratic discipline by the father, lack of maternal supervision, lack of parental affection, preference for excite-ment, tendency toward extroversion, and other factors be associated with delinquency in other sociocultural situations? In England? In Israel? Among middle-class Midwesterners? With the Gluecks' evidence one can only say that the factors operating in the setting studied are associated with delinquency.

Equally important, one must ask: Are other forms of "deviation" associated with those factors? The controls in the study were "normal" boys, but the factors are highly similar to those often found associated with mental illness, as well, of course, as with at least a minority of the normals. For example, many, but not all, of the background factors presumably predisposing an individual to delinquency were also characteristic of the lower-class schizophrenics studied by Myers and Roberts.[4] This fact suggests that "the same" tendencies are associated with different patterns of behavior, depending upon the context.

The principle of multiple possibilities applies equally well to situations. In describing the "Lower Class Culture as a Generating Milieu of Gang Delinquency," Miller in effect develops a sociological prediction table to match (or to supplant) the Gluecks' psychological prediction table, so far as it applies to lower-class gang activities. He sees delinquency as a normal expression of the search for status, conditions, and qualities that are "valued within the actor's most significant cultural milieu." [5] In the lower-class cultural situation as Miller describes it—a situation where trouble is endemic; where toughness, smartness, excitement, and autonomy are highly valued; where fate seems to control one's life chances; where the one-sex peer unit, not the two-sex parental family unit, is the dominating group—gang delinquency is a normal consequence of socialization. "Lower class culture is a distinctive tradition many centuries old with an integrity of its own." [6]

In developing his thesis, Miller draws on a long and strong tradition in delinquency research that emphasizes a sociological point of view in order to complement and correct individualistic interpretations. This tradition has sought to answer the question: What are the sociocultural conditions that maximize the likelihood of delinquent behavior? This is an essential question. To answer it, however, is not to answer equally important questions: Why do some of the persons brought up in such situations not become delinquent? What other patterns of behavior appear frequently in such contexts (religious or political movements, mental illness, drug addiction, high aspiration for upward social mobility)? Delinquent behavior is clearly not the inevitable consequence of any known environment. Although they vary in the support they give to delinquency, all environments have multiple possibilities, depending upon who (individuals with what tendencies) experience them.

These reciprocal relationships can be expressed in terms of scales which describe the fact that delinquency is most likely to occur when individuals with serious problems of adjustment to self and/or society are found in situations that facilitate illegal expression of those tendencies. On the one hand we need a measure of delinquency proneness; on the other a measure of the delinquency-encouraging aspects of the environment. Although explicit scales that take account of a wide range of individual and structural factors are lacking, important progress toward them has been made in the prediction tables designed by the Gluecks and in the rich, but somewhat less quantified, descriptions of delinquency areas and subcultures by Shaw, Thrasher, Cohen, Miller, Cloward, Ohlin, and many others. To improve upon present measures we need clear specification of the variables that define a delinquency-encouraging environment and a delinquency-prone individual, as well as a factoring out of the variables most critical in affecting behavior.

ENVIRONMENTAL SUPPORTS FOR DELINQUENCY

The extensive studies of recent years indicate several factors that seem to be important in describing a delinquency-encouraging environment. *First*, following W. B. Miller's emphasis, we would need to measure the range of social structures, traditions, and values—shared attitudes toward the law, individual characteristics that are esteemed and rewarded, and the groups that define one's major experiences. In a recent paper, for example, Cohen and Hodges have richly described the social world of the lower-lower class in a sample drawn from several California counties. Although these authors are not directly concerned with crime or delinquency, they lend support to the view that lower-class persons experience a sociocultural world which is significantly different in many ways from that of persons who have higher status. They note particularly the way in which the insecurities of lower-class existence tend to encourage a morality focused on the small group of friends and relatives set against the wide circle of threatening strangers. "The LL's stake, therefore, is in a morality of particularistic loyalties and reciprocities." [7] This is not a context in which respect for impersonal law is strongly supported.[8]

Second, the extent of anomie, both in the sense of interaction among persons who do not agree on the rules for guiding the interaction and in the somewhat narrower sense emphasized by Merton (disjunction between goals and socially structured means for achieving those goals), seems likely to be an environmental factor associated with delinquency. Unfortunately, as was noted in Chapter 9, no good measures of anomie have been designed. Partly because of that, value perspectives intrude easily into interpretations of its significance. At our present level of knowledge a plausible hypothesis is that in a society with a strong success ideology, "the threat of defeat motivates men to the use of those tactics, beyond the law or the mores, which promise 'success.' " [9] To support or refute this hypothesis definitely will be difficult, because each of the items is difficult to define and to measure.

An anomic situation is one in which a large number of persons, relative to some other situation, experience discrepancy between the social goals as they aspire to them and accessible means as they experience them. That is, anomie is measured by individual facts that have been aggregated into a social rate. It cannot be determined, therefore, simply by designating generally approved goals (for occupational advance, increased income, or whatever) and generally available means (educational or training institutions, open and competitive exams, and the like). The crucial discrepancy is the gap experienced by individuals between their goals and means. When many persons feel this discrepancy—that is, when the social setting is anomic—processes are set in motion (a spiraling of the use of illegitimate means, for example) which are less likely to arise when few persons experience a discrepancy. Thus anomie as a social fact is important in its own right, as Durkheim so strongly emphasized. Yet its very strength cannot be measured without accurate individual data.

Merton has noted that we need data on socially patterned differentials in *"exposure* to the cultural goal and norms regulating behavior oriented toward that goal," *acceptance* of the goal and norms, relative *accessibility* of means, and the extent of *discrepancy* between goals and opportunities (which when aggregated would indicate the degree of anomie), as well as data on rates of various kinds of deviant behavior (and, we might add, nondeviant behavior).[10] Each of the terms above is difficult to measure. For example, is education "accessible" to a Negro who attends an excellent integrated high school but whose family is able to furnish little motivational support because of the effects of past discrimination? Is a goal "accepted" if, as appears in several studies of achievement motivation, there is a clear distinction between what one aspires to and what he expects? These difficulties of definition and measurement must be solved if the hypothesis of a relationship between anomie and delinquency (and other forms of deviation) is to be tested.[11]

A *third* structural factor strongly emphasized in sociological studies of delinquency and carefully explored by Cohen can be put in the form of a question: Are there many persons faced with similar problems of adjustment (to perceived failure, to feelings of injustice and helplessness, and the like) in close interaction? Collectively they may evolve patterns of behavior that would not develop among them individually.[12]

Fourth, to what degree are criminal opportunities available, as compared with other forms of action? Cloward and Ohlin have explored this question as one way of determining the *type* of delinquency that is likely to occur in a given setting (see below). The same question is relevant to measuring the structural support for the *amount* of delinquency. If criminal patterns are lacking and if, conversely, the forces of supervision, crime prevention, and law enforcement are strong and effective, persons with high delinquency potential will tend to struggle with their problems in nondelinquent ways.

As a *fifth* structural factor, information is needed on the extent to which supports for delinquency exist in the dominant normative system itself. Matza and Sykes have noted that delinquent behavior often seems to be an exaggerated expression of "subterranean values" not at all uncommon in the dominant society. The search for excitement, the use of "pull" to get by without too much work, and aggression, all of which, when raised to a style of life, are antinormative, are by no means uncommon as second-level values in the general culture.[13] Societies doubtless vary in the extent to which their cultural systems furnish normative preparation and support—even if beneath the surface of their most highly emphasized values—for delinquent behavior.

I do not mean to suggest that this listing of five structural factors that seem to be important in delinquency is in any sense definitive. There are doubtless gaps on the one hand and unnecessary duplications on the other. Since the factors are drawn from a review of the research and commentary on delinquency, however, a scale prepared from a measure of them would probably be useful in indicating the qualities of a delinquency-supporting environment. Communities where norms and structures are geared to illegality as the normal way of life, where anomie is high, where many persons struggle with problems of adjustment, where opportunities for delinquency are frequent, and where the surrounding culture furnishes semilegitimate or subterranean values that challenge the dominant norms, are communities in which delinquent *rates* are likely to be high.

Since we have only poor measures for several of these variables, their comparative importance and the patterns into which they cluster cannot be precisely stated. It seems quite possible that the structural supports are scalable in the Guttman sense, perhaps along something like the following lines:

		Types of Structural Support				
		I	II	III	IV	V
	Level of Support	Sub-terranean values	Anomie	Low level of social control	Many persons in area with problems of adjustment	Criminal subculture present
Middle class areas	1 (low)	Yes	No	No	No	No
	2	Yes	Yes	No	No	No
	3	Yes	Yes	Yes	No	No
Lower class areas	4	Yes	Yes	Yes	Yes	No
	5 (high)	Yes	Yes	Yes	Yes	Yes

This imaginary scale is meant only to suggest a problem, not to solve it. The weaknesses of the scale are apparent: for purposes of simplicity, each of the structural supports is treated as an attribute, although in reality each is a variable. The ordering is a preliminary guess and may well be wrong; indeed, the factors listed may be simply additive and not subject to such ordering at all. The variables may not be analytically distinct, but merely different names for the same factor; while other important variables may be missing. Yet the scale may suggest a procedure by which current debates over the nature and extent of structural supports to delinquency can be resolved.

In placing a "yes" in every cell of column I, I am supposing that no community is without subterranean supports for delinquency (I am thinking particularly of the United States but certainly not limiting the situation to this country). The search for excitement (kicks), for a good break (pull), for demonstrations of masculinity and toughness (aggression) that Matza and Sykes discuss are undoubtedly widely distributed.

As was noted in Chapter 9, the extent of anomie in American society may be exaggerated (or assumed) in current discussions. Yet there is good reason to believe that a society which emphasizes achievement will be characterized by widespread anomie, for hope seems easier to create than opportunity. Although anomie may be slight in some middle- and upper-class areas, as indicated on the chart, it seems likely to be characteristic, at least to some degree, of many others.

The concept of social control is seldom employed in research, doubtless because the term is difficult to define with sufficient precision to make measurement possible. I have in mind not only the formal control institutions of courts and police, but also the whole network of institutions—schools, churches, families—capable of maintaining stable patterns of sanctions and rewards. By the overlapping curved lines drawn at the left of the chart I mean to suggest that such patterns may be relatively lacking in some middle-class area, while they may be present in some stable lower-class areas.

In column IV, the phrase "many persons in area with problems of adjustment" refers to a social fact that is aggregated from a series of individual facts. Cohen has effectively shown that the likelihood of delinquency is affected by the extent to which there are many persons in close interaction who face similar problems. This is related to the fact that many deviants face the problem of handling their own guilt and anxiety. Without group support—which is in part a product of shared problems of adjustment—an individual's deviation is less likely to be against the system (delinquency), and more likely to entail withdrawal from the system or attacks upon himself. The chart says, in effect (comparing lines 3 and 4): Even though two areas are alike in level of support for delinquency furnished by subterranean values, by anomie, and by lack of social control, if there are more individuals in one area facing problems of adjustment than in the other, delinquency is more likely to be the outcome in the former *even if their individual tendencies toward delinquency are no stronger than in the latter.* This is, of course, an illustration of the structural effects emphasized by Durkheim.[14]

Column V represents the subcultural support for delinquency emphasized by Thrasher, Shaw, Sutherland, Miller, and others in the sociological tradition. By placing it fifth on the scale I imply that subcultural support is likely to occur only where the other four supports are also present. Moreover, this placement suggests that a distinction can be drawn between areas where many persons share problems of adjustment which lead them to an *emergent* delinquent "solution" (column IV) and areas where these tendencies are supported by *traditional* delinquent patterns.

If some such scale as this had adequate reliability and validity, we could begin to measure the proportion and location of areas with various levels of support for delinquent behavior. By using such measurements, one might be able to predict with some accuracy the *rate* of delinquency. This statement should not be taken, however, as an assertion of the adequacy of a purely structural theory of delinquency, because prediction of which individuals will engage in what kinds of delinquent behavior requires additional information of another kind.

INDIVIDUAL TENDENCIES TOWARD DELINQUENCY

The task of identifying and measuring the environmental factors is matched by the task of identifying and measuring the individual tendencies that predispose a person to delinquency as a way of struggling with his problems or seeking his goals.[15] Here again a wealth of material is available, but each study tends to follow its own course. There has been, therefore, less accumulation and less rapid designation of the basic personality variables than the extent of the work might have brought about. A more serious drawback from the point of view of adequate theory is that some of the interpretations of the tendencies predisposing an individual to delinquency fail to take systematic account of alternative ways in which the same tendencies may be expressed. Assuming, as I believe is reasonable, that delinquency proneness varies (not all or even most persons in a "high-delinquency" environment are offenders), one must determine whether or not the tendencies to delinquency are also associated with higher rates of mental illness, with "corner-boy" gang activities that are more retreatist than illegal, with different religious behavior, or with other expressions of the tendencies that depend upon the opportunities or stimulations of the surrounding environment.

Undoubtedly the most ambitious attempt to discover delinquency-producing traits is the work of the Gluecks. They are more sensitive to environmental influences than some of their critics contend, but this is shown more by way of incidental remarks than by systematic research procedures. They state, for example: "In the exciting, stimulating, but little-controlled and culturally inconsistent environment of the underprivileged area, such boys readily give expression to their untamed impulses and their self-centered desires by means of various forms of delinquent behavior." [16] Presumably in some other environment the same "impulses" and "desires" might be expressed in other ways, but the Gluecks do not follow up this line of thought. Their next sentence is: "Their tendencies toward uninhibited energy-expression are deeply anchored in soma and psyche and in the malformations of character during the first few years of life." [17]

By taking this approach to the problem, they are unable to explore possible supports for delinquency that come from normal socialization to a subculture oriented to illegality. Nor are they alerted to the *range* of environmental support, perhaps as measured by the factors I have listed above. Their "matching" of the home areas of their nondelinquent "controls" and their delinquent subjects on the basis of equal disprivilege does not necessarily match the subareas or neighborhoods, which are the critical environments for the boys, for extent of anomie, the structure of delinquent opportunities, or other structural factors.

While the Gluecks have made a valuable contribution to the understanding of delinquency, I believe they have been prevented from unraveling the causal forces by the way they posed the question. They were looking for "delinquents" and for the "traits" that distinguished them from "nondelinquents." A field view affirms that delinquents do not exist: delinquent *behavior* emerges in the continuous transactions between persons with certain tendencies and other persons and social situations.

Once again it is clear that the use of "extreme" cases can lead to good prediction, even when the theoretical argument is weak. If one deals only with boys committed to correctional schools, most of whom have records of repeated delinquency, and disregards the boys who are in parental custody or on probation for occasional illegality,[18] one can get good prediction from measurement of personal tendency only. The reason is that among these "high-score" boys, even environments with a low score will produce a transaction above the minimum required. By the same token, high-score social factors will also predict well by themselves, as the Gluecks found even with their limited range of social factors (discipline, affection from parents, and family cohesion). A theory that is parsimonious, however, must explain results equally well when scores are in the middle or low range.

If, in investigating the extent to which social class affects the chances of going to college, one studied only those persons with IQs under 80, he would surely get this answer: Class has no importance for determining the likelihood of college attendance; persons from upper, middle, and lower classes are equally unlikely to attend. Similarly, one could "refute" the importance of IQ in controlling college entrance by studying only those from the top status group. Since a high proportion of persons from this group attend college in spite of their IQ scores, such scores have little significance. No one would be content with either of these propositions. Obviously, the most valuable question is: What is the rate of college attendance under all the various possible combinations of social class and intelligence (thinking in terms of a two-variable model only)? In delinquency theory, unfortunately, some researchers are still content with an explanation derived from study of extreme cases of individual proneness or environmental support generalized to a total theory.

If the field point of view is accepted, the task is to prepare an adequate index of proneness to match an index of environmental support. Rorschach measures used by the Gluecks or the psychiatric assessment of "traits" that they use (adventurous, extroverted, suggestible, stubborn, emotionally unstable) might enter into the index. The "self concept" as explored by Reckless and his associates [19] seems to provide a valuable index if it is treated as a predisposing tendency, not a causal trait. Several writers have noted the importance of feelings of alienation from parents (partly as a result, in many cases, of neglect and cruelty compounded by culture conflict).[20]

Yablonsky's study of the violent gang, for example, contrasts the disorganized slum, where such gangs are found, with the stable slum (which may be the focus of attention of Thrasher, Shaw, and Miller). In the disorganized slum, normal processes of socialization are weak; institutions of social control are seriously inadequate; prejudice and discrimination frequently build both hostility and self-rejection. The personal deficiencies in the ability to relate to others, which are the frequent result of such conditions, make it difficult for the youths thus affected to take part in what Yablonsky calls delinquent and social gangs as well as sharply reducing their ability to participate in law-abiding groups. The violent gang makes minimum demands on social skills.

"The selection of violence by the sociopathic youth in his adjustment process is not difficult to understand. Violent behavior requires limited training, personal ability, or even physical strength. (As one gang boy stated: 'A knife or a gun makes you ten feet high.') ... Moreover, violence requires characteristics gang boys have in quantity: limited social ability and training, considerable resentment and aggression, and a motivation to retaliate against others." [21] In a society that emphasizes the rapid climb and the fast buck, the pattern of the violent gang is readily seen as a search for "instant status."

Yablonsky is by no means unaware of the social origins of these tendencies. He interprets the individual tendencies, in fact, as dependent variables, the independent or causal forces being the anomie, culture conflict, family disorganization, discrimination, social control breakdown, and the like, which characterize the disorganized slum.[22] It is one thing, however, to note these social forces as past causes of present individual tendencies; it is something else to see them as contemporary structures which set the range of alternatives within which individual tendencies will be worked out. In the latter sense Yablonsky tends to neglect the sociological aspects of delinquency causation.

Several writers have emphasized the difficulties, particularly for boys, in establishing a clear sex-role identity among some segments of modern society. The problem looms largest, of course, where unstable family patterns leave the mother-child relationship the major continuing one, with a succession of "fathers" being added to the household, or with a permanent father being clearly subordinate to his wife in power to support the family, or with the father being absent entirely. This primary source of the difficulty, however, is supported by other factors: occupational patterns which keep many fathers away from the home and often working in "abstract" jobs that cannot directly be communicated to children as models; educational patterns which place few men as teachers of the lower grades; and stable family patterns which emphasize the mother as the primary socializing agent for boys as well as girls.

The hypothesis that some forms of delinquency are expressions of an effort to prove one's masculinity seems highly plausible. Parsons, Cohen, Miller, Rohrer, Edmonson, among others, have suggested that the hypervirility and aggressiveness of some male adolescents have qualities of reaction formation; these behavior patterns can be understood as an effort in the face of serious doubts to convince themselves, as well as others, of their full masculinity.[23] Before this observation can be accepted with confidence, we need more precise measures of sex-role identity and fuller testing of its relationship to delinquency, other things being equal.

One further critical individual variable is the extent to which delinquent values have been internalized. Internalizing these values is not identical with living in an area where such values are widespread, for I am speaking here of an individual tendency. If a delinquent subculture has been thoroughly socialized into a person, he responds differently to pressures from law-enforcing influences than the person who is ambivalent does. The first suffers no guilt and seeks only to avoid punishment from those who support the dominant values. This pattern, however, is probably not common. There is strong evidence of wide sharing of norms throughout a society, mingled, in many cases, with the acceptance of contradictory norms.[24] The ambivalence in this pattern helps to account for the inaccessibility of some delinquents to communication, their nonutilitarian attack on the symbols of the dominant community, their maliciousness and negativism even when they seem to have nothing to gain thereby.[25] The repression of all tendencies toward identification with the dominant, law-abiding world may be an effort to avoid a painful conflict. Just as neurotics resist self-knowledge, so some delinquents press their antagonistic activities to the full—to stop is to allow the painful conflict to reappear.

Yablonsky has noted that the aggressive "leaders" of violent gangs often insist that all members participate in an act of cruelty. Unanimity may help each one to repress his own feelings of guilt and thus validate the violence. They dare not open the violence to examination (which lack of unanimity would tend to do), because that would expose its function —to hide their painful sense of helplessness and failure in the powerful world around them.

Even Miller, whose interpretive statements tend to be heavily sociologistic (or more appropriately, anthropologistic), carefully describes the ambivalence felt by lower-class persons. His explanation is in terms of two levels of culture—an overt and a covert level. But if he were more prepared to incorporate psychodynamic elements into his theory, the facts he observed and recorded might lead him to reduce the emphasis on the traditional and purely cultural aspects of lower-class behavioral patterns and to see them, in part, as emergent norms that have developed as efforts to deal with difficult contemporary problems,

It is often true that a keen observer sees beyond the constraining influence of his own theory. Miller notes, for example, that the aggressive assertion of autonomy—"I don't need nobody to take care of me"—is not merely a cultural norm. In part it disguises covert dependency needs. Miller suggests that lower-class persons sometimes seek out restrictive environments: the armed forces, disciplinary schools, prisons. Even while protesting the rules, they sometimes act in ways to bring themselves back under the rules. Miller also notes that the emphasis on toughness and masculinity partly hides a persistent concern over homosexuality. The toughest gang will allow expressions of strongly affectionate feelings, disguised as verbal or physical aggression.[26]

These brief comments on various psychodynamic forces are not intended as an outline of an adequate index of delinquency proneness. There is probably much overlapping among them, and undoubtedly other tendencies are involved—perhaps some forms of alienation, or of "anomia" as Srole has defined it. If a long list of tendencies were measured and factor-analyzed, a few distinct and crucial variables might emerge on the basis of which individuals could be reliably classified.

On the basis of the variables noted above, however, such a scale as the following can be imagined:

TYPES OF INDIVIDUAL TENDENCY

Extent of tendency toward delin- quency	I Subterranean values strongly internalized	II Strong sex-role prob- lems	III Inade- quate self concept	IV Strong sense of deprivation and lack of a "fair break"	V Delinquent values strongly internalized	VI Serious problems of psycho- pathology
1 (low)	Yes	No	No	No	No	No
2	Yes	Yes	No	No	No	No
3	Yes	Yes	Yes	No	No	No
4	Yes	Yes	Yes	Yes	No	No
5	Yes	Yes	Yes	Yes	Yes	No
6 (high)	Yes	Yes	Yes	Yes	Yes	Yes

Obviously, this may be the wrong list. Or the factors may be additive, not scalable; or factoring might reveal overlapping. To state the problem in this fashion, however, may serve to point up the need for a tendency scale and to emphasize that it must be related to measures of structural support.

COMBINING SOCIOCULTURAL AND PERSONALITY THEORIES OF DELINQUENCY

Most contemporary students of delinquency recognize its multiple sources even if they do not equally explore the several variables or build them into research programs. One way to express this recognition is to describe types of "subcultures" of delinquency—which is one way of saying that the various causes combine in different ways. Unfortunately the term "subculture" is not fully adequate to the task of combining individual and group factors in delinquency causation. Those who use the word are forced either to underemphasize some of the factors or to stretch the meaning of subculture so far that one wonders why it is used at all.

As a core definition, we can refer to subculture as the shared norms of a subsociety, of a group smaller than a society (which alone has a full culture). Subculture should be distinguished clearly from "role," which designates the rights and duties assigned by a full culture to the occupants of a given position. Role norms interlock into a system with the role norms of persons who occupy other positions, thus furnishing the basis for shared expectancies in interaction. Subculture norms, however, are not tied into the larger cultural complex; in fact, they tend to set those who share them apart from the total society. As contrasted with role norms, subcultural norms are unknown to, looked down upon, or thought of as separating forces by other members of a society.

Introduction of the concept of subculture into delinquency research added a valuable dimension. By using this term one can say that delinquent behavior is not (or is more than) a result of poor socialization or individual hostility or maladjustment. It expresses, at least in part, normal socialization to the subculture of certain groups. Delinquent behavior seems deviant or a sign of maladjustment only from the perspective of the dominant society. The natural result of being brought up in a "delinquency area," where criminals may be important personages, police officers are looked upon as enemies, opportunities for success are limited, peer groups do much of the socializing, and the like, is to acquire a set of distinctive values.[27] "Delinquency is not a negative thing; it is not a result of the breakdown of society, nor of the failure to curb criminal instincts, nor of the failure of the family, the church, or the school. The same set of concepts, the same social processes, and the same set of logical assumptions account for both delinquency and lawfulness." [28]

Insofar as a statement such as this calls attention to the phenomenon of subculture, to the wide variation in patterns of socialization, it is a valuable part of delinquency theory. When it becomes a total explanation, however, serious difficulties arise, as can be suggested by posing the following questions: Why do only some of those who are exposed to the delinquent subculture learn it? [29] Why do those who follow the subculture often manifest ambivalence and guilt feelings? [30] Why do many of the same patterns of behavior occur in areas and among groups where the presence of the subculture is much less clear (middle-class delinquency)? [31] What is the significance of the fact that some aspects of the delinquent subculture are not only different from, but in fact a reversal of, the values of the dominant culture? [32]

One way to try to answer these questions is to suggest a typology of subcultures, a procedure followed most notably by Cohen and Short and by Cloward and Ohlin. The former authors distinguish five types of delinquent subculture: "parent male" (which may be thought of as the basic type), conflict-oriented, drug addict, semiprofessional theft, and middle class.[33] That these phenomena are sufficiently different to require some measure of separate analysis, despite their shared patterns of illegality, there seems little doubt. A critical question then arises: What are the analytic variables which account for the differences? Is it just a matter of being socialized to different subsocieties, so that the drug-addict subculture contrasts with the semiprofessional-theft subculture in the same way that the traditions of the Spanish-American Southwest contrast with the traditions of the French-Canadian Northeast? Is it a matter of the accident of birth or residence? If individuals from the Southwest and the Northeast have somewhat different language patterns, values, and styles of life, we do not explain this by different body builds or crises of masculinity or self concepts. An explanation in terms of culture and normal socialization seems adequate.

Clearly such an explanation will not cover delinquency. Despite his emphasis on cultural factors, Miller stresses the importance of the problem of sex-role identification for many lower-class boys in a female-dominated household (which is scarcely traditional in any sense except among some Negroes). Their response to this problem may be identification with a street gang that emphasizes toughness and independence from parental control; but these values are not traditional in their subsocieties so much as emergent from their shared problem.[34] Cohen emphasizes the emergent quality of the norms of the delinquent subculture more strongly, interpreting them as shared norms by means of which individuals with similar problems of status struggle in a world where they have few advantages. "The crucial condition for the emergence of new cultural forms is the existence, *in effective interaction with one another, of a number of actors with similar problems of adjustment.*" [35]

Despite the recognition by Cohen of both psychogenic and sociocultural sources of delinquency, when he and Short sought to explain the origin of variation in delinquent behavior, they relied primarily on the extent to which stable criminal values and organizations existed in the area,[36] and the degree to which these were integrated with conventional values and structures. And although Cloward and Ohlin also are well aware of psychogenic aspects of delinquency causation, in their analysis of three delinquent subcultures (criminal, conflict, and retreatist) they explain the differences primarily on the basis of the availability of illegitimate means, which is a property of the surrounding structure.

The specification of different types of delinquent subcultures has not contributed as much as it might to the analysis of delinquency, in my judgment, because it has fostered serious terminological confusion. "Subculture" has a nice sociological and anthropological ring, and perhaps for that reason we tend to use it with exuberance and to resist precise definition. Cloward and Ohlin write: "This book is about delinquent gangs, or subcultures [of three types]. . . . One is what we call the 'criminal subculture'—a type of gang." [37] But gangs are groups of people; subcultures are the shared norms of such groups. To use them as synonyms is to make difficult the study of the extent to which the norms of groups are involved in the behavior of their members. Types of subcultures have been derived, not from independent information on normative systems, but from the study of variations in *behavior,* which have then been used to infer variations in norms.

Delineation of types of subcultures is surely a useful process. It must be done, however, with full recognition that the range of delinquency is a product not only of the variation in types of norms (as suggested by the use of the concept subculture), but also of variation in individual tendencies toward deviation. Students who have developed the typologies of subcultures are aware of this and have taken it into account in their theories, but terminology represses some insights. A wiser approach might be to design types of delinquent behavior, rather than being led by the implications of the term "subculture" either into neglecting nonnormative influences in behavior or into squeezing them into the meaning of subculture, thus depriving the term of its analytic clarity.

Of course, the significance of group-supported guidelines and socialization processes is undeniable. Drug addiction, for example, can surely not be understood until one takes into account, along with the physiochemical and psychological factors, the influence of tradition-bearing groups, the techniques by which they socialize or train members to drug use, the values they uphold, and other sociocultural facts. This information, however, does not explain drug addiction as behavior until it is integrated with information about the individuals who experience it.[38] A difficult point to remember, when one uses the term "drug-addict subculture" or "criminal subculture," is that one is using an abstraction.

If the typologies of subcultures that I have mentioned were redefined as typologies of delinquent behavior, they might be placed on a chart in such a way as to emphasize how each is a product of interaction between cultural, subcultural and structural influences acting upon persons with various levels of predisposition. On the basis of such variables as are suggested above, quasi-mathematical scales for the two sets of forces can be designed. On the assumption that the behavioral result is a *product* of situation and tendency, if either score is zero or very low, delinquent behavior will not result even if the other score is high. On scales that range from 0 to 10, we might posit a "score" of 25 or more as necessary to make delinquent behavior likely. Then if the measure on one scale is less than 2.5, delinquent behavior will not occur even if the other measure reaches the top of the scale.

The relationship can be charted in the following way:

The behavioral situations bounded by the line *ABCDE* are those in which individual tendency, environmental support, or both are of sufficient strength to lead to delinquency. As will be discussed below, subregions may represent probabilities of certain types of delinquency.

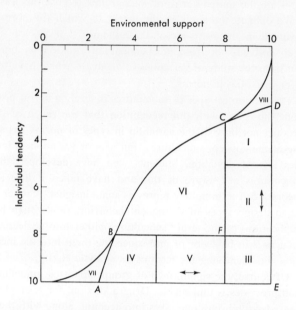

If the typologies of subcultures that have been mentioned were redefined as typologies of delinquent behavior, they might be placed on the chart in such a way as to emphasize how each is a product of interaction between cultural and subcultural influences acting upon persons with various levels of predisposition. Using the Cohen and Short typology, for example, the area designated by Roman numeral I might represent the core area for semiprofessional delinquencies. They would tend to occur under conditions of strong subcultural and group support (8 to 10 on the horizontal scale) and medium individual tendency (3 to 5 on the vertical scale). These are the situations emphasized by Miller.

Persons with strong psychodynamic tendencies toward delinquency (say, with a placement of 8 to 10 on the vertical scale, as indicated by such measures as those used by the Gluecks, or by Reckless's self-concept, or by strong signs of sex-role confusion, or by great alienation from parents—or by a combination of these), and who experience a powerful delinquency-supporting environment, might well be characterized by conflict-oriented behavior. This combination is designated by Roman numeral III on the chart. Yablonsky's description of the violent gang fits this pattern. In calling attention to the disturbed individuals who may be the core members of the violent gang, however, Yablonsky tends to underemphasize the group supports. Why is delinquency, rather than some alternative behavior, the outcome of the gang members' instabilities? This question draws our attention back again to the powerful structural supports for delinquency in the areas where violent gangs are found.[39]

Of the parent-male subculture, which is the core description in Cohen's *Delinquent Boys,* the "garden variety" can be thought of as falling between I and III, shading toward the semiprofessional pattern among the more "stable" boys and toward the conflict pattern among those with stronger tendencies toward deviance (shown by the double arrow in section II).

Among juveniles who experience little environmental support for delinquency, only those with strong individual tendencies are likely to be drawn into illegal activity. Continuing to use the categories of Cohen and Short, we can designate section IV as the area where middle-class delinquency (and I would add, delinquency in the stable lower class) is likely to occur. This is not to suggest that there are no structural supports in such an area. Attempts to explain middle-class delinquency on the basis of individual tendency alone are theoretically as inadequate as are such attempts applied to lower-class delinquency. The balance of forces is different, but both situational and personal factors are involved in each case.

Although we have little by way of firm evidence, the hypothesis emphasized by Cohen that sex-role identification is difficult for boys in a society where women are the chief socializers seems highly plausible. (I have noted that this is more of a problem in some lower-class settings than in the middle class.) Also, probably some children raised in comfort by relatively permissive methods may fail to develop the self-disciplines and deferred-gratification patterns that are required for the successes they have come to expect. For them, the anomic gap between means and ends will be large, because "availability of means" must refer not only to their presence in the environment, but also to individual tendencies that make the means accessible.

Supporting such personal influences are various sociocultural forces. Miller believes that lower-class values have diffused into the middle class, perhaps primarily through the mass media of communication. Bohlke notes that many persons who are "in the middle class" in terms of income may only recently have arrived there; the shared cultural values among such persons include many values from their points of origin.[40] Both scientific and literary descriptions have stressed the point that values and attitudes sometimes shift less rapidly than social status. Social control factors may be involved, since new and mobile communities often lack the institutions, services, and traditions that furnish part of the structure within which behavior occurs.[41]

Section V (high individual propensity, medium-high support from the situation) might promote a drug-addict response or, more broadly, escape patterns. And as indicated by the arrow, these patterns shade off toward conflict patterns on the one hand, and toward the illegal consumption of alcohol, the car thefts for joyrides, or other manifestations of what Cohen and Short identify as middle-class delinquencies on the other.

Of course, such a graphic presentation of the issues leaves many problems unexplored. The area bounded by *BCF* (VI), for example, represents situations with "scores" high enough to make delinquent behavior likely. Marginal to all five delinquency fields, this area is left open to suggest that tendencies toward particular types of delinquent behavior will be shaped by variables not shown in the model, particularly by the unique combination of influences that a given individual will experience. Area VI is also marginal to the nondelinquent field, suggesting that the situations near the line *BC,* although beyond the presumed critical score of 25, may result in nondelinquent behavior because of unmeasured influences.

Two other marginal areas suggest interesting theoretical problems. Area VII represents situations in which persons with high tendencies toward deviance experience a situation with very low support for delinquency. Some forms of mental illness (which I shall interpret in Chapter 12 as a field product, not something in the individual) or support for a "personal-salvation" religious movement might be frequent outcomes. In area VIII we have the opposite pattern: high environmental support for delinquency, but low individual tendency in that direction. Here we might expect the kind of activity described by Whyte in *Street Corner Society*— the marginally legal but unambitious behavior of the corner boy.[42]

Although I shall not undertake to interpret this chart further, a close relationship can be seen in it to Merton's paradigm of the types of response to anomie. The upper left quadrant, where values range from 0 to 5 on both scales, would indicate situations where conformist behavior is likely. The upper right quadrant contains the innovative situations, part of them within and part outside the delinquency area. And the lower left quadrant contains the ritualism-promoting combinations of tendency and situation. I have already suggested that various forms of retreatism and rebellion, Merton's last two types, fall in the lower right quadrant. Some of these may be deviant but not illegal and therefore not accurately identified as delinquent. From the social-psychological point of view, although not of course from other perspectives, the legal-illegal distinction may be quite unimportant. That drug addition as a form of retreat or escape involves one in illegal behavior while alcoholism may not has less social-psychological significance than their field similarities.[43]

A Process View of Delinquency

The discussion to this point has emphasized the need for simultaneous analysis of individual tendencies and structural factors. The picture I have drawn, however, has been essentially static. It can furnish the scaled background against which the dynamic transactions of life can be measured, but by itself it does not indicate what will take place. Process must be introduced into the system. This can be done by reference to the dynamic aspects of either the social system or the individual. Following Smelser and Smelser,[44] we can note that each has "directional tendencies"—learned and unlearned needs of the individual and functional prerequisites of social systems. Each has capacities, structures, and unifying principles related to the attempts to satisfy the needs and prerequisites. In those efforts each faces resistance, strain, and cost; responses to the strains are then set in motion. In these processes, the systems themselves undergo change.

Perhaps because it is difficult to avoid reification of society if these processes are viewed and discussed from the perspective of the social system, most discussions in delinquency theory and elsewhere are carried on from the point of the individuals' transactions. (We tend to be less sensitive to the danger of reifying individuals, who, after all, seem pretty real. From the perspective of a field view of behavior, however, individuals are as much abstractions as social systems are.) The individual's stable equilibrium of need satisfaction—hypothesized as a starting point—is upset by the periodic rhythm of many needs, by outside obstacles, or by the development of mutually contradictory needs. Efforts to reestablish equilibrium are based on past experience, built in as present tendency, and on the supports and resistances encountered from others.

Cohen has nicely described how a delinquent response may develop out of the tentative, exploratory gestures by which a group of boys, seeking satisfaction of various needs, tests the receptivity of those around them to various actions.[45] For boys with deeply established delinquent tendencies, the testing process is brief and not very tentative. Only definitive resistance from others and support for other activity will block delinquent behavior. Boys with few such tendencies will accept cues from other boys if they seem to lead to satisfactions, but delinquency is likely only if alternative paths to need satisfaction are blocked or "costly."

In exploring the way in which patterns of social control enter into delinquency, Maccoby, Johnson, and Church show how the outcome of a behavioral situation is a process of transaction between a subject and the environment (including other persons) around him:

If community disintegration is indeed a factor producing juvenile delinquency, how precisely are the effects produced?...we reasoned that something like the following process might occur: a child who, for a variety of reasons, has an interest in deviating [seeks to satisfy some need, remove some strain in a deviant manner], tries out one or two deviant acts in a tentative way, to see what the reaction of the community will be. If he lives in a disorganized community...there will be relatively little chance that he will be seen by someone who knows him or knows his parents, so long as the act is committed outside the walls of his own dwelling. The people who do see him may be deviants themselves, and may not consider the behavior especially reprehensible. But even if they do disapprove, they may nevertheless choose not to interfere, being reluctant to mention the incident directly to the child or his parents since they do not know them, and being afraid to attract the attention of the police to themselves by reporting the act to the authorities.[46]

The details of this transaction are different from those that occur where the strength of individual tendency or the situational factors are different; but the statement well suggests that the outcome was not "in" the person or in the sociocultural system, but in their interaction. A child starting the same series of acts in an environment that strongly sanctioned delinquency would move along a different sequence. And the same "others" confronting a different child, perhaps with more powerful tendencies toward delinquency, would respond in different ways.

CONTRACULTURE AND SUBCULTURE

I have suggested that the concept of subculture is often used in such a way that its analytic meaning (the shared norms of a subsociety) is lost. It sometimes becomes synonymous with "group"; and in a more serious confusion, it is sometimes used to refer to various kinds of behavior. Now there is no reason why a word, carefully used, cannot do all these things, provided the multiplicity of meanings is explictly chosen and precisely designated. In actuality, however, the gradual spreading out of the meaning of a word to cover related meanings (often on different levels) is usually not the result of explicit choice but of a limited theoretical perspective. For example, Chapter 6 noted that the failure to distinguish "role" from behavior on one hand, and from position on the other grew from—and contributed to—a failure to deal adequately with several levels of analysis. In this way important distinctions are lost.

If the concept of subculture is used to refer to the traditional norms that are passed on through processes of socialization among the members of a subsociety—norms that exist prior to and that are, in Durkheim's sense, external to individuals—it is a mistake to use the same term to refer to the shared guidelines for behavior that emerge out of the interaction of persons who have found that the norms to which they have been socialized either are inaccessible or fail to yield expected satisfactions. It is one thing to be socialized to a subculture of theft—trained in the necessary skills, taught the appropriate values, identified with supporting groups. It is something else for a group of boys who have been largely socialized to norms that oppose theft, but who face difficult problems of success in the dominant world and who struggle with problems of inadequacy, frustration, and a sense of injustice, to agree on norms of theft as their way of dealing with their difficult situation. In addition to the cultural element, norms in the latter sense introduce a social-psychological dimension, for they derive from the *contemporary* interaction of individuals faced with serious problems of adjustment in an anomic or otherwise culturally ambiguous setting.

Culture and personality are always interactive, to be sure. As Brewster Smith says:

Tendencies for parents to respond harshly to their children's aggressive behavior, for instance, if common to the members of a society, are to be referred equally to the culture and to the modal personality of the parents. But the result in the developing child is not a foregone conclusion: present knowledge suggests that under specifiable conditions outcomes as different as rigid politeness or touchy latent hostility may follow. These consequences in turn may lead to cultural elaborations that seem superficially remote from the cultural starting point, yet are dynamically linked with it....[47]

But although culture and personality are empirically tied together, the nature of the relation is not the same in all cases. Some conditions raise to prominence one particular kind of dynamic linkage between norms and personality: the creation of a series of inverse or countervalues (opposed to those of the surrounding society) in the face of serious frustration or conflict. To call attention to the special aspects of this kind of normative system, I have suggested the term *contraculture*.[48] Use of this concept in place of subculture seems appropriate wherever the normative system of a group contains, as a primary element, a theme of conflict with the values of the total society; wherever personality variables are directly involved in the development and maintenance of the group's values; and wherever its norms can be understood only by reference to the relationships of the group to a surrounding dominant culture.[49]

None of these criteria definitely, separates contraculture from subculture, because each is a continuum. Subsocieties fall along a range with respect to each criterion. The values of most subcultures probably conflict in some measure with the larger culture. In a contraculture, however, the conflict element is central; indeed, many of the values are specifically contradictions of the values of the dominant culture. Similarly, personality variables are involved in the development and maintenance of all cultures and subcultures, but usually the influence of personality is by way of variations around a theme that is part of the culture. In a contraculture, on the other hand, the theme itself expresses the tendencies of the persons who compose it. Finally, the norms of all subcultures are doubtless affected in some degree by the nature of the relationship with the larger culture. Understanding of subculture as a pure type, however, does not require intensive analysis of its interaction with the larger culture; that is, the subculture's norms are not to any significant degree a product of that interaction. But a contraculture can be understood only by giving full attention to the interaction of the group which is its bearer with the larger society.

It is one thing to say that the subculture of the rural lower-class Negro encourages slow, inefficient work. It is another thing to say, with Charles S. Johnson, that such a norm represents "pseudo-ignorant malingering," a contracultural way of describing the same phenomenon. Johnson stressed the conflict element, the extent to which the norm was a product of interaction of white and Negro. There is certainly an advantage in emphasizing the subcultural source of some of the values of Southern Negroes. Against racist views or individual explanations, the sociologist opposes the subcultural: "If Negroes strive less, have different sexual mores, or otherwise vary from standards of the dominant society, it is in part because they have been socialized in accordance with different norms." But this is not enough, for their similar behavior may be interpreted in part as a shared response to a frustrating environment.

Empirically, subcultural and contracultural influences may be mixed, of course. This is seen clearly in the phenomenon of delinquency. An emphasis on the subcultural aspects has beneficially corrected and complemented individualistic and moralistic interpretations. There is no need to review the extensive literature, some of which has been referred to above, to establish the importance of the normative element in delinquent behavior. To try to stretch a useful concept into a total theory is a mistake, however. As Cloward and Ohlin remark: "Once the pressure to adopt a polemical position is removed, it is possible to recognize delinquency as a product of the interaction between certain internalized orientations of the delinquent and the structure of definitions and evaluations with which he is confronted." [50]

Cohen's excellent work, although labeled a study of the culture of the gang, does not overlook the psychogenic sources of delinquency. In fact, his explanation of the origins of the subculture (contraculture) and its functions for the lower-class male makes clear that the norms of the gang are not learned, accepted, and taught in the same way that we learn what foods to eat, what clothes to wear, what language to speak. The very existence of the gang is a sign, in part, of blocked ambition. Because tensions which have been set in motion by this blockage cannot be resolved by achievement of dominant values, such values are repressed, their importance denied, and countervalues affirmed. The gang member is often ambivalent. Thwarted in his desire to achieve higher status by the criteria of the dominant society, he accepts criteria he can meet. But the reaction formation in this response is indicated by the content of the delinquent norms—nonutilitarian, malicious, and negativistic, in Cohen's terms. The negative polarity represents the need to repress his own tendencies to accept the dominant cultural standards.

This is not to say that the values of the gang cannot be explained partially by cultural analysis, by some extension of the idea that "the mores can make anything right." But I suggest that Cohen's multiple-factor analysis might have been clearer, and less subject to misinterpretation, had he introduced the concept of contraculture alongside the concept of subculture. The latter refers to a set of norms that are learned in standard socialization in a subsociety; the former stems from conflict and frustration in the experience of those who share some of the values of the whole society but are thwarted in their efforts to achieve those values.

Ambivalence is the key to the appearance of contracultural norms. A lower-class boy may have a sneaking suspicion that staying in school and trying to stay on the right side of the law are good ideas—because they will lead to better job opportunities, more satisfactory relations with others, and the like. But he is not prepared for school. He lacks language facility, skill in deferred-gratification disciplines, home support, and successful models close at hand. To avoid feelings of perpetual failure, he represses his sense of identity with the legitimate community. But this would be no "solution" at all if the repressed values came constantly back into his awareness. How can they be kept out most successfully?

First, a familiar quality of the human mind comes into play: Do not just deny the values, but reverse them. This is similar to projection, in which one attempts to rid himself of guilt by lodging responsibility for it not simply at random on someone else, but precisely on the victim of the act for which he feels guilty. Thus prejudiced white men see Negroes as violent and unrestrained in their interest in crossing the race line in sexual affairs. In a similar way, a person with paranoid tendencies *needs* enemies to help him justify and handle his hostility and to keep its origins in self-conflict repressed.[51]

Second, the reversal of values can be more "successful" in the individual's struggle with ambivalence if he can get others to share it. I have noted in Cohen's interpretation how contracultural norms (although Cohen does not use the term) emerge out of the tentative and ambiguous steps by which a group of persons sharing similar problems moves toward shared definitions.

Other types of contraculture. The creation of contracultural norms as a kind of innovation may take many forms other than delinquency. There is an extensive literature describing an adolescent subculture or "peer culture." [52] Many of the analyses of the control exercised by a youth group over its members employ the *concept* of contraculture, although the terminology and the assumptions are often those of subculture or culture. The emphasis is on the cross-pressures which young people feel: they want to be adults, yet fear to leave the securities of childhood; they experience contradictory adult treatment—a demand for grown-up behavior here, the prevention of it there; ambiguity of self-image leads to efforts to prove themselves full-fledged adults; there is sexual frustration. The peer group may help one struggle with these cross-pressures, as described by Parsons: "Perhaps the best single point of reference for characterizing the youth culture lies in its contrast with the dominant pattern of the adult male role. By contrast with emphasis on responsibility in this role, the orientation of the youth culture is more or less specifically irresponsible." [53]

This irresponsibility cannot be understood simply as another cultural norm, as part of the "role" of youth, although such are Parsons' terms. It must be studied in the context of strain, of role ambiguity. Some sociologists explain the irresponsibility as merely a manifestation of the youth culture, thus obscuring the personality factors also involved. The description and analysis of an adolescent subculture, to be sure, are an important contribution to the sociology of youth. Many adolescents spend a great deal of time in groups that sustain norms different from those of the adult world, and adults often respond to the behavior that follows these norms in an "ethnocentric" way. To rely on a subcultural explanation alone, however, is to disregard the emergent quality of many of the standards and to minimize the fact that they are often in direct conflict with adult standards (which most adolescents themselves will soon accept).

This sharp conflict of values requires explanation. Parsons states the facts clearly: "Negatively, there is a strong tendency to repudiate interests in adult things, and to feel at least a certain recalcitrance to the pressure of adult expectations and disciplines. . . . Thus the youth culture is not only, as is true of the curricular aspects of formal education, a matter of age status as such but also shows signs of being a product of tensions in the relationship of younger people and adults." [54] At several other points Parsons develops the "reaction" theme and later uses the concept of "reaction-formation." [55] Should these various phenomena be subsumed under the concept of culture? It is one thing for a society to train its youth to certain ways of behaving. It is quite another for a youth group to develop inverse values in an effort to struggle with role ambiguities and strains. The adolescent may experience both the cultural training and the youth-group values as normative sanctions; but that should scarcely lead the social analyst to disregard their differences. I suggest the term contra-culture in order to indicate the normative *and* the conflict aspects of this type of situation.

Many religious movements have contracultural qualities. If they are available to (known to, operating in the environment of) persons with strong tendencies toward deviation, they may serve as functional alternatives to illegal behavior. This is not to suggest that the several possibilities in an environment are equally congenial to a person with given tendencies. Undoubtedly an individual is more sensitive to some cues than to others. But there seems to be at least partial substitutability: When the Black Muslims appear, for example, some persons are drawn away from criminal behavior.

The contracultural quality of a religious movement may lead to disparagement of life on earth and emphasis on a reversal of status in heaven: the last shall be first; success as measured by worldly criteria is actually failure; the values by which the apparently successful live lead only to destruction.[56] Or the reversal and the contradiction may refer to the present life. Many of the beliefs and values of the Black Muslims are contracultural ways of struggling with problems of disprivilege here and now, not in heaven. If the dominant society says that to be white is good, the Muslims say that white is evil, that virtue is in black men, who are destined to rule the world. If, paradoxically, some white men say that integration is good, that race differences are unimportant, the Muslims declare that separation alone is good. Dominant values taboo violence (but not subterranean values, we should remember); the Black Muslims exalt violence as a necessary instrument for destroying an evil society. (It should be noted that in practice the violence is strongly curtailed, that the individuals who join the Muslims have in large measure been schooled in violence before their membership, and that, in fact, the movement probably inhibits violent activity. It is on the level of value that violence is made more explicit by the movement.)

Public response to the Black Muslims tends to be based on their official norms and policies—that is, the public tends to treat the Muslims in terms of a subcultural perspective. If the suggestion that there are contracultural qualities in the movement has merit, we need to look beneath the manifest level to latent processes. The literal meaning of the doctrines may require reinterpretation if we add psychodynamic questions: What are the functions of the reversal themes? Do they suggest an effort to repress feelings of attachment to the aspirations and values of the dominant world—an attachment that has to be broken for one's own self respect, because prejudice and discrimination keep success out of reach? Is it not likely, in fact, that the apparent attack on the white man and his society is, as Essien-Udom and Lincoln observe, an oblique attack on the feelings of inferiority of the black man? [57]

Such questions are difficult to answer definitively. One line of evidence strongly supports the hypothesis that sectarian behavior is not simply the result of subcultural training but also the result of shared problems of adjustment. This point of view is based on the account of the process of development from sect to church. Children of the first generation of sect members are socialized to the norms subculturally; their own personal tendencies have not gone into the process of shaping those norms. Since the children do not necessarily share the need for repression or reversal of values that had led their parents to found or join the sect, they tend to withdraw from it (many sects are short-lived) or to redefine its norms back toward those of the religious tradition from which the sect came.[58] Some sects, to be sure, become established with stable subcultural values and neither disintegrate nor return to churchlike definitions.[59] More commonly, however, they change. And the individuals who continue to experience disjunction between their own tendencies and the now more traditional sect-turned-church may found or join a new movement. Some persons move from group to group in a sequence of efforts to struggle with their problems.[60]

The varieties and transitions in types of delinquent behavior show some interesting parallels to religious behavior, even though the reference is often to the life of one person in the first case and to intergenerational changes in the second. Many, perhaps most, persons who have engaged in delinquent behavior move as adults "from sect to church"—that is, into the law-abiding community, with primary allegiance to its values. This is probably most true of middle-class delinquents, because the problems of adjustment of which their delinquency was an expression normally abate when they reach adulthood. Achieving a satisfying sex-role definition is a major problem for them, as Cohen suggests; but for most this problem is not a continuing or permanent issue. Just as the children of sect members may not have the tendencies that inclined their parents to the religious protest, so the twenty-one-year-old may not still be dealing with the problems of identity that inclined him, as a fifteen- or sixteen-year-old, to delinquent protest.

For some, however, the problems do not abate. Self-hatred, feelings of injustice, lack of economic opportunity may persist. They are likely to move "from sect to sect." As the delinquent gang becomes inaccessible (because its structure relates to the problems and tendencies of youth) other ways of struggling with one's problems must be sought. Drug addiction, mental illness, or other types of response may follow in sequence for those whose problems are most serious.[61]

Also, some delinquent gangs may become "established sects" with stable subcultures. They lose their contracultural qualities. That is, their norms are not primarily a result of the shared tendencies toward repression, ambivalence, and hostility of their contemporary members. Not all types of delinquent gang are equally likely to become established, with procedures for accepting and socializing new members, techniques of stable accommodation with the larger society, and traditional more than emergent norms. Aspects of the structural setting and of personal tendency both make such a development possible for some gangs, perhaps for those engaged in semiprofessional theft and drawing support from stable adult criminal groups. But tendency and setting may foreclose this possibility for others, perhaps for the violent gang, which gets little outside support and tends to lack internal structure. The violent gang is more readily seen as a series of loosely joined "near-groups" strongly affected by the immediate needs of the shifting membership, not as a stable organization with agreed-on procedures for socializing new members to a traditional subculture.[62]

CONCLUSION

This chapter represents an exercise in asking questions about delinquent behavior. After half a century of extensive and often brilliant research in this field, limited perspectives continue, in many instances, to block understanding. Many writers, of course, are specialists—and properly so; they eschew any effort to develop a total theory. But they do not always escape the temptation to stretch their specialized observations in an attempt to cover the total phenomenon, or to criticize others who have abstracted a different part of the whole.

Fortunately, multivariate research and broader theoretical perspectives are more common now than they used to be. Cohen's *Delinquent Boys,* for example, seems to me an important turning point because of the explicit recognition of both psychogenic and sociogenic forces. (It is interesting that Miller criticizes Cohen for failing to see the subcultural aspects of lower-class delinquency, while Sykes and Matza criticize him for exaggerating those aspects and failing to see the degree to which persons in the lower class have absorbed the dominant culture. The polemical—as contrasted with critical—quality of much social-scientific writing is manifest in the tendency to make our "opponents" appear to be more one-sided than in fact they are.)

Since Cohen is concerned with gangs, he denies any ambitions to develop a total theory to explain delinquent behavior. Paradoxically, he tends to assign that task to psychology: "To understand fully the behavior of a particular child, the proper task of the psychologist, it is necessary to take this uniqueness fully into account." [63] Uniqueness, I believe, is not the province of any science; yet all the sciences of human behavior must help to take it into account—that is, define its parameters—in order to state the limits of their own powers of prediction. From the point of view of field theory, psychology is not the behavioral science. It is an abstract discipline which seeks to discover the properties and processes of the individual as a system. If psychology's proper task were "to understand fully the behavior of a particular child," it would have to absorb biology, anthropology, and sociology. For behavior is the outcome of the interaction of all the systems studied by these sciences, plus the uniqueness which none of them encompasses.

Applying this statement to delinquency, one would say that in a field view, sociology and anthropology can isolate the social systems most highly correlated with delinquency; they can describe the cultural and subcultural values and the group processes that support it. But the formula for the explanation of delinquent *behavior* must always include reference to variation in inner tendency. Psychological study can isolate the individual propensities most highly associated with delinquency; but behavior is always situational. The extent of opportunity or stimulation on one hand, and the strength of preventive powers on the other, are always involved in the equation. "Many potentially delinquent or criminal persons do not engage in delinquent or criminal acts simply because a delinquency or crime-producing situation never arises." [64] Even the potential victim may be one of the "causes." "This is certainly true in many sex cases, confidence games, and even murder and assault cases." [65] Reckless states the problem well: "The S (situation) needs an I (individual) and I needs S. . . . As a matter of fact, we do not know what the I really is without the S, and we do not know what the S is without the I." [66]

Delinquency will occur when delinquent-prone individuals are found in situations that facilitate illegal expression of their tendencies. A theory of delinquent *behavior* must be continuously field-oriented.

FOOTNOTES

Note: The bracketed number following an author's name refers to the footnote in which the source is cited in full.

1. I shall make no effort to review the literature on delinquency. There are a number of excellent brief summaries. See Richard A. Cloward and Lloyd E. Ohlin, *Delinquency and Opportunity*, The Free Press of Glencoe, 1960, especially chap. 3; and David J. Bordua, "Delinquent Subcultures: Sociological Interpretations of Gang Delinquency," *Annals of the American Academy of Political and Social Science*, November, 1961, pp. 119–136.

2. Sheldon Glueck, "Crime Causation," *National Probation and Parole Association Yearbook*, 1941, p. 90. Note how precisely this statement reverses Durkheim's formulation of social causation. See also Sheldon Glueck and Eleanor Glueck, *Unraveling Juvenile Delinquency*, The Commonwealth Fund, 1950.

3. Albert K. Cohen and James F. Short, Jr., "Juvenile Delinquency," in Robert K. Merton and Robert A. Nisbet (eds.), *Contemporary Social Problems*, Harcourt, Brace & World, Inc., 1961, p. 89.

4. Jerome K. Myers and Bertram H. Roberts, *Family and Class Dynamics in Mental Illness*, John Wiley & Sons, Inc., 1959.

5. Walter B. Miller, "Lower Class Culture as a Generating Milieu of Gang Delinquency," *Journal of Social Issues*, vol. 14, 1958, p. 18.

6. *Ibid.*, p. 19; see also William Kvaraceus and Walter B. Miller, *Delinquent Behavior*, National Education Association of the United States, 1959; and Walter B. Miller, Hildred Geertz, and Henry S. G. Cutter, "Aggression in a Boys' Street-corner Group," *Psychiatry*, November, 1961, pp. 283–298. In this kind of problem we need more precise specification of the meaning of class membership. For an interesting exploration of this question, see Robert A. Ellis, W. C. Lane, and Virginia Olesen, "The Index of Class Position: An Improved Intercommunity Measure of Stratification," *American Sociological Review*, April, 1963, pp. 271–277.

7. Albert K. Cohen and Harold M. Hodges, Jr., "Characteristics of the Lower-blue-collar-class," *Social Problems*, Spring, 1963, p. 324. Similar observations have been made in other societies by Oscar Lewis, *Five Families: Mexican Case Studies in the Culture of Poverty*, Basic Books, Inc., Publishers, 1959; and Edward Banfield, *The Moral Basis of a Backward Society*, The Free Press of Glencoe, 1958.

8. Cohen and Hodges nicely show the interaction of social structure and character in describing a "vicious circle" that develops from the circumstances of the lower-lower class: " (1) A set of life conditions characterized by powerlessness, deprivation and insecurity. (2) The adoption of a view of the world as bleak and uncertain, partly a matter of realistic perception and partly an adaptive protection against disappointment. (3) On the basis of this world-view, the adoption of a style

of life characterized by 'improvidence,' etc. (4) In consequence of the style of life, the more certain recurrence of the experience of power-lessness, deprivation and insecurity. (5) A further intensification of the pessimistic world view, partly on the basis of the fact that things *did* turn out badly after all, and partly to protect the self against the criti-cism of having brought about one's plight through one's own moral defect." Cohen and Hodges [7], p. 323.

9. Robert K. Merton, *Social Theory and Social Structure,* rev. ed., The Free Press of Glencoe, 1957, p. 169.

10. *Ibid.,* p. 175.

11. For the most systematic application of anomie theory to delin-quency, see Cloward and Ohlin [1]. They seek to integrate this approach with the cultural or subcultural approach.

12. See Albert K. Cohen, *Delinquent Boys,* The Free Press of Glen-coe, 1955, especially pp. 59–62.

13. David Matza and Gresham M. Sykes, "Juvenile Delinquency and Subterranean Values," *American Sociological Review,* October, 1961, pp. 712–719; David Matza, "Subterranean Traditions of Youth," *Annals of the American Academy of Political and Social Science,* November, 1961, pp. 102–118. See also Robin M. Williams, Jr., *American Society,* Alfred A. Knopf, Inc., 1960, chap. 10, where the normative quality of some norm violations is discussed.

14. See Peter Blau, "Structural Effects," *American Sociological Review,* April, 1960, pp. 178–193; and James A. Davis, Joe L. Spaeth, and Carolyn Huson, "A Technique for Analyzing the Effects of Group Composition," *American Sociological Review,* April, 1961, pp. 215–225. For an interesting methodological commentary, see Arnold S. Tannen-baum and Jerald G. Bachman, "Structural versus Individual Effects," *American Journal of Sociology,* May, 1964, pp. 585–595.

15. Analysis of the processes whereby these tendencies are learned or internalized is a task for psychology and social psychology. For an interesting exploration of these processes, see Gordon Trasler, *The Explanation of Criminality,* Routledge and Kegan Paul, Ltd., 1962. See also Sheldon Glueck and Eleanor Glueck, *Family Environment and Delinquency,* Houghton Mifflin Company, 1962. In the latter work, how-ever, the search for "traits" and the emphasis on constitutional factors seem to me to lead to the wrong way of examining the questions con-cerning the source of tendencies.

16. Glueck and Glueck [2], p. 282.

17. *Ibid.*

18. Their "controls" were also from the extreme end of the range, for they sought persons with few "blemishes." See *ibid.,* p. 29.

19. See Edwin L. Lively, Simon Dinitz, and Walter C. Reckless, "Self Concept as a Predictor of Juvenile Delinquency," *American Journal of Orthopsychiatry,* January, 1962, pp. 159–168; Walter C. Reck-less, Simon Dinitz, and Ellen Murray, "Self Concept as an Insulator against Delinquency," *American Sociological Review,* December, 1956, pp. 744–746; Jon E. Simpson, Simon Dinitz, Barbara Kay, and Walter C. Reckless, "Delinquency Potential of Pre-adolescents in High Delin-quency Areas," *British Journal of Delinquency,* January, 1960, pp. 211–215.

20. Glueck and Glueck [2]; Lewis Yablonsky, *The Violent Gang,* The Macmillan Company, 1962, pp. 178–184.

21. *Ibid.,* p. 205.

22. See *ibid.,* p. 232. Casual sequences, however, are complicated. See Lee N. Robins, Harry Gyman, and Patricia O'Neal, "The Interaction of Social Class and Deviant Behavior," *American Sociological Review,* August, 1962, pp. 480–492.

23. See Talcott Parsons, "Certain Primary Sources and Patterns of Aggression in the Social Structure of the Western World," *Psychiatry,* May, 1947, pp. 167–181; Cohen [12], pp. 162–169; John H. Rohrer and Munro S. Edmonson (eds.), *The Eighth Generation: Cultures and Personalities of New Orleans Negroes,* Harper & Row, Publishers, Incorporated, 1960, chap. 6; and Miller [5]. Cohen discusses the problem primarily with respect to middle-class boys, missing the issue in lower-class situations where males are absent or subservient.

24. See Gresham M. Sykes and David Matza, "Techniques of Neutralization: A Theory of Delinquency," *American Sociological Review,* December, 1957, pp. 664–670; Fritz Redl and David Wineman, *Children Who Hate,* The Free Press of Glencoe, 1951, chap. 4; John P. Clark and Eugene P. Wenninger, "Goal Orientations and Illegal Behavior among Juveniles," *Social Forces,* October, 1963, pp 49–59; Martin Gold, *Status Forces in Delinquent Boys,* Institute for Social Research, University of Michigan, 1962; Robert A. Gordon, James F. Short, Jr., Desmond S. Cartwright, and Fred L. Strodtbeck, "Values and Gang Delinquency: A Study of Street-corner Groups," *American Journal of Sociology,* September, 1963, pp. 109–128; Aaron Antonovsky and Melvin J. Lerner, "Occupational Aspirations of Lower Class Negro and White Youth," *Social Problems,* Fall, 1959, pp. 132–138.

25. See Cohen [12], pp. 24–32.

26. See Miller [5].

27. Classic statements of this approach have been made by Clifford Shaw, *Delinquency Areas,* The University of Chicago Press, 1929; and Frederic M. Thrasher, *The Gang,* The University of Chicago Press, 1936. For an examination of recent literature on this topic, see Roland J. Chilton, "Continuity in Delinquency Area Research: A Comparison of Studies for Baltimore, Detroit, and Indianapolis," *American Sociological Review,* February, 1964, pp. 71–83.

28. Frank Hartung in a review of *Delinquent Boys* by Albert Cohen, *American Sociological Review,* December, 1955, p. 752.

29. See Solomon Korbin, "The Conflict of Values in Delinquency Areas," *American Sociological Review,* October, 1951, pp. 653–661; Alex Inkeles, "Personality and Social Structure," in Robert K. Merton, Leonard Broom, and Leonard S. Cottrell, Jr., (eds.), *Sociology Today,* Basic Books, Inc., Publishers, 1959, p. 254.

30. See Sykes and Matza [24].

31. John I. Kitsuse and David C. Dietrick, "Delinquent Boys: A Critique," *American Sociological Review,* April, 1959, pp. 208–215.

32. See Yablonsky [20].

33. Albert K. Cohen and James Short, "Research in Delinquent Subcultures," *Journal of Social Issues,* vol. 14, 1958, pp. 20–37.

34. See Miller [5]; and Rohrer and Edmonson [23].

35. Cohen [12], p. 59.

36. Cohen and Short [33]. See also Solomon Korbin [29].

37. Cloward and Ohlin [1], p. 1.

38. See Isidor Chein *et al.*, *The Road to H: Narcotics, Delinquency, and Social Policy*, Basic Books, Inc., Publishers, 1964; Howard S. Becker, "Becoming a Marihuana User," *American Journal of Sociology*, November, 1953, pp. 235–242; John A. Clausen, "Social Patterns, Personality, and Adolescent Drug Use," in Alexander Leighton, John A. Clausen, and Robert Wilson (eds.), *Explorations in Social Psychiatry*, Basic Books, Inc., Publishers, 1957, pp. 230–277.

39. Pfautz suggests the need for greater emphasis on collective behavior theory in explaining Yablonsky's data; added to that, I am implying, is the need for sociocultural theory. See Harold W. Pfautz, "Near-group Theory and Collective Behavior: A Critical Reformulation," *Social Problems*, Fall, 1961, pp. 167–174.

40. Robert H. Bohlke, "Social Mobility, Stratification Inconsistency and Middle Class Delinquency," *Social Problems*, Spring, 1961, pp. 351–363. This paper is a useful summary of several explanations of middle-class delinquency.

41. See *ibid.*

42. William F. Whyte, *Street Corner Society*, 2d ed., The University of Chicago Press, 1955.

43. See Merton [9], chaps. 4 and 5; and Robert Dubin, "Deviant Behavior and Social Structure," *American Sociological Review*, April, 1959, pp. 147–164.

44. Neil J. Smelser and William T. Smelser, *Personality and Social Systems*, John Wiley & Sons, Inc., 1963, pp. 1–18.

45. Cohen [12], pp. 59–65.

46. Eleanor E. Maccoby, Joseph P. Johnson, and Russell M. Church, "Community Integration and the Social Control of Juvenile Delinquency," *Journal of Social Issues*, vol. 14, 1958, pp. 38–39.

47. Brewster Smith, "Anthropology and Psychology," in John Gillin (ed.), *For a Science of Social Man*, The Macmillan Company, 1954, p. 61. See also Talcott Parsons and Edward A. Shils (eds.), *Toward a General Theory of Action*. Harvard University Press, 1951, especially the monograph by the editors; and Ralph Linton's preface to Abram Kardiner, *The Psychological Frontiers of Society*, Columbia University Press, 1945.

48. For a full discussion of this term and its relationship to subculture, see J. Milton Yinger, "Contraculture and Subculture," *American Sociological Review*, October, 1960, pp. 625–635, from which this section is partly drawn.

49. By the noun in "contraculture" I seek to call attention to the normative aspects of the phenomena under study, and by the qualifying prefix I wish to emphasize the conflict aspects. Similar terms are occasionally found in the literature, but they are either defined only by their use in context or are used differently from the meaning assigned to contraculture in this book. Harold D. Lasswell uses the term "countermores" to refer to "culture patterns which appeal mainly to the *id*" (*World Politics and Personal Insecurity*, McGraw-Hill, 1935, p. 64). He then designates "revolutionists, prostitutes, prisoners, obscene and subversive talk"—which scarcely suggests a clear analytic category. In *World Revolutionary Propaganda* (Knopf, 1939), Lasswell and Dorothy Blumenstock discuss the use of inverse values as a revolutionary propaganda weapon and comment on the presumed vulnerability of deprived persons to the countermores stressed in this propaganda. In *Power and*

Society (Yale University Press, 1950, p. 49), Lasswell uses the term somewhat differently: *"Countermores* are culture traits symbolized by the group as deviations from the mores, and yet are expected to occur." A certain amount of bribery, for example, is "normal" "and must be included by the candid observer as part of culture."

At various points, Talcott Parsons more nearly approaches the meaning of the concept contraculture as used here, although more by implication than by direct definition, and without distinguishing it from the concept of subculture. Referring to the ideological aspects of a subculture, he writes: "In such cases of an open break with the value-system and ideology of the wider society we may speak of a 'counter-ideology' " (*The Social System*, The Free Press of Glencoe, 1951, p. 355). And later: "If, however, the culture of the deviant group, like that of the delinquent gang, remains a 'counter-culture' it is difficult to find the bridges by which it can acquire influence over wider circles" (p. 522). It is not clear from these uses how counterideology and counterculture are to be defined; but the important place Parsons gives to the element of ambivalence in his use of the concept subculture suggests that he has in mind something similar to my concept of contraculture (see *ibid.*, p. 286).

50. Cloward and Ohlin [1], p. 130.

51. See Norman Cameron, "The Paranoid Pseudo-community Revisited," *American Journal of Sociology*, July, 1959, pp. 52–58.

52. See Talcott Parsons, *Essays in Sociological Theory Pure and Applied*, The Free Press of Glencoe, 1949, chap. 5; Howard Becker, *German Youth: Bond or Free*, Oxford University Press, 1946; S. N. Eisenstadt, *From Generation to Generation: Age Groups and the Social Structure*, The Free Press of Glencoe, 1956; David Riesman, with Nathan Glazer and Reuel Denney, *The Lonely Crowd*, Yale University Press, 1950; R. J. Havighurst and Hilda Taba, *Adolescent Character and Personality*, John Wiley & Sons, Inc., 1949; Kingsley Davis, "The Sociology of Parent-Youth Conflict," *American Sociological Review*, August, 1940, pp. 523–534; Ralph Linton, "Age and Sex Categories," *American Sociological Review*, October, 1942, pp. 589–603; Joseph R. Gusfield, "The Problem of Generations in an Organizational Structure," *Social Forces*, May, 1957, pp. 323–330; Jessie Bernard (issue ed.), *Teenage Culture: Annals of the American Academy of Political and Social Science*, November, 1961. For some contradictory evidence, see W. A. Westley and Frederick Elkin, "The Protective Environment and Adolescent Socialization," *Social Forces*, March, 1957, pp. 243–249; and Elkin and Westley, "The Myth of Adolescent Culture," *American Sociological Review*, December, 1955, pp. 680–684.

53. Talcott Parsons [52], p. 92.

54. *Ibid.*, pp. 92–93.

55. See *ibid.*, pp. 101–102, 189–190, 342–345, 355.

56. Liston Pope, *Millhands and Preachers*, Yale University Press, 1942.

57. See E. U. Essien-Udom, *Black Nationalism: A Search for Identity in America*, The University of Chicago Press, 1962; C. Eric Lincoln, *The Black Muslims in America*, Beacon Press, 1961; J. Milton Yinger, *Sociology Looks at Religion*, The Macmillan Company, 1963, chap. 2.

58. See H. Richard Niebuhr, *The Social Sources of Denomination-*

alism, Henry Holt and Company, Inc., 1929; Walter G. Muelder, "From Church to Sect," *Christendom*, Autumn, 1945, pp. 450–462; J. Milton Yinger, *Religion in the Struggle for Power*, The Duke University Press, 1946, pp. 31–34.

59. I cannot explore here the conditions under which that is likely to occur. See J. Milton Yinger, *Religion, Society, and the Individual*, The Macmillan Company, 1957, pp. 150–152.

60. See Eric Hoffer, *The True Believer*, Harper & Row, Publishers, Incorporated, 1951.

61. Lee N. Robins and Patricia O'Neal, "Mortality, Mobility, and Crime: Problem Children Thirty Years Later," *American Sociological Review*, April, 1958, pp. 162–170.

62. Lewis Yablonsky, "The Delinquent Gang as a Near-group," *Social Problems*, Fall, 1959, pp. 108–117.

63. Cohen [12], p. 74.

64. Marshall B. Clinard, "Criminological Research," in Merton, Broom, and Cottrell [29], p. 520.

65. *Ibid.*

66. Walter Reckless, *The Crime Problem*, Appleton-Century-Crofts, Inc., 1950, p. 80.

CHAPTER 11

The Field View of Prejudice and Discrimination

Few manifestations of human behavior have received more intensive study in the last two decades than discrimination and the related, but separate, phenomenon of prejudice. Two major lines of investigation have characterized this period, each of which can be illustrated by a basic volume. The cultural and institutional patterns of discrimination against Negroes were emphasized by Gunnar Myrdal in *An American Dilemma* [1] and in the monographs which were written in preparation for and in support of this central volume. The sources of prejudice in the insecurities and anxieties of individuals were emphasized by T. W. Adorno and his associates in *The Authoritarian Personality* [2] and in the large number of studies which preceded and followed it.

To some degree these are simply specialized documents which explore either the institutional supports or the individual tendencies that help to account for the behavior of a person toward the members of "out-groups." But such a description scarcely encompasses the full aims of the authors or the ways in which their books have been used. Myrdal paid some attention to individual tendencies, but the evidence on which he drew was not nearly so full as the evidence for institutional patterns which forms the greater part of his volumes. *The Authoritarian Personality* shows a more serious imbalance, for the authors used their evidence of individual tendencies to construct a theory of *behavior,* giving virtually no attention to the ways in which behavior is a function of the situation within which it occurs. These two major documents demonstrate that the schism so common to the study of human behavior is found in this field as elsewhere.

Two basic terms require definition before we can explore the issues involved in building an adequate theory of behavior toward the members of out-groups. By discrimination I shall mean "the differential treatment of individuals considered to belong to a particular social group," differential treatment of such a variety that it violates nominally universal norms of judgment.[3] Not all differential treatment is discrimination in this sense. Children are treated differently from adults, but this may be in accord with, not in violation of, a shared norm. Thus children are not allowed to drive cars or stay away from school (which sometimes leads them, without much success, to claim discrimination against them). The situation is not always well agreed upon, however, even among the adults. Some will say that children should not be permitted a given activity; others will say that children should not be denied such an opportunity "just because they are children"—which is to say that these persons believe the prohibition violates a norm. Persons under 21 years of age are not permitted to vote in most places, but the fact that 18- to 20-year-olds may vote in a few localities indicates that "nominally universal norms of judgment" are not entirely universal.

To say what behavior is discriminatory is not always easy, then; the standards being used must be clearly specified. In any event, discrimination is behavior. Prejudice, on the other hand, is an attitude, a predisposition to respond to the members of a human category (which may or may not be a group) in a uniformly unfavorable or uniformly favorable way. The term is often used only in the negative sense.

If we follow these definitions, then to account for prejudice is not to account for discrimination. By the same token, to document the structural supports for discrimination in an environment is not to describe behavior, because individuals vary in their responsiveness to various stimuli. Before developing a field view that encompasses both sets of influences, I shall outline the specialized "psychological" and "sociological" approaches, stating them without the major or minor qualifications that most writers would use.

THE "PERSONALITY" APPROACH TO PREJUDICE AND DISCRIMINATION

Few studies in the behavioral sciences have stimulated so much commentary, replication, modification, and controversy as *The Authoritarian Personality*. The importance of the subject matter, the decisive one-sidedness of its theoretical perspective, the ingenuity of the scales developed for the study (which can readily be used in replicative research), the richness of the data (if not their adequacy in representing any defined universe), and the imaginative use of Freudian and other "depth" theories—these are among the reasons for its influence.

Students who interpret prejudice from this perspective see it not as a primary cause of behavior, but at most as an intermediary influence that focuses a more fundamental sense of hostility and anxiety. "Beneath"

antagonistic attitudes toward out-groups (different races, religions, nations, etc.), according to those who describe an authoritarian or prejudiced personality, are fundamental questions of self-regard and orientation to the world. The "authoritarian" is threat-oriented, in Newcomb's
phrase. His experiences with other people, particularly in his earliest
years, were filled with so much unpredictability, hostility, neglect, or
crushing criticism that he views human relationships fundamentally in
terms of power: one is ruler or ruled. He is filled with hostility, which he
displaces onto the weak; he is filled with guilt, which he projects onto the
"inferior." Anxious for a secure status, he pushes away from anyone who
might cast doubt on his qualifications. Dominated by fear of a world that
has been cruel and unpredictable, he defines the "devil" clearly, in order
to know whom to fight and where to place the blame. Once such tendencies are set, they become, according to this thesis, the primary determinants of behavior:

**Although personality is a product of the social environment of the past,
it is not, once it has developed, a mere object of the contemporary environment. What has developed is a *structure* within the individual,
something which is capable of self-initiated action upon the social environment and of selection with respect to varied impinging stimuli,
something which though always modifiable is frequently very resistant
to fundamental change.[4]**

Knowing a person's fundamental traits, according to this view, allows
one to predict not simply attitudes or verbal behavior but many kinds of
actions toward minority groups, politics, religion, and members of the
opposite sex. There is no need to pay much attention to the sociopolitical
context, the groups to which the person belongs, his reference groups, the
patterns of sanctions and rewards in the environment, the position he is
occupying at the moment (with its implied structure of interpersonal
obligations and expectations), or the individuals with whom he is
interacting.

The syndrome of traits that presumably characterizes the power-
oriented, ego-alien authoritarian is well summarized by Himmelhoch:

**The person who scores high on the F scale [the major measuring instru-
ment used in *The Authoritarian Personality*] exhibits the following
seven traits: repression of hostile impulses, repression of sexual impulses, drive for power and status, rigidity of emotional control, conven-
tionality, emotional immaturity, and lack of insight. The high F scorer
makes a rigid division in his personality structure between a conscious
authorized social-self and an unconscious unauthorized impulse-self.
Because he represses or dissociates the impulsive aspect of his personality and therefore cannot look into his own deeper motives or conflicts,
we call him "self-rejecting." [5]**

Literally hundreds of studies have been built on the research leads
found in *The Authoritarian Personality*. Attempts have been made to map

its distribution through various segments of the population and to discover what other traits correlate with, and perhaps help to account for, authoritarianism. I shall not review those studies here,[6] but only note the fairly consistent findings of positive correlations of authoritarianism with age, maladjustment, and conformity; negative correlations with education, intelligence, and social class; and contradictory evidence concerning such variables as family experience and religiosity.

Many researchers have accepted the basic point of view that the underlying personality structure is the key to behavior, but have presented evidence which purports to show that some trait other than authoritarianism is fundamental. Thus acquiescence, mental rigidity, dogmatism, and anomia (feelings of self-to-other alienation) have variously been described as explaining a large part of the variation in prejudice instead of, or in addition to, authoritarianism.[7] Although these studies contribute to our knowledge of the tendency structure, the inclination that most of them show toward an explanation of behavior based on knowledge only of individuals reduces their value. Before considering how they might be incorporated into a field theoretical examination of prejudice and discrimination, we need to look at the social-structural and cultural approach to the problem.

THE SOCIOCULTURAL APPROACH TO PREJUDICE AND DISCRIMINATION

From the point of view of sociology, attempts to explain prejudice and discrimination by reference to types of personality are seriously inadequate. Two levels of criticism of the psychological approach are important to distinguish, however. Drawing on standard socialization theory and on observation of cultural and subcultural differences in *norms* of prejudice, some sociologists explain differences in individual attitudes not on the basis of variation in ego alienation or basic anxiety, but rather by reference to different learning environments. If some persons are more authoritarian than others, the reason is not primarily because they experienced an anxiety-laden childhood but because they have been taught such attitudes in their particular learning environment. This is a version of "subculture theory." Rhyne, for example, writes:

Since we cannot presume that each southerner experiences the same cultural constraints, it follows that variations on social attitudes may be a function of these variations within a culture. For some, the concatenation of family and friends, schoolbooks and arguments, accidents and recurrences, points toward prejudice; for others the concatenation is more neutral, and for some it must surely be anti-prejudicial. If we are willing to assume that within a culture each person is not given an equally uninstructed choice on prejudice, variations in cultural constraints can be as explanatory as certain personality constellations.[8]

Rhyne associates his explanation with Sutherland's differential-learning approach in criminology. Although he identifies it as "rigorously sociologistic," the explanation is more precisely social psychological, for Rhyne is still concerned with individual prejudices. It is simply that he focuses on the sources of those prejudices in the process of socialization to the norms of one's immediate environment rather than in ego-threatening trauma. A more explicitly social-psychological perspective is developed by Stewart and Hoult, who account for authoritarian tendencies by reference to inadequacies of role taking. Lack of practice and opportunities for "taking the role of the other" is associated with lack of understanding and sympathy for those in other positions, rejection of others, high rate of failure in interpersonal relations, and projection to rationalize the failures.[9]

Such commentaries modify in a useful way the concentration on anxiety-laden childhood experiences that has characterized the psychoanalytic approach to prejudice. They emphasize the importance of group memberships, cultural and subcultural norms, and standard processes of learning and socialization in the shaping of individual tendencies. They are still primarily concerned, nevertheless, with explanations of variation in individual tendencies.

A strictly sociological approach requires a more drastic modification of psychological interpretations. The *contemporary* social structure, the patterns of interacting individuals, strongly influences (determines, in some interpretations) discriminatory behavior. These structural forces affect individuals whose personal inclinations toward discrimination are slight as well as individuals whose inclinations are strong. The influence resides in the interaction among persons and cannot, therefore, be explained by reference to separate individuals. To know how a person will behave, one needs to know the group within which he is behaving, the position he occupies ("position" implies counterpositions and roles—*mutual* patterns of expectation), the sanctions and rewards of the surrounding environment (which facilitate the expression of certain tendencies and inhibit the expression of others), and the stream of events around him (which activate some predispositions while others remain latent).

Only by their ability to inhibit many tendencies can men live in societies. Particularly under conditions of rapid social change, but to some degree in all situations, individuals look to "significant others" for clues to guide their behavior, as if to ask, "Which of my many selves shall I wear here; which attitudes are appropriate; what behavior will maximize my satisfactions?" The answers to these questions depend in part upon the behavior of others.

In emphasizing the sociological factors that affect the level of discrimination, Reitzes notes their increased importance in modern societies. In the modern urban world, an increasing proportion of activities occur within specialized organizations, where individuals play specific roles.

Fewer dimensions of the total self are engaged in the interaction; role-specific behavior is more likely. "Because so many social situations in modern society have a limited and specific objective, the importance of rational considerations is increased." [10] The complexity of the decision-making process leads us to transfer more of our decisions to large organizations and their functionaries. One of the effects of such developments in social structure and process is the appearance of more "inconsistent" behavior on the part of the individuals, as they move among a wider circle of significant others and play a more diversified repertoire of roles.[11]

Resistance to desegregation, which is accounted for psychologically by reference to individual prejudices, is interpreted sociologically by reference to qualities of the social structure. Breed has recently noted, for example, that the South is our least pluralistic and "open" region. Fewer private associations exist; there is less political and policy controversy supported by diverse parties, labor unions, ethnic groups, and churches; lower rates of political participation are the rule; strong institutional supports for segregation prevail; and there are few organizations for opposing segregation. One need scarcely measure individual prejudices to recognize that such a setting promotes discrimination.[12] Dozens of demographic studies have demonstrated the close correlation between various demographic variables and the level of resistance to desegregation.[13] Low levels of education and per capita income, high proportion of nonwhites and rural residents, and population stability or decline are closely associated with resistance to desegregation.

One can argue, of course, that demographic and structural facts are significant only if they are perceived by individuals or if they are somehow influential in shaping individuals' tendencies: they are only *indexes* of individual data, insofar as they predict discriminatory behavior. Doubtless such a criticism has some truth to it. A purely structural influence can be isolated only by showing that individuals who vary in prejudice behave in a similar (not necessarily identical) way. That is, a researcher must show that the level of discrimination is partially independent of the distribution of individual prejudice scores. In my judgment, field-oriented studies dealing with the interaction of individual and situational factors would demonstrate this fact. Some studies have already done so, as will be discussed later in this chapter. But the definitive isolation of a pure structural influence must be carried out with full recognition that one is dealing with an analytic variable. There is some danger that a patriotic listing of sociologically significant influences will be taken for a demonstration of their importance—often in rebuttal to an equally patriotic listing of psychological influences. This danger is not entirely avoided, for example, by Herbert Blumer, Arnold Rose, and others who have recently reaffirmed the significance of sociological forces in the study of discrimination.[14]

MULTIPLE POSSIBILITIES IN
INDIVIDUAL AND SITUATION

Applying the principle of multiple possibilities will help us to avoid the exaggerations that develop when only one part of the total field is examined. A person who has a tendency to respond in an unfavorable way to those of another race may express that tendency in various ways. He may discriminate directly against them. If direct expression of prejudice is painful or costly, however, it may be deflected. He may instead attack institutions or powerful leaders, for example, if he identifies them as somehow connected with his difficulties. Thus the same tendency can result in different behavior, depending upon the "opportunity structure," to use the phrase that Cloward and Ohlin apply to delinquency.

In addition, persons who are prejudiced have many other tendencies which may be activated by particular situations involving interracial contact. Among such other attitudes might be the following: "Law should be obeyed; my children need good schools; my store needs customers; violence is bad; outsiders should not push us around; this place needs more industry; my mortgage is awfully heavy, but we've finally got into a respectable neighborhood." Individuals vary in the way such attitudes are patterned and in the comparative strength of the attitudes, but it would be an unusual attitudinal structure that did not contain several possibilities, often with quite different implications for behavior.

Complex individual tendency systems do not, however, leave the field completely open for situational influences to determine behavior by activating one of the tendencies. The principle of multiple possibilities applies also to situations. The case would be rare and limiting in which the setting strongly "engaged" one attitude, facilitating its expression as behavior, while blocking all other possible tendencies entirely. Such a rare setting is approached by some "total institutions," where the range of behavior is severely narrowed; i.e., the effect of variation in individual tendencies is sharply reduced. This is the institutional counterpart of the authoritarian personality. As Chapter 8 showed, however, even the concentration camp does not eliminate the influence of individual variation. Some slight range of possibilities, however narrow, does remain. A wider range exists in even the most severely discriminatory race relations situations—in the rural South of the United States or in South Africa, for example.

Thus I agree, in part, with the Adorno quotation cited above. Individuals have structure and capacity for self-initiated action with respect to the environment. But such a statement is subject to serious misinterpretation. Although individuals develop selector systems and are not mere creatures of the environment, the alternatives from which they can select and the costs of the selections are set by others—by the environment in which they behave. Many of life's transactions are like those of a child with a dime to buy "what he wants." He may discover that what he wants most is not there, or costs too much. The actual transaction, therefore, is a function both of his desires and of the situation. The social structure, in other words, also has selector systems: normatively approved behavior and sanctions to encourage such behavior, the desires and values of significant others, and the like. These do not operate on completely malleable individuals, however, but on persons with tendencies which set their own costs.

The task of field theory, then, is to apply the principle of multiple possibilities simultaneously to individual prejudices and situational influences. Perhaps this can be done by using our now familiar two-variable model, with quasi scales representing the structural supports for discrimination and the individual tendencies toward discrimination. For purposes of simplicity a scale for the latter might be built around answers to three questions: Has the individual internalized prejudicial attitudes? Is he struggling with strong feelings of status anxiety? Does he tend to view the world as a hostile and threatening place (in part because of ego alienation and accompanying tendencies toward projection)? If these questions are scalable, as I think they are, the distribution would appear as follows:

Level of prejudice	Tendencies that support prejudice		
	Internalized attitudes of prejudice	Strong feelings of status anxiety	Strong feelings of ego alienation
1 (low)	No	No	No
2	Yes	No	No
3	Yes	Yes	No
4 (high)	Yes	Yes	Yes

Answering the questions yes or no, that is, treating them as attributes rather than variables, is undoubtedly an oversimplification. A more sophisticated scale would require additional questions with different levels of answer, but the present statement may illustrate the procedure.

Level of support	Structural Supports for Discrimination		
	Traditional institutional segregation	Extensive normative justification for discrimination	Political, economic, and sexual rewards for discrimination built into institutions
1 (low)	No	No	No
2	Yes	No	No
3	Yes	Yes	No
4 (high)	Yes	Yes	Yes

A matching scale, again using three questions for simplicity, can be designed for the structural supports for discriminatory behavior.

Level 1 might be descriptive of a liberal university community and level 4 of the rural South in the traditional Black Belt areas, while levels 2 and 3 might refer to modal cities of the North and South.

Can these two scales now be put together in such a way that they form a field theoretical statement of prejudice and discrimination?

To characterize the four levels of tendency toward discrimination, I have used Merton's labels.[15] Hypothetical means (X) are noted for each class. Assuming again that the critical score is 25, on this two-variable model we would find all the behavioral situations falling below the curved line to be discrimination-producing.

The all-weather illiberal (the authoritarian) will discriminate in most situations; thus one can predict quite well from knowledge of his tendencies alone what his behavior will be. He is the person who, according to the quasi scale, has internalized attitudes of prejudice, has strong feelings of status anxiety, and is strongly ego-alienated. Only when structural supports are at the lowest level (column I) would prediction from individual data alone be poor. Use of such extreme cases has allowed some authors to be comfortable with limited theoretical schemes.

On the other end of the scale, the all-weather liberal will discriminate

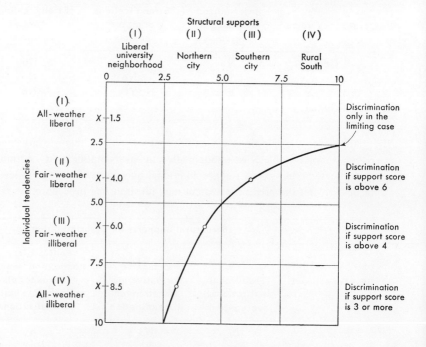

only in the limiting case: only when he is near the "border" of his group and the structural supports for discrimination are at a maximum on the range given here. A person with the mean score for this group (1.5) would never discriminate. The issue is thus stated in order to illustrate how one can get excellent prediction from a limited theory—for here we need no information about the situation—if the stated range of a neglected crucial variable is fairly narrow. By imagining settings in which the structural supports were 15 or 20, rather than the maximum of 10, we can arrive at the critical score of 25 for many persons of type I.

Viewing the scores from the point of view of structural support types, one sees that type IV (e.g., the rural South) will activate discrimination in almost everyone; therefore one can get good prediction from knowledge of situational forces alone. Most fair-weather liberals, as well as both types of illiberals, discriminate in such a setting. The liberal community, however, inhibits discrimination in everyone (again assuming the maximum prejudice score of 10), even the all-weather illiberal.

Thus parts of this range of possibilities can be predicted by reference to one of the variables alone. But a parsimonious theory that will account for the full distribution requires simultaneous reference to both variables seen as functions of each other.

These comments assume that stability exists in both environment and tendency; the model is static. Two kinds of process must be introduced into the system to bring it closer to reality: (1) variation in the potentialities of structure or person which are dominant in particular situations (without change in the potentialities), and (2) longer-run variations which indicate change in the potentialities themselves.

Let me illustrate each of these briefly. "Southern city" has been used as an example of type III structural support, a type which, according to the quasi scale, has traditional institutional segregation and extensive normative justification for discrimination (but which does not have political, economic, and sexual rewards for discrimination built into its institutions). The extent of emphasis on these supports varies from time to time, depending upon events affecting the city. A racial demonstration, for example, may call attention to a national norm of equality of treatment; it may also produce vivid reaffirmation of normative justification for discrimination. The balance of these two opposite norms will not always be the same. We need to think in terms of Southern city $_{April, 1963}$, Southern city $_{1935}$, and the like.

In the same way, the salience of individual tendencies will vary. There is some danger in using Merton's descriptive words for types of individuals, for the terms tend to focus on their "essence" and to overlook the complexity of the attitude structures. A critical event may bring an ordinarily latent attitude into a dominant position. A "fair-weather liberal" who has, according to the scale, internalized attitudes of prejudice, but who has no strong feelings of status anxiety or sense of ego alienation, may discriminate under conditions of fairly peaceful segregation. Under conditions of severe conflict, however, his latent attitudes ("Violence is bad, respect for law and order is essential") may become the crucial ones. A field view emphasis on the contemporary process requires that we think in terms of fair-weather liberal $_{1965}$ and fair-weather liberal $_{1935}$.

The second kind of process is a change, not simply in the salience of various potentialities, but in the potentialities themselves. The change can come about as a result either of mobility or of development on the individual or social level. For example, a fair-weather illiberal who always discriminates in the South may move to one of the more liberal Northern cities (scale score 4.0 or under), where he will discriminate less even if his prejudice remains the same, because of the reduction in structural support. Behavior of the fair-weather liberal who moves to the South will shift in the opposite direction. But on the other hand, if many fair-weather illiberals move into a Northern city, that city may discover that the structures for controlling discrimination are no longer so powerful; or migration into the South may bring persons insufficiently socialized to the norms of prejudice to be counted on in defending the traditional structures. When mobility occurs, in short, we must write new equations.

Developments in individuals or structures over time may produce the same results as mobility in space. In many Northern cities, upper-lower and lower-middle class individuals have struggled with heavy mortgages and have sacrificed other values in order to move to the suburbs. They seek better schools for their children, escape from spreading slums, and a more secure status. Their status anxiety is a product of many forces: long-run neglect of schools in the United States, job insecurity as a result of automation, rising hopes and aspirations. But the most visible source is the rapid increase in the number of nonwhite families in their neighborhoods and the sharp demands of these families for equality of treatment. These trends both increase and focus the status anxiety of the affected white persons. The result (if we disregard possible offsetting forces) is to increase the "scores" of such persons—to shift some of them from fair-weather liberals to fair-weather illiberals.

FIELD–ORIENTED RESEARCH
ON PREJUDICE AND DISCRIMINATION

The point of view I am developing here is gradually being incorporated into research designs that take account, simultaneously, of individual and structural variables. The appearance of a field perspective can perhaps best be described in terms of two stages of criticism of the thesis that discrimination is primarily a product of individual prejudice. In the first stage, the narrowly individualistic approach was countered by demonstrations that much of the variation in discrimination could be explained by variation in situational influences, without any reference to individual prejudices. The evidence on this, a small part of which I shall cite below, is full and decisive. In the second stage of criticism, individual tendencies are being "brought back in" and studied simultaneously with situational influences. Research along this line is recent and quite scarce; it is not always carried out with reference to explicit theory. But we have at least the beginnings of field-oriented research.

In the first stage, situational factors were introduced by showing that knowledge of individual attitudes as recorded in verbal behavior did not adequately predict nonverbal behavior; expressed prejudices did not correlate highly with discrimination. In his well-known study, LaPiere demonstrated that what hotel and restaurant managers said they would do with regard to accepting an interracial group (deny them accommodations) contradicted in almost all cases what they had actually done (accepted the group).[16] Schlesinger found that by controlling the messages "received from peers" (although actually coming from the experimenter), he could control agreement or disagreement of his subjects with anti-Semitic statements and expression of favorable or unfavorable opinions about Jews. The shifts in opinion in the direction of the presumed opinion of three peers were not significantly affected by the subjects' initial level of prejudice.[17]

Without implying that individual differences were unimportant, Cowen, Landes, and Schaet showed that a mildly frustrating environment increased the prejudice scores of thirty-two men and thirty-two women college students. The investigators measured their subjects' attitudes by a scale drawn from the Berkeley studies of the authoritarian personality (using questions from the F, anti-Negro, antiminority, and patriotism scales). After a mild frustration engendered by the assignment of two puzzles which were not solvable in the time allowed (during which period the experimenter was unsupporting and expressed disbelief that they could not finish), they were given a matched test from the same source. Anti-Negro scores went up significantly, especially for males. The other scores changed unreliably.[18]

The importance of the context in which prejudice is expressed was further emphasized by Feshbach and Singer, who hypothesized that discussion of a personally threatening situation would increase prejudice and that discussion of a shared threat would decrease it. Students enrolled in introductory psychology classes were randomly assigned to a control group, one of three personal-threat groups (dealing with problems of marriage, mental health, or fire), or one of two shared-threat groups (flood or atomic war). Prejudice toward Negroes had been measured by a scale of questions from the Berkeley studies and other sources. Four weeks later, each group was given a mimeographed discussion of a threat and asked to discuss it. Prejudice scores were then measured again. All three of the personal-threat groups gained significantly in prejudice over the control group (at .05 and .06 levels of significance). The flood-threat group lost significantly (at the .02 level). The atomic-war-threat group did not confirm the hypothesis, for their prejudice scores increased, although not significantly. Perhaps this was because war with Russia was included in the communication in such a way as to encourage the generalization of aggression to other groups.[19]

I shall not attempt to review here further studies of the ways in which situational forces affect the expressions of prejudice and the likelihood of discriminatory behavior.[20] For the most part, research along this line has not sought to deny the importance of variation in individual tendency, but has emphasized the need for adding attention to situational influences. Addition, however, is not enough. Only by simultaneous attention to tendencies and structures can the full range of outcomes be discovered.

This fact is nicely shown in research designed to test the hypothesis that prejudiced persons are characterized by a generalized "rigidity" of mind. Rokeach identified students who were high or low in "ethnocentrism" by use of the Berkeley E scale. He then showed them a complicated method for solving the kind of arithmetic puzzle which asks, for example, how one gets 22 quarts from three jars that hold 31, 61, and 4 quarts. Having taught them a six-step method, he then showed them a three-step method. But those with high scores on the E scale continued, in significantly greater numbers, to use the more complicated method. He concluded that rigidity as a quality of mind was associated with ethnocentrism.[21]

Unable in several replications to get the same results, Brown wondered if situational variables were involved. Rokeach had used a large lecture class, and the problems had a "test" quality; while Brown had carried out the experiment in small laboratory groups. Perhaps the former setting created an ego-involving atmosphere, so that the measures referred to a "defensive, situationally dependent rigidity," not a generalized trait. Following this lead, Brown gave the tests under two different sets of conditions in order to try out the hypothesis that an ego-involving atmosphere would yield a higher correlation between rigidity and authoritarianism than a relaxed atmosphere. In one test, the experimenter was aloof and formal in manner; he cautioned repeatedly against looking at the test ahead of time; he stressed its importance as a test of motivation and intelligence; names were written down before the test was given. In the relaxed atmosphere, the experimenter wore sports clothes, adopted a casual manner, showed little interest in the test, and did not ask for names until the end. Under the ego-involving conditions, those with high authoritarian scores did show a significantly greater tendency to cling to the original method than those with low authoritarian scores. The difference was not significant, however, under the relaxed conditions.[22]

Developing Brown's argument further, Maher sought to increase the anxiety of his subjects by creating more of a punishment-reward situation than the ego-involved setting described above. Success or failure for his subjects was related to marks in a course. Under these conditions, *both* the authoritarian and equalitarian subjects held rigidly to the original and more complicated method.[23]

Now we can make sense of these various findings by putting them together in a design that refers both to tendencies and to experimental situations:

LIKELIHOOD OF MENTAL RIGIDITY

Experimental conditions	Individual tendency		
	Authoritarian	Nonauthoritarian	
Relaxed	No	No	(Brown)
Ego-involving	Yes	No	(Rokeach, Brown)
Anxiety-producing	Yes	Yes	(Maher)

This is scarcely a definitive statement of the problem, of course. Our index of rigidity is fairly crude; the three-step scale of anxiety-creating conditions has not been tested for reliability; a simple dichotomy of tendencies is undoubtedly inadequate; and different measures of authoritarianism were used by the different experimenters. Yet field theory orders the observed data in a meaningful way. From it we can derive the hypothesis that mental rigidity as a form of behavior is a function of the *product* of authoritarian tendencies and anxiety-producing conditions.

In an ingenious series of experiments with boys' groups, Sherif and his associates have shown that prejudice and discrimination can be created and—with what appears to be somewhat greater difficulty—reduced by the manipulation of intergroup contacts.[24] Partly because the focus of their research was on intergroup relations (the conditions that produce intergroup hostility, shared stereotypes, and then cooperation again), and partly because their subjects were chosen from a fairly narrow range of individuals (boys with good school records and high levels of adjustment), they gave little systematic attention to individual differences. Yet they noted that the speed with which close identity with the in-group was adopted, the ease with which group lines were crossed in friendship choices, and particularly the rapidity with which a total-camp point of view was accepted (after experimental efforts to split the camp into two competing and antagonistic groups were stopped and reversed) all depended in part upon individual tendencies. For example, boys who were most insecure and who had only painfully won a feeling of identity in the smaller groups were slowest in shifting their allegiance to the larger group, wherein the task of establishing themselves had to be carried on all over again.

In a related study, Yarrow and her coworkers also showed how attitudes and behavior could be changed by variation in camp associations. In this case, the work was done in an interracial camp. The "equal-status contact" of the camp situation significantly reduced the use of race as a criterion of friendship and increased the self-esteem of the Negro children. But not all were affected in the same ways or to the same degree. Age, race, and sex all influenced the meaning of the interracial experience. And what is more important for our purposes here, individual tendencies did also. These tendencies can be seen, for example, in the process of choice of friends:

In the desegregated cabins some children make friendship choices along a simple, categorical line (either race or location within the cabin). Others seem to make more complicated appraisals of the individual characteristics of their peers.... For 30 per cent of the campers race was the prime determinant of friendship choice.... Among 38 per cent of the children, friendship choice was guided predominantly by cabin space.... Twenty-seven per cent of the children did not follow either of these categorical approaches; for them friendship was not precut to the measure of race or room; choice seemed to be more in terms of an appraisal of the individual....

It was hypothesized that children who appraise others on an individual basis tend themselves to be confident of their own social sensitivities and are interested in interpersonal experiences. Children who invoke a simple formula for guiding interpersonal relations tend to be less confident and less interested in social relations.[25]

Behavior was significantly changed, in short, by the interracial structure of the camp. But the nature of the change was not the same for everyone; it varied with individual characteristics, group membership, and ecological position.

A field perspective sometimes helps to make sense out of an otherwise puzzling series of observations. Pettigrew, for example, notes that there are contradictory findings concerning the relationship of downward social mobility and intolerance.[26] In the North, downward mobility generally has been found to be associated with intolerance. Comparing samples from four Northern and four Southern towns, Pettigrew found that in the former the downwardly mobile were significantly more anti-Negro ($p = .05$) and more anti-Semitic ($p = .15$) than the stationary or upwardly mobile. In the South, however, the downwardly mobile were significantly less anti-Negro ($p = .001$) and less anti-Semitic ($p = .20$).[27] The implications of downward mobility as an individual experience, in other words, cannot be explored until reference is made to the surrounding environment, which helps to define the meaning of this downward mobility. "Perhaps in a culture that emphasizes status and family background, that makes a sharp distinction between 'poor whites' and 'respectable whites,' and that cherishes its aristocratic traditions, the downwardly mobile southerner learns to reject much of his culture. And rejecting the culture's stress on tradition and status makes it easier to reject also the culture's dicta concerning the Negro." [28]

On the basis of this evidence it appears likely that many studies of the relationship between mobility and prejudice have not asked a sufficiently complicated question. Explorations of the general question, "Is downward mobility associated with intolerance?" yield only contradictory answers. But when we introduce structural dimensions to explore the conditions under which downward mobility is associated with higher or lower levels of tolerance, the apparent contradictions are resolved.

The significance of the interaction of tendency and situation variables is demonstrated again by Hamblin's factor analysis of a series of measures on a quota sample of 100 white adults in the St. Louis metropolitan area.[29] Although in most instances he discovered the expected simple correlations between a "discrimination index" and a series of nine possible antecedent variables, only three of the nine showed substantial independent relationship: fear of equal-status contact explained 17 per cent of the variance, family pressures to discriminate 32 per cent, and friends' pressures to discriminate 16 per cent.

The multiple regression correlation of these three with the discrimination index is .81, a figure that is raised to only .82 by the addition of the other six antecedents. Two of the three critical variables, family pressures and friends' pressures to discriminate, are situational factors (although, unfortunately, they are measured only in terms of the perceptions of the individuals being studied, not by actual behaviors of the significant others—thus we have an index rather than a direct measure). A multiple correlation treats the three variables as additive. Hamblin wisely notes, however, that their effects, and their relationships to the other six factors, may be interactive.

The comparative importance of family and friends, for example, varies with the level of "anomia" expressed by the individuals. The correlation between pressures from family and friends and the discrimination index remains high for persons at all levels of anomia, but when the relationship is "specified" (in the Lazarsfeld sense) by three different levels of anomia, interesting variations appear. As anomia goes up (from low to medium to high), the correlation between family pressure to discriminate and the discrimination index also goes up (from .68 to .73 to .83); but as anomia goes up, the correlation between friends' pressures to discriminate and the discrimination index goes down irregularly (from .77 to .59 to .62). Graphically, the relationships appear as follows: [30]

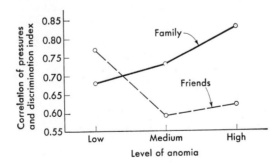

These data say: One cannot predict the level of the index to discriminate simply by knowledge of the situational pressures. These pressures act differently on persons with different tendencies (in this case, feelings of anomia). In a similar finding, Hamblin reports that as the individual tendency toward authoritarianism decreases, the correlation between friends' pressures and the discrimination index also decreases (from .83 to .68 to .58 for the three levels of authoritarianism). "The results indicate that authoritarianism has but an indirect effect on the tendency to discriminate; it appears to modify the effects of friends' pressures." [31] Hamblin might have noted also that friends' pressures have but an indirect effect, for they are modified by the level of authoritarianism. "Apparently authoritarianism, a personality factor, interacts with friends' pressures, a normative or cultural factor." [32]

If simultaneous attention to individual and structural factors is theoretically more adequate, it can be expected in most instances to be clinically more adequate as well. In attempts to reduce discrimination, for example, a given structural change may influence some persons one way, other persons in different ways. To ask whether equal-status contact will reduce discrimination is to ask an inadequate question. The experience may reduce the discriminations of the self-confident though ill-informed person but increase the discrimination of the person filled with status anxiety.

Mussen studied the effects of a twenty-eight-day interracial camping experience on the attitudes of 106 white boys, most of them lower-class. Mean prejudice scores before and after the camp showed no change, but individual measures indicated that 28 had moved significantly in the direction of less prejudice while 27 boys had moved in the direction of more prejudice. Comparing these two groups, Mussen noted that the boys whose prejudices had increased expressed more aggressive feelings and needs, as well as stronger needs to defy authority, than those whose prejudices had declined. The boys whose prejudices had grown felt themselves to be the victims of aggression, believed that others were not kind and helpful, and expressed more dissatisfaction with the camp and disagreement with its values. Their adjustment to camp was poorer.[33]

In this equal-status contact situation, the effects on attitudes were a function not of the original prejudice score, but of personal insecurities and anxieties. On the basis of scattered evidence, one might guess that shifts in prejudice or discrimination under different status-contact conditions might be distributed as follows for ego-alien, anxious persons and for self-confident, self-accepting persons:

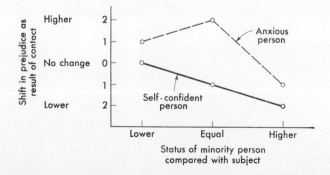

This is by no means an adequate formulation of the problem. The initial level of prejudice, as well as the degree of status insecurity, is no doubt an important individual variable. The nature of the contact situation and the definitions of the situation furnished by significant others are probably factors that influence the way in which the status comparison operates.[34] The need is for several measures of individual tendency and of structural influence applied simultaneously to various kinds of contact situations. With adequate data it would not be difficult, for example, to program computer analyses of shifts in prejudice scores under two structural conditions (comparative status levels and degree of support for discrimination from significant others) and two individual conditions (initial level of prejudice and level of anxiety). Stated in tabular form, the design would appear as shown on the following page.

For the beginnings of an adequate treatment of the problem, we need data for the 24 columns noted here.[35] On the basis of the research done to the present, we can only cautiously record probable outcomes in a few of the columns. Using a scale from −2 (large reduction of prejudice) to +2 (large increase) one might list, taking Mussen's study for example, a +2 in columns 13 and 15 and a −2 in columns 14 and 16. This would be to say that under conditions of equal-status contact, where significant others offer little support for discrimination (information on this is slight), anxious persons showed more antipathy and self-confident persons less antipathy to minority persons whether or not the initial level of prejudice had been high. Various studies cited above offer evidence for other columns, but our knowledge of such multivariate situations is sketchy.

CONCLUSION

In the last two decades an impressive body of research and commentary dealing with minority-majority relations has accumulated. During this period formerly separate, even contradictory, modes of interpretation have been brought into confrontation, and we are beginning to see the development of a behavioral science of prejudice and discrimination which subsumes the formerly separate viewpoints. I have attempted in this chapter to sketch the outlines of a field perspective that I believe accounts well for the evidence in hand and promises to be valuable in future research.[36] It now seems clear that to explain the dramatic events involving racial and cultural relations which are commanding such attention around the world, we must explore cultural and subcultural norms, the prevailing structures of interaction, the distribution of personal tendencies —and the interaction of these forces. Effective action, no less surely, requires a multidisciplinary view.

Factors	Effects of contact on prejudice and discrimination																							
Comparative status of minority	Lower								Equal								Higher							
Support for discrimination from significant others	H (high)				L (low)				H (high)				L (low)				H (high)				L (low)			
Prejudice level of subjects	H		L		H		L		H		L		H		L		H		L		H		L	
Anxiety level of subjects	H	L	H	L	H	L	H	L	H	L	H	L	H	L	H	L	H	L	H	L	H	L	H	L
	(1)	(2)	(3)	(4)	(5)	(6)	(7)	(8)	(9)	(10)	(11)	(12)	(13) $+2$	(14) -2	(15) $+2$	(16) -2	(17)	(18)	(19)	(20)	(21)	(22)	(23)	(24)

FOOTNOTES

Note: The bracketed number following an author's name refers to the footnote in which the source is cited in full.

1. Gunnar Myrdal, with the assistance of Richard Sterner and Arnold Rose, *An American Dilemma,* Harper & Row, Publishers, Incorporated, 1944, 2 vols.

2. T. W. Adorno, Else Frenkel-Brunswik, D. J. Levinson, and R. N. Sanford, *The Authoritarian Personality,* Harper & Row, Publishers, Incorporated, 1950.

3. Robin M. Williams, Jr., *The Reduction of Intergroup Tensions,* Social Science Research Council, 1947, p. 39.

4. Adorno, Frenkel-Brunswik, Levinson, and Sanford [2], p. 6.

5. Jerome Himmelhoch, "Tolerance and Personality Needs," *American Sociological Review,* February, 1950, p. 81.

6. See Richard Christie and Peggy Cook, "A Guide to Published Literature Relating to the Authoritarian Personality through 1956," *Journal of Psychology,* April, 1958, pp. 171–199; George E. Simpson and J. Milton Yinger, *Racial and Cultural Minorities: An Analysis of Prejudice and Discrimination,* 3d ed., Harper & Row, Publishers Incorporated, 1965, chap. 3.

7. See *ibid.,* for an analysis of the research dealing with authoritarianism and the studies which qualify its thesis. Representative works include Donn Byrne and Terry Wong, "Racial Prejudice, Interpersonal Attraction, and Assumed Dissimilarity of Attitudes," *Journal of Abnormal and Social Psychology,* October, 1962, pp. 246–253; Loren Chapman and Donald Campbell, "The Effect of Acquiescence Response-set upon Relationships among the F Scale, Ethnocentrism, and Intelligence, *Sociometry,* June, 1959, pp. 153–161; Richard Christie, Joan Havel, and Bernard Seidenberg, "Is the F Scale Irreversible?" *Journal of Abnormal and Social Psychology,* March, 1958, pp. 143–159; Milton Rokeach, *The Open and Closed Mind,* Basic Books, Inc., Publishers, 1960; Ivan Steiner and Homer Johnson, "Authoritarianism and Conformity," *Sociometry,* March, 1963, pp. 21–34; Frank Jacobson and Salomon Rettig, "Authoritarianism and Intelligence," *Journal of Social Psychology,* September, 1959, pp. 213–219; John Photiadis and Jeanne Biggar, "Religiosity, Education, and Social Distance," *American Journal of Sociology,* May, 1962, pp. 666–672; Edward McDill, "Anomie, Authoritarianism, Prejudice, and Socio-economic Status: An Attempt at Clarification," *Social Forces,* March, 1961, pp. 239–245; Mervin Freedman, Harold Webster, and Nevitt Sanford, "A Study of Authoritarianism and Psychopathology," *Journal of Psychology,* April, 1956, pp. 315–322; and Norman Prentice, "Ethnic Attitudes, Neuroticism, and Culture," *Journal of Social Psychology,* June, 1961, pp. 75–82.

8. Edwin H. Rhyne, "Racial Prejudice and Personality Scales: An Alternative Approach," *Social Forces,* October, 1962, p. 46.

9. Don Stewart and Thomas Hoult, "A Social-Psychological Theory of the Authoritarian Personality," *American Journal of Sociology,* November, 1959, pp. 274–279.

10. Dietrich C. Reitzes, "Institutional Structure and Race Relations," *Phylon,* Spring, 1959, p. 49.

11. See *ibid.,* pp. 48–66; Arnold M. Rose, "Inconsistencies in Attitudes toward Negro Housing," *Social Problems,* Spring, 1961, pp. 287–292; Isidor Chein, Morton Deutsch, Herbert Hyman, and Marie Jahoda (issue eds.), "Consistency and Inconsistency in Intergroup Relations," *Journal of Social Issues,* vol. 5, 1949, no. 3; M. L. Kohn and Robin M. Williams, Jr., "Situational Patterning in Intergroup Relations," *American Sociological Review,* April, 1956, pp. 164–174.

12. Warren Breed, "Group Structure and Resistance to Desegregation in the Deep South," *Social Problems,* Summer, 1962, pp. 84–94.

13. See, e.g., Melvin M. Tumin, *Desegregation: Resistance and Readiness,* Princeton University Press, 1958; Thomas F. Pettigrew, "Demographic Correlates of Border-state Desegregation," *American Sociological Review,* December, 1957, pp. 683–689.

14. Herbert Blumer, "Race Prejudice as a Sense of Group Position," *Pacific Sociological Review,* vol. 1, 1958; Arnold M. Rose, "Intergroup Relations vs. Prejudice," *Social Problems,* October, 1956, pp. 173–176; Edwin H. Rhyne [8].

15. See Robert K. Merton in R. M. MacIver (ed.), *Discrimination and National Welfare,* Institute for Religious and Social Studies, 1949, pp. 99–126.

16. Richard LaPiere, "Attitudes vs. Actions," *Social Forces,* December, 1934, pp. 230–237; for a useful extension of this design, see Bernard Kutner, Carol Wilkins, and P. R. Yarrow, "Verbal Attitudes and Overt Behavior Involving Racial Prejudice," *Journal of Abnormal and Social Psychology,* July, 1952, pp. 649–652.

17. Lawrence E. Schlesinger, *The Influence of Exposure to Peer Group Opinions on the Expression of Attitudes toward a Minority Group,* unpublished doctoral dissertation, Boston University, 1955, described by Melvin Tumin in *An Inventory and Appraisal of Research on American Anti-Semitism,* Anti-Defamation League of B'nai B'rith, 1961, p. 60.

18. Emory L. Cowen, Judah Landes, and Donald E. Schaet, "The Effects of Mild Frustration on the Expression of Prejudiced Attitudes," *Journal of Abnormal and Social Psychology,* January, 1959, pp. 33–38. This study supports the earlier work of Neal Miller and B. R. Bugelski, and others, who had demonstrated the effects of situational frustration on prejudice. See John Dollard, *et al., Frustration and Aggression,* Yale University Press, 1939, pp. 43–44.

19. Seymour Feshbach and Robert Singer, "The Effects of Personal and Shared Threats upon Social Prejudice," *Journal of Abnormal and Social Psychology,* May, 1957, pp. 411–416.

20. For illustrative work see J. D. Lohman and D. C. Reitzes, "Deliberately Organized Groups and Racial Behavior," *American Sociological Review,* June, 1954, pp. 342–344; Lewis M. Killian, "The Adjustment of Southern White Migrants to Northern Urban Norms," *Social Forces,* October, 1953, pp. 66–69; Alvin Winder, "White Attitudes toward Negro-White Interaction in a Number of Community Situations," *Journal of Social Psychology,* August, 1956, pp. 15–32.

21. Milton Rokeach, "Generalized Mental Rigidity as a Factor in

Ethnocentrism," *Journal of Abnormal and Social Psychology*, July, 1948, pp. 259–278.

22. Roger W. Brown, "A Determinant of the Relationship between Rigidity and Authoritarianism," *Journal of Abnormal and Social Psychology*, October, 1953, pp. 469–476. Because he used the F rather than the E scale, Brown's study is not an exact replication of Rokeach's.

23. Brendan A. Maher, "Personality, Problem Solving, and the Einstellung Effect," *Journal of Abnormal and Social Psychology*, January, 1957, pp. 70–74.

24. Muzafer Sherif and Carolyn W. Sherif, *Groups in Harmony and Tension*, Harper & Row, Publishers, Incorported, 1953; Muzafer Sherif et al., *Intergroup Conflict and Cooperation: The Robbers Cave Experiment*, University of Oklahoma Book Exchange, 1961.

25. John D. Campbell and Marian Radke Yarrow in "Interpersonal Dynamics in a Desegregation Process," in Marian Radke Yarrow (issue ed.), *Journal of Social Issues*, vol. 14, 1958, pp. 40–51.

26. Thomas F. Pettigrew, "Regional Differences in Anti-Negro Prejudice," *Journal of Abnormal and Social Psychology*, July, 1959, pp. 28–36. For discussions of social mobility and intolerance, see also Fred B. Silberstein and Melvin Seeman, "Social Mobility and Prejudice," *American Journal of Sociology*, November, 1959, pp. 258–264; Harold L. Wilenski and Hugh Edwards, "The Skidder: Ideological Adjustments of Downward Mobile Workers," *American Sociological Review*, April, 1959, pp. 215–231; and Thomas F. Pettigrew, "Personality and Sociocultural Factors in Intergroup Attitudes: A Cross-National Comparison," *Journal of Conflict Resolution*, March, 1958, pp. 29–42.

27. See Thomas F. Pettigrew, "Regional Differences in Anti-Negro Prejudice" [26].

28. Thomas F. Pettigrew, "Personality and Sociocultural Factors in Intergroup Attitudes: A Cross-national Comparison" [26], p. 39.

29. Robert L. Hamblin, "The Dynamics of Racial Discrimination," *Social Problems*, Fall, 1962, pp. 103–121.

30. Based on data from *ibid.*, p. 113.

31. *Ibid.*, p. 117.

32. *Ibid.*, p. 118.

33. Paul H. Mussen, "Some Personality Factors Related to Changes in Children's Attitudes toward Negroes," *Journal of Abnormal and Social Psychology*, July, 1950, pp. 423–441.

34. See Daniel M. Wilner; Rosabelle P. Walkley, and Stuart W. Cook, *Human Relations in Interracial Housing*, University of Minnesota Press, 1955; Morton Deutsch and Mary Evans Collins, *Interracial Housing: A Psychological Evaluation of a Social Experiment*, The University of Minnesota Press, 1951; Gordon W. Allport, *The Nature of Prejudice*, Addison-Wesley Publishing Company, Inc., 1954, pp. 262–263; Frank W. Westie, "Negro-White Status Differentials and Social Distance," *American Sociological Review*, October, 1952, pp. 550–558; and Robert Coles, *The Desegregation of Southern Schools: A Psychiatric Study*, Anti-Defamation League and Southern Regional Council, 1963.

35. By the addition of other variables—e.g., the proportion of the interacting group that is of minority status—or by more refined sub-

division of the factors, the 24 columns could rapidly be expanded. Only cumulative research can show which differences are significant and which therefore require further attention.

36. For a more extensive commentary and review of research to date, see George E. Simpson and J. Milton Yinger [6], especially chaps. 3–5.

CHAPTER 12

The Field View of Abnormal Behavior

Contemporary research on abnormal behavior is perhaps more thoroughly multidisciplinary than any other branch of behavioral science. At the same time, what one can say with full confidence about the systems of causes is quite limited. In this chapter, therefore, I shall be exploring a question of great significance for field theory, but I shall have to speak in even more tentative terms than were required for other topics.

Prevailing interpretations of abnormal behavior have shifted so extensively that it is not uncommon to speak of "revolutions" in psychiatry (thinking of psychiatry both as a theory of causes and as a body of techniques of healing). Although some observers disagree about the critical turning points, I shall refer to three major shifts. Perhaps the most significant was the first—the restatement of abnormality or mental illness (which I shall use to mean severe abnormality) as a medical rather than a moral problem. With the development of modern medicine in the nineteenth century, physicians and the educated public gradually came to think of abnormality not as a sign of moral weakness or sin, but as a disease or a series of diseases. Congruent with more general theories of the period, strong emphasis was placed upon inherited weaknesses and biological processes.

The Freudian revolution shifted attention away from genetic weakness, physical lesion, poison, and microbe. Organic illnesses and weaknesses were not denied, but psychodynamic processes were emphasized. Abnormality is the awkward but vital effort of the self to protect itself against a threatening and uncertain world. Caught between the often mutually contradictory demands of the body and the social world, everyone struggles with whatever tactics of compromise, escape, or radical denial seem capable of reducing the conflict. People are abnormal who have been deprived, by the nature of their early experiences with others, of the possibilities of developing socially acceptable ways of dealing with life's inherent tensions. Freud is linked at the same time both to the earlier theories of abnormality by his orientation to neurology and the body, and to the beginnings of the third "revolution" by his emphasis on the importance of these interpersonal dramas from which so much of life is formed.

This third movement in psychiatry, however, required far more attention to society and culture, to class and race, and to the effects of shared values and opportunities than the Freudian view encompassed. Much of this material, to be sure, can be added to psychodynamic theory without destroying it. With the candor he frequently used about his own theoretical ambiguities and incomplete resolutions, Freud gives a powerful impression in his work of a mind seeking to break the boundaries set by his time and place. "If we cannot see clearly, at least we see the obscurities clearly." [1] A latent theory capable of encompassing more aspects of the sociocultural world was hinted at. But his involvement in late nineteenth-century biology and physics was dominant.

I do not fully share the enthusiasm shown by many contemporary scholars for Freud as a social scientist. Scholarship is perhaps too often devoted to digging out in his work the ambiguous hints of ideas that got much fuller emphasis and demonstration from later scientists. I am relatively unsympathetic to exegesis and prefer to go directly to contemporary research and theory for evidence of psychiatry's third revolution. It is enough that Freud was the major figure in accomplishing the second revolution, that he hinted at the third, and that he designed a system capable of the extension and reformulation necessary to encompass the work of later theorists.

The third transformation of psychiatry has been the combined product of physicians and social scientists—anthropologists, psychologists, and more recently, sociologists. No one decisive event marks the beginning of this period, but I would be inclined to emphasize the publication of Mead's lectures, particularly *Mind, Self, and Society*,[2] the work of Karen Horney,[3] the collaboration of Kardiner, Linton, and others,[4] and the attention given group structure and process by Lewin and Moreno.[5] Thus by the end of the 1930s, strong foundations for "social psychiatry" had been laid.[6] Stimulated by the demands and research opportunities of wartime and by the enormous expansion of behavioral research since World War II, this discipline has become a significant part of the theory and practice of psychiatry.

In the succession of revolutions, earlier perspectives have been not so much repudiated as absorbed into a larger framework. Even the shift to the definition of abnormality in medical and scientific rather than in moral terms has not been completed. And the organic-biological, the psychodynamic, and the social-psychiatric points of view are all maintained, in somewhat uneasy alliance, on the contemporary scene. Most students of the problem, however much they may emphasize one process or structure over the others, are ready to grant that organic, characterological, and sociocultural forces must all be considered in the development of a theory of mental illness. Clausen summarizes well this multi-dimensional view when he writes: "The amount of mental illness in any society or population will depend, then, upon the genetic composition of the population, the prevalence of certain organic diseases, the nutritional practices, the prevalence of certain types of trauma or pathogenic processes in early family life, the kinds of stresses to which adults are exposed late in life, cultural definitions of deviant behavior, and the exercise of potential controls which may limit the development of illness." [7]

From a field perspective, the task is to bring these several dimensions into one system so that the effects of their *interaction* can be given full attention. Before I undertake some observations along this line, however, I shall examine the problem of definition, because once a sociocultural perspective was brought into the study of abnormality, the boundaries of the phenomenon were no longer so self-evident as they seemed when only organic and psychodynamic processes were considered.

ABNORMALITY VERSUS ATYPICALITY

One of the most difficult and important tasks of a science is so to define those parts of nature with which it is concerned that phenomena which are fundamentally different will be classified separately, despite impressive superficial similarities, and phenomena which are fundamentally alike will be classified together, despite impressive superficial differences. When anthropologists began to extend their interests to include the study of personality, they were quick to warn against any assumption that a given type of behavior had the same implications for personality among persons from different cultural settings. Homosexuality in one setting, for example, may be a defensive maneuver to neutralize unconscious hatred of one's father; or an effort to avoid adult responsibilities (a childish craving for love and attention); or a demonstration of fear of the opposite sex and of low self-esteem—that is, a manifestation of inner fears and tensions. In another setting, it may be the product of normal socialization to a particular role (a Samurai warrior, e.g.); or a culturally acceptable compromise with the demands of an unattainable status (as was the *berdache* position among some Plains Indians); or a situationally induced response to sexual deprivation (as among some prisoners). Whether or not homosexuality represents abnormality, in other words, cannot be known until the cultural and situational influences are studied.

This is the point of Ruth Benedict's well-known paper on "Anthropology and the Abnormal." [8] Abnormality is not simply "in" the behavior of a person, but in the culturally defined meaning of the behavior accepted by him and by those around him. The paranoid-like delusions of grandeur shown by some of the Kwakiutl or the pervading suspicions among the Dobu do not express personality disorganization. They are the product of normal socialization. Horney took much the same position:

"... the term neurotic, while originally medical, cannot be used now without its cultural implications. One can diagnose a broken leg without the cultural background of the patient, but one would run a great risk in calling an Indian boy psychotic because he told us that he had visions in which he believed." [9]

Horney was more cautious in her use of this idea than was Benedict. The latter, in her effort to emphasize the importance of cultural influences, tended to define abnormality *solely* as a segment of human behavior which the individual's society does not culturally prescribe. This definition led her to imply that abnormality is behavior that departed from the cultural norm, behavior that is unusual in a given group; thus equating abnormality with atypicality. In my judgment this reflects a confusion of an individual fact with a social fact, or an unjustified assumption of a one-to-one relationship between them. Benedict tried to do too much with an important idea. She correctly observed that without knowledge of culture one can easily misread the significance of a given action, because what is symptom of abnormality in one society is folkway in another. The Kwakiutl insult complex is not a paranoid delusion of persecution but a culturally learned way of responding to competition.

One cannot reverse this statement, however. The absence of such a complex among some Kwakiutl, even if it were statistically unusual, would not be proof of abnormality as usually defined. Abnormal behavior is an indication of individual malintegration, of tensions incapable of release, of mutually inconsistent desires. One's sociocultural experiences are of great importance in creating individual tendencies in those directions, as I shall discuss; and knowledge of cultural norms assists the researcher in understanding the significance of a given act for an individual. Deviation from the standards or the common practices of one's group, however, is not *ipso facto* proof of abnormality. One needs to know the internal meaning of the deviation. Does it show that the individual is at odds with himself, torn by inconsistent desires, confused by an unconscious conflict beyond the articulation and control of ego? [10]

Whatever terms one uses, two concepts are needed: behavior that departs from the statistically and culturally normal, which I shall call atypical, and behavior that expresses intraindividual conflicts and malintegration, which I shall call abnormal. The possible relationships between the two should also be specified. If we think of each as a variable with many possible scale values, their relationships could be sketched as follows:

One would know a great deal about a society or other group if he knew how its members were distributed along these two scales. In a stable, homogeneous society, most might fall quite closely along line *AC*. This would indicate that the person who behaves abnormally is likely also to be atypical, and vice versa. (If the chart were three-dimensional, one might show the distribution all along the line, perhaps in the form of a normal curve, somewhat skewed to the right, with a peak at point *X*.) In a heterogeneous, changing society, however, there may be wider scatter around the line, with some persons at every point in the whole area bounded by *ABCD*. This is to say, under some conditions there can be normal-atypical persons and abnormal-typical persons. The former deviate from the prevailing standards and practices in their society, but are sustained by a real or imaginary subsociety; they are not ego-alien. The latter do not deviate, yet they are torn by conflict; they are perhaps "compulsively normal."

RELATIONSHIPS BETWEEN THE ABNORMAL AND ATYPICAL

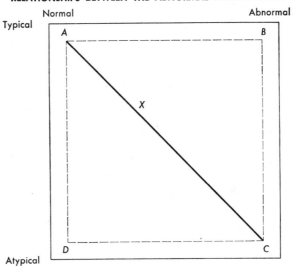

A field definition of abnormal behavior. We must distinguish between abnormality as tendency, which is an individual fact, and abnormal behavior, which requires a field construct. The distinction is difficult to maintain because of our inclination, particularly when referring to the more extreme manifestations, to think in terms of abnormal *persons*, as if their whole beings were intrinsically characterized by abnormality. The principle of multiple possibilities is useful to remember here: Persons characterized by abnormal tendencies are characterized also by other tendencies. Whether certain tendencies will be activated and then defined as abnormal depends upon self-other interactions.

Fried and Lindemann, for example, suggest this operational definition for extreme mental illness: Impulses break through the regulations of the ego and superego; behavior cannot be controlled by the usual regulatory agencies—family, peers, work colleagues—and thus a crisis is precipitated; efforts to support the ego-superego system by the usual agencies of control fail, endangering the normal institutional structure and patterns of interaction; extraordinary institutional resources are drawn in.[11] This is no mere adding together of individual and group factors; it is a *process* definition that requires simultaneous attention to the various levels of influence.

The Continuum of Health and Illness

Implicit in a definition of illness is some conception of health. Jahoda points out that we have the option, in defining mental health, of thinking of "a relatively constant and enduring function of the personality," or of "a momentary function of personality and situation." [12] The latter is a field conception. In her review of many definitions of mental health, Jahoda identifies six major categories found among those who think of health as individual tendency, not behavior: attitudes of an individual toward self; growth, development, or self-actualization; integration of component parts of self; autonomy, independence from undue social influence; adequate reality perception; and environmental mastery.[13] Many definitions of mental health combine several of these categories into a syndrome analogous to the clustering of symptoms that constitutes a disease.

Since I prefer a field definition, I would modify the reference to individual characteristics by stating that mental health consists of behavior in a situation that facilitates the expression of tendencies toward self-respect, growth, integration, autonomy, and independence. Health, in this view, does not reside in the individual, just as redness does not reside in the rose. Health, or illness, is behavior that emerges from the individual-situation interaction.[14]

Health and illness are variables, of course, not attributes; hence the problem of drawing a line arises. Where does health end and illness begin? This raises the further problem: How many persons suffer from mental illness? The tendency in recent years has been to include a larger proportion of the population in the "ill" category than was formerly believed necessary. This has resulted partly from increased information and partly from an inclination to pay more attention to moderate disturbances. Careful studies of large populations have found that half or more of the adults are "psychiatrically impaired" to some degree. Dealing with a rural and small-town sample, the authors of the Stirling County research reported that approximately two-thirds suffer at some time from a psychiatric disorder and that most of the illnesses are so persistent that "at least half of the adults in Stirling County are *currently* suffering from some psychiatric disorder defined in the APA Diagnostic and Statistical Manual." [15] Srole and his associates classified a sample of adults in mid-Manhattan into four groups: well, 18.5 per cent; mild symptom formation, 36.3 per cent; moderate symptom formation, 21.8 per cent; and severe symptom formation, 23.4 per cent.[16] This classification does not include the 1.3 per cent who were under treatment for mental illness. Such studies use very inclusive definitions of impairment. When more stringent tests which refer only to the seriously ill are applied, rates from 10 to 25 per cent may be found.[17]

The different figures indicate the use of different "cutting points" and disagreements in diagnostic practices, as well as differing samples. Further research will doubtless narrow the range of estimates. Even as they stand, however, the disagreements are not overwhelming when the variation in degree of impairment being studied is recognized. All studies give one common impression: the rate of abnormality is high. Conceivably, we have tended to think in terms of a distribution of mental health approximating a reverse J curve and are now discovering that a normal curve, skewed to the right, is a more accurate representation. Thus data in hand seem startling if judged against chart A below, but not if judged against chart B. The latter seems to represent the actual situation better.

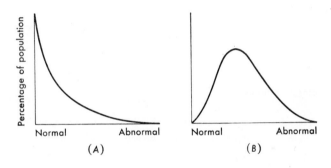

(A) (B)

THE MULTIPLE CAUSES OF ABNORMALITY

A field definition of abnormality takes a step from designation toward explanation; it points to causes as well as characteristics. Speaking in general terms, without reference to particular types of abnormality, we can note that knowledge of heredity alone, or of the presence or absence of microbe or poison in the system, or of the degree of stress during the ego-formation process, or of the nature of the sociocultural environment, without knowledge of the other factors, would seldom yield good prediction. In extreme cases we can afford to act *as if* abnormality were a result of influence from one level only; but insofar as we attempt to build a theory of causes out of such cases, we must be aware of the assumption we make of stability on the other levels.

Severe genetic or organic weakness, for example, may be closely associated with some forms of abnormality whatever the influence from the other factors, *within the presently known range*. But if knowledge of modes of training and socialization grows beyond what we now can imagine, or if we learn to control some of the presently "inevitable" biological processes—that is, if the sociocultural environment is significantly changed—then we will find that we have been able to speak of "organic" illnesses only because of stability in some of the factors. This is to note again that a field approach is particularly necessary when two or more systems of variables can have significantly different scale values.

Even under present conditions, the tendency may be to draw too sharp a line between "organic" and "functional" illness. Since some of the symptoms of presumed organic illness respond to psychotherapy, it appears that functional factors are involved.[18] Karl Menninger has noted that ". . . even general paresis, the classical clinical entity of psychiatry, can occur without spirochetal encephalitis, that most syphilitic infections of the brain do not produce the picture of 'general paresis,' and that the symptoms of paresis sometimes respond to psychotherapy and *not* to spirocheticides. . . . In short, we know that syphilis alone does not 'cause' the mental disorder 'general paresis.' Syphilitic and other toxins which injure the brain can contribute to the production of a variety of symptoms which in a given culture have a certain general similarity. But this is a far cry from our once cherished and 'established' paradigm of a specific psychosis." [19]

The Etiology of Schizophrenia

The difficulties in isolating the biological or organic aspect of abnormality from the environmental are well known. Since no direct controls are possible, the interpretations are based on statistical operations, with all the hazards that such interpretations carry. Where definitive identification and measurement of variables is impossible, the likelihood of presupposition and theoretical bias entering into an explanation is increased. These dangers are well shown, in my judgment, in the studies of schizophrenia. Because of the high rates and the extensive study of this disorder, it is a good "case" to use in testing an interdisciplinary view.

The comparison of twins with siblings and unrelated persons seems to offer an effective way to "control" the hereditary factor. What is more difficult to measure and is often disregarded, however, is the extent to which being a twin is a sociocultural experience.[20] Before any hereditary factor in schizophrenia can be isolated, in fact, we need three sets of information: (1) a completely reliable classification of twins into monozygotic and dizygotic, (2) "blind" diagnoses among which any unreliability can at least be randomized, and (3) extensive information about the similarities and differences in the social experiences of twins and any comparison groups. Almost never are these criteria met to a degree that permits confident judgments.

Kallmann's well-known studies of twins illustrate the possibilities and difficulties in this kind of research. He reports, in general, that the closer the biological relationship between two individuals, the greater the likelihood that if one has schizophrenia, the other will also. Against a general incidence of 0.85 per cent in his studies (the range is from 0.3 per cent to

3.0 per cent in other studies), he reports concordance indexes of 11.5 for siblings, 12.5 for dizygotic twins, 17.6 for dizygotic twins of the same sex, and 81.7 for monozygotic twins.[21] These figures seem to argue impressively for a genetic factor in the etiology of schizophrenia. By a more or less random list of statements, however, one can indicate the difficulty in assessing just how impressive they are:

To some degree, diagnosis as "schizophrenic" is a matter of time, place, and psychiatric "fashion," not of symptoms.

Schizophrenics are more likely to have mothers who were also thus afflicted than fathers who were. Since there has been no argument for a sex-linked relationship, this fact does not fit the genetic model.

Concordance indexes for same-sex dizygotic twins are higher than for opposite-sex twins, as Kallmann's data show. Again, this fact can have no genetic base, although it has implications for a cultural and interactional interpretation.

The twins who have been studied have almost without exception been reared together for the first several years of life. In his exhaustive review of the literature, Jackson found reference to only two pairs of identical twins who had been separated early in life and who had become schizophrenic. In his reports Kallmann distinguishes between twins who were "separated for over 5 years prior to onset" and not so separated, but he does not make this distinction by age, thus obscuring its value. (The concordance indexes for the two groups were 77.6 and 91.5; on genetic grounds one would expect no difference.)

Female dizygotic twins show more concordance than male dizygotic twins, a finding that cannot be explained on genetic grounds but suggests the hypothesis that a culturally supported "closeness" between sisters, contrasted with a more open relationship between brothers, is involved.

Significant differences in rates of schizophrenia by class, race, culture, and patterns of family interaction cut across genetic and organic explanations and tend to qualify them.[22]

How much such observations qualify the genetic approach to schizophrenia is impossible to say, but they indicate clearly the need for research on psychodynamic and sociocultural factors. In one of the pioneer studies in social psychiatry, Faris and Dunham directed attention to the structure of the city as a possible factor in the origin of mental illness. They observed not only that rates of illness varied from area to area within Chicago, but also that specific illnesses had characteristic patterns of distribution. Schizophrenic disorders, for example, were heavily over-represented in the transient, rooming-house areas. The authors hypothesize, after examining alternative explanations, that the nature of the social life—the isolation, the loss of meaningful social contacts—accounts for the high rate.[23] Later studies have not uniformly substantiated their findings, however. Jaco found a significant statistical relationship between various measures of isolation and rates of schizophrenia, for example, but Gerard and Houston concluded that area differences were due to the drift of ill or potentially ill persons into disorganized areas.[24]

Clausen and Kohn have summarized well the questions that must be answered before the possible etiological significance of isolation for schizophrenia can be definitely established: What is sufficient isolation to produce the presumed result? What types of isolation are there (absence of peers, of siblings; extensive mobility; overprotective parents)? What are the *differential* consequences of isolation in different settings for persons with different tendencies? At what period in life is isolation most influential? [25] How does isolation fit into the development of schizophrenia— is it a symptom, a reinforcer, or an essential condition? [26]

More recent work has shifted attention from spatial to social isolation, from the structure of neighborhoods to the patterns of interaction within families. In the thesis of Bateson and others, isolation is a product of faulty communication resting upon feelings of ambivalence and hostility. The essential ingredient in Bateson's interpretation is the "double bind" into which children are placed when powerful others send them one message, with threatened sanctions if they do not act upon it, and simultaneously send them (perhaps by gesture or act) a contrary message, also with sanctions attached, all the while blocking any escape from the field. Under these conditions, adequate discrimination of messages is prevented, because each interpretation involves threat; there is no way out. A mother who feels hostile toward her child might say:

"Go to bed, you're very tired and I want you to get your sleep." This overtly loving statement is intended to deny a feeling which could be verbalized as "Get out of my sight because I'm sick of you." If the child correctly discriminates her metacommunicative signals, he would have to face the fact that she both doesn't want him and is deceiving him by her loving behavior. He would be "punished" for learning to discriminate orders of messages accurately. He therefore would tend to accept the idea that he is tired rather than recognize his mother's deception. This means that he must deceive himself about his own internal state in order to support mother in her deception. To survive with her he must falsely discriminate his own internal messages as well as falsely discriminate the messages of others.[27]

The double-bind hypothesis and the more general emphasis on family interaction are intriguing and highly plausible. Until we have several types of comparative data, however, we do not know how large a place they can be assigned in the explanation of schizophrenia. Do all children who experience persistent and painful double messages develop schizophrenic tendencies? (This cannot be answered simply by studying patients.) Is there some critical point at which the double bind, which is doubtless experienced to some degree by everyone, becomes a decisive factor? Is family stress completely lacking in the experience of some persons who nevertheless develop the symptoms?

These brief references to some of the theories of schizophrenia may indicate the range of etiological factors under investigation in current studies of mental illness. No one factor or combination of factors has been established as the decisive cause. Within the limits of present knowledge, there are two rather sharply different interpretations and many positions between them. Some say: "With the tremendous strides being made in neurophysiology, neurochemistry, and neuropharmacology, there is every reason to believe that the problem of mental disease can eventually be defined and dealt with in terms of purely biological concepts." [28] But on the other hand: ". . . one might say that the etiology of lower socio-economic-status-group mental illness (and crime) is generally sociogenic in nature, whereas in the upper strata of society, mental illness is generally more psychogenic. Thus, the etiology of middle class mental disorders, being somewhere in between, i.e., more or less equally sociogenic and psychogenic, or simply *social-psychogenic* in origin, reflects characteristics of both the extreme strata of society." [29]

In my judgment, a genetic or biochemical interpretation cannot be defended until one has controlled for group membership and experience, which have been demonstrated to be associated with rates of schizophrenia. Nor can a strictly psychogenic and sociogenic position be defended without more careful family and twin studies to measure the degree to which "twinness" is a sociocultural fact as well as a biological fact. On the evidence to date, it seems reasonable to assume that variation exists in predisposition, whether of genetic, physiological, or chemical origin. It seems equally likely that schizophrenic tendencies are associated with certain kinds of stressful interpersonal experiences and with certain kinds of response from significant others to early manifestations of distress. At the moment it is difficult to go beyond eclecticism; but eclecticism seems wiser than the assumption that when the evidence is better, a genetic, neurochemical, psychodynamic, or sociocultural explanation will prove to be the decisive one. Many persons may carry the vulnerability in damaged gene or "twisted molecule" who do not develop the tendencies or the symptoms because of a favorable environment. Others may face problems of ego repression in psychoanalytic terms, of double bind in the communication experience with powerful others, of a cold and domineering mother and a passive father, and still not develop schizophrenic tendencies because they lack vulnerability as organisms.

Abnormal Behavior as a Product of the Contemporary Field

The need for combining predisposing factors with precipitating factors to explain the origin of tendencies toward schizophrenia or other abnormalities is now widely, if not universally, accepted.[30] A field approach, however, goes somewhat further: not only must one adopt a multidimensional view to account for the origin of abnormal *tendencies,* but the same perspective must also be maintained in the explanation of abnormal *behavior*. I have noted above that mental illness as behavior is not *in* the person; it is a process that results from the interaction of the person with the situation. Two persons equally vulnerable as a result of genetic weakness, equally burdened by doubt and guilt, equally torn by mutually contradictory inclinations, equally confused by ego-alienating desires (or however one may want to describe the abnormality-prone individual), are not necessarily equally likely to express these tendencies by abnormal behavior. One person may live in a supportive environment that blunts the edge of his anxieties or furnishes socially and ego-approved outlets for their expression. Another may be caught in a situation which compounds his anxieties. The task of behavioral science is to isolate on the one hand the sociocultural conditions that minimize and those that maximize the likelihood of abnormal behavior, and on the other hand the conditions that establish tendency systems immune to or vulnerable to "abnormality-prone" environments.

Knowledge of predisposition alone cannot explain abnormal behavior, both because alternative ways of expressing the inner tendencies are available to the individual and because the strength of precipitating forces varies. The positions one occupies, his class environment, and the total situation of which he is a part all help to account for the path he will follow.

Knowledge of the situation within which interaction is occurring cannot alone explain abnormal behavior, because different inner-tendency systems respond differently to the same external circumstances. Among persons equally anxious, one may become delinquent, another neurotic or a drug addict, and another deeply religious, depending upon situational variation. Conversely, however, the same situation may precipitate neurosis in one, delinquency in another, and unusual effort in a third, because of different "selector systems" within individuals.

When we conceive of personality as process, not as a system of inner traits, the study of abnormality takes on new dimensions. To say that a given individual *is* paranoic is different from saying that he behaves paranoically under certain conditions. The latter statement leads us—with Cameron, for example—to seek out the precipitating conditions. If the suspicions, threats, and aggressive actions of the paranoia-prone individual heighten the anxiety of those around him, "he inevitably arouses defensive and retaliatory hostility in others." [31] This response seems to confirm his interpretation of the situation and promotes his aggressive tendencies. If, however, hostility-promoting responses are lacking, if a neutral therapist serves as a bridge to reality, the paranoia-prone individual "can begin to entertain doubts and consider alternative interpretations." [32]

The point of view being developed here requires a more drastic departure from disciplinary perspectives than is sometimes realized. To say that social interactional and cultural factors are involved in the origins of mental illness is not the same as saying that the situation in which a person with abnormal tendencies behaves *now* affects the likelihood of and the forms of abnormal responses. Quite traditional psychiatry, except that which is fully tied to a biological view, can accept the former statement, particularly if the reference is to the social experiences in early life. The field view—that abnormality is a function of the current situation as well as of current tendencies—is a more "radical" position, as judged against prevailing ideas.

A Multiple-disciplinary Interpretation of Suicide

The field view presented here can help to bring some order into the conflicting interpretations of many forms of abnormality. Suicide, for example, has been accounted for in many different ways. Of course, suicide is not always a sign of abnormality as I have defined it. It may be a culturally supported act of heroism or a socially prescribed event that is best accounted for by knowledge of the society involved and of the usual processes of socialization to its culture. In many societies, however, suicide generally demonstrates individual malintegration and internal conflict. It is abnormal and not simply atypical behavior, although the abnormality is seldom so severe that one speaks of mental illness.

What kinds of information are needed to account for suicide? Since most interpretations of abnormality started with the individual and have only slowly added a social dimension, let us begin with a strictly sociological theory and ask how it might be modified by study of individual facts. When Durkheim sought the explanation of suicide, he examined various theories one by one and found each inadequate until he came to the influences of the social structure. After a careful analysis of extensive, but unreliable, data, he concluded that anomie, the state of normlessness in society, was the key to the explanation. No psychopathic state, he found, "bears a regular and indisputable relation to suicide." Nor did the analysis of "normal psychological states" prove valuable, although he recognized differences in aptitude for suicide, "permitting but not necessarily implying suicide and therefore giving no explanation for it." [33]

With good reason, this study has been used for decades as a prime example of sociological research. But the tendency is often to think of it, not as an attempt to isolate the social structural aspect of suicide causation, but as a complete theory of suicide. Durkheim does come near to a blending of individual and social factors.[34] He notes that individual tendency is a necessary if not a sufficient cause (although he does not use these terms). What he fails to make clear is that the sociocultural forces are also necessary but insufficient. His development of the idea of "productive cause" (*la cause productrice*) gives primacy to the social structural factor; but this is meaningful only in the explanation of a social *rate* of suicide, not in the social-psychological task of explaining the behavior of the individual in the group setting. To restate the brief quotation from Durkheim, one can with as much justice say that an anomic setting "permits but does not necessarily imply suicide." Not everyone in such settings commits suicide.

Durkheim helped to eliminate an excessively individualistic theory by demonstrating the influence of sociological factors in a dramatic way. As an illustration of the new light that can be thrown on old facts by the use of sociological perspective, *Le Suicide* is a masterpiece. But when we try to use the study as a behavioral theory we get into difficulty, for it is no more adequate as an explanation of behavior than the individualistic interpretations it so successfully attacked.[35]

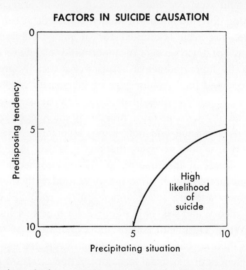

FACTORS IN SUICIDE CAUSATION

The field point of view can be described in the two-variable diagram, using the familiar terms "predisposing" factors (located in the individual) and "precipitating" factors (located in the situation): [36] The likelihood of suicide (or of any other act being interpreted by the use of this scheme) is measured by the product of the values on these two presumed scales. The zero point and the 10 represent theoretically limiting cases. Since the likelihood of an act occurring is indicated by the product of two measures, if either is zero the act will not occur no matter how high the score on the other measure. Thus a person caught in a thoroughly anomic situation and surrounded by other social forces strongly precipitating him toward suicide will not perform the act if his "predisposal" score is zero. Similarly, if he is as thoroughly predisposed as can be theoretically imagined, but is surrounded by a situation that contains no precipitating influences whatsoever, suicide will not occur.

To think of more likely cases, we can hypothesize a "score" of 50 as the point at which suicide is likely to occur. A person with a "predisposal" score of 1 to 4 will be immune even in a context as anomic and stressful as we can imagine. If his score rises to 5, however, he becomes vulnerable in situations with the highest possible score. One can successfully predict a high *rate* (that is, a group measure) when such precipitating influences as anomie are strong (let us say arbitrarily, when the "precipitating" score is above 7), because the product scores of many persons-in-situations may be brought above the assumed critical point of 50. A precipitating score of 5 will affect only those with a predisposal score of 10; but if the precipitating score rises to 7, all those above 7 in the predisposal measure are affected.[37]

Knowledge of anomie therefore, as Durkheim demonstrated, allows one to predict rates better, but is of little value in the larger behavioral science task of understanding how particular individuals will behave in the social context. This statement can be reversed, of course: Knowledge of individual tendencies tells us who is vulnerable, but does not indicate the likelihood of a given act, which is always situationally influenced. The situation may be so constant that we have learned to take it for granted, but that is no indication of its irrelevance. And as we seek to extend our propositions in time and space, we are inevitably confronted with variation in situational influence.

Freud, and many who have elaborated his theory, viewed suicide as an expression of hostile impulses toward a loved and powerful other— impulses which are severely threatening and are "handled" by turning them in upon one's self. Others think in terms of an individual need to atone for guilt or of a final desperate call for recognition and sympathy. Granted such inner tendencies, why do they take the form of suicide? Do the high rate in Denmark and the low rate in Ireland demonstrate wide variation in individual tendency, or does this contrast indicate variation in the forms which hostile impulses or guilt feelings take in different situations? Do the structure of sanctions and rewards in the surrounding society, the nature of its culture, and the extent of its support for the individual channel individual tendencies in particular directions? Variation in suicide rates by class, occupational group, and culture indicates the need for knowledge of the sociocultural situation.

If alternative ways of expressing one's hostility are "available" (in the sense both of individual acceptability and of low social sanctions opposing them), suicide is not the inevitable outcome of certain individual tendencies. Thus, as Henry and Short have shown, suicide and homicide can in part be seen as alternative responses, depending upon the balance of internal and external restraints. Where the rate for one is low, the rate for the other may be high.[38]

An adequate theory of suicide, recognizing the multiple possibilities in every character and in every situation, encompasses both individual and setting in its unit of analysis. Only thus can the results of their interaction be assessed.

The Field View of Drug Addiction

A multidimensional approach to the study of drug addiction is also developing. Gradually we are learning to ask the more complicated series of questions necessary to bring the full range of influences into view. If our general problem is to discover who will become addicted under what conditions, then clearly, to know the chemical properties of particular drugs or the neurochemical processes set in motion by their consumption is not enough. These factors establish the possibility of addiction, but scarcely its probability. Since about 50,000 persons in the United States, for example, are addicted [39] (approximately 1 in 3,000 of the population over 14 years of age), we need some way to differentiate the one addict from the other 2,999. What are the sources of resistance on one hand and vulnerability on the other? Incidence is obviously not randomly scattered through the population. What combination of biological, characterological, social, and cultural forces is involved?

On the basis of present information, perhaps these four levels of influence should again be condensed into two and referred to as the psychobiological and the sociocultural forces. Individual variation may exist in biological sensitivity to drugs; but at the present level of knowledge, this is buried as one of the dimensions of character.[40] Research to separate the influence of cultural norms from the influence of patterns of social interaction is difficult to design; most studies blend these two levels of influence into one environmental level. As information grows, we may be able to fill in the necessary reference to all levels in some such formula as this: $A = f(B,P,G,C)$. (Addiction is a function of biological propensity, personal tendency, group influence, and culture.) Indeed, each of the four levels may be characterized by several dimensions requiring separate analysis.

In any event, the need is for measures of the strength of drug-inducing environmental influences and drug-permitting individual tendencies. On the environmental level, the drug must be available, not simply in the physical sense, but in the sense that there are agents of persuasion and instruction (who are more likely in contemporary America to be associates than "pushers"); attitudes and values in one's groups must support drug use (e.g., the desirability of searching for kicks); and there must be a tenuous connection in the surrounding community with the values and opportunities of the dominant society.[41]

The legal and medical structures are also of great importance on the environmental level. Medical facilities that promote early detection and treatment, for example, affect prevalence rates. Any comparison of individuals or groups must control for this variable if an attempt is being made to study other causes. A legal definition of the possession or transfer of drugs as a crime also affects the likelihood of detection, since such a definition drives the traffic underground. The legal structure partially determines the kinds of persons likely to use drugs, because those who are willing to employ drugs even if they are illegal are probably different from those who might make use of drugs under conditions of cultural approval or legal acceptability. To assess the environmental influence one would need to know also the extent to which a situation furnishes individuals with the weapons needed to struggle with problems of employment, status, and identity. Closely related to this is the structure of the primary-group system: a strong family pattern which maximizes adult-child interaction is less conducive to addiction than peer-dominated interaction.

Even in environments where all these conducive forces prevail, however, the majority of persons will not become addicts, although most of them will have been in association with persons who are drug users. A sociocultural explanation, therefore, is insufficient. Why do some persons get involved in drug use while others who are surrounded by a relatively similar environment do not? (One cannot, of course, assume environmental equivalence, since some of the situational forces I have listed may influence one person and not another who lives in "the same" neighborhood. Until the situations of particular persons are specified, the precise effects of the surrounding sociocultural influences cannot be measured.[42] Many of the environmental forces mentioned above, however, apply to a neighborhood or even to a whole society and thus are relevant for all the individuals in the specified groups.)

Interpretations of the way in which individual differences are involved vary quite widely. Theorists who stress social influences minimize the importance of inner tendencies. Lindesmith, for example, emphasizes the way in which a person, once he has learned to recognize his dependence upon a drug, develops a different self-conception. In American society, at any rate, he sees himself as an addict, is drawn into close interaction with other addicts, and comes to share their values, language, and concerns. In this view, personality factors are a dependent variable, at least in the first stages of drug use.

Becker takes a similar position in his explanation of the process of becoming a marihuana user.[43] He rejects an explanation based on a presumed predispositional or motivational influence, because such a theory is unable to explain why some users do not exhibit the presumed necessary personal tendencies and because it cannot account for the variability of an individual's behavior at different times. He focuses attention on "the sequence of social experiences" during which the meaning of the experience is defined for the individual. "Thus, the motivation or disposition to engage in the activity is built up in the course of learning to engage in it and does not antedate this learning process." [44]

This is a valuable emphasis on the social and cultural forces involved in drug use. But the interpretations of Lindesmith and Becker insufficiently distinguish between the forces that promote initial trials and those that lead to continuing use, perhaps to full addiction. In some environments, many persons will experiment with drugs who do not become regular users or do not move from marihuana to heroin. Combining personality theory with social interactional theory at this point, we can ask, "Among those who make some use of drugs as a result of participation in groups that permit or encourage drug taking, are the persons who become continuing users distinguishable on predispositional grounds?"

Unfortunately, we do not have the kind of longitudinal study, with independent measures of predisposition of a defined population *before* some of them become addicted to drugs, that would permit a definitive answer to this question. Chein and his associates, on the basis of their study of family environments, give a cautiously affirmative reply: "In contrast to our control cases, the addicts were reared in a family milieu which, in terms of our psychological theorizing, we would regard as contributing to the development of weak ego functioning, defective superego, inadequate masculine identification, lack of realistic levels of aspiration with respect to long-range goals, and a distrust of major social institutions." [45] Characterological factors emerge more distinctly when the addicts studied come from groups within which sociocultural support for their drug use is weak, as among physicians.[46]

None of these facts suggest that personality tendencies exist which by themselves lead to drug addiction. There are many alternative ways in which the person with "weak ego functioning" or "inadequate masculine identification," for example, might struggle with his problems. Some cultural and group situations facilitate the use of drugs as a mode of struggle; others strongly block such action.

Moreover, to suggest that individual tendencies are involved in the determination of who, among those with access to drugs, will become users and addicts is not to state that those tendencies are abnormal, in the sense in which I have defined this term. The degree of abnormality of drug users is a separate question. Lindesmith believes that most addicts were normal prior to their addiction.[47] Investigators more generally hold, however, that the persons in a conducive environment who become drug users are those who are particularly susceptible to "escape" as a way of struggling with their problems. Referring to young male addicts in New York, Chein and his associates state:

The evidence indicates that all addicts suffer from deep-rooted, major personality disorders. Although psychiatric diagnoses are apt to vary, a particular set of symptoms seems to be common to most juvenile addicts. They are not able to enter prolonged, close friendly relations with either peers or adults; they have difficulties in assuming a masculine role; they are frequently overcome by a sense of futility, expectation of failure, and general depression; they are easily frustrated and made anxious; and they find both frustration and anxiety intolerable.[48]

It is their view, in short, that in a situation where drug use is physically and culturally possible, the individuals who feel most insecure, least sure of their sexual identity, and most rejected are the ones who learn to use drugs as a source of relief from their misery.

In part, disagreement over the importance of abnormality may reflect the different social circumstances of the various addict groups which have been studied.[49] Under conditions of strong environmental support, persons of relatively lesser insecurity may become drug addicts. If the socio-cultural supports suggested above are weak, however, only more seriously disturbed individuals will seek relief through drug use. Certainly no personality type inevitably becomes addicted; the insecure and miserable person may struggle with his problems in many different ways. Certainly no environment inevitably produces addiction; some persons will respond to addiction-conducive environments by withdrawal from them, by attack upon them, or by attempts to change them; others will become drug users in such a situation.

In our urban slums there are many young people with severe problems of adjustment and there are social forms which dispose many adolescents to seek "kicks" or escapes. Some of these persons become habitual delinquents, some experiment with drugs (and may become hooked), and some develop neurotic defenses and psychotic states. It is hardly to be doubted that drug use among adolescents and young adults only develops where drugs are relatively accessible and where conventional controls are lax. Further, it is hardly to be doubted that in areas where the same values and personality tendencies are found but drugs are not readily available, other types of behavior which offer "kicks" and provide props for the anxious will be explored and exploited.[50]

In short, probably any theory is inadequate which places exclusive emphasis on either the processes of interaction within a group which support drug use or the predispositions of individuals inclining them toward "escape" and lack of realism. Neither by itself can account for the full range of facts.

A Methodological Note

I have referred at several points to methodological problems in the study of abnormal behavior. Hereditary and environmental influences are always empirically mixed; research in many instances deals only with persons brought to public attention by the treatment processes; differences in definition create situations in which similar phenomena are given different names, and vice versa, with resulting confusion.

To emphasize the tentativeness imposed on us by methodological questions, I shall focus on some of them explicitly. Several are illustrated by recent research designed to isolate the cultural element in alcoholism. I have suggested in the previous section that it is difficult to separate a purely cultural aspect of drug use from the social interactional complex in which it is embedded. This is scarcely less true of alcoholism, but since a greater number of comparative studies have been made of alcohol use, we can more nearly approximate a statement dealing with the normative element alone and may thereby isolate some general principles that are valuable in other contexts.[51] Because a theory of alcoholism on the most general level involves the same set of variables as those related to other drugs, I shall not refer to broader questions of the etiology of alcoholism. My concern is not with the specialized study of addiction or with an examination of the extensive literature dealing with it, but with certain methodological issues raised by current research.

No one argues that variation in cultural norms regarding the use of alcohol *determines* variation in rates of consumption or of alcoholism. Nor are there many who argue that culture is not involved. The question is "How important are the norms regarding drinking in influencing rates of consumption and of addiction, *all other things being equal?*" Snyder, who emphasizes the cultural factor, also notes its relationship to other factors. He accepts Bales's theory, for example, that extreme drinking pathologies are a function of the extent of acute psychic tension, the availability of alternative forms of dealing with them, and the cultural norms regarding drinking.[52] It may be necessary to add that they are a function also of physiological factors.

Present evidence seems to indicate that a group's norms regarding alcohol consumption influence the rate of pathological use. Ullman states the thesis well: "The groups which are low in alcoholism are clearly the very ones which introduce their members to alcohol comparatively early —*usually before their young are concerned with problems of adult role-assumption.* Thus, there is no opportunity for drinking to become a *rite de passage,* as is so often the case with high-alcoholism groups whose members first drink during adolescence." [53] When drinking is related to the family, to occasions of ritual, it does not become a symbol of one's "declaration of independence"; it is accepted as a positive good. Therefore, the argument runs, the individual has low ambivalence about it, a lack of guilt, and less likelihood of high consumption leading him to a cycle of guilt repression.

This very plausible thesis needs to be regarded with reservations because some contradictory data exist (e.g., France has early and accepted use, but high alcoholism), because other variables are difficult to control, and because the data used to support it are not entirely adequate. Although I think that a cultural element is involved in rates of addiction, I would like to mention three methodological problems that impose limitations on present knowledge:

1. Comparison of groups must carefully specify the base populations being studied. If one takes two groups, for example, and studies only the

drinkers (not the nondrinkers) within each in order to see if drinking pathologies are more numerous in one than in the other, he may get a different result from what he would have obtained if he had compared the total groups. This would be true if the nondrinkers in a group which proscribed the use of alcohol were the people who, because of their lack of "acute psychic tension," would be least likely to become alcoholic if they did drink.

For example, assume that 40 per cent of those in a group which taboos drinking nevertheless do drink, and that 90 per cent of those in a permitting group drink. Assume that the nondrinkers in each group would be moderate, nonaddicted users of alcohol if they did drink. And assume, finally, that 5 per cent in each group become alcoholic. If drinkers only are used as the base of comparison, one-eighth of those from the proscribing group become alcoholic (5 per cent out of 40 per cent), while only one-eighteenth of those in the prescribing group become alcoholic (5 per cent out of 90 per cent). If the total groups are used as the base, however, one-twentieth of each group becomes addicted.

I do not know whether this comparison is the correct one, because the hypothesis given above, although reasonable, is only a hypothesis. One can state, however, that any study of the presumed influence of normative factors must include abstainers as well as users. Although this is noted by Snyder, his data generally refer to drinkers only. He reports the following percentages for one of his college studies: [54]

	Never drunk	Drunk over 5 times	Drunk 1 to 4 times (inferred)	N
Jewish-affiliated	51%	4%	45%	253
Methodist (white)	33%	16%	51%	752

He states that the pattern of the data . . . is not an artifact resulting from the exclusion of abstainers. . . ." The proportion of abstainers for each group, however, is not given (the range among Protestant groups is from 31 to 50 per cent). If we assume that it is 40 per cent for the Methodist and 10 per cent for the Jewish students, and assume further that the abstainers are the persons least likely to become drunk were they to drink, the percentages then would be as follows:

	Never drunk	Drunk over 5 times	Drunk 1 to 4 times
Jewish-affiliated	55.9%	3.6%	40.5%
Methodist (white)	59.8%	9.6%	30.6%

Granted the assumptions we have made, the differences between these two religious groups would be much less decisive than those found in the original data. Equivalent shifts would be found in the comparison of other religious groups referred to in Snyder's study.

I do not mean to imply that cultural norms, represented here by religious traditions, do not affect rates of alcoholism. Even under the assumptions made above, which are favorable to the reduction of religious differences, a clear contrast remains in the proportions "drunk over 5 times." I want simply to call attention to the effect of the chosen base and the implications for an explanation of causes.

Decision on the appropriate base also requires careful statement of the meaning of group membership. Normative regulations scarcely apply to an individual who is a nominal member only. This is recognized in Snyder's study of the influence of the Jewish tradition,[55] but it requires application to other groups as well.

2. A second methodological question concerns the possibility of the "ecological error." Drinkers who are members of a group which proscribes drinking may not themselves, as individuals, have been trained to accept this norm. One cannot describe their presumed ambivalence on the basis of knowledge about their group's norms. Knowledge of the individual's values is also needed.

The cultural element can be isolated, finally, only by study of the functionally alternative responses to stress which are available in the groups being compared. For example, perhaps the subcultures of Jews and Italians, who have low rates of alcoholism, may permit more verbal aggression, while groups that inhibit the use of alcohol also inhibit verbal aggression. If this were true, rates of alcoholism might reflect comparative styles of aggression control and not the norms of drinking.

3. In several connections I have referred to the difficulties that arise when an interpretation is based primarily on the study of extreme cases. Much of the research on abnormal behavior deals with such material. A great deal can be learned, of course, by studying a variable where it is decisive and by the related process of "deviant case analysis." This is a resource for testing and refining a theory, however, and not a source of general theory. Researchers frequently take the top and bottom quartiles —selecting for study those with the highest authoritarian scores, those who have become seriously addicted to drugs, those who suffer from extreme mental disorder, and the like—to test the adequacy of causal statements. Extreme cases tend to give good prediction even when only one variable is taken into account. The danger comes when one seeks to derive from the study of extreme cases a general proposition concerning the importance of that variable.

Suppose one seeks to answer this question: To what degree is drug addiction the direct result of the biochemical influence of the drug? The hypothesis might be that continuous use over a given period of time leads to addiction regardless of variation in personality tendencies (anxiety, values, etc.) or variation in the amount of group support. Investigation of

persons who have become addicted might reveal wide variation in personality tendencies and group support, thus seeming to rule them out as
causes, on the grounds that one cannot account for a constant (the
addiction) by a variable (the range of personality tendencies and group
supports). Yet the imputation that the direct effect of the drug is a
sufficient cause is not warranted, because the researchers used only
"extreme cases"—namely, those who have become addicted. Persons who
received the drug the requisite length of time but did not become addicted
and persons who never received the drug are not in the sample. Perhaps
biochemical sensitivity or vulnerability is a variable. Those at the high
end of the range may become addicted even if the personality and group
influences are relatively weak, while those at the low end of the range
become addicted only if the personality and/or group factors are strong.

Assume a range of 0 to 10 on three potential "causes," biochemical
sensitivity, personality tendency, and group support. Assume further that
a "score" of 100 will produce addiction. For all persons with a sensitivity
score above 8, addiction will occur if the combined score from the other
two variables is 12 or more. On the premise that these influences are
interactive, not merely additive, their influence is expressed by multiplying
the scores. Thus a 3×4 combination, a 2×6 combination, or any other
with larger numbers would produce the requisite influence. Since these
two variables might range from 3 to 10 among addicted persons, the
researcher concentrating on the biochemical influence alone and using
only extreme cases might be tempted to rule out both variables. But if
persons with a low "biochemical score" were included in the sample (an
extremely difficult research task, it should be noted), the significance of
the other variables would be clearly revealed.

If we make the further assumption that co-acting variables have normal
distributions, then an extreme score in one can make prediction possible
in an extraordinarily high proportion of the cases. In a two-variable
situation, if an "interaction score" of 24 is needed to produce a given
result, reference to cases with a score of 8 or more in variable A will
predict 93 per cent of the time if variable B is distributed relatively
normally, as follows:

Score on Variable B	Per cent	
0	1	
1	2	
2	4	
Variable $A = 8 \times 3$	8	93%
4	16	predicted
5	38	
6	16	
7	8	
8	4	
9	2	
10	1	

There is no intent here to equate all variables. One variable may indeed be so critical that others can be disregarded. This would be expressed mathematically by giving it a higher range, perhaps 40 to 50, so that only the lowest imaginable scores on the other variables—empirically perhaps highly unlikely—would hold the product below the critical point. What I am seeking to emphasize is that even this condition cannot be discovered by the use of extreme cases alone.

FOOTNOTES

Note: The bracketed number following an author's name refers to the footnote in which the source is cited in full.

1. Sigmund Freud, *The Problem of Anxiety,* The Psychoanalytic Quarterly Press and W. W. Norton & Company, Inc., 1936, p. 60.

2. George Herbert Mead, *Mind, Self, and Society,* The University of Chicago Press, 1934. Anselm Strauss has prepared a valuable anthology drawn from this work and from *Movements of Thought in the Nineteenth Century* and *Philosophy of the Act,* under the title *The Social Psychology of George Herbert Mead* (The University of Chicago Press, 1956).

3. See especially Karen Horney, *The Neurotic Personality of Our Time,* W. W. Norton & Company, Inc., 1937; *New Ways in Psychoanalysis,* Norton, 1939; and *Our Inner Conflicts,* Norton, 1945. In many ways, Horney is my "favorite" among the revisionists.

4. Abram Kardiner, with Ralph Linton, *The Individual and His Society: The Psychodynamics of Primitive Social Organization,* Columbia University Press, 1939; Abram Kardiner, with the collaboration of Ralph Linton, Cora DuBois, and James West, *The Psychological Frontiers of Society,* Columbia University Press, 1945.

5. See Kurt Lewin, *A Dynamic Theory of Personality,* McGraw-Hill Book Company, 1935; Kurt Lewin in Dorwin Cartwright (ed.), *Field Theory in Social Science,* Harper & Row, Publishers, Incorporated, 1951; J. L. Moreno, *Who Shall Survive? A New Approach to the Problems of Human Interrelations,* Nervous and Mental Disease Publishing Co., 1934.

6. "Social psychiatry" is not an entirely happy choice of term. If we define psychiatry as "healing the mind" (disregarding for the moment its theoretical dimensions), then social psychiatry perhaps heals the mind by giving attention to social forces causing abnormality. In some measure, however, the referent is not to intraindividual questions but to interpersonal tensions. For L. K. Frank and Harry S. Sullivan, for example, and to a lesser degree for Erich Fromm, Karen Horney, and many others, it is to "society as the patient" that attention should be directed. This might more accurately be called "sociatry"—healing the interpersonal patterns that block the achievement of mutual goals and individual development. In an incautious moment one might even refer to psychosociatry: healing the interpersonal relationships by giving attention to individual tendencies that disrupt them. I shall not use these terms; but noting them may alert us to necessary distinctions. "Social psychiatry" is neologism enough, but we shall have to define it broadly

enough to mean the study of the relationships of social and individual factors in the etiology and cure of behavioral disorders. The next chapter will be concerned with some of these problems.

7. John A. Clausen in Robert K. Merton and Robert A. Nisbet (eds.), *Contemporary Social Problems,* Harcourt, Brace & World, Inc., 1961, p. 156. The chapter headings in *Causes of Mental Disorders: A Review of Epidemiological Knowledge,* 1959, The Milbank Memorial Fund, 1961, suggests much the same series of causes: "Genetic, Damage to Fetus, Damage to Brain after Birth, Family and Mental Disorder, Precipitating Proximal Factors, Social Structures and Mental Disorders, Social Change and Mental Health, and Cultures as Causative of Mental Disorder."

8. *Journal of Genetic Psychology,* vol. 10, 1934, pp. 59–82.

9. Horney, *The Neurotic Personality of Our Time* [3], p. 14.

10. See Henry J. Wegrocki, "A Critique of Cultural and Statistical Concepts of Abnormality," *Journal of Abnormal and Social Psychology,* vol. 34, 1939, pp. 166–178; reprinted in Clyde Kluckhohn, Henry A. Murray, and David Schneider (eds.), *Personality in Nature, Society, and Culture,* Alfred A. Knopf, Inc., 1953, pp. 691–701; see also Paul Benedict and Irving Jacks, "Mental Illness in Primitive Societies," *Psychiatry,* November, 1954, pp. 377–389.

11. Marc Fried and Erich Lindemann, "Sociocultural Factors in Mental Health and Illness," *American Journal of Orthopsychiatry,* January, 1961, pp. 87–101.

12. Marie Jahoda, *Current Concepts of Positive Mental Health,* Basic Books, Inc., Publishers, 1958, pp. 7–8.

13. *Ibid.,* p. 23.

14. This point of view is implied in Redlich's statement that "behavior will approximate normality if it simultaneously gratifies and does not frustrate instinctual needs, leads to success rather than to failure, and produces social praise rather than punishment." See Frederick C. Redlich in Alexander Leighton, John A. Clausen, and Robert Wilson (eds.), *Explorations in Social Psychiatry,* Basic Books, Inc., Publishers, 1957, p. 150.

15. Dorothea C. Leighton *et al., The Character of Danger* (The Stirling County Study of Psychiatric Disorder and Sociocultural Environment, vol. III), Basic Books, Inc., Publishers, 1963, p. 356.

16. Leo Srole, *et al., Mental Health in the Metropolis: The Midtown Manhattan Study* (Thomas A. C. Rennie Series in Social Psychiatry, vol. I), McGraw-Hill Book Company, 1962, p. 138.

17. See Commission on Chronic Illness, *Chronic Illness in a Large City: The Baltimore Study,* Harvard University Press, 1957; and J. G. Manis, M. J. Brawer, C. L. Hunt, and L. C. Kercher, "Estimating the Prevalence of Mental Illness," *American Sociological Review,* February, 1964, pp. 84–89. For a discussion of the likelihood that the Baltimore data underrepresent true incidence, see Srole *et al.* [16], pp. 139–145.

18. See Robert W. Wallerstein, "Treatment of the Psychosis of General Paresis with Combined Sodium Amytal and Psychotherapy: Report of a Case," *Psychiatry,* vol. 14, 1951, pp. 307–317.

19. Karl Menninger, with Martin Mayman and Paul Bruyser, *The Vital Balance,* The Viking Press, Inc., 1963, p. 61.

20. Jackson makes some astute observations on this problem. See

"A Critique of the Literature on the Genetics of Schizophrenia," in Don D. Jackson (ed.), *The Etiology of Schizophrenia*, Basic Books, Inc., Publishers, 1960, pp. 37–87.

21. See Franz J. Kallmann, "The Genetic Theory of Schizophrenia," *American Journal of Psychiatry*, November, 1946, pp. 309–322. See also the summary of several such studies in Jackson [20], p. 60.

22. These statements are based on observations found in a number of sources. See, in addition to the cited works of Kallman [21] and Jackson [20], Eliot H. Rodnick, "Clinical Psychology, Psychopathology, and Research on Schizophrenia," in Sigmund Koch (ed.), *Psychology: A Study of a Science*, McGraw-Hill Book Company, 1963, vol. 5, pp. 738–779; Jacob Tuckman and Robert J. Kleiner, "Discrepancy between Aspiration and Achievement as a Predictor of Schizophrenia," *Behavioral Science*, October, 1962, pp. 443–447; Victor D. Sanau, "Sociocultural Factors in Families of Schizophrenics," *Psychiatry*, August, 1961, pp. 246–265; A. B. Hollingshead, "Some Issues in the Epidemiology of Schizophrenia," *American Sociological Review*, February, 1961, pp. 5–13; Jerome K. Myers and Bertram H. Roberts, *Family and Class Dynamics in Mental Illness*, John Wiley & Sons, Inc., 1959; and David Rosenthal, "Some Factors Associated with Concordance and Discordance with Respect to Schizophrenia in Monozygotic Twins," *Journal of Nervous and Mental Disease*, vol. 129, 1959, pp 1–10.

23. R. E. L. Faris and H. W. Dunham, *Mental Disorders in Urban Areas*, The University of Chicago Press, 1939.

24. E. Gartly Jaco, "The Social Isolation Hypothesis and Schizophrenia," *American Sociological Review*, October, 1954, pp. 567–577; Donald L. Gerald and Lester G. Houston, "Family Setting and the Social Ecology of Schizophrenia," *Psychiatric Quarterly*, vol. 27, 1953, pp. 90–101.

25. For a discussion of the importance of age differentials, see Marjorie F. Lowenthal, "Social Isolation and Mental Illness in Old Age," *American Sociological Review*, February, 1964, pp. 54–74.

26. John A. Clausen and Melvin L. Kohn, "The Ecological Approach in Social Psychiatry," *American Journal of Sociology*, September, 1954, pp. 145–146; see also Melvin L. Kohn and John A. Clausen, "Social Isolation and Schizophrenia," *American Sociological Review*, June, 1955, pp. 265–273.

27. Gregory Bateson, Don D. Jackson, Jay Haley, and John Weakland, "Toward a Theory of Schizophrenia," *Behavioral Science*, October, 1956, pp. 251–264; reprinted in Neil J. Smelser and William T. Smelser, *Personality and Social Systems*, John Wiley & Sons, Inc., 1963, pp. 172–187; quote from p. 179 of latter. See also Lyman Wynne, Irving Rycoff, Julian Day, and Stanley Hirsch, "Pseudo-mutuality in the Family Relations of Schizophrenics," *Psychiatry*, May, 1958, pp. 205–220; Jackson [20], pp. 323–440; Melvin J. Kohn and John A. Clausen, "Parental Authority Behavior and Schizophrenia," *American Journal of Orthopsychiatry*, April, 1956, pp. 297–313. For a vivid description of the communicative pattern of schizophrenics, demonstrating the systematic distortion of messages, see Jay Haley, "An Interactional Description of Schizophrenia," *Psychiatry*, November, 1959, pp. 321–332.

28. L. G. Abood, in Jackson [20], p. 111.

29. R. M. Frumkin, "Occupation and Major Mental Disorders," in Arnold Rose (ed.), *Mental Health and Mental Disorder: A Sociological Approach*, W. W. Norton & Company, Inc., 1955, p. 155.

30. See Jackson [20], John Clausen [7], and Rodnick [22].

31. Norman Cameron, "The Paranoid Pseudo-community Revisited," *American Journal of Sociology*, July, 1959, p. 58.

32. *Ibid.*

33. Émile Durkheim, *Suicide*, The Free Press of Glencoe, 1951, p. 103.

34. See *ibid.*, pp. 102–103 and 323–324, for example.

35. On this question, see Alex Inkeles, "Personality and Social Structure," in Robert K. Merton, Leonard Broom, and Leonard S. Cottrell, Jr. (eds.), *Sociology Today*, Basic Books, Inc., Publishers, 1959, pp. 251–253; George Simpson's preface to his translation of Durkheim's *Suicide* (The Free Press of Glencoe, 1951); Talcott Parsons, *The Structure of Social Action*, McGraw-Hill Book Company, 1937, p. 326; Maurice Halbwachs, *Les Causes du Suicide*, F. Alcan, 1930; and A. F. Henry and J. F. Short, *Suicide and Homicide*, The Free Press of Glencoe, 1954.

36. See Jaco [24]; and T. A. C. Rennie, "The Yorkville Community Mental Health Research Study," *Interrelations between the Social Environment and Psychiatric Disorders*, Milbank Memorial Fund, 1953, pp. 213 ff.

37. In this greatly oversimplified scheme, I have assumed two arithmetic scales and precision in measurement. I have also disregarded the question of functionally equivalent types of behavior.

38. Henry and Short [35]. For other recent studies and commentaries, see Louis Dublin, *Suicide: A Sociological and Statistical Study*, The Ronald Press Company, 1963; Raymond Firth, "Suicide and Risk-taking in Tikopia Society," *Psychiatry*, February, 1961, pp. 1–17; Jack Gibbs, "Suicide," in Merton and Nisbet [7], pp. 222–261; Herbert Hendin, "Suicide in Denmark," in Eric and Mary Josephson (eds.), *Man Alone: Alienation in Modern Society*, Dell Publishing Co., Inc., 1962, pp. 447–458; Martin Gold, "Suicide, Homicide, and the Socialization of Aggression," *American Journal of Sociology*, May, 1958, pp. 651–661; Warren Breed, "Occupational Mobility and Suicide among White Males," *American Sociological Review*, April, 1963, pp. 179–188. A basic psychodynamic interpretation is given in Karl Menninger, *Man against Himself*, Harcourt, Brace and Company, Inc., 1938.

39. See *Traffic in Opium and Other Dangerous Drugs*, Bureau of Narcotics, Government Printing Office, 1959. On the problem of estimates, see Isidor Chein, Donald L. Gerard, Robert S. Lee, and Eva Rosenfeld, with the collaboration of Daniel M. Wilner, *The Road to H: Narcotics, Delinquency, and Social Policy*, Basic Books, Inc., Publishers, 1964, chap. 2. At this point I am defining "drugs" administratively, referring to those that come under the authority of the Bureau of Narcotics. On biological and sociological grounds, of course, there is often need for both broader and narrower definitions, to encourage study of similarities and differences among various chemical agents. Since I am focusing on general theory, such an examination of types of definition is not necessary here.

40. During the period before the Harrison Act when the rate of addiction in the United States was much higher than it is now, there were as many female as male addicts. Now females make up a small part of the total. This casts doubt on variation in biological vulnerability as an important cause. Since males and females have approximately equal rates of personality instability, as measured by serious mental illness, some other variable must be added to account for the large

difference between them in drug use. It is at this point that the importance of the negativistic subculture into which males are drawn in our most disprivileged communities is demonstrated.

41. See Chein *et al.* [39], especially chaps. 3 and 4; Alfred R. Lindesmith, *Opiate Addiction,* Principia Press, 1947; Harold Finestone, "Cats, Kicks, and Color," *Social Problems,* July, 1957, pp. 3–13; Albert K. Cohen and James F. Short, Jr., "Research in Delinquent Subcultures," *Journal of Social Issues,* vol. 14, 1958, pp. 20–37; Howard S. Becker, *Outsiders: Studies in the Sociology of Deviance,* The Free Press of Glencoe, 1963; John A. Clausen, "Social Patterns, Personality, and Adolescent Drug Use," in Leighton, Clausen, and Wilson [14], pp. 230–277.

42. See Chein *et al.* [39], chap. 5.

43. Howard S. Becker, "Becoming a Marihuana User," *American Journal of Sociology,* November, 1953, pp. 235–242; reprinted in his essays, *Outsiders* [41].

44. Becker, "Becoming a Marihuana User," [43], p. 235.

45. Chein *et al.* [39], p. 268.

46. Charles Winick, "Physician Narcotic Addicts," *Social Problems,* Fall, 1961, pp. 174–186.

47. He cites several studies which indicate that a high proportion of addicts were not normal, but he notes the lack of any control group. See Lindesmith [41], pp. 141–164. More recent studies are alert to this need for controls.

48. Chein *et al.* [39], p. 14.

49. See Cohen and Short [41].

50. Clausen [41], p. 269.

51. See David J. Pittman and Charles R. Snyder (eds.), *Society, Culture, and Drinking Patterns,* John Wiley & Sons, Inc., 1962; Donald Horton, "The Function of Alcohol in Primitive Societies," in Clyde Kluckhohn, Henry A. Murray, and David M. Schneider (eds.), *Personality in Nature, Society, and Culture,* Alfred A. Knopf, Inc., 1953, pp. 680–690; Ruth Bunzel, "The Role of Alcoholism in Two Central American Cultures," *Psychiatry,* vol. 3, 1940, pp. 361–387; William McCord and Joan McCord, *Origins of Alcoholism,* Stanford University Press, 1960; Charles R. Snyder, *Alcohol and the Jews,* The Free Press of Glencoe, 1958; and Albert D. Ullman, "Ethnic Differences in the First Drinking Experience," *Social Problems,* Summer, 1960, pp. 45–56.

52. See Charles R. Snyder in Pittman and Snyder [51], p. 189; and Robert F. Bales in *ibid.,* chap. 10, and "Cultural Differences in Rates of Alcoholism," *Quarterly Journal of Studies on Alcohol,* vol. 6, 1946, pp. 480–499.

53. Ullman [51], p. 54.

54. Based on a table in Snyder, *Alcohol and the Jews* [51], p. 190.

55. See *ibid.,* chap. 2.

CHAPTER 13

Social Psychiatry

At the beginning of the preceding chapter the interdisciplinary quality of psychiatry was noted. This has not long been true, however, for its origins are in the field of medicine, and most students of the theory and practice of psychiatry have been medical men. It was only with difficulty that they brought psychoanalysis and other functional points of view into full consideration. If one were arbitrarily to designate a time when this occurred, I have suggested that the period of World War I might be the appropriate point. Of course, general developments in psychology, as well as the work of Freud, Janet, and others, had been preparing the way for many years.

The addition of a sociocultural dimension to the study of mental illness requires an even sharper reformulation of traditional views. And in the last twenty-five years we have begun to see its assimilation into a holistic conception of psychiatry. This process has not gone far; social psychiatry is still best described as marginal to the thought and interests of most clinicians and many theoreticians of mental disorder. Important beginnings have been made, nevertheless; and in these beginnings we see the possibilities for the rounding out of a field view of abnormality.

Taking for granted the established positions of organic and psychodynamic theories and therapies (without, of course, implying that they are finished products), I shall ask how, in field perspective, social psychiatry might be added to them. What new dimensions come into view when attention is given to social and cultural facts? Much of Chapter 12 is related to that question, but I want now to focus on it more specifically. Although the meaning of the term "social psychiatry" varies widely, most usages can probably be subsumed under three headings: social and cultural factors in the etiology of mental illness; the effects of mental illness on society and culture; and social and cultural influences in the therapeutic process. Each of these has several dimensions. By reference to a few of them I may be able to indicate something of the scope and method of social psychiatry as part of the larger study of etiology and therapy related to mental disorders.

SOCIAL AND CULTURAL FORCES IN ETIOLOGY OF MENTAL ILLNESS

The basic approach to etiological work in social psychiatry is comparative. How do societies and subsocieties differ in rates and types of mental illness? What aspects of their normative systems and their patterns of interaction may help to account for these differences? Common-sense notions on these questions have not always survived careful examination. It appears not to be true, for example, that stable rural societies necessarily have low rates of mental illness while urban mobile societies exhibit high rates.[1] Pathological symptoms vary from group to group;[2] but they also vary from time to time within the same group. Sometimes in a group they shift extensively in a few years' time, which suggests the operation of sociocultural influences.[3]

Social psychiatry first became prominent in the form of a critique and modification of the Freudian emphasis on the universal traumas of human experience. What Freud saw as the inevitable product of tension between the needs and desires of individuals and the demands and requirements of social order as a generic fact, others began to describe as partly "the neurotic personality of *our time*," "the loneliness and anxiety of *modern* man," the crisis of identity in a depersonalizing society, or the burden of freedom among those who had failed to achieve full maturity.[4] The discussions along this line have usually been concerned both with culture (its contradictions and its requirements) as a source of maladjustment and with society (the dominant patterns of interaction).

Recently the broad sweep of this approach has been modified. More differentiated questions have emerged and systematic empirical work has been undertaken to test and modify the exciting but somewhat imprecise work of some of the earlier writers. The range of the questions related to sociocultural factors and mental disorder is suggested by the list prepared by Leighton and Hughes. Culture (in our terminology, the sociocultural system) may be thought to determine the pattern of specific mental disorders; to produce basic personality types, some of which are especially vulnerable to mental disorder; and to produce abnormality through certain child-training practices, through types of sanctions used (shame versus guilt), through rewarding abnormality in certain prestigeful roles, through maintaining stressful roles, through processes of change, and through indoctrination of members with certain sentiments. Culture per se may also be thought to produce psychiatric disorder; culture may be seen as affecting the distribution of disorders through patterns of breeding and through practices which result in poor physical hygiene.[5]

Socialization and Mental Disorder

Perhaps the most extensive explorations of social factors in mental disorder have been concerned with the task of identifying the anxiety-producing patterns of socialization. This was also a major problem in Freud's work, of course; [6] but his studies of the family dramas basic to human experience were so oriented to an instinctual view that the range of variation was obscured. Viewed sociologically, a normal person is the product of a process of identification in which a child accepts the major definitions of the world from those around him. He has learned to "take the role of the other" because he has found satisfactions from this process. If "the other" is cruel or neglectful, however, the child resists his definitions of the world. If, when looking back upon his self from the perspective of another, the child sees an unwanted image, he does not develop the skill in role playing that social life requires. Such social emotions as loyalty, shame, and contrition, which require that one measure his own behavior by group standards, do not develop; communication is blocked.[7]

Almost at the moment of birth, and certainly when they begin to move about, to talk, and to interact with others, infants begin to get a picture of orderliness in the world. Spatial and temporal relations are learned; environmental structures that they can count on furnish a sense of relatedness. Part of this process is the learning of patterns of interpersonal behavior. For some, however, it is a matter of nonpattern, of caprice and unpredictability; for some others, it is a matter of self-crushing pain. And children develop strategies of defense appropriate to these conceptions.

In the field view, explaining the origin of such tendencies is not enough, because socialization is a continuous process and behavior is a result of continuous interaction with the environment. As Boss has said: "What matters most, therapeutically, is not the recalling of the occasion when a neurotic pattern of relating to fellow men was acquired in childhood, but finding the answer to two questions: Why has the patient remained, right up to the present time, caught within this same, restricted way of communicating? What is keeping him a prisoner of his neurotic behavior patterns right now?" [8] The answer to these questions does not lie wholly within the individual. "Becoming a mental patient is a socially structured event." [9] And avoiding this outcome is also socially structured.

The cycles of interaction with others vitally influence which of a person's various tendencies will be brought into play. Lemert notes that the suspicions and hostilities of a person with paranoid tendencies interact with the exclusion, evasion, and blocked communication he experiences from others. Under such conditions of "spurious interaction," his suspicions and hostilities are given some substance, are thus reinforced, and feed back into the cycle.[10] The deviant patterns of behavior of the mentally ill may thus be stabilized by societal reaction to them.[11] Most children, Scheff points out, exhibit in a tentative way many of the kinds of behavior which, if they become established tendencies, are the symptoms of mental illness. Temper tantrums, head banging, fantasy playmates, illusory physical complaints, unrealistic fears, and the like are quite common. Like mental disorder, they are strategies for seeking help from others; responses of others to these strategies are critical forces in determining whether they will become stable tendencies.

Social Class and Mental Illness

In heterogeneous societies, one would expect to find variation among groups both in the frequency with which pathological tendencies are formed and in the patterns of response which deepen and activate, or alleviate and inhibit, those tendencies. Contemporary social psychiatry is greatly interested in this question, particularly in its application to social classes, which I shall use for illustration, but also with reference to racial, religious, and other groups.

One can hypothesize a number of possible relationships between class and mental illness. Classes might vary in the distribution of biological tendencies toward mental illness or toward particular forms of abnormality. At the present time, such a hypothesis is beyond definitive testing. Classes might vary in the incidence of illness (whatever the sources), the prevalence, the attitudes toward treatment of various kinds, the availability of treatment, the range of responses toward persons with abnormal tendencies, and the kinds of stresses to which their members are subjected.

We are beginning to get evidence on many of these issues. Students have long recognized that many physical illnesses are "social diseases with medical aspects," as William Osler said with reference to tuberculosis. This appears to be no less true of mental illnesses. Even before birth, infants in lower-status groups face more of the risks of injury, malnutrition, maternal illness and hypertension, and the like, that are related to abnormality than infants born into higher-status groups.[12] Whether later conditions of stress are also unequally distributed so that total rates of abnormality vary by class has been a subject of controversy. Various investigators have found general rates to be negatively correlated, positively correlated, and uncorrelated with socioeconomic status.[13] Kleiner and Parker have suggested that the inconsistencies in the studies of social class and abnormality may be caused by failure to take "goal discrepancy" into account as an intervening social-psychological variable. They cite evidence to support the hypothesis that the discrepancy between education, as a measure of aspiration, and occupation, as an indicator of achievement, is significantly related to rates of schizophrenia.[14]

Social mobility as well as contemporary class status must also be taken into account. The midtown Manhattan data indicate that the upward mobile have a somewhat higher mental health rating than those with stable socioeconomic positions and that both groups have significantly higher ratings than the downward mobile. Without panel data, of course, we cannot determine whether mobility is the cause or effect of these relationships. Srole and Langner see support for both hypotheses in their material: ". . . on the whole healthier adolescents tend to be more heavily drawn into the traffic of upward-moving adults, whereas more disturbed adolescents tend to be shunted into the downward traffic.... [And] those in the ascending traffic stream are subsequently less likely to show exogenous deterioration in mental health than those in the descending stream." [15]

Several of the problems and possibilities connected with the study of social class and mental illness are shown in the work of Hollingshead, Redlich, and their associates.[16] When they used total prevalence rates, the enumeration of psychiatric patients in the New Haven area did not reveal great differences among the classes.[17] Types of illness, however, varied widely, with the higher classes being over-represented among the neurotic patients and the lower classes being over-represented among the psychotics. Those diagnosed as schizophrenic, for example, showed the following indexes of prevalence for the five classes, ranging from the highest status position, I, to the lowest, V (with 100 representing a proportionate share): I, 22; II, 33; III, 43; IV, 88; V, 246.[18] Prevalence of an illness in a hospitalized or treated group, of course, is not identical with its incidence. Hollingshead and Redlich found little differences by class in the incidence rates of neuroses. Yet the upper-class rates of prevalence exceeded lower-class rates by more than three to one, indicating greater likelihood of continuous treatment for the higher-status persons. Opposite effects are found in the study of psychoses. Later detection or treatment of cases in the lower classes may lead to greater severity, longer hospitalization or persistence, and hence to greater prevalence at any given time. Clausen and Kohn, in a study of Hagerstown, Maryland, found no difference among classes in average annual rates of schizophrenia based on first admission to hospitals—a measure closer to true total incidence than prevalence data. They do not conclude from this that there were in fact no class differences in rates; they believe that rates were somewhat higher in the lower classes, but the lack of "collecting areas" for unattached persons in a relatively small city led to some outward migration of lower-status schizophrenics.[19]

We can tentatively accept the idea that there is some difference in rate of schizophrenia by class and that this difference is magnified in prevalence data as result of longer illnesses among those from the lower class. The difference is as difficult to account for as to measure. Is a diagnosis of schizophrenia more likely to be used in connection with a lower-class person? Are lower-class persons more seriously ill when treatment begins? Do they receive less adequate treatment? Are they less responsive, as a result of their values and attitudes, to the treatment process? Is the medical staff less ready to discharge them? Are there class-related differences in the tendency to take or permit another to take the "sick role"? Do families and friends vary, by class, in the ways in which they receive a member after a hospital experience—thus affecting the likelihood of his symptoms returning?

A definitive answer to any of these questions is not possible. For some of them the evidence contains clear contradictions. But the "leaning" of the evidence suggests that the answer to all but the last two questions is yes; variation in class rates is partly a function of treatment procedures and attitudes.[20] Class subcultures and variation in the patterns of interaction are also involved. Persons vulnerable to schizophrenia are more likely to develop in lower-class settings because of the more frequent frustration produced by the gap between actual status and aspiration, because of subculturally allowable responses to that frustration, because of differential family experiences, and because of other sociocultural facts.

From a field perspective, to measure class differences in the origin of tendencies is not enough. One needs also to measure class differences in contemporary situations which may facilitate different types of response. If two groups, one lower- and one middle-class, with equal predispositions were compared, one group might have a higher rate, not because of what is in the persons (tendencies having been matched), but because of differences in precipitating forces. The responses of families and communities to illness and treatment vary by class; therapeutic demands are to some degree class-oriented; functionally alternative forms of response are not equally available. These may be among the situational ingredients which facilitate a schizophrenic response more frequently in one group than in another.

In a content analysis of mental health pamphlets, Gursslin, Hunt, and Roach found the material strongly oriented toward middle-class perspectives. Lower-class persons, with somewhat different cultural perspectives, may not be well served by a movement which attempts to bring about a middle-class model of health. "The 'message' sets forth a way of life which is most unrealistic for lower-class people, who must make some adjustment to the conditions and culture of the lower class." [21] This should not be read as a moral commentary. One can readily argue that the circumstances should be changed. But under present conditions, prevailing conceptions of mental health differentially affect social classes. "Lower-class people who take on forms of behavior implied in the mental health model are apt to find themselves alienated from lower-class society as well as subjected to other stresses of upwardly mobile types." [22]

This point is well supported by the evidence in the Stirling County studies. The authors state as a hypothesis, for which they think the evidence is good, that an individual's adjustment is affected not only by his own class level, but by the class level of his community. Thus they emphasize the influence of the surrounding social structure. "An individual's adoption of one or another of major possible reaction patterns as his 'life style' is settled fairly early in his career, *primarily on the basis of what is going on in the community around him.*" [23] In a well-integrated community, an individual may keep working, keep hoping, keep mentally healthy, because the kind of success he expects seems to be within the reach of most people. "On the other hand a young man in a much better occupational position in a disintegrated community—a Depressed Areas storekeeper, for example—may take much less interest in his work and much more in his liquor because in this community economic success, even should he manage to gain a little despite the obstacles, is resented rather than admired by his neighbors, and it would isolate him still more." [24]

Although we cannot yet describe precisely the nature of the relationship between social class and mental illness, it now seems abundantly clear that class location and class mobility must be taken into account in any full etiological investigation. Research on other forms of group membership is somewhat less extensive, but race, religion, sex, ethnicity, residence, and other group identities clearly are significantly related to differences in sociocultural experiences pertinent to the level of mental illness. Attempts to explain the origins of abnormality that do not control for or take account of such groups are, on the basis of present evidence, seriously deficient.[25]

EFFECTS OF MENTAL ILLNESS ON SOCIETY AND CULTURE

In stressing the interaction of the individual and society, field-oriented psychiatry is led to examine the effects of mental illness as well as its causes. These effects, in turn, become part of a new situation and thereby influence future rates of illness. This cyclical view of causation does not come easily for most of us. Perhaps we are oriented to a mechanical model of causation in circumstances where an organic model is more appropriate. In any event, much less research has been directed toward the measurement of the effects of abnormality on social structure and process than on its causes in social structure and process. My aim here is simply to point briefly to this topic to indicate its importance and encourage further study.

From general role theory we would expect that deviations from anticipated performance caused by abnormality would intrude into the whole role network, affecting the performances of others and their role definitions. I have suggested above, following Fried and Lindemann, that the very definition of mental illness involves attention to the disruption of role relationships and the adjustment of affected groups to the disruption. There is no doubt that small, intimate groups are strongly affected by the presence of abnormal individuals and that the response of others, in turn, influences the development of the abnormalities.[26] The influence of a group member's abnormal behavior can be illustrated by an experiment made by Redl. He introduced a new boy who had serious behavior problems into a group which over the course of a year had worked out democratic methods of operation and built up a large amount of group pride. He believed that this smoothly functioning group could handle the masochistic tendencies of the new boy. Yet within a week they were bickering and fighting, quarrelsome in their discussions, aggressive toward the adult leader, and in general acting "like a bunch of sadistic bullies." [27]

The need is to isolate the conditions under which the effects of an individual are maximal and the conditions which allow a group to absorb disruptive role performance with minimum change. The extensive literature of small-group studies contains many suggestions concerning the influence of individuals on group functioning.[28] In terms of our present interest, we need to apply these suggestions in realistic settings in which one or more of the participants have abnormal tendencies. The most common effect of individual pathological behavior on the group is probably to lower morale. The pathology may spread, developing into a *folie à deux,* a shared mania, or group delusion.[29] But we should not overlook the possibility that the mentally ill may form a group; and their challenge to the stability of group structure may promote activities which increase, rather than lower, morale.

The influence of abnormality on large groups is also important, although one speaks on this topic with even more caution than on small-group effects. Economic costs can be recorded (care of the seriously ill and their lost earnings amount to several billion dollars annually in the United States), but other consequences for the economy, for politics, and for religion cannot be stated so easily. We have learned to take cautiously, for example, the sweeping generalizations concerning the political effects of "paranoid" leaders or of the direct political consequences of "authoritarian personalities" (not all of whom are psychiatrically impaired). Even their own activity is not deducible from their tendencies alone; and their influence on group life is not a simple function of their characteristics. Nevertheless there is an individual dimension to institutional life which we would be unwise to disregard. Perhaps more than those who are seriously ill, whose deviations are so bizarre that they produce counteraction, the person with "subclinical" abnormalities is the one who influences group life through his deviant role performances and motivations.[30] The level of deviation is then affected by the new roles and norms, or the role confusion and anomie, thus developed.

THERAPEUTIC ASPECTS OF SOCIAL PSYCHIATRY

If social and cultural forces are involved in the development of abnormal tendencies and if they influence the probability that those tendencies will be expressed in behavior, any total program of treatment must have a sociocultural dimension. Of course, from the point of view of strategy in any given context, one or another of a series of causal forces may be more accessible to change. It may be more efficient, for example, to disregard the tendencies of mildly disturbed children entirely and to concentrate on changing the situations within which they live.[31] On the other hand, it may be necessary under some circumstances to take the social structures and cultural values as fairly fixed, so far as a deeply disturbed person is concerned, and to concentrate on the modification of his tendencies.

Such strategic decisions should not obscure the continuing presence of both sets of forces in the causal equation. In fact, if both sets are strong, treatment of one of them alone will be unavailing. Reduction of one may constrain a given form of pathology only to facilitate another; or the success may prove to be temporary. Inhibit the discriminations of deeply prejudiced persons, and one may increase the rate of alcoholism or the exuberance of chauvinistic sentiments. If the anxieties of a disturbed person are reduced in the specialized environment of the hospital and he is then placed back in the situations which had fostered those anxieties, his difficulties are liable to reappear. The high rate of recidivism among criminals is not proof of the extreme tenacity of their tendencies any more than it demonstrates the persistent supports to criminality in the environments to which they are returned.

A field-oriented therapy, in short, must deal with both character structure and social structure, with the body and with the group. Therapies based on the findings of social psychiatry are complements—of what comparative significance it is still impossible to say—of organic therapy and psychotherapy.

Milieu Therapy

If mental illness is embedded not simply in an individual but in the whole system of relationships of which he is a part, an adequate program of treatment must deal with those relationships. Of vital importance are the kinds of associations one has, not simply with the physician, but also with other members of one's family, with other patients if one is hospitalized, with staff members on every level of influence. Cultural definitions of the meaning of mental illness affect the response of significant others to the person who is ill. These normative and interactional dimensions are now being given serious attention.

Some of the concepts of milieu therapy were implicit in the "moral treatment" that developed in the mid-nineteenth century in opposition to punishment and incarceration as dominant modes of handling the mentally ill.[32] This would warn us against any overly simple picture of stages in clinical practice. Yet the dominance of organic and biological theories until well into the twentieth century, and the powerful influence of biologically oriented psychodynamic theories for the last several decades, blocked the growth of the earlier insights into the value of a humane environment that facilitated normal interaction. More recently, the full range of the treatment experience has been given increasing attention. Evidence is growing that where, when, and in what group context one is treated for mental illness and other deviations significantly influence the process of rehabilitation.

Some of the evidence comes from experience gained during World War II. Persons removed from the front lines because of neurotic or psychotic symptoms had a low rate of recovery if they were taken to a hospital far from battle. "Any therapy, including usual interview methods that sought to uncover basic emotional conflicts or attempted to relate current behavior and symptoms with past personality patterns, seemingly provided patients with logical reasons for their combat failure. The insights obtained by even such mild depth therapy readily convinced the patient and often his therapist that the limit of combat endurance had been reached as proved by vulnerable personality traits." [33] But when the men were treated in the combat zone, with ventilation, reassurance, and persuasion, many more returned to combat. Maintenance of ties with their outfit helped to preserve a picture of themselves as capable of combat.[34]

A conception of personality that leads one to think of neurotic or psychotic persons as separate entities cannot easily interpret such observations. When we conceive of personality as behavior, however, and speak of tendencies toward abnormality that are expressed under certain conditions, the full range of the facts can be accounted for. It is this perspective that governs milieu therapy. The tendencies of individuals are not disregarded, but their intricate connections with the setting are emphasized. This is well illustrated in a study of six hyperaggressive boys in a residential treatment center.[35] Their behavior was observed in six different settings on two occasions eighteen months apart. Behavior varied both with the settings and with the individual boys. When average change for a given boy, or average influence of a given setting, is the factor under study, the *interaction* of a particular setting with a particular boy is obscured. For example, 34 per cent of all the responses of the children toward adults were hostile. For Frank it was 37 per cent; yet his rate was only 9 per cent in the arts and crafts setting, where the average for all the boys was 28 per cent. The authors conclude: "We would view traits not as a once-and-for-all-time exclusive property of the organism irrespective of the environment but as directional potentialities under certain environmental circumstances; similarly, situations would be viewed as having arousal potential only for certain traits." [36]

One expression of milieu therapy is the development of treatment centers in which the full range of activity is considered part of the healing process. The work of such men as Maxwell Jones, Bruno Bettelheim, Fritz Redl, and David Wineman is based on the theory that every contact and activity has potential influence on the level of anxiety.[37] Bettelheim, for example, attempts to maintain a "total therapeutic milieu" for disturbed children. Their symptoms range from schizoid withdrawal to murderous assault, but they have in common a view that the world is dangerous, frustrating, and capricious. In the treatment center they find themselves in a completely nonpunitive situation. The constant love and patience of adults belies their previous experience and leads them to test reality in new ways. These ways may be destructive; but they also find, perhaps almost for the first time, that conventional and cooperative behavior is rewarding.[38]

Family therapy. A somewhat different form of milieu therapy takes the family as its unit of treatment. Some of the treatment centers which emphasize milieu therapy attempt to simulate a constructive family environment, but they do not usually deal directly with the patterns of relationships among family members. To the extent that illness resides not in the individual alone but also in the disturbed relationships of which he is a part, therapy must attempt to reconstruct those relationships.

Ackerman has pointed out that a generation ago, work with "problem families" emphasized social therapy more than psychotherapy. It was carried on mostly by social agencies in which a "variety of social techniques for therapeutic intervention in the family" had been developed. Attention to occupational, recreational, and other social needs, however, often proved quite ineffective, at least within the limits of the techniques used. Partly as a result of disillusionment, there was a rapid and drastic shift in many social agencies toward a psychiatric and often strictly psychoanalytic emphasis. "The influence of social and economic factors on the mental health of families was minimized"; individual therapy was given prime attention, with little regard to the reciprocities so critical in family life.[39]

Effective family therapy avoids these extreme formulations of the problem. In recent years, attention to the fact that mental illness is partly a property of the family as a social system has highlighted the several levels on which therapeutic work must proceed. To treat one person's neurotic anxieties independently of the role relationships which support them is often useless; to disregard the way those anxieties disrupt the role reciprocities is equally unwise. Within the family, relationships between the spouses, between parents and children, and among the children affect each other in intricate ways. Therapeutic efforts that concentrate on one of these without regard to the others are liable to failure. Focusing on mother-child relationships, for example, and overlooking the father-child relationships or the interaction of husband and wife, may prove ineffective. Bell, Trieschman, and Vogel found that when fathers were brought into the therapy work with disturbed children, additional cultural as well as interactional factors were revealed.[40] Class differences in patterns of discipline and training, for example, proved to be important. Knowledge of the subcultural traditions toward which parents are oriented is essential, as well as knowledge of the larger sociocultural environment within which the family lives, knowledge of the networks of interpersonal relationships among its members, and knowledge of the abnormal tendencies of the individuals.[41]

The hospital as a social system. Concern for the several levels on which therapy must operate leads naturally to the study of the hospital, not simply as a collection of individual patients and medical agents, but also as a social organization, with a complex of roles and cultural values, and with relationships to the larger society. We have come to see that the whole structure of relationships—between patient and patient, between patients and members of the staff on every level, and among the staff members—affects the therapeutic process for better or worse. "Treatment" is continuous. Not only the explicit culture of medicine, but many implicit cultural norms are involved. There are role assignments, but also role conflicts; there is a formal structure ostensibly designed to cure illness, but also an informal structure which may support custodial or even punishment norms more than therapy. The physician may see his patients only a few minutes a day, so that the impact of the hospital is governed by the attitudes and values of the attendants to an important degree.

Many of the consequences may be entirely unintended by-products of the search for efficiency and order or of the competition for influence among the attendants. As Goffman notes, the patient may find it difficult to maintain any sense of identity in a system where one "finds himself cleanly stripped of many of his accustomed affirmations, satisfactions, and defenses, and is subjected to a rather full set of mortifying experiences: restriction of free movement, communal living, diffuse authority of a whole echelon of people, and so on." [42]

Attention to the therapeutic consequences of the hospital has been quite explicitly field theoretical, as I use that term. Cumming and Cumming write: "We shall attempt to . . . develop a theory that will enable us to practice a milieu therapy which is *a scientific manipulation of the environment aimed at producing changes in the personality of the patient.* This theory will have to be general enough to include social structure, culture, and personality, all in the same terms." [43] Caudill takes the same perspective. His study of the psychiatric hospital as a small society demonstrates "a theoretical concern with the linkage between related open systems of physiological, personality, meaningful small groups, and wider social structures." [44] This could well stand as a general statement of the field approach.

Once alerted to the fact that every dimension of the hospital milieu has therapeutic significance, we broaden the range of concerns for theory and clinical practice. We begin to add to our interest in physical health, organic therapy, and ego-strengthening processes (to categorize traditional psychiatry overly simply) an interest in the physical setting of the hospital, patterns of authority and control, roles and role relationships, culture, and lines of communication.[45] We study the processes of staff recruitment and the values staff members bring to their tasks. We investigate the *collective* behavior that develops in the ward. We examine the effects of work and idleness, of recreation, of frequent or infrequent contacts with family and friends. We relate life in the hopsital to the culture and social process of the outside world. On each of these topics, significant research is being carried on. Although careful attention to the full range of influences of the treatment setting is a recent development —and therefore presents more questions than definitive answers—one sees in contemporary studies of hospitals and other treatment centers a valuable complement to the more established therapeutic methods.[46]

Posthospital behavior. The interest of milieu therapy does not end when patients leave the hospital. A third or more will return for further treatment; many others will function in their families and communities only with difficulty; and those who show no continuing impairment are of interest because of what they can reveal concerning the sources of recovery. One speaks with caution on the causes of posthospital behavior, because there are a number of interacting variables, several of which are difficult to measure.

In their excellent studies on this subject, Freeman and Simmons note that among the male patients whom they investigated, successful adjustment to family and community was not a function simply of the extent of recovery. The personalities of relatives (particularly female relatives), the man's place in his home (whether he lives with parents or with a wife), the availability of other males for work, the class level of the family, the expectations of relatives and their tolerance of deviation, all influenced posthospital performance. None of these relationships was decisive. Rehospitalization was most significantly related to bizarre behavior, which did not correlate highly with adjustment to family or to work. Perhaps, Freeman and Simmons suggest, once a family has experienced the problems associated with having to deal with a person who is mentally ill, it becomes quite similar to other families in its response to bizarre behavior, regardless of differences in class, job situation, or family structure. This research may not have answered the questions, but it has sharpened the hypotheses. And the authors are led to a field orientation: Behavior of a person who has been discharged from a mental hospital (and specifically, the likelihood of his full recovery or rehospitalization) is a function of his personality, the attitudes and other tendencies of family members, cultural and subcultural norms, particularly those related to tolerance of deviation, and the structure of social relationships in which he is placed.[47]

Group Therapy

The previous section has developed some aspects of the thesis that being restored to health, as well as becoming ill, is in part a socially structured process. A more specific application of this thesis than milieu therapy is group therapy, which involves a narrower range of forces and a more limited attention to interactional factors. It is, nevertheless, a group process designed to reduce or cure abnormality by application of knowledge of the effects of interaction. The basic hypothesis, in Beck's formulation, is that favorable therapeutic results can be produced in an artificially structured, temporary social system and subculture which are as different as possible from the settings in which maladaptive learning took place.[48]

Practices of group therapy vary widely. The groups may vary in size from 3 to over 50, with a mode, perhaps, in the 6 to 8 range. The groups may be homogeneous or heterogeneous with respect to the pathology of the members or their age, sex, race, and religion. The activity may vary from simple rhythmic exercises together—a major step in social communication for some schizophrenics—to enacting a plot containing an anxiety-laden problem, to uninhibited and even destructive play in which disturbed children test the limits of acceptance, to a lengthy series of discussions in which patients seek insight into and control over their problems by examining them openly in the presence of others who have similar problems.

The theoretical guidelines are also diverse. There are Freudian but perhaps more particularly Adlerian concepts dealing with the reestablishment of the ego in control over the coercions of id or superego. Group therapy, according to this view, helps to free the individual from repression and guilt; it unlocks his energies. Psychological learning theory combines with this by noting that intense but blocked responses are permitted by the removal of the usual sanctions, thus bringing the responses to awareness; new behavior of self-examination and self-expression is rewarded. Sociologically, the therapy session can be seen as a temporary subsociety, with a specialized subculture of roles and norms designed to reshape self-images and patterns of social interaction. Many of the theoretical concerns of group dynamics, which cut across the disciplines I have mentioned, are relevant to group therapy. And finally, in a somewhat different sense, there is a religious conception underlying some manifestations of group therapy. The function of the group is to encourage the individual to control himself, to inspire him to find identity in work or human associations, thus freeing him from the problems that burden him. The Oxford Movement, some elements of Christian Science, and in a more secular sense, Alcoholics Anonymous can be described in these terms.

Disregarding the diversity of structure and of theoretical perspective, which should not, of course, be forgotten, one can describe an underlying unity in the various group therapy settings. From its origins in drama and religion to its application to physical illness and then to abnormality, the emphasis is on the rediscovery of self by destroying the sense of isolation. The group, by facilitating interaction, encourages the adoption of new roles and new perspectives from which one's own problems are viewed. Sharing symptoms with others gives one a sense of security; the unconditional acceptance of words and, within limits, actions, weakens the feelings of rejection and isolation. When norms and rules emerge from the group, they are seen as ways of achieving individual and group goals, not as the repressive ideas of other people.

Group therapy is no panacea, although there are some who support it with faddist enthusiasm. A person may be so strongly in need of acceptance that he dare not attempt the deviations or open expressions permitted in the group, having learned too well from past experience the penalties of deviation. Another, in a search for reassurance, may be so anxious to test the limits of the therapist or the group that he carries his deviation beyond the point that others are able to accept. More controlled research is needed, such as that of Singer and Goldman, who compared the behavior of ten long-hospitalized male schizophrenics in a series of unstructured, "democratic" therapy sessions with the behavior of a matched group in a series of "authoritarian" sessions, where seats were assigned, a lecture approach employed, attendance taken, etc.[49] The long-run therapeutic effects of the former were superior to the latter, but this was not true during the early weeks, a fact which suggests the possibility that for such groups a structured pattern followed by growing participation and democratic processes may be best.

And finally, to illustrate some of the problems connected with group therapy, the very success of the open and accepting sessions may create the possibility that participants, on returning to the dominant social world, may find themselves too uninhibited or outspoken. As Beck points out, their former symptoms, however painful and awkward, were not wholly out of joint with the social systems of which they were a part; the symptoms were indeed efforts to struggle with the social systems. A marriage may have rested upon "a dovetailing of neurotic traits"; a formerly submissive employee of an authoritarian boss may run into new difficulties; parents may suffer severe losses as the power balance of the family is swung away from them.[50]

This is not to argue against therapy, of course, but only to stress the need for attention to the whole system of interactions within which abnormality is embedded. While commenting on the possible dysfunctions of group therapy, Beck notes that they are not typically serious. Therapy ends short of full transformation of the person; the outside world continues to restrain him; the restraints may be more acceptable if therapy has lowered self-deprecation and rigidities; and if the group processes have taught a patient to see social clues better, he may interact more adequately with others.[51]

Group therapy is based on an interest both in individual tendency and group process. It is implicitly, and sometimes explicitly, field theoretical. Used with proper caution, it is a major therapeutic instrument and can, indeed, contribute to the development of the theoretical base on which it is built.[52]

Society as the Patient

If cultural and interactional forces are involved both in forming abnormal tendencies and in facilitating their expression, then part of any therapeutic program should deal with "society as the patient." [53] This concept shares much in common with milieu therapy and group therapy, but it differs in several ways. There is a stronger emphasis on prevention, rather than cure. Attention is paid to the etiological and therapeutic implications of the full range of social structures, and not simply to those of treatment structures (hospitals, for example). And the degree to which various forms of pathology—illness, crime, family disorganization, and the like—are alternative responses to the same disordered social system is stressed. Considering the traditional emphasis on *cure* of *specific pathologies* in *specialized environments,* these are valuable additions to psychiatry.

On the basis of his work with children, Plant has declared: "In what might be termed the personality-culture balance the desired changes in the total picture can . . . be more simply and effectively initiated at the cultural than at the individual level." [54] From his clinical practice he found that where anxieties were not severe he often could disregard the individual entirely. By adjusting school placement, recommending more play with children of the same age rather than with an older sibling, or showing parents how they were promoting conflicts among their children, Plant has often been able to reduce a field-supported anxiety by restructuring the situation rather than treating the individual.

Individual and social therapies are complementary, of course, not contradictory. The need for attention to abnormal tendencies is most clearly seen when the problems of the individual are severe. Even under those conditions, however, failure to deal with environmental forces sharply reduces the effectiveness of therapy. With regard to drug use, for example, Leighton, Clausen, and Wilson write:

Nothing seems more futile than to base a therapeutic program for adolescent drug users in deprived population groups primarily upon treatment of the individual user. He is seldom motivated to seek such treatment. The realities of his world are so grossly different from those of the middle-class psychiatrist that treatment goals in psychotherapy seem destined to be unattainable as long as the user remains within an untreated social environment. Yet to attempt to change that environment is a larger task of social engineering than man has yet achieved. It would be utopian to assume that such a change can be brought about in a short time, but it would be defeatist to assume that purposive modifications of the total environment are beyond our power.[55]

If we take seriously the estimates that 10 to 25 per cent of the population is seriously impaired and another 50 per cent handicapped to some degree by psychiatric disorder, we must find some position between utopianism and defeatism in designing programs of prevention. It would be difficult to estimate how much of our control over physical illness rests upon prevention—on the purification of water supplies, dietary controls, regular examinations, and innoculations. But to compare morbidity rates of a society which has modern health practices with that society's own rates at an earlier period or with the rates of societies without such preventive measures leads one to believe that an ounce of prevention is indeed worth a pound of cure.

We have not yet learned the same lesson with regard to mental illness or other forms of behavioral deviation. In a wave of economy we may cut out the "frills" from a public housing project—that is, dispense with the counselors who might have been able to assist a group of culturally deprived and insecure persons to deal with a difficult environment. (We do not avoid the costs. We pay them later, out of a different pocket, and probably at a heavy rate of interest.) Governors take pride in "sound, businesslike budgets," and we elect them for their talents along those lines, without regard for the fact that the budgets often imply such curtailment of services for those who are being treated for their first deviation that the chances of preventing entrenchment of the patterns are sharply reduced.

Children spend a large proportion of their waking hours in school for ten or more years. If several "vicious circles" are to be broken up, I believe that many children should be started in school at age two or three. But even in the wealthiest societies, there is little readiness to invest in the educational process past the minimum,[56] despite evidence of the power of enriched education to "innoculate" children against the deviations so punishing to themselves and their communities.[57] Social psychiatry is the least developed branch of psychiatry, and its preventive dimension is the most poorly understood and supported. Yet I should judge that in the long run we have more to gain by greatly increasing our efforts to create health-giving environments than by any other psychiatric endeavor. Perhaps there will come a time when we are as concerned with the quality of our "character supply" as with the purity of our water supply.

CONCLUSION

I shall not try to summarize further what is already a highly condensed statement. I would like to express, however, my sense of excitement at the close of many months of intensive study built upon a quarter century of "undisciplined" investigation in behavioral science. Students of human behavior are not likely to achieve a decisive breakthrough which suddenly reveals the significance of many different relationships and dramatically makes sense out of many puzzling observations. The variables with which we deal are so numerous and the patterns of interaction so complex that no one or two master laws are likely to bring clarity to our views of human nature.

We shall have to learn to live with complexity. And on my reading of the evidence, we are learning to do so. Despite separation of the disciplines, dedication to partial explanations, and a desire for a simple, definitive theory that fits our preconceptions, we are developing a behavioral science. If we can train new generations of researchers to build upon the common foundation, and not simply to struggle toward cooperation and understanding from different positions, the important beginnings of a unified view of man in his world that are in hand can rapidly be extended. From the richness of the work being done and the speed with which several areas of research have become interdisciplinary, we have reason to be quietly confident.

FOOTNOTES

Note: The bracketed number following an author's name refers to the footnote in which the source is cited in full.

1. See Herbert Goldhamer and Andrew Marshall, *Psychosis and Civilization*, The Free Press of Glencoe, 1953; Joseph W. Eaton and Robert J. Weil, *Culture and Mental Disorder*, The Free Press of Glencoe, 1955; and the three volumes of the Stirling County Study of Psychiatric Disorder and Sociocultural Environment (Basic Books, Inc., Publishers): Alexander H. Leighton, *My Name is Legion*, 1959; Charles C. Hughes, Marc-Adelard Tremblay, Robert N. Rapoport, and Alexander H. Leighton, *People of Cove and Woodlot*, 1960; and Dorothea C. Leighton *et al.*, *The Character of Danger: Psychiatric Symptoms in Selected Communities*, 1963.

2. See Ralph Linton in George Devereux (ed.), *Culture and Mental Disorders*, Charles C Thomas, Publisher, 1956; Paul Benedict and Irving Jacks, "Mental Illness in Primitive Societies," *Psychiatry*, November, 1954, pp. 377–389.

3. See Marvin K. Opler, *Culture, Psychiatry and Human Values: The Methods and Values of a Social Psychiatry*, Charles C Thomas, Publisher, 1956, p. 86.

4. There is, of course, a vast literature on this topic. See Erich Fromm, *Escape from Freedom*, Holt, Rinehart and Winston, Inc., 1941; Karen Horney, *The Neurotic Personality of our Time*, W. W. Norton & Company, Inc., 1937; Erik H. Erikson, *Childhood and Society*, 2d ed., W. W. Norton & Company, Inc., 1963; Rollo May, *Man's Search for Himself*, W. W. Norton & Company, Inc., 1953; Maurice R. Stein, Arthur J. Vidich, and David M. White (eds.), *Identity and Anxiety*, The Free Press of Glencoe, 1960. Much of the existential psychiatry and the philosophy with psychiatric interests stands in this tradition. See Ludwig Binswanger, *Being-in-the-World*, Jacob Needleman (trans. and ed.), Basic Books, Inc., Publishers, 1963; Rollo May, Ernest Angel, and Henri F. Ellenberger (eds.), *Existence: A New Dimension in Psychiatry and Psychology*, Basic Books, Inc., Publishers, 1958; Medard Boss, *Psychoanalysis and Daseinsanalysis*, Basic Books, Inc., Publishers, 1963; Abraham H. Maslow, *Toward a Psychology of Being*, D. Van Nostrand Company, Inc., 1963; Maurice Merleau-Ponty, *The Structure of Behavior*, Beacon Press, 1963; Jean-Paul Sartre, *Being and Nothingness*, Philosophical Library, Inc., 1956. Many of these writers, it should be noted, were strongly influenced by the Freudian tradition and sought to extend and correct it, not to destroy it.

5. Alexander H. Leighton and Jane M. Hughes in *Causes of Mental Disorders: A Review of Epidemiological Knowledge*, 1959, Milbank Memorial Fund, 1961, pp. 341–383.

6. See Sigmund Freud, *New Introductory Lectures on Psychoanalysis*, W. W. Norton & Company, Inc., 1933, chap. 4; and *The Problem of Anxiety*, The Psychoanalytic Quarterly Press and W. W. Norton & Company, Inc., 1936.

7. Simon Dinitz, A. R. Mangus, and Benjamin Pasamanick, "Integration and Conflict in Self-Other Conceptions as Factors in Mental Illness," *Sociometry*, March, 1959, pp. 44–55; Lyman C. Wynne, Irving M. Rycoff, Julian Day, and Stanley Hirsch, "Pseudo-mutuality in the Family Relations of Schizophrenics," *Psychiatry*, May, 1958, pp. 205–220; Hubert Bonner, "Sociological Aspects of Paranoia," *American Journal of Sociology*, November, 1950, pp. 255–262; Melvin Kohn and John A. Clausen, "Parental Authority Behavior and Schizophrenia," *American Journal of Orthopsychiatry*, April, 1956, pp. 297–313; H. G. Gough, "A Sociological Theory of Psychopathy," *American Journal of Sociology*, March, 1948, pp. 359–366. For some contradictory evidence on role playing, see Sheldon Stryker, "Role-taking Accuracy and Adjustment," *Sociometry*, December, 1957, pp. 286–296.

8. Medard Boss [4], p. 243.

9. Harold Sampson, Sheldon L. Messinger, and Robert D. Towne, "Family Processes and Becoming a Mental Patient," *American Journal of Sociology*, July, 1962, pp. 88–96.

10. Edwin M. Lemert, "Paranoia and the Dynamics of Exclusion," *Sociometry*, March, 1962, pp. 2–19.

11. See Thomas J. Scheff, "The Role of the Mentally Ill and the Dynamics of Mental Disorder: A Research Framework," *Sociometry*, December, 1963, pp. 436–453; and Robert Sommer and Humphry Osmond, "Symptoms of Institutional Care," *Social Problems*, Winter, 1960–1961, pp. 254–263.

12. See Benjamin Pasamanick, H. Knobloch, and A. M. Lilienfield, "Socioeconomic Status and Precursors of Neuropsychiatric Disorder,"

American Journal of Orthopsychiatry, vol. 26, 1956, pp. 594–602; see also Brian MacMahon and James M. Sowa, "Psychical Damage to the Fetus," in Leighton and Hughes [5], pp. 51–110. Although class is not used as a variable in the latter work, several class-correlated causes are examined.

13. See Leo Srole and Thomas Langner, in Srole *et al., Mental Health in the Metropolis,* McGraw-Hill Book Company, 1962, pp. 210–212, for a summary of several studies. Their own data from a midtown Manhattan sample show a decisive negative correlation between their measures of mental health and parental socioeconomic status. See also Thomas Langner and Michael Stanley, *Life Stress and Mental Health,* The Free Press of Glencoe, 1963 (vol. II of the Midtown Manhattan study).

14. Robert J. Kleiner and Seymour Parker, "Goal-striving, Social Status, and Mental Disorder: A Research Review," *American Sociological Review,* April, 1963, pp. 189–203; see also Jacob Tuckman and Robert J. Kleiner, "Discrepancy between Aspiration and Achievement as a Predictor of Schizophrenia," *Behavioral Science,* October, 1962, pp. 443–447.

15. Srole and Langner [13], p. 228; see also William H. Sewell, "Social Class and Childhood Personality," *Sociometry,* December, 1961, pp. 340–356; E. Douvan and Joseph Adelson, "The Psychodynamics of Social Mobility in Adolescent Boys," *Journal of Abnormal and Social Psychology,* January, 1958, pp. 31–44. For a Study of the related problem of status consistency, see Elton F. Jackson, "Status Consistency and Symptoms of Stress," *American Sociological Review,* August, 1962, pp. 469–480. For a longitudinal study, see Lee N. Robins, Harry Gyman, and Patricia O'Neal, "The Interaction of Social Class and Deviant Behavior," *American Sociological Review,* August, 1962, pp. 480–492.

16. A. B. Hollingshead and Frederick C. Redlich, *Social Class and Mental Illness: A Community Study,* John Wiley & Sons, Inc., 1958; Lawrence Z. Freedman and A. B. Hollingshead, "Neurosis and Social Class I: Social Interaction," *American Journal of Psychiatry,* March, 1957, pp. 769–775; Jerome K. Myers and Bertram H. Roberts, *Family and Class Dynamics in Mental Illness,* John Wiley & Sons, Inc., 1959.

17. In the light of studies of total incidence, it seems likely that the listing of patients seriously underestimates the actual number of mentally ill persons, thus making group comparisons difficult. I shall not explore that question here. See Hollingshead and Redlich [16], especially pp. 233–237; and Leighton, *et al.* [1].

18. A. B. Hollingshead and Frederick C. Redlich, "Social Stratification and Psychiatric Disorders," *American Sociological Review,* April, 1953, p. 168.

19. See John A. Clausen and Melvin L. Kohn, "The Relation of Schizophrenia to the Social Structure of a Small City," in Benjamin Pasamanick (ed.), *Epidemiology of Mental Disorder,* American Association for the Advancement of Science, 1959, pp. 69–86. See also Hollingshead and Redlich [16], who found that class contrasts, although they remained significant, were reduced when based on incidence instead of prevalence.

20. See Orville R. Gursslin, Raymond G. Hunt, and Jack L. Roach, "Social Class and the Mental Health Movement," *Social Problems,* Winter, 1959–1960, pp. 210–218; Alexander Leighton, John A. Clausen, and Robert Wilson (eds.), *Explorations in Social Psychiatry,* Basic

Books, Inc., Publishers, 1957, p. 393; Myers and Roberts [16], pp. 208–209. Some contrary evidence is found in R. H. Hardt and S. J. Feinhandler, "Social Class and Mental Hospitalization Prognosis," *American Sociolgical Review*, December, 1959, pp. 815–821. They report an inverse relationship between class level and "risk of continuous long-term hospitalization" for schizrophrenia that could not be explained by "class differences in admission procedures, clinical characteristics, or condition at the time of discharge." Contradiction of an expected class difference in reception of returned hospital patients is found in Howard E. Freeman and Ozzie G. Simmons, *The Mental Patient Comes Home*, John Wiley & Sons, Inc., 1963; and in Mark Lefton, Shirley Angrist, Simon Dinitz, and Benjamin Pasamanick, "Social Class, Expectations, and Performance of Mental Patients," *American Journal of Sociology*, July, 1962, pp. 79–87.

21. Gursslin, Hunt, and Roach [20], p. 215.

22. *Ibid.*

23. Leighton *et al.* [1], p. 380.

24. *Ibid.*

25. For representative studies and commentaries, see Eugene B. Brody, "Social Conflict and Schizophrenic Behavior in Young Adult Negro Males," *Psychiatry*, November, 1961, pp. 337–346; R. M. Dreger and K. S. Miller, "Comparative Psychological Studies of Negroes and Whites in the United States," *Psychological Bulletin*, September, 1960, sec. 7; Raymond G. Hunt, "Socio-cultural Factors in Mental Disorder," *Behavioral Science*, April, 1959, pp. 96–106; Kiyoshi Ikeda, Harry V. Ball, and Douglas S. Yamamura, "Ethnocultural Factors in Schizophrenia," *American Journal of Sociology*, September, 1962, pp. 242–248; Abram Kardiner and Lionel Ovesey, *The Mark of Oppression; A Psychological Study of the American Negro*, W. W. Norton & Company, Inc., 1951; E. Gartley Jaco, *The Social Epidemiology of Mental Disorders*, Russell Sage Foundation, 1960; Robert J. Kleiner, Jacob Tuckman, and Martha Lavell, "Mental Disorder and Status Based on Race," *Psychiatry*, August, 1960, pp. 271–274; Robert J. Kleiner, Jacob Tuckman, and Martha Lavell, "Mental Disorder and Status Based on Religious Affiliation," *Human Relations*, September, 1959, pp. 273–276; Eleanor Leacock, "Three Social Variables and the Occurrence of Mental Illness," in Leighton, Clausen, and Wilson [20], chap. 10; Marvin K. Opler, *Culture and Mental Health*, The Macmillan Company, 1959; Ann Hallman Pettigrew and Thomas F. Pettigrew, "Race, Disease and Desegregation: A New Look," *Phylon*, Winter, 1963, pp. 315–333; William A. Scott, "Social Psychological Correlates of Mental Illness and Mental Health," *Psychological Bulletin*, March, 1958, pp. 65–87; and Srole *et al.* [13], part III.

26. Sampson, Messinger, and Towne [9]; Ernest Gruenberg and S. Bellin, "The Impact of Mental Disease on Society," in Leighton, Clausen, and Wilson [20], chap. 11; John A. Clausen and Marian R. Yarrow (issue eds.), "The Impact of Mental Illness on the Family," *Journal of Social Issues*, vol. 11, 1955, no. 4; Norman Cameron, "The Paranoid Pseudo-community," *American Journal of Sociology*, July, 1943, pp. 32–38; Norman Cameron, "The Paranoid Pseudo-community Revisited," *American Journal of Sociology*, July, 1959, pp. 52–58; and Hughes, Tremblay, Rapoport, and Leighton [1].

27. Cited by Ernest Gruenberg, "Socially Shared Pathology," in Leighton, Clausen, and Wilson [20], p. 221.

28. See William Haythorn, "The Influence of Individual Members on the Characteristics of Small Groups," *Journal of Abnormal and Social Psychology,* vol. 48, 1953, pp. 276–284; Ralph K. White and Ronald Lippitt, *Autocracy and Democracy: An Experimental Inquiry,* Harper & Row, Publishers, Incorporated, 1960; William J. Gnagey, "Effects on Classmates of a Deviant Student's Power and Response to a Teacher-exerted Control Technique," *Journal of Educational Psychology,* vol. 51, 1960, pp. 1–8.

29. See Ernest Gruenberg [27], pp. 201–229.

30. See Anthony F. C. Wallace, *Culture and Personality,* Random House, Inc., 1961, pp. 195–198; Leo Lowenthal and Norbert Guterman, *Prophets of Deceit: A Study in the Techniques of the American Agitator,* Harper & Row, Publishers, Incorporated, 1949; Daniel Bell (ed.), *The Radical Right,* Doubleday & Company, Inc., 1963; Gruenberg and Bellin [26].

31. See James S. Plant, *Personality and the Culture Pattern,* The Commonwealth Fund, 1937.

32. See Karl Menninger, with Martin Mayman and Paul Pruyser, *The Vital Balance,* The Viking Press, Inc., 1963, pp. 67–71. For a discussion of the history of social factors in medicine generally, see George Rosen, "The Evolution of Social Medicine," in Howard E. Freeman, Sol Levine, and Leo G. Reeder (eds.), *Handbook of Medical Sociology,* Prentice-Hall, Inc., 1963, pp. 17–61.

33. Albert J. Glass, quoted by John Clausen in Robert Merton, Leonard Broom, and Leonard Cottrell, Jr. (eds.), *Sociology Today,* Basic Books, Inc., Publishers, 1959, p. 503.

34. See *ibid.*

35. H. L. Raush, A. T. Dittmann, and T. J. Taylor, "Person, Setting, and Change in Social Interaction," *Human Relations,* vol. 12, 1959, pp. 361–378.

36. *Ibid.,* p. 373.

37. See Maxwell Jones, *The Therapeutic Community,* Basic Books, Inc., Publishers, 1953; Bruno Bettelheim, *Love Is Not Enough,* The Free Press of Glencoe, 1950; Bruno Bettleheim, *Truants from Life,* The Free Press of Glencoe, 1955; Fritz Redl and David Wineman, *Children Who Hate,* The Free Press of Glencoe, 1951; Alfred H. Stanton, "Milieu Therapy and the Development of Insight," *Psychiatry,* vol. 24, supplement to no. 2, May, 1961, pp. 19–29; Howard Jones, "A Contribution to the Evaluation of Some Methods of Residential Therapy," *Human Relations,* vol. 11, 1958, pp. 55–65.

38. See Bruno Bettelheim, *Truants from Life* [37].

39. Nathan W. Ackerman, "Interpersonal Disturbances in the Family: Some Unsolved Problems in Psychotherapy," *Psychiatry,* vol. 17, 1954, pp. 359–369.

40. See Norman Bell, Albert Trieschman, and Ezra Vogel, "A Sociocultural Analysis of the Resistances of Working-class Fathers Treated in a Child Psychiatric Clinic," *American Journal of Orthopsychiatry,* April, 1961, pp. 388–405.

41. See Nathan W. Ackerman, *Psychodynamics of Family Life,* Basic Books, Inc., Publishers, 1958; J. P. Spiegel, "The Resolution of Role Conflict within the Family," *Psychiatry,* vol. 20, 1957, pp. 1–16; Stephen Fleck *et al.,* "The Family as the Unit of Study and Treatment,"

American Journal of Orthopsychiatry, January, 1961, pp. 40–86; John E. Bell, "Recent Advances in Family Group Therapy," in Max Rosenbaum and Milton Berger (eds.), *Group Psychotherapy and Group Function*, Basic Books, Inc., Publishers, 1963, pp. 635–652. There are a number of references to therapy as well as etiology in the papers of part VI, "Family Dynamics," in *The Etiology of Schizophrenia*, Don D. Jackson (ed.), Basic Books, Inc., Publishers, 1960.

42. Erving Goffman, *Asylums: Essays on the Social Situation of Mental Patients and Other Inmates*, Doubleday & Company, Inc., 1961, p. 148.

43. John Cumming and Elaine Cumming, *Ego and Milieu*, Atherton Press, 1962, p. 5.

44. William Caudill, *The Psychiatric Hospital as a Small Society*, Harvard University Press for the Commonwealth Fund, 1958, p. 17.

45. These are the chapter topics of part II in Cumming and Cumming [43].

46. In addition to the works of Goffman [42], Cumming and Cumming [43], and Caudill [44], see Alfred H. Stanton and Morris S. Schwartz, *The Mental Hospital*, Basic Books, Inc., Publishers, 1954; Ivan Belknap, *Human Problems of a State Mental Hospital*, McGraw-Hill Book Company, 1956; Milton Greenblatt, Daniel J. Levinson, and Richard Williams (eds.), *The Patient and the Mental Hospital*, The Free Press of Glencoe, 1957; and Freeman, Levine, and Reeder [32].

47. See Freeman and Simmons [20].

48. Dorothy F. Beck, "The Dynamics of Group Psychotherapy as Seen by a Sociologist," *Sociometry*, June, 1958, pp. 98–128. If our theoretical perspective is correct, the principles involved in group therapy should apply to forms of deviation other than abnormality. There are, in fact, some fascinating applications of group theory to delinquency and crime. See LaMar T. Empey and Jerome Rabow, "The Provo Experiment in Delinquency Rehabilitation," *American Sociological Review*, October, 1961, pp. 679–695; Donald R. Cressey, "Changing Criminals: The Application of the Theory of Differential Association," *American Journal of Sociology*, September, 1955, pp. 116–120; S. R. Slavson, *Re-educating the Delinquent*, Harper & Row, Publishers, Incorporated, 1954. A valuable interpretation of parallels between group processes in treatment of criminality and drug addiction is found in Rita Volkman and Donald R. Cressey, "Differential Association and the Rehabilitation of Drug Addicts," *American Journal of Sociology*, September, 1963, pp. 129–142.

49. Jerome L. Singer and George E. Goldman, "Experimentally Contrasted Social Atmospheres in Group Psychotherapy with Chronic Schizophrenics," *Journal of Social Psychology*, August, 1954, pp. 23–37.

50. Beck [48], pp. 191–195.

51. *Ibid.*

52. For some of the background of group therapy see Trigant Burrow, *The Social Basis of Conciousness: A Study in Organic Psychology*, Basic Books, Inc., Publishers, 1927; J. L. Moreno, *Who Shall Survive? A New Approach to the Problem of Human Interrelations*, Nervous and Mental Disease Publishing Co., 1934; Kurt Lewin, *Resolving Social Conflicts*, Harper & Row, Publishers, Incorporated, 1948; and the extensive literature on group dynamics, for example, Dorwin Cartwright and Alvin Zander (eds.), *Group Dynamics*, 2d ed., Harper & Row,

Publishers, Incorporated, 1960. More specifically on contemporary group therapy, see Florence B. Powdermaker and Jerome D. Frank, *Group Psychotherapy,* Harvard University Press for the Commonwealth Fund, 1953; S. R. Slavson (ed.), *The Fields of Group Psychotherapy,* International Universities Press, Inc., 1956; S. R. Slavson, *Analytic Group Psychotherapy,* Columbia University Press, 1950; Raymond J. Corsini, *Methods of Group Psychotherapy,* McGraw-Hill Book Company, 1957; Beck [48], and "The Dynamics of Group Psychotherapy as Seen by a Sociologist: Part II, Some Puzzling Questions on Leadership, Contextual Relations, and Outcomes," *Sociometry,* September, 1958, pp. 180–197; Rosenbaum and Berger [41]; and the several issues of the *International Journal of Group Psychotherapy.*

53. L. K. Frank, *Society as the Patient: Essays on Culture and Personality,* Rutgers University Press, 1948. See also Erich Fromm, *The Sane Society,* Holt, Rinehart and Winston, Inc., 1955; and Alexander H. Leighton, *An Introduction to Social Psychiatry,* Charles C Thomas, Publisher, 1960.

54. Plant [31], p. 43. He uses the term culture to refer to the patterns of interpersonal relations.

55. Leighton, Clausen, and Wilson [20], pp. 394–395.

56. I will leave it to the reader, if he shares my discomfort with this situation, to make his own comparison of expenditure ratios. There is the familiar one between education and tobacco-alcohol-cosmetics; or one can compare expenditures for schooling with our readiness to remodel automobiles annually and to demand high horsepower; perhaps the most poignant comparison is between education and the accumulation of "overkill" in our atomic arsenal and other weapons.

57. See *1961 Commission on Civil Rights Report,* Government Printing Office, 1962, vol. 2, pp. 126–131; Harold Baron, "Samuel Shepard and the Banneker Project," *Integrated Education,* April, 1963, pp. 25–27.

BIBLIOGRAPHY

Aberle, David, *et al.:* "The Functional Prerequisites of Society," *Ethics,* vol. 60, 1950, pp. 100–111.

Ackerman, Nathan W.: "Interpersonal Disturbances in the Family: Some Unsolved Problems in Psychotherapy," *Psychiatry,* vol. 17, 1954, pp. 359–369.

———: *Psychodynamics of Family Life.* New York: Basic Books, Inc., Publishers, 1958.

Adler, Franz: "A Unit Concept for Sociology," *American Journal of Sociology,* January, 1960, pp. 356–364.

Adorno, T. W., Else Frenkel-Brunswik, D. J. Levinson, and R. N. Sanford: *The Authoritarian Personality.* New York: Harper & Row, Publishers, Incorporated, 1950.

Alexander, Leo: "War Crimes: Their Social-Psychological Aspects," *American Journal of Psychiatry,* September, 1948, pp. 170–177.

Allport, Gordon W.: *Personality.* New York: Henry Holt and Company, Inc., 1937.

———: *Becoming: Basic Considerations for a Psychology of Personality.* New Haven, Conn.: Yale University Press, 1955.

———: *Personality and Social Encounter.* Boston: Beacon Press, 1960.

Almond, Gabriel: *The Appeals of Communism.* Princeton, N.J.: Princeton University Press, 1954.

Alport, Floyd: *Theories of Perception and the Concept of Structure.* New York: John Wiley & Sons, Inc., 1955.

Angell, Robert C.: "Preferences for Moral Norms in Three Problem Areas," *American Journal of Sociology,* May, 1962, pp. 650–660.

Antonovsky, Aaron, and Melvin J. Lerner: "Occupational Aspirations of Lower Class Negro and White Youth," *Social Problems,* Fall, 1959, pp. 132–138.

Bachman, Carl W., and Paul F. Secord: "Liking, Selective Interaction, and Misperception in Congruent Interpersonal Relations," *Sociometry,* December, 1962, pp. 321–335.

———, ———, and Jerry R. Pierce: "Resistance to Change in the Self-concept as a Function of Consensus among Significant Others," *Sociometry,* March, 1963, pp. 102–111.

Bales, Robert F.: "Cultural Differences in the Rates of Alcoholism," *Quarterly Journal of Studies in Alcohol,* vol. 6, 1949, pp. 480–499.

———: *Interaction Process Analysis.* Reading, Mass.: Addison-Wesley Publishing Company, Inc., 1951.

Bandura, Albert, and Richard H. Walters: *Social Learning and Personality Development.* New York: Holt, Rinehart and Winston, Inc., 1963.

Banfield, Edward: *The Moral Basis of a Backward Society.* New York: The Free Press of Glencoe, 1958.

Barnouw, Victor: *Culture and Personality.* Homewood, Ill.: The Dorsey Press, 1963.

Bates, Allan P. and Jerry Cloyd: "Toward the Development of Operations for Defining Group Norms and Member Roles," *Sociometry,* March, 1956, pp. 26–39.

Bates, Fredrick L.: "Position, Role, and Status: A Reformulation of Concepts," *Social Forces,* May, 1956, pp. 313–321.

———: "Some Observations concerning the Structural Aspect of Role Conflict," *Pacific Sociological Review,* Fall, 1962, pp. 76–82.

Bateson, Gregory, Don D. Jackson, Jay Haley, and John Weakland: "Toward a Theory of Schizophrenia," *Behavorial Science,* October, 1956, pp. 251–264.

Bauer, Raymond: "The Communicator and the Audience," *Conflict Resolution,* March, 1958, pp. 67–77.

Beck, Dorothy Fahs: "The Dynamics of Group Psychotherapy as Seen by a Sociologist," *Sociometry,* June, 1958, pp. 98–128.

———: "The Dynamics of Group Psychotherapy as Seen by a Sociologist, Part II: Some Puzzling Questions on Leadership, Contextual Relations, and Outcomes," *Sociometry,* September, 1958, pp. 180–197.

Becker, Howard P.: "Normative Reactions to Normlessness," *American Sociological Review,* December, 1960, pp. 803–810.

Becker, Howard S.: *Outsiders: Studies in the Sociology of Deviance.* New York: The Free Press of Glencoe, 1963.

———: "Personal Change in Adult Life," *Sociometry,* March, 1964, pp. 40–53.

——— and Blanche Geer: "The Fate of Idealism in Medical School," *American Sociological Review,* February, 1958, pp. 50–56.

Belknap, Ivan: *Human Problems of a State Mental Hospital.* New York: McGraw-Hill Book Company, 1956.

Bell, Daniel: *The End of Ideology.* New York: The Free Press of Glencoe, 1960.

Bell, Norman, Albert Trieschman, and Ezra Vogel: "A Sociocultural Analysis of the Resistances of Working-class Fathers Treated in a Child Psychiatric Clinic," *American Journal of Orthopsychiatry,* April, 1961, pp. 388–405.

Bell, Wendell: "Anomie, Social Isolation, and the Class Structure," *Sociometry,* June, 1957, pp. 105–116.

Bellin, Seymour S., and Robert H. Hardt: "Marital Status and Mental Disorders among the Aged," *American Sociological Review,* April, 1958, pp. 155–162.

Bendix, Reinhard: "Compliant Behavior and Individual Personality," *American Journal of Sociology,* November, 1952, pp. 292–303.

Benedict, Paul K., and Irving Jacks: "Mental Illness in Primitive Societies," *Psychiatry,* November, 1954, pp. 377–389.

Benedict, Ruth: "Anthropology and the Abnormal," *Journal of Genetic Psychology,* vol. 10, 1934, pp. 59–82.

———: *Patterns of Culture.* Boston: Houghton Mifflin Company, 1934.

———: "Continuities and Discontinuities in Cultural Conditioning," *Psychiatry,* vol. 1, 1938, pp. 161–167.

———: *The Chrysanthemum and the Sword.* Boston: Houghton Mifflin Company, 1946.

Bennett, John W.: "The Interpretation of Pueblo Culture," *Southwestern Journal of Anthropology,* vol. 24, 1946, pp. 361–374.

Berelson, Bernard, and Gary A. Steiner: *Human Behavior: An Inventory of Scientific Findings.* New York: Harcourt, Brace & World, Inc., 1964.

Berg, Irwin, and Bernard Bass (eds.): *Conformity and Deviation.* New York: Harper & Row, Publishers, Incoporated, 1961.

Berkowitz, Leonard: *Aggression: A Social Psychological Analysis.* New York: McGraw-Hill Book Company, 1962.

Bertrand, Alvin L.: "The Stress-Strain Element of Social Systems: A Micro Theory of Conflict and Change," *Social Forces,* October, 1963, pp. 1–9.

Bettelheim, Bruno: "Individual and Mass Behavior in Extreme Situations," *Journal of Abnormal and Social Psychology,* October, 1943, pp. 417–452.

———: *Love Is Not Enough.* New York: The Free Press of Glencoe, 1950.

———: *Truants from Life.* New York: The Free Press of Glencoe, 1955.

Biddle, Bruce J.: *The Present Status of Role Theory,* vol. A, *Studies in the Role of the Public School Teacher.* Columbia, Mo.: Social Psychology Laboratory, The University of Missouri, 1961.

Biderman, Albert, and Herbert Zimmer (eds.): *The Manipulation of Human Behavior.* New York: John Wiley & Sons, Inc., 1961.

Binswanger, Ludwig: *Being-in-the-World,* trans. and ed. by Jacob Needleman. New York: Basic Books, Inc., Publishers, 1963.

Birren, James (ed.): *Handbook of Aging and the Individual: Psychological and Biological Aspects.* Chicago: The University of Chicago Press, 1959.

Blake, Robert R., and Glenn V. Ramsey (eds.): *Perception: An Approach to Personality.* New York: The Ronald Press Company, 1951.

Blalock, H. M., Jr.: "Correlated Independent Variables: The Problem of Multicollinearity," *Social Forces,* December, 1963, pp. 233–237.

Blau, Peter: "Structural Effects," *American Sociological Review,* April, 1960, pp. 178–193.

———: "A Theory of Social Integration," *American Journal of Sociology,* May, 1960, pp. 545–556.

Blau, Zena Smith: "Structural Constraints on Friendships in Old Age," *American Sociological Review,* June, 1961, pp. 429–439.

Bohlke, Robert H.: "Social Mobility, Stratification Inconsistency and Middle Class Delinquency," *Social Problems,* Spring, 1961, pp. 351–363.

Bolton, Charles D.: "Is Sociology a Behavioral Science?" *The Pacific Sociological Review,* Spring, 1963, pp. 3–9.

Bonner, Hubert: "Sociological Aspects of Paranoia," *American Journal of Sociology,* November, 1950, pp. 255–262.

Bordua, David J.: "Delinquent Subcultures: Sociological Interpretations of Gang Delinquency," *Annals of the American Academy of Political and Social Science,* November, 1961, pp. 119–136.

Borgatta, Edgar F.: "Role-playing Specification, Personality, and Performance," *Sociometry,* September, 1961, pp. 218–233.

———, Leonard Cottrell, Jr., and Henry J. Meyer: "On the Dimensions of Group Behavior," *Sociometry,* December, 1956, pp. 223–240.

Boss, Medard: *Psychoanalysis and Daseinsanalysis,* trans. by Ludwig B. Lefebre. New York: Basic Books, Inc., Publishers, 1963.

Bott, Elizabeth: "Urban Families: Conjugal Roles and Social Networks," *Human Relations,* vol. 8, 1955, pp. 345–384.

Braude, Lee: "Professional Autonomy and the Role of the Layman," *Social Forces,* May, 1961, pp. 297–301.

Breed, Warren: "Occupational Mobility and Suicide among White Males," *American Sociological Review,* April, 1963, pp. 179–188.

Brim, Orville G., Jr.: "Family Structure and Sex Role Learning by Children: A Further Analysis of Helen Koch's Data," *Sociometry,* March, 1958, pp. 1–16.

———: "Personality Development as Role-learning," in Ira Iscoe and Harold Stevenson (eds.), *Personality Development in Children.* Austin, Tex.: University of Texas Press, 1960.

———, David C. Glass, David E. Lavin, and Norman Goodman: *Personality and Decision Processes.* Stanford, Calif.: Stanford University Press, 1962.

——— and David B. Hoff: "Individual and Situational Differences in Desire for Certainty," *Journal of Abnormal and Social Psychology,* March, 1957, pp. 225–229.

Brittain, Clay V.: "Adolescent Choices and Parent-Peer Cross-pressures," *American Sociological Review,* June, 1963, pp. 385–391.

Brody, Eugene B.: "Social Conflict and Schizophrenic Behavior in Young Adult Negro Males," *Psychiatry,* November, 1961, pp. 337–346.

Bronfenbrenner, Urie: "Toward an Integrated Theory of Personality," in Robert R. Blake and Glenn V. Ramsey (eds.), *Perception: An Approach to Personality.* New York: The Ronald Press Company, 1951.

———: "Socialization and Social Class through Time and Space," in Eleanor E. Maccoby, T. M. Newcomb, and E. L. Hartley (eds.), *Readings in Social Psychology,* 3d ed., New York: Holt, Rinehart and Winston, 1958.

———: "The Changing American Child: A Speculative Analysis," *Journal of Social Issues,* vol. 17, 1961, pp. 6–18.

Brown, Roger W.: "A Determinant of the Relationship between Rigidity and Authoritarianism," *Journal of Abnormal and Social Psychology,* October, 1953, pp. 469–476.

Bruner, Edward M.: "Cultural Transmission and Cultural Change," *Southwestern Journal of Anthropology,* vol. 12, 1956, pp. 191–199.

Bruner, Jerome: "On Perceptual Readiness," *Psychological Review,* vol. 64, 1957, pp. 123–152.

——— and Leo Postman: "On the Perception of Incongruity: A Paradigm," *Journal of Personality,* vol. 18, 1949, pp. 206–223.

Bunzel, Ruth: "The Role of Alcoholism in Two Central American Cultures," *Psychiatry,* vol. 3, 1940, pp. 361–387.

Bureau of Narcotics: *Traffic in Opium and Other Dangerous Drugs.* Washington: Government Printing Office, 1959.

Byrne, Donn, and Terry J. Wong: "Racial Prejudice, Interpersonal

Attraction, and Assumed Dissimilarity of Attitudes," *Journal of Abnormal and Social Psychology,* October, 1962, pp. 246–253.

Cameron, Norman, "The Paranoid Pseudo-community," *American Journal of Sociology,* July, 1943, pp. 32–38.

———: "The Paranoid Pseudo-community Revisited," *American Journal of Sociology,* July, 1959, pp. 52–58.

Campbell, Donald T., and Donald W. Fiske: "Convergent and Discriminant Validation by the Multitrait-Multimethod Matrix," *Psychological Bulletin,* vol. 56, 1959, pp. 81–105.

Canning, Ray R., and James M. Baker: "Effect of the Group on Authoritarian and Non-authoritarian Persons," *American Journal of Sociology,* May, 1959, pp. 579–581.

Cantril, Hadley: *The Politics of Despair.* New York: Basic Books, Inc., Publishers, 1958.

Cartwright, Dorwin, and Alvin Zander (eds.): *Group Dynamics.* New York: Harper & Row, Publishers, Incorporated, 1960.

Cattell, R. B.: *Personality: A Systematic, Theoretical, and Factual Study.* New York: McGraw-Hill Book Company, 1950.

———: *Personality and Motivation Structure and Measurement of Behavior.* New York: Harcourt, Brace & World, Inc., 1957.

Caudill, William: *The Psychiatric Hospital as a Small Society.* Cambridge, Mass.: Harvard University Press, for The Commonwealth Fund, 1958.

Centers, Richard: "An Examination of the Riesman Social Character Typology: A Metropolitan Survey," *Sociometry,* September, 1962, pp. 231–240.

Chapman, Loren J., and Donald T. Campbell: "The Effect of Acquiescence Response-set upon Relationships among the F Scale, Ethnocentrism, and Intelligence," *Sociometry,* June, 1959, pp. 153–161.

Chein, Isidor, Morton Deutsch, Herbert Hyman, and Marie Jahoda (issue eds.): "Consistency and Inconsistency in Intergroup Relations," *Journal of Social Issues,* vol. 5, 1949.

———, D. L. Gerard, R. S. Lee, and Eva Rosenfeld, with the collaboration of D. M. Wilner: *The Road to H: Narcotics, Delinquency, and Social Policy.* New York: Basic Books, Inc., Publishers, 1964.

Child, Charles M.: *Physiological Foundations of Behavior.* New York: Henry Holt and Company, Inc., 1924.

Child, Irwin L.: "Socialization," in Gardner Lindzey (ed.), *Handbook of Social Psychology,* vol. 2, chap. 18. Reading, Mass.: Addison-Wesley Publishing Company, Inc., 1954.

———: "Problems of Personality and Some Relations to Anthropology and Sociology," in Sigmund Koch (ed.), *Psychology: A Study of A Science,* vol. 5, pp. 593–638. New York: McGraw-Hill Book Company, 1963.

Chilton, Roland J.: "Continuity in Delinquency Area Research: A Comparison of Studies for Baltimore, Detroit, and Indianapolis," *American Sociological Review,* February, 1964, pp. 71–83.

Christie, Richard, and Peggy Cook: "A Guide to Published Literature Relating to the Authoritarian Personality through 1956," *The Journal of Psychology,* April, 1958, pp. 171–199.

————, Joan Havel, and Bernard Seidenberg: "Is the F Scale Irreversible?" *The Journal of Abnormal and Social Psychology*, March, 1958, pp. 143–159.

———— and Marie Jahoda (eds.): *Studies in the Scope and Method of "The Authoritarian Personality."* New York: The Free Press of Glencoe, 1954.

Clark, Burton: "The 'Cooling-out' Function in Higher Education," *American Journal of Sociology*, May, 1960, pp. 569–576.

————: *Educating the Expert Society*. San Francisco: Chandler Publishing Company, 1962.

Clark, John P. and Eugene P. Wenninger: "Socio-economic Class and Area as Correlates of Illegal Behavior among Juveniles," *American Sociological Review*, December, 1962, pp. 826–834.

———— and ————: "Goal Orientations and Illegal Behavior among Juveniles," *Social Forces*, October, 1963, pp. 49–59.

Clausen, John A.: *Sociology and the Field of Mental Health*. New York: Russell Sage Foundation, 1956.

————: "Social Patterns, Personality, and Adolescent Drug Use," in Alexander Leighton, John Clausen, and Robert Wilson (eds.), *Explorations in Social Psychiatry*. New York: Basic Books, Inc., Publishers, 1957.

————: "Mental Disorders," chap. 3 in Robert K. Merton and Robert A. Nisbet (eds.), *Contemporary Social Problems*. New York: Harcourt, Brace & World, Inc., 1961.

———— and Melvin L. Kohn: "The Ecological Approach in Social Psychiatry," *American Journal of Sociology*, September, 1954, pp. 140–151.

———— and Marian R. Yarrow (issue eds.): "The Impact of Mental Illness on the Family," *Journal of Social Issues*, vol. 11, 1955.

Clinard, Marshall B.: "Criminological Research," in Robert K. Merton, Leonard Broom, and Leonard Cottrell, Jr. (eds.), *Sociology Today*. New York: Basic Books, Inc., Publishers, 1959.

Cloward, Richard A., and Lloyd E. Ohlin: *Delinquency and Opportunity*. New York: The Free Press of Glencoe, 1960.

Cohen, Albert K.: *Delinquent Boys: The Culture of the Gang*. New York: The Free Press of Glencoe, 1955.

———— and Harold M. Hodges, Jr.: "Characteristics of the Lower-blue-collar-class," *Social Problems*, Spring, 1963, pp. 303–334.

———— and James F. Short, Jr.: "Research in Delinquent Subcultures," *The Journal of Social Issues*, vol. 14, 1958, pp. 20–37.

Cohen, E. A.: *Human Behavior in the Concentration Camp*. New York: W. W. Norton & Company, Inc., 1953.

Cohen, Yehudi A. (ed.): *Social Structure and Personality*. New York: Holt, Rinehart and Winston, Inc., 1961.

Coleman, James S.: *The Adolescent Society*. New York: The Free Press of Glencoe, 1961.

Coles, Robert: *The Desegregation of Southern Schools: A Psychiatric Study*. New York: Anti-Defamation League and Southern Regional Council, 1963.

Commission on Chronic Illness: *Chronic Illness in a Large City: The Baltimore Study.* Cambridge, Mass.: Harvard University Press, 1957.

Corsini, Raymond J.: *Methods of Group Psychotherapy.* New York: McGraw-Hill Book Company, 1957.

Coser, Rose Laub: "Insulation from Observability and Types of Social Conformity," *American Sociological Review,* February, 1961, pp. 28–39.

Coutu, Walter: *Emergent Human Nature: A Symbolic Field Interpretation.* New York: Alfred A. Knopf, Inc., 1949.

Cowen, Emory L., Judah Landes, and Donald E. Schaet: "The Effects of Mild Frustration on the Expression of Prejudiced Attitudes," *Journal of Abnormal and Social Psychology,* January, 1959, pp. 33–38.

Cressey, Donald R.: "Changing Criminals: The Application of the Theory of Differential Association," *American Journal of Sociology,* September, 1955, pp. 116–120.

Crockett, Harry J., Jr.: "The Achievement Motive and Differential Occupational Mobility in the United States," *American Sociological Review,* April, 1962, pp. 191–204.

Crutchfield, Richard S.: "Conformity and Character," *American Psychologist,* May, 1955, pp. 191–198.

Cumming, Elaine, and William E. Henry: *Growing Old: The Process of Disengagement.* New York: Basic Books, Inc., Publishers, 1961.

Cumming, John, and Elaine Cumming: *Ego and Milieu.* New York: Atherton Press, 1962.

Davis, Allison W., and Robert J. Havighurst: *Father of the Man: How Your Child Gets His Personality.* Boston: Houghton Mifflin Company, 1947.

Davis, Fred: "The Cabdriver and His Fare: Facets of a Fleeting Relationship," *American Journal of Sociology,* September, 1959, pp. 158–165.

Davis, James A., Joe L. Spaeth, and Carolyn Huson: "A Technique for Analyzing the Effects of Group Composition," *American Sociological Review,* April, 1961, pp. 215–225.

Dean, Dwight G.: "Alienation: Its Meaning and Measurement," *American Sociological Review,* October, 1961, pp. 753–758.

———— and Jon A. Reeves: "Anomie: A Comparison of a Catholic and a Protestant Sample," *Sociometry,* June, 1962, pp. 209–212.

DeFleur, Melvin L., and Frank R. Westie: "Attitude as a Scientific Concept," *Social Forces,* October, 1963, pp. 17–31.

Deutsch, J. A.: *The Structural Basis of Behavior.* Chicago: The University of Chicago Press, 1960.

Deutsch, Morton, and Solomon Leonard: "Reactions to Evaluations by Others as Influenced by Self-evaluations," *Sociometry,* June, 1959, pp. 93–112.

Dinitz, Simon, A. R. Mangus, and Benjamin Pasamanick: "Integration and Conflict in Self-Other Conceptions as Factors in Mental Illness," *Sociometry,* March, 1959, pp. 44–55.

Dohrenwend, Bruce P.: "Egoism, Altruism, Anomie, and Fatalism: A Conceptual Analysis of Durkheim's Types," *American Sociological Review,* August, 1959, pp. 466–473.

Dollard, John: *Caste and Class in a Southern Town.* New Haven, Conn.: Yale University Press, 1937.

―――― and Neal E. Miller: *Personality and Psychotherapy.* New York: McGraw-Hill Book Company, 1950.

Douvan, E., and Joseph Adelson: "The Psychodynamics of Social Mobility in Adolescent Boys," *Journal of Abnormal and Social Psychology,* January, 1958, pp. 31–44.

Dreger, R. M., and K. S. Miller: "Comparative Psychological Studies of Negroes and Whites in the United States," *Psychological Bulletin,* September, 1960, pp. 361–402.

Dubin, Robert: "Deviant Behavior and Social Structure," *American Sociological Review,* April, 1959, pp. 147–164.

Dublin, Louis: *Suicide: A Sociological and Statistical Study.* New York: The Ronald Press Company, 1963.

Dunphy, Dexter C.: "The Social Structure of Urban Adolescent Peer Groups," *Sociometry,* June, 1963, pp. 230–246.

Durkheim, Émile: *The Rules of Sociological Method,* 8th ed., trans. by S. A. Solovay and John H. Mueller, ed. by G. E. G. Catlin. Chicago: The University of Chicago Press, 1938.

―――――: *Suicide,* trans. by John A. Spaulding and George Simpson. New York: The Free Press of Glencoe, 1951.

Eaton, Joseph W., and Robert J. Weil: *Culture and Mental Disorders.* New York: The Free Press of Glencoe, 1955.

Eggan, Dorothy: "The General Problem of Hopi Adjustment," *American Anthropologist,* vol. 45, 1943, pp. 357–373.

Ehrlich, Howard J., James W. Rinehart, and John C. Howell: "The Study of Role Conflict: Explorations in Methodology," *Sociometry,* March, 1962, pp. 85–97.

Elkins, Stanley M.: *Slavery: A Problem in American Institutional and Intellectual Life.* Chicago: The University of Chicago Press, 1959.

Ellis, Robert A., W. Clayton Lane, and Virginia Olesen: "The Index of Class Position: An Improved Intercommunity Measure of Stratification," *American Sociological Review,* April, 1963, pp. 271–277.

Empey, Lemar T., and Jerome Rabow: "The Provo Experiment in Delinquency Rehabilitation," *American Sociological Review,* October, 1961, pp. 679–695.

Erikson, Erik H.: *Childhood and Society,* 2d ed. New York: W. W. Norton & Company, Inc., 1963.

Essien-Udom, E. U.: *Black Nationalism: A Search for Identity in America.* Chicago: The University of Chicago Press, 1962.

Etzioni, Amitai (ed.): *Complex Organizations.* New York: Holt, Rinehart and Winston, Inc., 1961.

Evans-Pritchard, E. E.: *Social Anthropology.* New York: The Free Press of Glencoe, 1952.

Eysenck, H. J.: *The Structure of Human Personality.* New York: John Wiley & Sons, Inc., 1953.

Farber, I. E., Harry F. Harlow, and Louis J. West: "Brainwashing,

Conditioning, and DDD (Debility, Dependency, Dread)," *Socio metry*, December, 1957, pp. 271–285.

Faris, Rcbert E. L.: "Reflections on the Ability Dimension in Human Society," *American Sociological Review*, December, 1961, pp. 835–843.

———— and H. W. Dunham: *Mental Disorders in Urban Areas*. Chicago: The University of Chicago Press, 1939.

Feshbach, Seymour, and Robert Singer: "The Effects of personal and Shared Threats upon Social Prejudice," *Journal of Abnormal and Social Psychology*, May, 1957, pp. 411–416.

Festinger, Leon: *Theory of Cognitive Dissonance*. New York: Harper & Row, Publishers, Incorporated, 1957.

Field, Mark G.: "Structured Strain in the Role of the Soviet Physician," *American Journal of Sociology*, March, 1953, pp. 493–502.

Firth, Raymond: "Suicide and Risk-taking in Tikopia Society," *Psychiatry*, February, 1961, pp. 1–17.

Flavell, John H.: *The Developmental Psychology of Jean Piaget*. Princeton, N.J.: D. Van Nostrand Company, Inc., 1963.

Fleck, Stephen, *et al.*, "The Family as the Unit of Study and Treatment," *American Journal of Orthopsychiatry*, January, 1961, pp. 40–86.

Frank, Lawrence K.: *Society as the Patient: Essays on Culture and Personality*. New Brunswick, N.J.: Rutgers University Press, 1948.

Freedman, Lawrence Z., and August B. Hollingshead: "Neurosis and Social Class," *The American Journal of Psychiatry*, March, 1957, pp. 769–775.

Freedman, M. B., T. F. Leary, A. G. Ossorio, and H. S. Coffey: "The Interpersonal Dimension of Personality," *Journal of Personality*, vol. 20, 1951, pp. 143–161.

————, Harold Webster, and Nevitt Sanford: "A Study of Authoritarianism and Psychopathology," *Journal of Psychology*, April, 1956, pp. 315–322.

Freeman, Howard E., Sol Levine, and Leo G. Reeder (eds.): *Handbook of Medical Sociology*. Englewood Cliffs, N.J.: Prentice-Hall, Inc., 1963.

———— and Ozzie G. Simmons: *The Mental Patient Comes Home*. New York: John Wiley & Sons, Inc., 1963.

Freud, Sigmund: *Group Psychology and the Analysis of the Ego*. London: The Hogarth Press, 1922.

————: *The Ego and the Id*, trans. by Joan Riviere. London: The Hogarth Press, 1927.

————: *Civilization and its Discontents*, trans. by Joan Riviere. New York: Jcnathan Cape and Harrison Smith, 1930.

————: *New Introductory Lectures in Psychoanalysis*. New York: W. W. Norton & Company, Inc., 1933.

————: *The Problem of Anxiety*, trans. by Henry A. Bunker. New York: The Psychoanalytic Quarterly Press and W. W. Norton & Company, Inc., 1936.

Fried, Marc, and Erich Lindemann: "Sociocultural Factors in Mental Health and Illness," *American Journal of Orthopsychiatry*, January, 1961, pp. 87–101.

Fromm, Erich: *Escape from Freedom.* New York: Holt, Rinehart and Winston, Inc., 1941.
———: *The Sane Society.* New York: Holt, Rinehart and Winston, Inc., 1955.
Gerard, Donald L., and Lester G. Houston: "Family Setting and the Social Ecology of Schizophrenia," *Psychiatric Quarterly,* vol. 27, 1953, pp. 90–101.
Gerard, Harold B.: "Some Effects of Status, Role Clarity, and Group Goal Clarity upon the Individual's Relations to Group Processes," *Journal of Personality,* June, 1957, pp. 475–488.
Gerth, Hans, and C. Wright Mills: *Character and Social Structure.* New York: Harcourt, Brace & World, Inc., 1953.
Getzels, Jacob W., and Philip W. Jackson: *Creativity and Intelligence.* New York: John Wiley & Sons, Inc., 1962.
Gibbs, Jack P.: "Suicide," in Robert K. Merton and Robert A. Nisbet (eds.), *Contemporary Social Problems.* New York: Harcourt, Brace & World, Inc., 1961.
Gilbert, Doris C., and Daniel J. Levinson: "Ideology, Personality, and Institutional Policy in the Mental Hospital," *Journal of Abnormal and Social Psychology,* 1956, pp. 263–271.
Gillin, John (ed.): *For a Science of Social Man.* New York: The Macmillan Company, 1954.
Glueck, Sheldon, and Eleanor Glueck: *Unraveling Juvenile Delinquency.* New York: The Commonwealth Fund, 1950.
——— and ———: *Predicting Delinquency and Crime.* Cambridge, Mass.: Harvard University Press, 1959.
——— and ———: *Family Environment and Delinquency.* Boston: Houghton Mifflin Company, 1962.
Gnagey, William J.: "Effects on Classmates of a Deviant Student's Power and Response to a Teacher-exerted Control Technique," *Journal of Educational Psychology,* vol. 51, 1960, pp. 1–8.
Goffman, Erving: "On Cooling the Mark out: Some Aspects of Adaptation to Failure," *Psychiatry,* November, 1952, pp. 451–463.
———: *The Presentation of Self in Everyday Life.* Edinburgh: University of Edinburgh Social Sciences Research Center, Monograph No. 2, 1956.
———: *Asylums.* Garden City, N.Y.: Doubleday & Company, Inc., 1961.
Gold, Martin: *Status Forces in Delinquent Boys.* Ann Arbor, Mich.: Institute for Social Research, University of Michigan, 1962.
Goldberg, Solomon: "Three Situational Determinants of Conformity to Social Norms," *Journal of Abnormal and Social Psychology,* July, 1954, pp. 325–329.
Goldfrank, Esther: "Socialization, Personality, and the Structure of Pueblo Society," *American Anthropologist,* vol. 47, 1945, pp. 516–539.
Goldhamer, Herbert, and Andrew Marshall: *Psychosis and Civilization.* New York: The Free Press of Glencoe, 1953.
Goode, William J.: "A Theory of Role Strain," *American Sociological Review,* August, 1960, pp. 483–496.
———: "Norm Commitment and Conformity to Role-status Obliga-

tions," *American Journal of Sociology,* November, 1960, pp. 246–258.

———: "Illegitimacy, Anomie, and Cultural Penetration," *American Sociological Review,* December, 1961, pp. 910–925.

Gordon, Robert A., James F. Short, Jr., Desmond S. Cartwright, and Fred L. Strodtbeck: "Values and Gang Delinquency: A Study of Street-corner Groups," *The American Journal of Sociology,* September, 1963, pp. 109–128.

Gorer, Geoffrey: *The American People.* New York: W. W. Norton & Company, Inc., 1948.

———: *Exploring English Character.* London: The Cresset Press, 1955.

Goslin, David A.: "Accuracy of Self Perception and Social Acceptance," *Sociometry,* September, 1962, pp. 283–296.

Gough, H. G.: "A Sociological Theory of Psychopathy," *American Journal of Sociology,* March, 1948, pp. 359–366.

Gouldner, Alvin W.: "Cosmopolitans and Locals: Toward an Analysis of Latent Social Roles, I," *Administrative Science Quarterly,* December, 1957, pp. 281–306.

———: "Cosmopolitans and Locals: Toward an Analysis of Latent Social Roles, II," *Administrative Science Quarterly,* March, 1958, pp. 444–480.

Greenblatt, Milton, Daniel J. Levinson, and Richard H. Williams (eds.): *The Patient and the Mental Hospital.* New York: The Free Press of Glencoe, 1957.

Grinker, Roy R.: *Toward a Unified Theory of Human Behavior.* New York: Basic Books, Inc., Publishers, 1956.

Grodzins, Morton: *The Loyal and the Disloyal: Social Boundaries of Patriotism and Treason.* Chicago: The University of Chicago Press, 1956.

Gross, Llewellyn (ed.): *Symposium on Sociological Theory.* New York: Harper & Row, Publishers, Incorporated, 1959.

Gross, Neal, Ward S. Mason, and Alexander W. McEachern: *Explorations in Role Analysis: Studies of the School Superintendent Role.* New York: John Wiley & Sons, Inc., 1958.

Grusky, Oscar: "The Effects of Formal Structure on Managerial Recruitment: A Study of Baseball Organization," *Sociometry,* September, 1963, pp. 345–353.

Gursslin, Orville R., Raymond G. Hunt, and Jack L. Roach: "Social Class and the Mental Health Movement," *Social Problems,* Winter, 1959–1960, pp. 210–218.

Hagen, Everett E.: "Analytical Models in the Study of Social Systems," *American Journal of Sociology,* September, 1961, pp. 144–151.

Hajda, Jan: "Alienation and Integration of Student Intellectuals," *American Sociological Review,* October, 1961, pp. 758–777.

Halbwachs, Maurice: *Les Cadres Sociaux de la Mémoire.* Paris: F. Alcan, 1925.

———: *Les Causes du Suicide.* Paris: F. Alcan, 1930.

Haley, Jay: "An Interactional Description of Schizophrenia," *Psychiatry,* November, 1959, pp. 321–332.

Hall, Calvin, and Gardner Lindzey: *Theories of Personality*. New York: John Wiley & Sons, Inc., 1957.

Hall, Robert L., and Ben Willerman: "The Educational Influence of Dormitory Roommates," *Sociometry*, September, 1963, pp. 294–318.

Haller, A. O., and I. W. Miller: "The Occupational Aspiration Scale: Theory, Structure and Correlates," *Technical Bulletin 288*, Michigan State University, Agricultural Experiment Station.

—— and Shailer Thomas: "Personality Correlates of the Socioeconomic Status of Adolescent Males," *Sociometry*, December, 1962, pp. 398–404.

Hallowell, A. Irving: "The Rorschach Technique in the Study of Personality and Culture," *American Anthropologist*, vol. 47, 1945, pp. 195–210.

——: *Culture and Experience*. Philadelphia: University of Pennsylvania Press, 1955.

Hamblin, Robert L.: "The Dynamics of Racial Discrimination," *Social Problems*, Fall, 1962, pp. 103–121.

Hanson, Robert C.: "The Systematic Linkage Hypothesis and Role Consensus Patterns in Hospital-Community Relations," *American Sociological Review*, June, 1962, pp. 304–313.

Harding, John (issue ed.): "New Light on Delinquency," *The Journal of Social Issues*, vol. 14, 1958.

Hardt, R. H., and S. J. Feinhandler: "Social Class and Mental Hospitalization Prognosis," *American Sociological Review*, December, 1959, pp. 815–821.

Hare, A. Paul: *Handbook of Small Group Research*. New York: The Free Press of Glencoe, 1962.

——, Edgar F. Borgatta, and Robert F. Bales: *Small Groups*. New York: Alfred A. Knopf, Inc., 1955.

Haring, Douglass G. (ed.): *Personal Character and Cultural Milieu*, 3d rev. ed. Syracuse, N.Y.: Syracuse University Press, 1956.

Harvey, O. J.: "Personality Factors in Resolution of Conceptual Incongruities," *Sociometry*, December, 1962, pp. 336–352.

——, Harold H. Kelley, and Martin M. Shapiro: "Reactions to Unfavorable Evaluations of the Self Made by Other Persons," *Journal of Personality*, June, 1957, pp. 393–411.

Havighurst, Robert J., et al.: *Growing up in River City*, New York: John Wiley & Sons, Inc., 1962.

Haythorn, William: "The Influence of Individual Members on the Characteristics of Small Groups," *Journal of Abnormal and Social Psychology*, vol. 48, 1953, pp. 276–284.

Heider, Fritz: *The Psychology of Interpersonal Relations*. New York: John Wiley & Sons, Inc., 1958.

Henry, Andrew F.: "Sibling Structure and Perception of the Disciplinary Roles of Parents," *Sociometry*, March, 1957, pp. 67–74.

—— and James F. Short, Jr.: *Suicide and Homicide: Some Economic, Sociological and Psychological Aspects of Aggression*. New York: The Free Press of Glencoe, 1954.

Henry, Jules: *Culture against Men*. New York: Random House, Inc., 1963.

Hilgard, E. R.: *Introduction to Psychology.* New York: Harcourt, Brace & World, Inc., 1953.

Himelhoch, Jerome: "Tolerance and Personality Needs: A Study of the Liberalization of Ethnic Attitudes among Minority Group College Students," *American Sociological Review,* February, 1950, pp. 71–88.

Hinkle, Lawrence E., Jr.: "The Physiological State of the Interrogation Subject as It Affects Brain Function," in Albert Biderman and Herbert Zimmer (eds.), *The Manipulation of Human Behavior.* New York: John Wiley & Sons, 1961.

Hollingshead, A. B.: "Some Issues in the Epidemiology of Schizophrenia," *American Sociological Review,* February, 1961, pp. 5–13.

——— and F. C. Redlich: "Social Stratification and Psychiatric Disorders," *American Sociological Review,* April, 1953, pp. 163–169.

——— and F. C. Redlich: *Social Class and Mental Illness.* New York: John Wiley & Sons, Inc., 1958.

Homans, George C.: *The Human Group.* New York: Harcourt, Brace & World, Inc., 1950.

———: *Social Behavior: Its Elementary Forms.* New York: Harcourt, Brace & World, Inc., 1961.

Honigmann, John J.: *Culture and Personality.* New York: Harper & Row, Publishers, Incorporated, 1954.

Horney, Karen: *The Neurotic Personality of Our Time.* New York: W. W. Norton & Company, Inc., 1937.

———: *New Ways in Psychoanalysis.* New York: W. W. Norton & Company, Inc., 1939.

———: *Our Inner Conflicts.* New York: W. W. Norton & Company, Inc., 1945.

Horton, Donald: "The Functions of Alcohol in Primitive Societies," in Clyde Kluckhohn, H. A. Murray, and David M. Schneider (eds.), *Personality in Nature, Society, and Culture.* New York: Alfred A. Knopf, Inc., 1953.

Hovland, Carl I., Irving L. Janis, and Harold H. Kelley: *Communication and Persuasion: Psychological Studies of Opinion Change.* New Haven, Conn.: Yale University Press, 1953.

Hovland, Carl I., A. A. Lumsdaine, and F. D. Sheffield: *Studies in Social Psychology in World War II,* vol. III, *Experiments on Mass Communication.* Princeton, N.J.: Princeton University Press, 1949.

Hsu, Francis L. K.: *Psychological Anthropology.* Homewood, Illinois: The Dorsey Press, 1961.

———: *Clan, Caste, and Club.* Princeton, N.J.: D. Van Nostrand Company, Inc., 1963.

Hughes, Charles C., Marc-Adelard Tremblay, Robert N. Rapoport, and Alexander H. Leighton: *People of Cove and Woodlot.* New York: Basic Books, Inc., Publishers, 1960.

Hughes, Everett Cherrington: *Men and Their Work.* New York: The Free Press of Glencoe, 1958.

Hull, C. L.: *Principles of Behavior.* New York: Appleton-Century-Crofts, Inc., 1953.

Hunt, J. McV. (ed.): *Personality and the Behavior Disorders,* 2 vols. New York: The Ronald Press Company, 1944.

Hunt, Raymond G.: "Socio-cultural Factors in Mental Disorder," *Behavioral Science,* April, 1959, pp. 96–106.

Hyman, Herbert: *Political Socialization: A Study in the Psychology of Political Behavior.* New York: The Free Press of Glencoe, 1959.

Ikeda, Kiyoshi, Harry V. Ball, and Douglas S. Yamamura: "Ethnocultural Factors in Schizophrenia," *American Journal of Sociology,* September, 1962, pp. 242–248.

Inkeles, Alex: "Social Change and Social Character: The Role of Parental Mediation," *Journal of Social Issues,* vol. 11, 1955, pp. 12–23.

——: "Personality and Social Structure" in Robert K. Merton, Leonard Broom, and Leonard S. Cottrell, Jr. (eds.), *Sociology Today.* New York: Basic Books, Inc., Publishers, 1959.

——: "Industrial Man: The Relation of Status to Experience, Perception, and Value," *American Journal of Sociology,* July, 1960, pp. 1–31.

—— and Daniel J. Levinson, "National Character: The Study of Modal Personality and Sociocultural Systems," in Gardner Lindzey (ed.), *Handbook of Social Psychology,* vol. 2. Reading, Mass.: Addison-Wesley Publishing Company, Inc., 1954.

—— and ——: "The Personal System and the Sociocultural System in Large-scale Organizations," *Sociometry,* June, 1963, pp. 217–229.

Iscoe, Ira, and Harold W. Stevenson (eds.): *Personality Development in Children.* Austin, Tex.: University of Texas Press, 1960.

Jackson, Don D. (ed.): *The Etiology of Schizophrenia.* New York: Basic Books, Inc., Publishers, 1960.

Jackson, Elton F.: "Status Consistency and Symptoms of Stress," *American Sociological Review,* August, 1962, pp. 469–480.

Jaco, E. Gartley: "The Social Isolation Hypothesis and Schizophrenia," *American Sociological Review,* October, 1954, pp. 567–577.

——: *The Social Epidemiology of Mental Disorders.* New York: Russell Sage Foundation, 1960.

Jahoda, Marie: *Current Concepts of Positive Mental Health.* New York: Basic Books, Inc., Publishers, 1958.

——: "Conformity and Independence," *Human Relations,* vol. 12, 1959, pp. 99–120.

Janis, Irving L., and Carl I. Hovland (eds.): *Personality and Persuasibility.* New Haven, Conn.: Yale University Press, 1959.

Janowitz, Morris: *Sociology and the Military Establishment.* New York: Russell Sage Foundation, 1959.

Jennings, H. S.: *The Biological Basis of Human Nature.* New York: W. W. Norton & Company, Inc., 1930.

Jessor, Richard, *et al.*: "Theory and Method in the Study of Deviance in a Tri-ethnic Community," *Research Report No. 25,* Tri-Ethnic Research Project, University of Colorado, 1963.

Jones, Edward E., Keith E. Davis, and Kenneth J. Gergen: "Role Playing Variations and Their Informal Value for Person Perception," *Journal of Abnormal and Social Psychology,* September, 1961, pp. 302–310.

———— and Richard deCharms: "Changes in Social Perception as a Function of the Personal Relevance of Behavior," *Sociometry,* March, 1957, pp. 75–85.

Jones, Howard: "A Contribution to the Evaluation of Some Methods of Residential Therapy," *Human Relations,* vol. 11, 1958, pp. 55–65.

Jones, Maxwell: *The Therapeutic Community.* New York: Basic Books, Inc., 1953.

Josephson, Eric, and Mary Josephson (eds.): *Man Alone: Alienation in Modern Society.* New York: Dell Publishing Co., Inc., 1962.

Kallmann, Franz J.: "The Genetic Theory of Schizophrenia," *American Journal of Psychiatry,* November, 1946, pp. 309–322.

Kaplan, Bert (ed.): *Studying Personality Cross-culturally.* New York: Harper & Row, Publishers, Incorporated, 1961.

Kardiner, Abram, with Ralph Linton: *The Individual and His Society: The Psychodynamics of Primitive Social Organization.* New York: Columbia University Press, 1939.

———— (with collaboration of Ralph Linton, Cora DuBois, and James West): *The Psychological Frontiers of Society.* New York: Columbia University Press, 1945.

———— and Lionel Ovesey: *The Mark of Oppression: A Psychological Study of the American Negro.* New York: W. W. Norton & Company, Inc., 1951.

Kassarjian, W. M.: "A Study of Riesman's Theory of Social Character," *Sociometry,* September, 1962, pp. 213–230.

Katz, Elihu, Peter M. Blau, Morton L. Brown, and Fred L. Strodtbeck: "Leadership Stability and Social Change: An Experiment with Small Groups," *Sociometry,* March, 1957, pp. 36–50.

———— and Paul F. Lazarsfeld: *Personal Influence: The Part Played by People in the Flow of Mass Communications.* New York: The Free Press of Glencoe, 1955.

Kelly, E. Lowell: "Consistency of the Adult Personality," *American Psychologist,* November, 1955, pp. 659–681.

Kelman, H. C.: "Effects of Success and Failure on 'Suggestability' in the Autokinetic Situation," *Journal of Abnormal and Social Psychology,* vol. 45, 1950, pp. 267–285.

Kerckhoff, Alan C.: "Anomie and Achievement Motivation: A Study of Personality Development within Cultural Disorganization," *Social Forces,* March, 1959, pp. 196–202.

Kimble, Gregory A.: *Hilgard and Marquis' Conditioning and Learning,* 2d ed. New York: Appleton-Century-Crofts, Inc., 1961.

Kitsuse, John I., and David C. Dietrick: "Delinquent Boys: A Critique," *American Sociological Review,* April, 1959, pp. 208–215.

Klapp, Orrin E.: *Heroes, Villains, and Fools: The Changing American Character.* Englewood Cliffs, N.J.: Prentice-Hall, Inc., 1962.

Klapper, Joseph T.: "What We Know about the Effects of Mass Communication: The Brink of Hope," *Public Opinion Quarterly,* Winter, 1957–1958, pp. 453–474.

Klein, G. S., and David Krech: "The Problem of Personality and Its Theory," *Journal of Personality,* vol. 20, 1951, pp. 2–23.

Kleiner, Robert J., and Seymour Parker: "Goal-striving, Social Status, and Mental Disorder: A Research Review," *American Sociological Review*, April, 1963, pp. 189–203.

━━━, Jacob Tuckman, and Martha Lavell: "Mental Disorder and Status Based on Religious Affiliation," *Human Relations*, September, 1959, pp. 273–276.

━━━, ━━━, and ━━━: "Mental Disorder and Status Based on Race," *Psychiatry*, August, 1960, pp. 271–274.

Klinberg, Otto: *Tensions Affecting International Understanding*. New York: Social Science Research Council, 1950.

Kluckhohn, Clyde: *Culture and Behavior*, ed. by Richard Kluckhohn. New York: The Free Press of Glencoe, 1962.

━━━, H. A. Murray, and David Schneider (eds.): *Personality in Nature, Society, and Culture*, rev. ed. New York: Alfred A. Knopf, Inc., 1953.

Kluckhohn, Florence R., and Fred L. Strodtbeck, with the assistance of John M. Roberts, A. Kimball Romney, Clyde Kluckhohn, and Harry A. Scarr: *Variations in Value Orientations*. New York: Harper & Row, Publishers, Incorporated, 1961.

Kobrin, Solomon: "The Conflict of Values in Delinquency Areas," *American Sociological Review*, October, 1951, pp. 653–661.

Koch, Helen L.: "Sissiness and Tomboyishness in Relation to Sibling Characteristics," *Journal of Genetic Psychology*, June, 1956, pp. 231–244.

Koch, Sigmund (ed.): *Psychology: A Study of a Science*, 7 vols. New York: McGraw-Hill Book Company, 1959–1964.

━━━, and ━━━: "Parental Authority Behavior and Schizophrenia," *American Journal of Orthopsychiatry*, April, 1956, pp. 297–313.

Kohn, Melvin L., and John A. Clausen: "Social Isolation and Schizophrenia," *American Sociological Review*, June, 1955, pp. 265–273.

━━━ and Robin M. Williams, Jr.: "Situational Patterning in Intergroup Relations," *American Sociological Review*, April, 1956, pp. 164–174.

Komarovsky, Mirra: *Women in the Modern World*. Boston: Little, Brown, and Company, 1953.

Kornhauser, Arthur, Harold L. Sheppard, and Albert J. Mayer: *When Labor Votes*. New York: University Books, 1956.

Kornhauser, William: *The Politics of Mass Society*. New York: The Free Press of Glencoe, 1959.

Krech, David, Richard S. Crutchfield, and Egerton L. Ballachey: *Individual in Society*. New York: McGraw-Hill Book Company, 1962.

Kroeber, A. L. (ed.): *Anthropology Today*. Chicago: The University of Chicago Press, 1953.

━━━ and Clyde Kluckhohn: *Culture: A Critical Review of Concepts and Definitions*. Cambridge: Peabody Museum Papers, vol. 47, 1952.

━━━ and Talcott Parsons: "The Concepts of Culture and of Social System," *American Sociological Review*, October, 1958, pp. 582–583.

Kuhn, Manford H.: "Self-attitudes by Age, Sex and Professional Training," *Sociological Quarterly*, January, 1960, pp. 39–56.

━━━ and Thomas S. McPartland: "An Empirical Investigation of Self

Attitudes," *American Sociological Review,* February, 1954, pp. 68–76.

Kutner, Bernard, Carol Wilkins, and P. R. Yarrow: "Verbal Attitudes and Overt Behavior Involving Racial Prejudice," *Journal of Abnormal and Social Psychology,* July, 1952, pp. 649–652.

Kvaraceus, William, and Walter B. Miller: *Delinquent Behavior.* Washington: National Education Association of the United States, 1959.

La Barre, Weston: "The Influence of Freud on Anthropology," *American Imago,* vol. 15, 1958, pp. 275–328.

Lane, Robert: *Political Life: Why People Get Involved in Politics.* New York: The Free Press of Glencoe, 1959.

Langner, Thomas, and Stanley Michael: *Life Stress and Mental Health.* New York: The Free Press of Glencoe, 1963.

LaPiere, Richard: "Attitudes vs. Actions," *Social Forces,* December, 1934, pp. 230–237.

Lecky, Prescott: *Self-consistency: A Theory of Personality.* New York: Island Press, 1951.

Lefton, Mark, Shirley Angrist, Simon Dinitz, and Benjamin Pasamanick: "Social Class, Expectations, and Performance of Mental Patients," *American Journal of Sociology,* July, 1962, pp. 79–87.

Leighton, Alexander H.: *My Name Is Legion.* New York: Basic Books, Inc., Publishers, 1959.

————: *An Introduction to Social Psychiatry.* Springfield, Ill.: Charles C Thomas, Publisher, 1960.

————, John A. Clausen, and Robert N. Wilson (eds.): *Explorations in Social Psychiatry.* New York: Basic Books, Inc., Publishers, 1957.

Leighton, Dorothea, *et al.: The Character of Danger.* New York: Basic Books, Inc., Publishers, 1963.

Lemert, Edwin M.: "Paranoia and the Dynamics of Exclusion," *Sociometry,* March, 1962, pp. 2–19.

Lerner, Daniel: *The Passing of Traditional Society.* New York: The Free Press of Glencoe, 1959.

Levinson, Daniel J.: "Role, Personality, and Social Structure in the Organizational Setting," *Journal of Abnormal and Social Psychology,* vol. 58, 1959, pp. 170–180.

Lewin, Kurt: *A Dynamic Theory of Personality,* trans, by Donald K. Adams and Karl E. Zener. New York: McGraw-Hill Book Company, 1935.

————: *Field Theory in Social Science,* ed. by Dorwin Cartwright. New York: Harper & Row, Publishers, Incorporated, 1951.

Lewis, Oscar: Five Families: *Mexican Case Studies in the Culture of Poverty.* New York: Basic Books, Inc., Publishers, 1959.

Lieberman, Seymour: "The Effects of Changes in Roles on the Attitudes of Role Occupants," *Human Relations,* vol. 9, 1956, pp. 385–402.

Lifton, Robert J.: *Thought Reform and the Psychology of Totalism.* New York: W. W. Norton & Company, Inc., 1963.

Lincoln, C. Eric: *The Black Muslims in America.* Boston: Beacon Press, 1961.

Lindesmith, Alfred R.: *Opiate Addiction.* Evanston, Ill.: Principia Press, 1947.

———— and Anselm L. Strauss, "A Critique of Culture-Personality Writings," *American Sociological Review,* October, 1950, pp. 587–600.

——— and ———: *Social Psychology,* rev. ed. New York: Holt, Rinehart and Winston, Inc., 1956.

Lindzey, Gardner (ed.): *Handbook of Social Psychology,* 2 vols. Reading, Mass.: Addison-Wesley Publishing Company, Inc., 1954.

Linton, Ralph: *Study of Man.* New York: D. Appleton–Century Company, Inc., 1936.

———: *The Cultural Background of Personality.* New York: Appleton-Century-Crofts, Inc., 1945.

———: *Culture and Mental Disorders,* ed. by George Devereux. Springfield, Ill.: Charles C Thomas, Publisher, 1956.

Lipset, Seymour M.: "Democracy and Working-class Authoritarianism," *American Sociological Review,* August, 1959, pp. 482–501.

———: *Political Man: The Social Bases of Politics.* Garden City, N.Y.: Doubleday & Company, Inc., 1960.

——— and Leo Lowenthal (eds.): *Culture and Social Character: The Work of David Riesman Reviewed.* New York: The Free Press of Glencoe, 1961.

Lively, Edwin L., Simon Dinitz, and Walter C. Reckless: "Self Concept as a Predictor of Juvenile Delinquency," *American Journal of Orthopsychiatry,* January, 1962, pp. 159–168.

Lowenthal, Marjorie Fiske: "Social Isolation and Mental Illness in Old Age," *American Sociological Review,* February, 1964, pp. 54–74.

Lynd, Helen Merrell: *On Shame and the Search for Identity.* New York: Science Editions, Inc., 1961.

McClelland, David C.: *The Achieving Society.* Princeton, N.J.: D. Van Nostrand Company, Inc., 1961.

———, J. W. Atkinson, R. A. Clark, and E. L. Lowell: *The Achievement Motive.* New York: Appleton-Century-Crofts, Inc., 1953.

———, Alfred L. Baldwin, Urie Bronfenbrenner, and Fred L. Strodtbeck: *Talent and Society.* Princeton, N.J.: D. Van Nostrand Company, Inc., 1958.

McClintock, Charles G.: "Personality Syndromes and Attitude Change," *Journal of Personality,* December, 1958, pp. 479–493.

Maccoby, Eleanor E.: "Role-taking in Childhood and Its Consequences for Social Learning," *Child Development,* June, 1959, pp. 239–252.

———: "The Choice of Variables in the Study of Socialization," *Sociometry,* December, 1961, pp. 357–371.

———, Joseph P. Johnson, and Russell M. Church: "Community Integration and the Social Control of Juvenile Delinquency," *The Journal of Social Issues,* vol. 14, 1958, pp. 38–51.

———, Theodore M. Newcomb, Eugene L. Hartley (eds.): *Readings in Social Psychology,* 3d ed. New York: Holt, Rinehart and Winston, Inc., 1958.

McCord, William (issue ed.): "New Light on Delinquency," *The Journal of Social Issues,* vol. 14, 1958.

——— and Joan McCord: *Origins of Alcoholism.* Stanford, Calif.: Stanford University Press, 1960.

——— and ———, with Irving K. Zola: *Origins of Crime: New Evaluation of the Cambridge-Sommerville Youth Study.* New York: Columbia University Press, 1959.

McCurdy, H. G.: "Coin Perception Studies and the Concept of Schemata," *Psychological Review,* vol. 63, 1956, pp. 160–168.

McDill, Edward L.: "Anomie, Authoritarianism, Prejudice, and Socioeconomic Status: An Attempt at Clarification," *Social Forces,* March, 1961, pp. 239–245.

——— and James Coleman: "High School Social Status, College Plans, and Interest in Academic Achievement: A Panel Analysis," *American Sociological Review,* December, 1963, pp. 905–918.

McGranahan, Donald G.: "A Comparison of Social Attitudes among American and German Youth," *Journal of Abnormal and Social Psychology,* vol. 41, 1946, pp. 245–257.

MacIver, R. M. (ed.): *Discrimination and National Welfare.* New York: Institute for Religious and Social Studies; distributed by Harper & Row, Publishers, Incorporated, 1949.

McPartland, Thomas S., John H. Cumming, and Wynona S. Garretson: "Self-conception and Ward Behavior in Two Psychiatric Hospitals," *Sociometry,* June, 1961, pp. 111–124.

Maddox, George L.: "Activity and Morale: A Longitudinal Study of Selected Elderly Subjects," *Social Forces,* December, 1963, pp. 195–204.

Maehr, Martin L., Josef Mensing, and Samuel Nafzger: "Concept of Self and the Reaction of Others," *Sociometry,* December, 1962, pp. 353–357.

Maher, Brendan A.: "Personality, Problem Solving, and the Einstellung Effect," *Journal of Abnormal and Social Psychology,* January, 1957, pp. 70–74.

Malof, Milton, and Albert J. Lott: "Ethnocentrism and the Acceptance of Negro Support in a Group Pressure Situation," *Journal of Abnormal and Social Psychology,* October, 1962, pp. 254–258.

Mandelbaum, D. G.: "On the Study of National Character," *American Anthropologist,* vol. 52, 1953, pp. 174–187.

Mangus, A. R.: "Role Theory and Marriage Counseling," *Social Forces,* March, 1957, pp. 200–209.

Manis, J. G., M. J. Brawer, C. L. Hunt, and L. C. Kercher: "Estimating the Prevalance of Mental Illness," *American Sociological Review,* February, 1964, pp. 84–89.

Mann, John H.: "Experimental Evaluations of Role Playing," *Psychological Bulletin,* May, 1956, pp. 227–234.

Maslow, Abraham H. (issue ed.): "American Culture and Personality," *Journal of Social Issues,* vol. 7, 1951.

———: *Toward a Psychology of Being.* Princeton, N.J.: D. Van Nostrand Company, Inc., 1962.

Matza, David: "Subterranean Traditions of Youth," *The Annals of the American Academy of Political and Social Science,* November, 1961, pp. 102–118.

——— and Gresham Sykes: "Juvenile Delinquency and Subterranean Values," *American Sociological Review,* October, 1961, pp. 712–719.

May, Rollo: *Man's Search for Himself.* New York: W. W. Norton & Company, Inc., 1953.

———, Ernest Angel, and Henri F. Ellenberger (eds.): *Existence: A*

New Dimension in Psychiatry and Psychology. New York: Basic
Books, Inc., Publishers, 1958.

Mead, George Herbert: *Mind, Self, and Society,* ed. by C. W. Morris
Chicago: The University of Chicago Press, 1934.

———: *The Social Psychology of George Herbert Mead,* ed. by Anselm
Strauss. Chicago: The University of Chicago Press, 1956.

Mead, Margaret: *From the South Seas.* New York: William Morrow
and Company, Inc., 1939.

———: *And Keep Your Powder Dry.* New York: William Morrow and
Company, Inc., 1942.

——— and Martha Wolfenstein (eds.): *Childhood in Contemporary
Cultures.* Chicago: The University of Chicago Press, 1955.

Mechanic, David, and Edmund H. Volkart: "Stress, Illness Behavior,
and the Sick Role," *American Sciological Review,* February, 1961,
pp. 51–58.

Meier, Dorothy L., and Wendell Bell: "Anomia and Differential Access
to the Achievement of Life Goals," *American Sociological Review,*
April, 1959, pp. 189–202.

Menninger, Karl, with Martin Mayman and Paul Pruyser: *The Vital
Balance.* New York: The Viking Press, Inc., 1963.

Merleau-Ponty, Maurice: *The Structure of Behavior.* Boston: Beacon
Press, 1963.

Merton, Robert K.: "The Role-set: Problems in Sociological Theory,"
British Journal of Sociology, June, 1957, pp. 106–120.

———: *Social Theory and Social Structure,* rev. ed. New York: The
Free Press of Glencoe, 1957.

———, Leonard Broom, and Leonard S. Cottrell, Jr. (eds.): *Sociology
Today: Problems and Prospects.* New York: Basic Books, Inc.,
Publishers, 1959.

Middleton, Russell: "Alienation, Race, and Education," *American Sociological Review,* December, 1963, pp. 973–977.

——— and Snell Putney: "Religion, Normative Standards, and Behavior," *Sociometry,* June, 1962, pp. 141–152.

Milbank Memorial Fund: *Causes of Mental Disorders: A Review of
Epidemiological Knowledge,* 1959. New York: Milbank Memorial
Fund, 1961.

Milgram, Stanley: "Nationality and Conformity," *Scientific American,*
December, 1961, pp. 45–51.

Miller, Daniel R.: "The Study of Social Relationships: Situation, Iden-
tity, and Social Interaction," in Sigmund Koch (ed.), *Psychology:
A Study of a Science,* vol. v, pp. 639-737. New York: McGraw-Hill
Book Company, 1963.

——— and Guy E. Swanson: *The Changing American Parent.* New York:
John Wiley & Sons, Inc., 1958.

——— and ———: *Inner Conflict and Defense.* New York: Holt, Rinehart and Winston, Inc., 1960.

Miller, James G.: "Toward a General Theory for the Behavioral Sciences," *American Psychologist,* September, 1955, pp. 513–531.

Miller, Walter B.: "Lower Class Culture as a Generating Milieu of Gang
Delinquency," *The Journal of Social Issues,* vol. 14, 1958, pp. 5–19.

————, Hildred Geertz, and Henry S. G. Cutter: "Aggression in a Boys' Street-corner Group," *Psychiatry,* November, 1961, pp. 283–298.

Mills, C. Wright: *White Collar: The American Middle Classes.* Fair Lawn, N.J.: Oxford University Press, 1951.

Milosz, Czeslaw: *The Captive Mind.* New York: Alfred A. Knopf, Inc., 1953.

Mizruchi, Ephraim H.: "Social Structure and Anomia in a Small City," *American Sociological Review,* October, 1960, pp. 645–654.

———— and Robert Perrucci: "Norm Qualities and Differential Effects of Deviant Behavior: An Exploratory Analysis," *American Sociological Review,* June 1962, pp. 391–399.

Moloney, J. C.: "Psychic Self-abandon and Extortion of Confession," *International Journal of Psycho-Analysis,* vol. 35, 1955, pp. 53–60.

Moreno, J. L.: *Who Shall Survive? A New Approach to the Problems of Human Interrelations.* New York: Nervous and Mental Disease Publishing Company, 1934.

Murphy, Gardner: *Personality: A Biosocial Approach to Origins and Structure.* New York: Harper & Row, Publishers, Incorporated, 1947.

Murphy, Raymond J., and Richard T. Morris: "Occupational Situs, Subjective Class Identification, and Political Affiliation," *American Sociological Review,* June, 1961, pp. 383–392.

Mussen, Paul H.: "Some Personality and Social Factors Related to Changes in Children's Attitudes toward Negroes," *Journal of Abnormal and Social Psychology,* July, 1950, pp. 423–441.

————: "Some Antecedents and Consequents of Masculine Sex-typing in Adolescent Boys," *Psychological Monographs,* vol. 75, 1961.

———— and J. Kagan: "Group Conformity and Perceptions of Parents," *Child Development,* vol. 29, 1958, pp. 57–60.

Myers, Jerome K., and Bertram H. Roberts: *Family and Class Dynamics in Mental Illness.* New York: John Wiley & Sons, Inc., 1959.

Myrdal, Gunnar: with the assistance of Richard Sterner and Arnold Rose: *An American Dilemma: The Negro Problem and Modern Democracy,* 2 vols. New York: Harper & Row, Publishers, Incorporated, 1944.

Nadel, S. F.: *The Theory of Social Structure.* New York: The Free Press of Glencoe, 1957.

Nagel, Ernest: *The Structure of Science.* New York: Harcourt, Brace & World, Inc., 1961.

Neal, Arthur G., and Salomon Rettig: "Dimensions of Alienation among Manual and Non-manual Workers," *American Sociological Review,* August, 1963, pp. 599–608.

Nett, Emily M.: "An Evaluation of the National Character Concept in Sociological Theory," *Social Forces,* May, 1958, pp. 297–303.

Nettler, Gwynn: "A Measure of Alienation," *American Sociological Review,* December, 1957, pp. 670–677.

———— and James R. Huffman: "Political Opinion and Personal Security," *Sociometry,* March, 1957, pp. 51–66.

Newcomb, Theodore M.: *Social Psychology.* New York: Holt, Rinehart and Winston, Inc., 1950.

————: *The Acquaintance Process.* New York: Holt, Rinehart and Winston, Inc., 1950.

————, Ralph H. Turner, and Philip E. Converse: *Social Psychology* New York: Holt, Rinehart and Winston, Inc., 1965.

Olds, James: *The Growth and Structure of Motives.* New York: The Free Press of Glencoe, 1956.

Opler, Marvin K.: *Culture, Psychiatry and Human Values: The Methods and Values of a Social Psychiatry.* Springfield, Ill.: Charles C Thomas, Publishers, 1956.

————: *Culture and Mental Health.* New York: The Macmillan Company, 1959.

Orlansky, Harold: "Infant Care and Personality," *Psychological Bulletin,* January, 1949, pp. 1–48.

Parsons, Talcott: *The Social System.* New York: The Free Press of Glencoe, 1950.

————: *Essays in Socological Theory Pure and Applied,* rev. ed. New York: The Free Press of Glencoe, 1954.

————: "Social Structure and the Development of Personality: Freud's Contribution to the Integration of Psychology and Sociology," *Psychiatry,* vol. 21, 1958, pp. 321–340.

————: *Social Structure and Personality.* New York: The Free Press of Glencoe, 1964.

———— and Robert F. Bales, in collaboration with James Olds, Morris Zelditch, Jr., and Philip E. Slater: *Family, Socialization and Interaction Process.* New York: The Free Press of Glencoe, 1955.

————, R. F. Bales, and E. A. Shils: *Working Papers in the Theory of Action.* New York: The Free Press of Glencoe, 1953.

————, Kasper D. Naegele, and Jesse R. Pitts: *Theories of Society: Foundation of Modern Sociological Theory,* 2 vols. New York: The Free Press of Glencoe, 1961.

———— and Edward A. Shils (eds.): *Toward a General Theory of Action.* Cambridge, Mass.: Harvard University Press, 1951 (reprinted as Harper Torchbook, 1962).

Pasamanick, Benjamin (ed.): *Epidemiology of Mental Disorder.* Washington: American Association for the Advancement of Science, 1959.

————, H. Knobloch, and A. M. Lilienfield: "Socioeconomic Status and Precursors of Neuropsychiatric Disorder," *American Journal of Orthopsychiatry,* vol. 26, 1956, pp. 594–602.

Payne, Donald E., and Paul H. Mussen: "Parent-Child Relations and Father Identification among Adolescent Boys," *Journal of Abnormal and Social Psychology,* May, 1956, pp. 358–362.

Pearlin, Leonard I.: "Alienation from Work: A Study of Nursing Personnel," *American Sociological Review,* June, 1962, pp. 314–326.

————: "Sources of Resistance to Change in a Mental Hospital," *American Journal of Sociology,* November, 1962, pp. 325–334.

Perry, Stewart E., and Lyman C. Wynne: "Role Conflict, Role Definition, and Social Change in a Clinical Research Organization," *Social Forces,* October, 1959, pp. 62–65.

Pettigrew, Ann Hallman, and Thomas F. Pettigrew: "Race, Disease and Desegregation: A New Look," *Phylon,* Winter, 1963, pp. 315–333.

Pettigrew, Thomas F.: "Demographic Correlates of Border-state Desegregation," *American Sociological Review,* December, 1957, pp. 683–689.

————: "Personality and Sociocultural Factors in Intergroup Attitudes: A Cross-national Comparison," *The Journal of Conflict Resolution,* March, 1958, pp. 29–42.

————: "Regional Differences in Anti-Negro Prejudice," *Journal of Abnormal and Social Psychology,* July, 1959, pp. 28–36.

————: *A Profile of the Negro American.* Princeton, N.J.: D. Van Nostrand Company, Inc., 1964.

Pfautz, Harold W.: "Near-group Theory and Collective Behavior: A Critical Reformulation," *Social Problems,* Fall, 1961, pp. 167–174.

Phillips, Derek L.: "Rejection: A Possible Consequence of Seeking Help for Mental Disorders," *American Sociological Review,* December, 1963, pp. 963–972.

Photiadis, John D., and Jeanne Bigger: "Religiosity, Education, and Social Distance," *American Journal of Sociology,* May, 1962, pp. 666–672.

Piaget, Jean: *The Language and Thought of the Child.* New York: Harcourt, Brace and Company, Inc., 1926.

————: *The Moral Judgment of the Child.* London: Kegan Paul, 1932.

Pittman, David J., and Charles R. Snyder (eds.): *Society, Culture, and Drinking Patterns.* New York: John Wiley & Sons, Inc., 1962.

Plant, James S.: *Personality and the Culture Pattern.* New York: The Commonwealth Fund, 1937.

Pollack, O.: *Integrating Sociological and Psychoanalytic Concepts.* New York: Russell Sage Foundation, 1956.

Powdermaker, Florence B., and Jerome D. Frank: *Group Psychotherapy.* Cambridge, Mass.: Harvard University Press, for the Commonwealth Fund, 1953.

Powell, Elwin H.: "Occupation, Status, and Suicide: Toward a Redefinition of Anomie," *American Sociological Review,* April, 1958. pp. 131–139.

Prentice, Norman M.: "Ethnic Attitudes, Neuroticism, and Culture," *Journal of Social Psychology,* June, 1961, pp. 75–82.

Pye, Lucian: *Guerilla Communism in Malaya: Its Social and Political Meaning.* Princeton, N.J.: Princeton University Press, 1956.

Radcliffe-Brown, A. R.: *A Natural Science of Society.* New York: The Free Press of Glencoe, 1957.

Raush, H. L., A. T. Dittmann, and T. J. Taylor: "Person, Setting, and Change in Social Interaction," *Human Relations,* vol. 12, 1959, pp. 361–378.

Raven, Bertram H., and John R. P. French, Jr.: "Legitimate Power, Coercive Power, and Observability in Social Influence," *Sociometry,* June, 1958, pp. 83–97.

Reckless, Walter: *The Crime Problem.* New York: Appleton-Century-Crofts, Inc., 1950.

————, Simon Dinitz, and Ellen Murray: "Self Concept as an Insulator against Delinquency," *American Sociological Review*, December, 1956, pp. 744–746.

Redl, Fritz, and David Wineman: *Children Who Hate*. New York: The Free Press of Glencoe, 1951.

Reeder, Leo G., George A. Donohue, and Arturo Biblarz: "Conceptions of Self and Others," *American Journal of Sociology*, September, 1960, pp. 153–159.

Reitzes, Dietrich C.: "Institutional Structure and Race Relations," *Phylon*, Spring, 1959, pp. 48–66.

Rhyne, Edwin Hoffman: "Racial Prejudice and Personality Scales: An Alternative Approach," *Social Forces*, October, 1962, pp. 44–53.

Rieff, Philip: *Freud: The Mind of the Moralist*. New York: The Viking Press, Inc., 1959.

Riesman, David: *Individualism Reconsidered*. New York: The Free Press of Glencoe, 1954.

————, with Nathan Glazer and Reuel Denney: *The Lonely Crowd*, rev. ed. New Haven, Conn.: Yale University Press, 1961.

Riley, Matilda White, and Richard Cohn: "Control Networks in Informal Groups," *Sociometry*, March, 1958, pp. 30–49.

———— and S. H. Flowerman: "Group Relations as a Variable in Communications Research," *American Sociological Review*, April, 1951, pp. 174–180.

Roberts, A. H., and Milton Rokeach: "Anomie, Authoritarianism, and Prejudice: A Replication," *American Journal of Sociology*, January, 1956, pp. 355–358.

Roberts, B. H., and J. K. Myers: "Schizophrenia in the Youngest Male Child of the Lower Middle Class," *American Journal of Psychiatry*, August, 1955, pp. 129–134.

Robins, Lee N., Harry Gyman, and Patricia O'Neal: "The Interaction of Social Class and Deviant Behavior," *American Sociological Review*, August, 1962, pp. 480–492.

———— and Patricia O'Neal: "Mortality, Mobility, and Crime: Problem Children Thirty Years Later," *American Sociological Review*, April, 1958, pp. 162–170.

Rocheblave-Spenlé, Anne-Marie: *La Notion du Rôle en Psychologie Sociale: Étude Historico-critique*. Paris: Presses Universitaires de France, 1962.

Rogers, Carl R.: *Client-centered Therapy*. Boston: Houghton Mifflin Company, 1951.

Rohrer, John H., and Munro Edmonson (eds.): *The Eighth Generation: Cultures and Personalities of New Orleans Negroes*. New York: Harper & Row, Publishers, Incorporated, 1960.

———— and Muzafer Sherif (eds.): *Social Psychology at the Crossroads*. New York: Harper & Row, Publishers, Incorporated, 1951.

Rokeach, Milton: "Generalized Mental Rigidity as a Factor in Ethnocentrism," *Journal of Abnormal and Sociol Psychology*, July, 1948, pp. 259–278.

————: *The Open and Closed Mind.* New York: Basic Books, Inc., Publishers, 1960.

Rose, Arnold M. (ed.): *Mental Health and Mental Disorder: A Sociological Approach.* New York: W. W. Norton & Company, Inc., 1955.

————: "Inconsistencies in Attitude toward Negro Housing," *Social Problems,* Spring, 1961, pp. 287–292.

———— (ed.): *Human Behavior and Social Processes.* Boston: Houghton Mifflin Company, 1962.

Rosen, Bernard C.: "The Achievement Syndrome: A Psychocultural Dimension of Social Stratification," *American Sociological Review,* April, 1956, pp. 203–211.

————: "Race, Ethnicity, and the Achievement Syndrome," *American Sociological Review,* February, 1959, pp. 47–60.

————: "Family Structure and Achievement Motivation," *American Sociological Review,* August, 1961, pp. 574–585.

———— and Roy D'Andrade: "The Psychosocial Origins of Achievement Motivation," *Sociometry,* September, 1959, pp. 185–218.

Rosenbaum, Max, and Milton Berger (eds.): *Group Psychotherapy and Group Function.* New York: Basic Books, Inc., Publishers, 1963.

Rosenberg, Larry: "Social Status and Participation among a Group of Chronic Schizophrenics," *Human Relations,* November, 1962, pp. 365–377.

Rosenberg, Morris: *Occupations and Values.* New York: The Free Press of Glencoe, 1957.

————: "Parental Interest and Children's Self-conceptions," *Sociometry,* March, 1963, pp. 35–49.

Rosenthal, David: "Some Factors Associated with Concordance and Discordance with Respect to Schizophrenia in Monozygotic Twins," *Journal of Nervous and Mental Disease,* vol. 129, 1959, pp. 1–10.

Sampson, Edward E.: "Status Congruence and Cognitive Consistency," *Sociometry,* June, 1963, pp. 146–162.

Sampson, Harold, Sheldon L. Messinger, and Robert D. Towne: "Family Processes and Becoming a Mental Patient," *American Journal of Sociology,* July, 1962, pp. 88–96.

Sanau, Victor D.: "Sociocultural Factors in Families of Schizophrenics," *Psychiatry,* August, 1961, pp. 246–265.

Sanford, Nevitt: "Personality: Its Place in Psychology," in Sigmund Koch (ed.), *Psychology: A Study of a Science,* vol. 5, pp. 488–592. New York: McGraw-Hill Book Company, 1963.

Sartre, Jean-Paul: *Being and Nothingness: An Essay on Phenomenological Ontology,* trans. by Hazel E. Barnes. New York: Philosophical Library, Inc., 1956.

Schachter, Stanley: "Birth Order, Eminence and Higher Education," *American Sociological Review,* October, 1963, pp. 757–768.

Scheff, Thomas J.: "The Role of the Mentally Ill and the Dynamics of Mental Disorder: A Research Framework," *Sociometry,* December, 1963, pp. 436–453.

Schein, Edgar H.: "The Chinese Indoctrination Program for Prisoners of War: A Study of Attempted 'Brainwashing,'" *Psychiatry*, May, 1956, pp. 149–172.

———, with Inge Schneier and Curtis H. Barker: *Coercive Persuasion*. New York: W. W. Norton & Company, Inc., 1961.

Schlesinger, Lawrence E.: *The Influence of Exposure to Peer Group Opinions on the Expression of Attitudes toward a Minority Group*. Unpublished doctoral dissertation, Boston University, 1955.

Schneider, Louis, and Sverre Lysgaard: "The Deferred Gratification Pattern: A Preliminary Study," *American Sociological Review*, April, 1953, pp. 142–149.

Schramm, Wilbur (ed.): *The Process and Effects of Mass Communication*. Urbana, Ill.: The University of Illinois Press, 1954.

Schutz, William C.: *Firo: A Three-dimensional Theory of Interpersonal Behavior*. New York: Holt, Rinehart and Winston, Inc., 1958.

Scott, William A.: "Social Psychological Correlates of Mental Illness and Mental Health," *Psychological Bulletin*, March, 1958, pp. 65–87.

Sears, Robert R.: "A Theoretical Framework for Personality and Social Behavior," *American Psychologist*, August, 1951, pp. 476–483.

———, E. E. Maccoby, and Harry Levin: *Patterns of Child Rearing*. New York: Harper & Row, Publishers, Incorporated, 1957.

Sebald, Hans: "Studying National Character through Comparative Content Analysis," *Social Forces*, May, 1962, pp. 318–322.

Secord, Paul F., and Carl W. Backman: "Personality Theory and the Problem of Stability and Change in Individual Behavior: An Interpersonal Approach," *Psychological Review*, January, 1961, pp. 21–32.

Seeman, Melvin: "Role Conflict and Ambivalence in Leadership," *American Sociological Review*, August, 1953, pp. 373–380.

———: "On the Meaning of Alienation," *American Sociological Review*, December, 1959, pp. 783–791.

——— and John W. Evans: "Alienation and Learning in a Hospital Setting," *American Sociological Review*, December, 1962, pp. 772–782.

Segal, H. A.: "Initial Psychiatric Findings of Recently Repatriated Prisoners of War," *American Journal of Psychiatry*, vol. III, 1954, pp. 358–363.

Selvin, Hanan C.: *The Effects of Leadership*. New York: The Free Press of Glencoe, 1960.

——— and Warren O. Hagstrom: "The Empirical Classification of Formal Groups," *American Sociological Review*, June, 1963, pp. 399–411.

Sewell, William H.: "Infant Training and the Personality of the Child," *American Journal of Sociology*, September, 1952, pp. 150–159.

———: "Social Class and Childhood Personality," *Sociometry*, December, 1961, pp. 340–356.

———: "Some Recent Developments in Socialization Theory and Research," *Annals of the American Academy of Political and Social Science*, September, 1963, pp. 163–181.

——— and A. O. Haller: "Social Status and the Personality Adjustment of the Child," *Sociometry*, June, 1956, pp. 114–125.

——— and ———: "Factors in the Relationship between Social Status and the Personality Adjustment of the Child," *American Sociological Review*, August, 1959, pp. 511–520.

Shaw, Clifford: *Delinquency Areas.* Chicago: The University of Chicago Press, 1929.

Sherif, Muzafer: *The Psychology of Social Norms.* New York: Harper & Brothers, 1936.

—— (ed.): *Intergroup Relations and Leadership.* New York and London: John Wiley & Sons, Inc., 1962.

—— et al.: *Intergroup Conflict and Cooperation: The Robbers Cave Experiment.* Norman, Okla.: The University Book Exchange, 1961.

—— and Carolyn W. Sherif: *Groups in Harmony and Tension.* New York: Harper & Row, Publishers, Incorporated, 1953.

—— and M. O. Wilson (eds.): *Group Relations at the Crossroads.* New York: Harper & Row, Publishers, Incorporated, 1953.

Sherman, Murray H. (ed.): *A Rorschach Reader.* New York: International Universities Press, Inc., 1960.

Sherwood, Rae: "The Bantu Clerk: A Study of Role Expectations," *Journal of Social Psychology,* May, 1958, pp. 285–316.

Shibutani, Tamotsu: "Reference Groups as Perspectives," *American Journal of Sociology,* May, 1955, pp. 562–569.

——: *Society and Personality.* Englewood Cliffs, N.J.: Prentice-Hall, Inc., 1961.

Silberstein, Fred B., and Melvin Seeman: "Social Mobility and Prejudice," *American Journal of Sociology,* November, 1959, pp. 258–264.

Simpson, George E., and J. Milton Yinger: *Racial and Cultural Minorities,* 3d ed. New York: Harper & Row, Publishers, Incorporated, 1965.

Simpson, Jon E., Simon Dinitz, Barbara Kay, and Walter C. Reckless: "Delinquency Potential of Pre-adolescents in High Delinquency Areas," *British Journal of Delinquency,* January, 1960, pp. 211–215.

Simpson, Richard L.: "Parental Influence, Anticipatory Socialization, and Social Mobility," *American Sociological Review,* August, 1962, pp. 517–522.

—— and H. Max Miller: "Social Status and Anomia," *Social Problems,* Winter, 1963, pp. 256–264.

Singer, Jerome L., and George D. Goldman: "Experimentally Contrasted Social Atmospheres in Group Psychotherapy with Chronic Schizophrenics," *Journal of Social Psychology,* August, 1954, pp. 23–37.

Skinner, B. F.: *Science and Human Behavior.* New York: The Macmillan Company, 1953.

Slater, Philip E.: "On Social Regression," *American Sociological Review,* June, 1963, pp. 339–364.

Slavson, S. R.: *Analytic Group Psychotherapy.* New York: Columbia University Press, 1950.

——: *Re-educating the Delinquent: Through Group and Community Participation.* New York: Harper & Row, Publishers, Incorporated, 1954.

—— (ed.): *The Fields of Group Psychotherapy.* New York: International Universities Press, Inc., 1956.

Slotkin, J. S.: *Personality Development.* New York: Harper & Row, Publishers, Incorporated, 1952.

————: "Life Course in Middle Age," *Social Forces,* December, 1954, pp. 171–177.

Smelser, Neil J., and William T. Smelser: *Personality and Social Systems.* New York: John Wiley & Sons, Inc., 1963.

Smelser, William T.: "Adolescent and Adult Occupational Choice as a Function of Family Socioeconomic History," *Sociometry,* December, 1963, pp. 393–409.

Snyder, Charles R.: *Alcohol and the Jews: A Cultural Study of Drinking and Sobriety.* New York: The Free Press of Glencoe, 1958.

Solomon, Herbert (ed.): *Mathematical Thinking in the Measurement of Behavior.* New York: The Free Press of Glencoe, 1960.

Sommer, Robert, and Humphry Osmond: "Symptoms of Institutional Care," *Social Problems,* Winter, 1960–1961, pp. 254–263.

Sorokin, P. A.: *Society, Culture, and Personality.* New York: Harper & Row, Publishers, Incorporated, 1947.

Southall, Aidan: "An Operational Theory of Role," *Human Relations,* vol. 12, 1959, pp. 17–34.

Spiegel, John P.: "The Resolution of Role Conflict within the Family," *Psychiatry,* February, 1957, pp. 1–16.

Spier, Leslie, A. I. Hallowell, and S. S. Newman (eds.): *Language, Culture, and Personality* (essay in memory of Edward Sapir). Menasha, Wis.: Sapir Memorial Publication Fund, 1941.

Spindler, George D.: "Personality and Peyotism in Menomini Indian Acculturation," *Psychiatry,* 1952, pp. 151–159.

————: *Sociocultural and Psychological Processes in Menomini Acculturation.* Berkeley, Calif.: University of California Publications in Culture and Society, 1955.

———— and Louise S. Spindler: "American Indian Personality Types and Their Sociocultural Roots," *Annals of the American Academy of Political and Social Science,* May, 1957, pp. 147–157.

Spindler, Louise, and George Spindler: "Male and Female Adaptations in Culture Change," *American Anthropologist,* vol. 60, 1958, pp. 217–233.

Spiro, M. E.: "Culture and Personality: The Natural History of a False Dichotomy," *Psychiatry,* vol. 14, 1951, pp. 19–46.

Sprey, Jetse: "Sex Differences in Occupational Choice Patterns among Negro Adolescents," *Social Problems,* Summer, 1962, pp. 11–23.

Srole, Leo: "Social Integration and Certain Corollaries: An Exploratory Study," *American Sociological Review,* December, 1956, pp. 709–716.

———— et al.: *Mental Health in the Metropolis.* New York: McGraw-Hill Book Company, 1962.

Stanton, Alfred H.: "Milieu Therapy and the Development of Insight," *Psychiatry,* May, 1961, pp. 19–29.

———— and Morris S. Schwartz: *The Mental Hospital.* New York: Basic Books, Inc., Publishers, 1954.

Stein, Maurice R., Arthur J. Vidich, and David Manning White (eds.): *Identity and Anxiety.* New York: The Free Press of Glencoe, 1960.

Steiner, Ivan D., and William L. Field: "Role Assignment and Inter-
personal Influence," *Journal of Abnormal and Social Psychology*,
September, 1960, pp. 239–245.
—— and Homer H. Johnson: "Authoritarianism and Conformity,"
Sociometry, March, 1963, pp. 21–34.
Stern, George G., Morris I. Stein, and Benjamin S. Bloom: *Methods in
Personality Assessment: Human Behavior in Complex Social Sit-
uations.* New York: The Free Press of Glencoe, 1956.
Stewart, Don, and Thomas Hoult: "A Social-Psychological Theory of
the Authoritarian Personality," *American Journal of Sociology*,
November, 1959, pp. 274–279.
Stoetzel, Jean: *Without the Chrysanthemum and the Sword: A Study
of the Attitudes of Youth in Post-war Japan.* UNESCO, 1955.
Stoodley, Bartlett H. (ed.): *Society and Self.* New York: The Free
Press of Glencoe, 1962.
Stotland, Ezra *et al.*: "The Effects of Group Expectations and Self-
esteem upon Self-evaluation," *Journal of Abnormal and Social Psy-
chology*, January, 1957, pp. 55–63.
Stouffer, Samuel, and Jackson Toby: "Role Conflict and Personality,"
American Journal of Sociology, March, 1951, pp. 395–406.
Straus, Murray A.: "Subcultural Variation in Ceylonese Mental Ability:
A Study in National Character," *Journal of Social Psychology*,
February, 1954, pp. 129–141.
——: "Deferred Gratification, Social Class, and the Achievement Syn-
drome," *American Sociological Review*, June, 1962, pp. 326–335.
Strauss, Anselm: *Mirrors and Masks: The Search for Identity.* New
York: The Free Press of Glencoe, 1959.
Strong, E. K., Jr.: "Permanence of Interest Scores over 22 Years," *Jour-
nal of Applied Psychology*, vol. 35, 1951, pp. 89–91.
Stryker, Sheldon: "Role-taking Accuracy and Adjustment," *Sociometry*,
December, 1957, pp. 286–296.
Suchman, Edward A.: "A Conceptual Analysis of the Accident Phenom-
enon," *Social Problems*, Winter, 1960–1961, pp. 241–253.
Sullivan, Harry Stack: *The Interpersonal Theory of Psychiatry.* New
York: W. W. Norton & Company, Inc., 1953.
Sussman, Maurice: *Animal Growth and Development.* Englewood Cliffs,
N.J.: Prentice-Hall, Inc., 1960.
Swanson, G. E.: "Mead and Freud: Their Relevance for Social Psy-
chology," *Sociometry*, December, 1961, pp. 319–339.
Swinehart, James W.: "Socio-economic Level, Status Aspiration, and
Maternal Role," *American Sociological Review*, June, 1963, pp.
391–399.
Sykes, Gresham M.: *The Society of Captives.* Princeton, N.J.: Princeton
University Press, 1958.
—— and David Matza: "Techniques of Neutralization: A Theory of
Delinquency," *American Sociological Review*, December, 1957, pp.
664–670.
Tagiuri, Renato, and Luigi Petrullo (eds.): *Person Perception and
Interpersonal Behavior.* Stanford, Calif.: Stanford University Press,
1958.

Tajfel, H.: "Value and the Perceptual Judgment of Magnitude," *Psychological Review,* vol. 64, 1957, pp. 192–204.

Tannenbaum, Arnold S., and Jerald G. Bachman: "Structural versus Individual Effects," *American Journal of Sociology,* May, 1964, pp. 585–595.

Thomas, W. I.: *Social Behavior and Personality: Contributions of W. I. Thomas to Theory and Social Research,* ed. by Edmund H. Volkart. New York: Social Science Research Council, 1951.

Thompson, Wayne E., and John E. Horton: "Political Alienation as a Force in Political Action," *Social Forces,* March, 1960, pp. 190–195.

Thrasher, Frederic M.: *The Gang.* Chicago: The University of Chicago Press, 1936.

Tibbetts, Clark (ed.): *Handbook of Social Gerontology: Societal Aspects of Aging.* Chicago: The University of Chicago Press, 1960.

Toby, Jackson: "Some Variables in Role Conflict Analysis," *Social Forces,* March, 1952, pp. 323–327.

Trasler, Gordon: *The Explanation of Criminality.* London: Rutledge & Kegan Paul, Ltd., 1962.

Trow, Martin: "Small Businessman, Political Tolerance, and Support for McCarthy," *American Journal of Sociology,* November, 1958, 270–281.

Tuckman, Jacob, and Robert J. Kleiner: "Discrepancy between Aspiration and Achievement as a Predictor of Schizophrenia," *Behavioral Science,* October, 1962, pp. 443–447.

Tumin, Melvin M.: *Desegregation: Resistance and Readiness.* Princeton, N.J.: Princeton University Press, 1958.

Turk, Herman: "Social Cohesion through Variant Values: Evidence from Medical Role Relations," *American Sociological Review,* February, 1963, pp. 28–37.

Turner, Ralph H.: "Role-taking, Role Standpoint, and Reference-group Behavior," *American Journal of Sociology,* January, 1956, pp. 316–328.

———: "Sponsored and Contest Mobility and the School System," *American Sociological Review,* December, 1960, pp. 855–867.

Ullman, Albert D.: "Ethnic Differences in the First Drinking Experience," *Social Problems,* Summer, 1960, pp. 45–56.

Veroff, Joseph, Sheila Feld, and Gerald Gurin: "Achievement Motivation and Religious Background," *American Sociological Review,* April, 1962, pp. 205–217.

Videbeck, Richard: "Self-conception and the Reaction of Others," *Sociometry,* December, 1960, pp. 351–359.

——— and Alan P. Bates: "An Experimental Study of Conformity to Role Expectations," *Sociometry,* March, 1959, pp. 1–11.

Voget, Fred W.: "Man and Culture: An Essay in Changing Anthropological Interpretation," *American Anthropologist,* December, 1960, pp. 943–965.

Volkman, Rita, and Donald R. Cressey: "Differential Association and the Rehabilitation of Drug Addicts," *The American Journal of Sociology,* September, 1963, pp. 129–142.

Vroom, Victor H.: "Projection, Negation, and the Self Concept," *Human Relations,* vol. 12, 1959, pp. 335–344.

Wallace, Anthony F. C.: *Culture and Personality.* New York: Random House, Inc., 1961.

Wallerstein, Robert W.: "Treatment of the Psychosis of General Paresis with Combined Sodium Amytal and Psychotherapy: Report of a Case," *Psychiatry,* vol. 14, 1951, pp. 307–317.

Warner, W. L., B. H. Junker, and W. A. Adams: *Color and Human Nature.* Washington, D.C.: American Council on Education, 1941.

Warriner, C. K.: "Groups are Real: A Reaffirmation," *American Sociological Review,* October, 1956, pp. 549–554.

Weber, Max: *The Protestant Ethic and the Spirit of Capitalism,* trans. by Talcott Parsons. London: George Allen and Unwin, 1930.

———: *From Max Weber,* ed. with an introduction by Hans Gerth and C. Wright Mills. Fair Lawn, N.J.: Oxford University Press, 1947.

Wegrocki, Henry J.: "A Critique of Cultural and Statistical Concepts of Abnormality," *Journal of Abnormal and Social Psychology,* vol. 34, 1939, pp. 166–178.

Westley, William A., and Frederick Elkin: "The Protective Environment and Adolescent Socialization," *Social Forces,* March, 1957, pp. 243–249.

White, Ralph K., and Ronald Lippitt: *Autocracy and Democracy: An Experimental Inquiry.* New York: Harper & Row, Publishers, Incorporated, 1960.

Whiting, Beatrice B. (ed.): *Six Cultures: Studies of Child Rearing.* New York: John Wiley & Sons, Inc., 1963.

Whiting, John W. M.: "Resource Mediation and Learning by Identification," in Iscoe and Stevenson (eds.), *Personality Development in Children.* Austin, Tex.: University of Texas Press, 1960.

——— and I. L. Child: *Child Training and Personality.* New Haven, Conn.: Yale University Press, 1953.

Whyte, William F.: *Street Corner Society,* 2d ed. Chicago: The University of Chicago Press, 1955.

Whyte, William H., Jr.: *The Organization Man.* Garden City, N.Y.: Doubleday & Company, Inc., 1957.

Wilensky, Harold L.: "Orderly Careers and Social Participation: The Impact of Work History on Social Integration in the Middle Mass, *American Sociological Review,* August, 1961, pp. 521–539.

——— and Hugh Edwards: "The Skidder: Ideological Adjustments of Downward Mobile Workers," *American Sociological Review,* April, 1959, pp. 215–231.

Williams, Robin M., Jr.: *The Reduction of Intergroup Tensions.* New York: Social Science Research Council, 1947.

———: *American Society: A Sociological Interpretation,* 2d ed. New York: Alfred A. Knopf, Inc., 1960.

Willis, Richard H.: "Two Dimensions of Conformity-Nonconformity." *Sociometry,* December, 1963, pp. 499–513.

Wilson, Alan B.: "Residential Segregation of Social Classes and Aspirations of High School Boys," *American Sociological Review,* December, 1959, pp. 836–845.

Winick, Charles: "Physician Narcotic Addicts," *Social Problems,* Fall, 1961, pp. 174–186.

Wrong, Dennis H.: "The Oversocialized Conception of Man in Modern Sociology," *American Sociological Review,* April, 1961, pp. 183–193.

Wylie, Ruth C.: *The Self Concept: A Critical Survey of Pertinent Research Literature.* Lincoln, Nebr.: University of Nebraska Press, 1961.

Wynne, Lyman C., Irving M. Rycoff, Julian Day, and Stanley I. Hirsch: "Pseudo-mutuality in the Family Relations of Schizophrenics," *Psychiatry,* May, 1958, pp. 205–220.

Yablonsky, Lewis: "The Delinquent Gang as a Near-group," *Social Problems,* Fall, 1959, pp. 108–117.

————: *The Violent Gang.* New York: The Macmillan Company, 1962.

Yarrow, Marian Radke (issue ed.): "Interpersonal Dynamics in a De-segregation Process," *Journal of Social Issues,* 1958.

Yinger, J. Milton: *Religion, Society, and the Individual.* New York: The Macmillan Company, 1957.

————: "Contraculture and Subculture," *American Sociological Review,* October, 1960, pp. 625–635.

————: "Research Implications of a Field View of Personality," *American Journal of Sociology,* March, 1963, pp. 580–592.

————: *Sociology Looks at Religion.* New York: The Macmillan Company, 1963.

Bugelski, B. R., 264
Bunzel, Ruth, 294
Burgess, Ernest W., 67
Burke, Kenneth, 49
Burrow, Trigant, 317
Byrne, Donn, 263

Cameron, Norman, 242, 278, 292, 315
Campbell, Angus, 36
Campbell, Donald T., 16, 49, 263
Campbell, John D., 265
Camus, Albert, 144
Canning, Ray R., 65
Cantril, Hadley, 36
Caplow, Theodore, 32
Cartwright, Desmond S., 240
Cartwright, Dorwin, 35, 50, 93, 317
Cattell, R. B., 24, 32
Caudill, William, 35, 306, 317
Centers, Richard, 90, 96
Chapman, Loren, 49, 263
Chein, Isidor, 183, 241, 264, 284, 293, 294
Child, Charles M., 42, 50
Child, Irvin L., 139, 158, 160, 161
Chilton, Roland J., 240
Christie, Richard, 263
Church, Russell M., 229, 241
Clark, Burton, 67, 92, 97, 202, 209
Clark, John P., 240
Clark, R. A., 66
Clausen, John A., 32, 183, 241, 269, 276, 290–292, 294, 299, 310, 313–316, 318
Clinard, Marshall B., 243
Cloward, Richard A., 210, 213, 215, 224, 225, 232, 238–240, 242, 250
Cloyd, Jerry, 133
Coch, Lester, 183
Cohen, Albert K., 95, 212–215, 217, 221, 224, 226–229, 232, 233, 236–241, 243, 293, 294
Cohen, Arthur, 169, 178
Cohen, E. A., 182, 184
Cohen, Yehudi A., 80, 94
Cohn, Richard, 157, 162
Coleman, James S. (Gov't.), 35
Coleman, James S. (Soc.), 24, 32, 60, 67, 105, 134
Coles, Robert, 184, 265
Collins, Mary Evans, 265
Comas, Juan, 66
Comte, Auguste, 27, 28
Converse, Philip E., 36, 107, 134
Cook, Peggy, 263

Cook, Stuart W., 265
Cooley, Charles H., 4, 27, 58, 66, 78, 144, 145
Corsini, Raymond J., 318
Coser, Lewis, 209
Coser, Rose Laub, 120, 137, 209
Cottrell, Leonard S., Jr., 16, 32, 34, 51, 98, 134, 137, 240, 292, 316
Coutu, Walter, 39, 49, 51, 134
Cowen, Emory L., 255, 264
Cressey, Donald R., 317
Crutchfield, Richard S., 26, 33, 54, 65
Cumming, Elaine, 67, 306, 317
Cumming, John H., 161, 306, 317
Cutter, Henry S. G., 238

D'Andrade, Roy, 66
Davies, James C., 36
Davis, Allison W., 160
Davis, Beverly, 32
Davis, Fred, 94
Davis, James A., 239
Davis, Keith E., 135
Davis, Kingsley, 27, 183, 242
Day, Julian, 292, 313
Dean, Dwight G., 210
de Charms, Richard, 55, 65
Demerath, N. J., III, 66
Denney, Reuel, 96, 137, 242
Dennis, Wayne, 66
Dernburg, Thomas, 15, 17
Deutsch, Morton, 46, 51, 147, 152, 159–161, 264, 265
Devereux, George, 97, 312
Dewey, John, 145
Dietrick, David C., 240
Dinitz, Simon, 239, 313, 315
Dittmann, A. T., 316
Dollard, John, 160, 264
Donahue, Wilma, 67
Donald, David, 37
Donohue, George A., 159
Dornbusch, Sanford M., 138
Douvan, E., 314
Dreger, R. M., 66, 315
Dubin, Robert, 208, 210, 241
Dublin, Louis, 293
Du Bois, Cora, 96, 290
Duncan, Otis D., 32
Dunham, H. W., 275, 292
Durkheim, Emile, 13, 21, 22, 27, 32, 34, 74, 76–78, 170, 188, 190, 192, 197, 198, 206, 209, 215, 217, 230, 279–281, 292

Kercher, L. C., 291
Kerckhoff, Alan C., 210
Key, V. O., Jr., 36
Khaldun, Ibn, 72
Killian, Lewis M., 210, 264
Kimble, Gregory A., 50
Kitsuse, John I., 240
Klapper, J. T., 169, 182
Klein, G. S., 158
Kleiner, Robert J., 292, 298, 314, 315
Klineberg, Otto, 33, 66, 96
Kluckhohn, Clyde, 5, 17, 27, 50, 74, 76,
  80, 81, 93–95, 159, 161, 181, 184, 291
Kluckhohn, Florence, 93
Knobloch, H., 313
Koch, Sigmund, 16, 17, 31, 33, 34, 50,
  51, 64, 158, 159, 292
Koffka, K., 27
Köhler, W., 27
Kohn, Melvin, 32, 264, 276, 292, 299,
  313, 314
Komarovsky, Mirra, 133
Korbin, Solomon, 240
Kornhauser, William, 36, 198, 209
Korzybski, Alfred, 25, 33
Krech, David, 26, 33, 158
Kroeber, A. L., 34, 74, 93
Kubzansky, P. E., 183
Kuhn, Manford H., 35, 159
Kutner, Bernard, 264
Kuznets, Simon, 35
Kvaraceus, William, 238

Landes, Judah, 255, 264
Lane, Robert, 36
Lane, W. C., 238
Langner, Thomas, 299, 314
LaPiere, Richard, 255, 264
Lasswell, Harold D., 36, 241, 242
Lauterbach, Albert, 35
Lavell, Martha, 315
Lazarsfeld, Paul, 16, 23, 24, 27, 32, 36,
  182, 259
Leacock, Eleanor, 315
Lee, Robert S., 293
Lefton, Mark, 315
Leibnitz, Gottfried, 143, 144
Leiderman, P. H., 183
Leighton, Alexander, 183, 241, 291, 296,
  310, 312–315, 318
Leighton, Dorothea C., 291, 312, 314, 315
Lemert, Edwin M., 297, 313
Lenski, Gerhard, 36
Lerner, Daniel, 35

Lerner, Eugene, 167
Lerner, Melvin J., 66, 240
Levin, Harry, 137, 160, 161
Levine, Sol, 316, 317
Levinson, Daniel J., 17, 67, 88, 89, 94,
  96, 98, 112, 132, 135, 159, 263, 317
Lewin, Kurt, 5, 13, 27, 34, 39, 40, 43,
  46, 47, 49–51, 94, 163, 164, 183, 268,
  290, 317
Lewis, Oscar, 238
Lieberman, Seymour, 114, 135
Lifton, Robert J., 184
Lilienfield, A. M., 313
Lincoln, C. Eric, 235, 242
Lindemann, Erich, 271, 291, 301
Lindesmith, Alfred R., 51, 94, 147, 159,
  283, 284, 293, 294
Lindzey, Gardner, 34, 51, 65, 94, 95, 131,
  160, 161
Linton, Ralph, 27, 67, 74–77, 83, 87, 93,
  96, 98, 102, 104, 105, 132, 135, 241,
  242, 268, 290, 312
Lippitt, Ronald, 40, 41, 50, 316
Lippmann, Walter, 65
Lipset, S. M., 36, 96, 97
Lively, Edwin L., 239
Locke, John, 143
Lohman, J. D., 264
Lott, Albert J., 53, 54, 65
Lowell, E. L., 66
Lowenthal, Leo, 96, 97, 316
Lowenthal, Marjorie F., 292
Lumsdaine, A. A., 182
Lynd, Helen, 50

McClelland, David C., 36, 59, 61, 66
Maccoby, Eleanor E., 65, 98, 134, 137,
  138, 160, 161, 183, 229, 241
McCord, Joan, 181, 294
McCord, William, 66, 181, 294
McCurdy, H. G., 65
McDill, Edward L., 67, 210, 263
McDougall, William, 4, 13, 26, 34
McEachern, A. W., 20, 32, 104, 105, 115,
  116, 123, 124, 131–137
McGinnis, Robert, 16
McGranahan, D. G., 90, 97
McGuinness, B. F., 33
MacIver, R. M., 27, 264
MacMahon, Brian, 314
MacMurray, John, 159
McPartland, Thomas S., 159, 161
McPhee, William, 36
Maehr, Martin L., 159, 161